For the Gay Stage

ALSO BY DREWEY WAYNE GUNN
AND FROM MCFARLAND

*Gay American Novels, 1870–1970:
A Reader's Guide* (2016)

*Gay Novels of Britain, Ireland and the Commonwealth,
1881–1981: A Reader's Guide* (2014)

For the Gay Stage

*A Guide to 456 Plays,
Aristophanes to Peter Gill*

Drewey Wayne Gunn

McFarland & Company, Inc., Publishers
Jefferson, North Carolina

LIBRARY OF CONGRESS CATALOGUING-IN-PUBLICATION DATA

Names: Gunn, Drewey Wayne, 1939– author.
Title: For the gay stage : a guide to 456 plays, Aristophanes to Peter Gill / Drewey Wayne Gunn.
Description: Jefferson, North Carolina : McFarland & Company, Inc., Publishers, 2017 | Includes bibliographical references and index.
Identifiers: LCCN 2017019140 | ISBN 9781476670195 (softcover : acid free paper) ∞
Subjects: LCSH: Homosexuality in literature. | Drama—Stories, plots, etc.
Classification: LCC PN1650.H66 G86 2017 | DDC 809.2/990866—dc23
LC record available at https://lccn.loc.gov/2017019140

BRITISH LIBRARY CATALOGUING DATA ARE AVAILABLE

ISBN (print) 978-1-4766-7019-5
ISBN (ebook) 978-1-4766-2893-6

© 2017 Drewey Wayne Gunn. All rights reserved

No part of this book may be reproduced or transmitted in any form or by any means, electronic or mechanical, including photocopying or recording, or by any information storage and retrieval system, without permission in writing from the publisher.

Front cover: (left to right) Leonard Frey, Robert La Tourneaux and Kenneth Nelson in the Mart Crowley play *The Boys in the Band*, from a 1969 staging on London's West End (Photofest)

Printed in the United States of America

McFarland & Company, Inc., Publishers
Box 611, Jefferson, North Carolina 28640
www.mcfarlandpub.com

Table of Contents

Overview of Entries   vii
Preface   1
Introduction   3

THE PLAYS

Pre-Modern, 5th c. BCE–18th c. CE   13
Early Modern, 1891–1943   19
Post–World War II, 1945–1969   32
Post-Stonewall, 1970–1981   48
AIDS, 1982–1989   70
Early Nineties, 1990–1994   91
Pre-Millennium, 1995–2000   112
Early Contemporary, 2001–2007   134
Recent Contemporary, 2008–2014   156

Appendix A: Performance Pieces   179
Appendix B: Musical Theater   181
General Bibliography   185
Index of Authors and Titles   187

Overview of Entries

1. *Knights*, 424 BCE | Aristophanes, Athenian
2. *Women at the Thesmophoria*, 411 BCE | Aristophanes, Athenian | Socratic Dialogues
3. *The Tale of Orpheus*, 1480 | Poliziano, Tuscan
4. *The Marescalco*, 1526 | P. Aretino, Tuscan
5. *Edward II*, 1593 | C. Marlowe, English
6. *Troilus and Cressida*, 1603 | W. Shakespeare, English
7. *Sodom*, w. 1671? | J. Wilmot, 2nd Earl of Rochester, English
8. *The Relapse*, 1696 | J. Vanbrugh, English
9. *Spring's Awakening*, 1891 | F. Wedekind, German
10. *The Blackmailers*, 1894 | J. Gray and M.-A. Raffalovich, English
11. *At Saint Judas's*, 1896 | H. B. Fuller, American
12. *When the King Comes He Is Welcome*, 1896 | Lord A. Douglas, English
13. *Saul*, 1903 | A. Gide, French
14. *"Mistakes,"* 1906 | H. Hirschberg, German
15. *The Dangerous Precaution*, 1907 | M. Kuzmin, Russian
16. *The Gentleman of the Chrysanthemums*, 1908 | Armory, French
17. *The Madras House*, 1910 | H. Granville-Barker, English
18. *The Venetian Madcaps*, 1914 | M. Kuzmin, Russian
19. *The Princess Zoubaroff*, 1920 | R. Firbank, English
20. *Baal*, 1922–26 | B. Brecht, German
21. *Mustn't Do It!*, 1922 | J. M. Goedhart-Becker, Dutch
22. *Spring Cleaning*, 1923 | F. Lonsdale, English
23. *The Life of Edward the Second of England*, 1924 | B. Brecht, German
24. *The Prisoners of War*, 1925 | J. R. Ackerley, English
25. *Semi-Monde*, w. 1926 | N. Coward, English
26. *The Drag*, 1927 | M. West, American
27. *Oscar Wilde*, 1928 | L. Cohen, American
28. *The Pleasure Man*, 1928 | M. West, American
29. *Strange Interlude*, 1928 | E. O'Neill, American
30. *Rope*, 1929 | P. Hamilton, English
31. *The Public*, w. 1930? | F. García Lorca, Spanish
32. *But It Still Goes On*, 1931 | R. Graves, English
33. *Vile Bodies*, 1931 | H. D. Bradley, English
34. *Dangerous Corner*, 1932 | J. B. Priestley, English
35. *Queer People*, 1932 / *Tragedy in Jermyn Street*, 1934 | M. Hill, English
36. *Design for Living*, 1933 | N. Coward, English
37. *The Green Bay Tree*, 1933 | M. Shairp, English
38. *The Rats of Norway*, 1933 | K. Winter, Welsh
39. *Oscar Wilde*, 1936 | L. Stokes and S. Stokes, English
40. *Whiteoaks*, 1936 | M. de la Roche, Canadian
41. *Outrageous Fortune*, 1943 | R. Franken, American
42. *Auto-da-Fé*, 1945 | T. Williams, American
43. *Deathwatch*, 1947 | J. Genet, French
44. *"Now Barabbas...,"* 1947 | W. D. Home, Scot
45. *The Fire That Consumes*, 1951 | H. de Montherlant, French
46. *Third Person*, 1951 | A. Rosenthal, American
47. *Camino Real*, 1953 | T. Williams, American
48. *One Foot to the Sea*, 1953 | H. Levitt, American
49. *South*, 1953 | J. Green, American
50. *Tea and Sympathy*, 1953 | R. Anderson, American
51. *The Immoralist*, 1954 | R. Goetz and A. Goetz, American
52. *Cat on a Hot Tin Roof*, 1955 | T. Williams, American
53. *Game of Fools*, 1955 | J. B. Fugaté, American

54. *Quaint Honour*, 1958 | R. Gellert, English
55. *Suddenly Last Summer*, 1958 | T. Williams, American
56. *A Taste of Honey*, 1958 | S. Delaney, English
57. *Big Fish, Little Fish*, 1961 | H. Wheeler, American
58. *Look: We've Come Through*, 1961 | H. Wheeler, American
59. *Now She Dances!*, 1961–2003 | D. Wilson, American
60. *The Boy in the Basement*, 1962 | W. Inge, American
61. *Man and Boy*, 1963 | T. Rattigan, English
62. *The Toilet*, 1963 | L. Jones, American
63. *The Baptism*, 1964 | L. Jones, American
64. *Entertaining Mr. Sloane*, 1964 | J. Orton, English
65. *The Haunted Host*, 1964 | R. Patrick, American
66. *The Madness of Lady Bright*, 1964 | L. Wilson, American
67. *The Sign in Sidney Brustein's Window*, 1964 | L. Hansberry, American
68. *The Bed*, 1965 | R. Heide, American
69. *A Patriot for Me*, 1965 | J. Osborne, English
70. *Degrees*, 1966 | G. Birimisa, American
71. *A Song at Twilight*, 1966 | N. Coward, English
72. *Staircase*, 1966 | C. Dyer, English
73. *When Did You Last See My Mother?*, 1966 | C. Hampton, English
74. *Where's Daddy?*, 1966 | W. Inge, American
75. *Fortune and Men's Eyes*, 1967 | J. Herbert, Canadian
76. *White Lies*, 1967 / *White Liars*, 1968 | P. Shaffer, English
77. *Wise Child*, 1967 | S. Gray, English
78. *Boys in the Band*, 1968 | M. Crowley, American
79. *The Death and Resurrection of Mr. Roche*, 1968 | T. Kilroy, Irish
80. *Total Eclipse*, 1968 | C. Hampton, English
81. *Change*, 1969 | W. Bauer, Austrian
82. *Enemy!*, 1969 | R. Maugham, English
83. *The Clash of Cymbals*, 1970 | W. M. Guerrero, Filipino
84. *Confessional*, 1970 / *Small Craft Warnings*, 1972 | T. Williams, American
85. *Find Your Way Home*, 1970 | J. Hopkins, English
86. *Norman, Is That You?*, 1970 | R. Clark and S. Bobrick, American
87. *Blow Job*, 1971 | S. Wilson, English
88. *Butley*, 1971 | S. Gray, English
89. *The Gentle Island*, 1971 | B. Friel, Irish
90. *Coming Out!*, 1972 | J. Katz, American
91. *The End*, 1972 | J. Palmer, Canadian
92. *Satyricon*, 1972 | P. Foster, American
93. *Elagabalus*, 1973 | M. Duberman, American
94. *The Enclave*, 1973 | A. Laurents, American
95. *Hosanna*, 1973 | M. Tremblay, Canadian
96. *Kennedy's Children*, 1973–75 | R. Patrick, American
97. *How Does Your Garden Grow*, 1973 | J. McNeil, Australian
98. *The Ritz*, 1974–75 | T. McNally, American
99. *Human Remains*, 1975 | L. Fineberg, Canadian
100. *Mates*, 1975 | P. Kenna, Australian
101. *Passing By*, 1975 | M. Sherman, American
102. *P.S. Your Cat Is Dead*, 1975–78 | J. Kirkwood, American
103. *The Return of A. J. Raffles*, 1975 | G. Greene, English
104. *The Shadow Box*, 1975 | M. Cristofer, American
105. *Caprice*, 1976 | C. Ludlam, American
106. *Confession*, 1976 | J. Patrick, American
107. *Conpersonas*, 1976 | P. Steven Lim, American
108. *Gemini*, 1976 | A. Innaurato, American
109. *Pogey Bait*, 1976 | G. Birimisa, American
110. *Streamers*, 1976 | D. Rabe, American
111. *As Time Goes By*, 1977 | N. Greig and D. Griffiths, English
112. *Chinchilla*, 1977 | R. D. MacDonald, Scot
113. *A Day after the Fair*, 1977 | J. Purdy, American
114. *Privates on Parade*, 1977 | P. Nichols, English
115. *Vieux Carré*, 1977 | T. Williams, American
116. *Fifth of July*, 1978 | L. Wilson, American
117. *Furtive Love*, 1978 | P. Kenna, Australian
118. *Lord Alfred's Lover*, 1978 | E. Bentley, American
119. *The Man with Straight Hair*, 1978–94 | G. Birimisa, American
120. *A Perfect Relationship*, 1978 | D. Wilson, American
121. *A Prayer for My Daughter*, 1978 | T. Babe, American
122. *A Tower near Paris*, 1978 | Copi, French
123. *T-Shirts*, 1978 | R. Patrick, American
124. *Bent*, 1979 | M. Sherman, American
125. *Cloud 9*, 1979 | C. Churchill, English
126. *Latin! or Tobacco and Boys*, 1979 | S. Fry, English

127. *News Boy*, 1979 | A. Brown, American
128. *Rents*, 1979 | M. Wilcox, English
129. *Richmond Jim*, 1979 | C. Yeomans, American
130. *Beer and Rhubarb Pie*, 1980–90 | D. Curson, American
131. *Forever After*, 1980 | D. Wilson, American
132. *Another Country*, 1981 | J. Mitchell, English
133. *Beyond Therapy*, 1981 | C. Durang, American
134. *Cock-Ups*, 1981–83 | S. Moss, English
135. *Forty-Deuce*, 1981 | A. Bowne, American
136. *Kiss of the Spider Woman*, 1981 | M. Puig, Argentine
137. *Niagara Falls*, 1981 | V. Bumbalo, American
138. *Pines '79*, 1981 | T. Miller, American
139. *Remember Me*, 1981 | M. Tremblay, Canadian
140. *Something Cloudy, Something Clear*, 1981 | T. Williams, American
141. *Torch Song Trilogy*, 1981 | H. Fierstein, American
142. *Coming Clean*, 1982 | K. Elyot, English
143. *Easy Terms*, 1982 | F. Vickery, Welsh
144. *Happy Birthday, Daddy*, 1982 | R. Hall, American
145. *If This Isn't Love!*, 1982 | S. Morris, American
146. *Snow Orchid*, 1982–93 | J. Pintauro, American
147. *Street Theater*, 1982 | D. Wilson, American
148. *Auto-Erotic Misadventure*, 1983 | F. J. Hartland, American
149. *Finding the Sun*, 1983 | E. Albee, American
150. *Webster*, 1983 | R. D. MacDonald, Scot
151. *Bearclaw*, 1984 | T. Mason, American
152. *The Dressing Gown*, 1984 | S. Gilbert, Canadian
153. *Levitation*, 1984 | T. Mason, American
154. *Night Sweat*, 1984 | R. Chesley, American
155. *Progress*, 1984 | D. Lucie, English
156. *As Is*, 1985 | W. M. Hoffman, American
157. *Being at Home with Claude*, 1985 | R.-D. Dubois, Canadian
158. *Coming of Age in Soho*, 1985 | A. Innaurato, American
159. *In the Blue*, 1985 / *Certain Young Men*, 1999 | P. Gill, Welsh
160. *It's All Due to Leprechauns*, 1985 | G. Branson, English
161. *The Lisbon Traviata*, 1985–90 | T. McNally, American
162. *Never the Sinner*, 1985–94 | J. Logan, American
163. *The Normal Heart*, 1985 | L. Kramer, American
164. *Observe the Sons of Ulster Marching towards the Somme*, 1985 | F. McGuinness, Irish
165. *Raw Youth*, 1985 | N. Bell, American
166. *When She Danced*, 1985 | M. Sherman, American
167. *Breaking the Code*, 1986 | H. Whitemore, English
168. *Diary of a Somebody*, 1986 | J. Lahr, American
169. *Innocence*, 1986 | F. McGuinness, Irish
170. *Irving*, 1986 | M. Piñero, Puerto Rican
171. *Jerker*, 1986 | R. Chesley, American
172. *A Quiet End*, 1986 | R. Swados, American
173. *Touch*, 1986 | D. Demchuk, Canadian
174. *A Bright Room Called Day*, 1987 | T. Kushner, American
175. *Burn This*, 1987 | L. Wilson, American
176. *Compromised Immunity*, 1987 | A. Kirby, English
177. *Lilies*, 1987 | M. M. Bouchard, Canadian
178. *Mean Tears*, 1987 | P. Gill, Welsh
179. *Mr. Universe*, 1987 | J. Grimsley, American
180. *Nasty Little Secrets*, 1987 | L. Robertson, American
181. *Round 2*, 1987 | E. Bentley, American
182. *Steel Kiss*, 1987 | R. Fulford, Canadian
183. *Straight and Narrow*, 1987 | J. Chinn, English
184. *Theatrelife*, 1987 | S. Gilbert, Canadian
185. *Absolute Hell*, 1988 | R. Ackland, English
186. *Carthaginians*, 1988 | F. McGuinness, Irish
187. *Eastern Standard*, 1988 | R. Greenberg, American
188. *The Heidi Chronicles*, 1988 | W. Wasserstein, American
189. *Polygraph*, 1988 | R. Lepage and M. Brassard, Canadian
190. *Single Spies*, 1988 | A. Bennett, English
191. *This Island's Mine*, 1988 | P. Osment, English
192. *Zero Positive*, 1988 | H. Kondoleon, American
193. *Adam and the Experts*, 1989 | V. Bumbalo, American
194. *Amulets against the Dragon Forces*, 1989 | P. Zindel, American
195. *Ancient Boys*, 1989–90 | J.-C. van Itallie, American
196. *The Death of Peter Pan*, 1989 | B. Lowe, Australian
197. *Hyde in Hollywood*, 1989 | P. Parnell, American
198. *Saint Oscar*, 1989 | T. Eagleton, English
199. *The Sum of Us*, 1989 | D. Stevens, Australian

200. *Unidentified Human Remains and the True Nature of Love*, 1989 | B. Fraser, Canadian
201. *Advice from a Caterpillar*, 1990–91 | D. C. Beane, American
202. *The American Plan*, 1990 | R. Greenberg, American
203. *The Baltimore Waltz*, 1990 | P. Vogel, American
204. *Blood and Honour*, 1990 | A. Harding, Australian
205. *La Maison Suspendue*, 1990 | M. Tremblay, Canadian
206. *Once in a While the Odd Thing Happens*, 1990 | P. Godfrey, English
207. *Six Degrees of Separation*, 1990 | J. Guare, American
208. *The Stanley Parkers*, 1990 | G. Aron, Irish
209. *Angels in America*, 1991–92 | T. Kushner, American
210. *The Best of Schools*, 1991 | J.-M. Besset, French
211. *Brave Hearts*, 1991 | H. Rintoul, Canadian
212. *Bravely Fought the Queen*, 1991 | M. Dattani, Indian
213. *Flesh and Blood*, 1991 | C. Thomas, Canadian
214. *Furious*, 1991 | M. Gow, Australian
215. *Mongrels*, 1991 | N. Enright, Australian
216. *The Old Boy*, 1991 | A. R. Gurney, American
217. *Raft of the Medusa*, 1991 | J. Pintauro, American
218. *The Saints and Apostles*, 1991 | R. Storey, Canadian
219. *Whale Riding Weather*, 1991 | B. MacDonald, Canadian
220. *The Baddest of Boys*, 1992 | D. Holsclaw, American
221. *The Fastest Clock in the Universe*, 1992 | P. Ridley, English
222. *Flaubert's Latest*, 1992 | P. Parnell, American
223. *Heartbreak*, 1992 | J. Heifner, American
224. *Jeffrey*, 1992 | P. Rudnick, American
225. *John, I'm Only Dancing*, w. 1992 | K. Duncum, New Zealander
226. *Lake Street Extension*, 1992 | L. Blessing, American
227. *The Law of Remains*, 1992 | R. Abdoh, American
228. *My Night with Tennessee*, 1992 | S. Gilbert, Canadian
229. *Party*, 1992 | D. Dillon, American
230. *Porcelain*, 1992 | C. Yew, American
231. *The School of Night*, 1992 | P. Whelan, English
232. *Trafficking in Broken Hearts*, 1992 | E. Sánchez, Puerto Rican
233. *Two Weeks with the Queen*, 1992 | M. Morris, Australian
234. *Beat the Sunset*, 1993 | M. L. MacLennan, Canadian
235. *Beautiful Thing*, 1993 | J. Harvey, English
236. *Blue Dragons*, 1993 | G. Armstrong, Canadian
237. *Box 27*, 1993 | M. N. Mann, American
238. *Lonely Planet*, 1993 | S. Dietz, American
239. *Pterodactyls*, 1993 | N. Silver, American
240. *The Rainy Season*, 1993 | D. Okita, American
241. *Stephen & Mr. Wilde*, 1993 | J. Bartley, Canadian
242. *The Stillborn Lover*, 1993 | T. Findley, Canadian
243. *The Twilight of the Golds*, 1993 | J. Tolins, American
244. *What's Wrong with Angry?*, 1993 | P. Wilde, English
245. *As the Beaver*, 1994 | J. D. Johnson, American
246. *Babies*, 1994 | J. Harvey, English
247. *Bad Company*, 1994 | S. Bent, English
248. *The Beloved Disciple*, 1994 | T. Jacobson, American
249. *Blade to the Heat*, 1994 | O. Mayer, American
250. *The Food Chain*, 1994–95 | N. Silver, American
251. *Good Works*, 1994 | N. Enright, Australian
252. *Joy*, 1994 | J. Fisher, American
253. *A Language of Their Own*, 1994 | C. Yew, American
254. *Love! Valour! Compassion!*, 1994 | T. McNally, American
255. *My Night with Reg*, 1994 | K. Elyot, English
256. *What Are Tuesdays Like?*, 1994 | V. Bumbalo, American
257. *You Should Be So Lucky*, 1994 | C. Busch, American
258. *Boom Bang-a-Bang*, 1995 | J. Harvey, English
259. *Clean*, 1995 | E. Sánchez, Puerto Rican
260. *Comfort and Joy*, 1995 | J. Heifner, American
261. *The Coronation Voyage*, 1995 | M. M. Bouchard, Canadian
262. *Dog Opera*, 1995 | C. Congdon, American
263. *Jim Dandy*, 1995 | S. Gilbert, Canadian
264. *Minutes from the Blue Route*, 1995 | T. Donaghy, American

Overview of Entries

265. *Raised in Captivity*, 1995 | N. Silver, American
266. *The Rise and Fall of Peter Gaveston*, 1995 | G. MacArthur, Canadian
267. *Roots and Wings*, 1995 | F. Vickery, Welsh
268. *Clocks and Whistles*, 1996 | S. Adamson, English
269. *Deporting the Divas*, 1996 | G. Reyes, American
270. *Flipzoids*, 1996 | R. B. Peña, American
271. *The Gay Detective*, 1996 | G. Stembridge, Irish
272. *Shopping and Fucking*, 1996 | M. Ravenhill, English
273. *Some Sunny Day*, 1996 | M. Sherman, American
274. *Sordid Lives*, 1996–2005 | D. Shores, American
275. *The Undertaking*, 1996 | P. Osment, English
276. *Visiting Mr. Green*, 1996 | J. Baron, American
277. *As Bees in Honey Drown*, 1997 | D. C. Beane, American
278. *Civil Sex*, 1997–2000 | B. Freeman, American
279. *The Convergence of Luke*, 1997 | H. Rintoul, Canadian
280. *Grace*, 1997 | M. L. MacLennan, Canadian
281. *Gross Indecency*, 1997 | M. Kaufman, American
282. *In Mortality*, 1997 | L. Cabranes-Grant, Puerto Rican
283. *The Invention of Love*, 1997 | T. Stoppard, English
284. *Martin Yesterday*, 1997 | B. Fraser, Canadian
285. *A Question of Mercy*, 1997 | D. Rabe, American
286. *The Secret Fall of Constance Wilde*, 1997 | T. Kilroy, Irish
287. *The Soldier Dreams*, 1997 | D. MacIvor, Canadian
288. *Corpus Christi*, 1998 | T. McNally, American
289. *Dogeaters*, 1998–2001 | J. Hagedorn, American
290. *Down Dangerous Passes Road*, 1998 | M. M. Bouchard, Canadian
291. *The Dying Gaul*, 1998 | C. Lucas, American
292. *Family Values*, 1998 | C. Deemer, American
293. *Four*, 1998 | C. Shinn, American
294. *Handbag*, 1998 | M. Ravenhill, English
295. *The Judas Kiss*, 1998 | D. Hare, English
296. *The Most Fabulous Story Ever Told*, 1998 | P. Rudnick, American
297. *On a Muggy Night in Mambai*, 1998 | M. Dattani, Indian
298. *The Backroom*, 1999 | A. Pagan, English
299. *Chat Room*, 1999 | L. Cabranes-Grant, Puerto Rican
300. *Coffeehouse*, 1999 | M. D. Jackson, American
301. *Compleat Female Stage Beauty*, 1999 | J. Hatcher, American
302. *Die Mommie Die!*, 1999 | C. Busch, American
303. *Dolly West's Kitchen*, 1999 | F. McGuinness, Irish
304. *Hushabye Mountain*, 1999 | J. Harvey, English
305. *Kilt*, 1999 | J. Wilson, Canadian
306. *Night Queen*, 1999 | M. Dattani, Indian
307. *Rescue and Recovery*, 1999 | S. Murray, American
308. *Somewhere in the Pacific*, 1999 | N. Bell, American
309. *Wonderland*, 1999 | C. Yew, American
310. *The Beginning of August*, 2000 | T. Donaghy, American
311. *The Crumple Zone*, 2000 | B. Thomas, American
312. *Elizabeth Rex*, 2000 | T. Findley, Canadian
313. *Hijra*, 2000 | A. Kotak, English
314. *In Extremis*, 2000 | N. Bartlett, English
315. *Kit Marlowe*, 2000 | D. Grimm, American
316. *The Laramie Project*, 2000 | M. Kaufman, American
317. *Mambo Italiano*, 2000 | S. Galluccio, Canadian
318. *Other People*, 2000 | C. Shinn, American
319. *The Queen & Peacock*, 2000 | L. Deegan, Irish
320. *Singapore*, 2000 | J., Canadian
321. *Southern Baptist Sissies*, 2000 | D. Shores, American
322. *Thief River*, 2000 | L. Blessing, American
323. *Vincent River*, 2000 | P. Ridley, English
324. *Flamingos*, 2001 | J. Hall, English
325. *Mouth to Mouth*, 2001 | K. Elyot, English
326. *Out in the Open*, 2001 | J. Harvey, English
327. *Prok*, 2001 | B. Drader, Canadian
328. *Say You Love Satan*, 2001 | R. Aguirre-Sacasa, American
329. *The Shooting Stage*, 2001 | M. L. MacLennan, Canadian
330. *The York Realist*, 2001 | P. Gill, Welsh
331. *The Coffee Lover's Guide to America*, 2002 | J. Hall, English
332. *Gates of Gold*, 2002 | F. McGuinness, Irish

333. *Lovesong of the Electric Bear*, 2002 | S. Wilson, English
334. *The Men from the Boys*, 2002 | M. Crowley, American
335. *Original Sin*, 2002 | P. Gill, Welsh
336. *Take Me Out*, 2002 | R. Greenberg, American
337. *Where Do We Live*, 2002 | C. Shinn, American
338. *Big Bill*, 2003 | A. R. Gurney, American
339. *Cherish*, 2003 | K. Duncum, New Zealander
340. *The End of the Tour*, 2003 | J. D. Johnson, American
341. *Hardcore*, 2003 | J. Hall, English
342. *Last Romantics*, 2003 | M. L. MacLennan, Canadian
343. *The Last Sunday in June*, 2003 | J. Tolins, American
344. *Mr Elliott*, 2003 | J. Hall, English
345. *My Big Gay Italian Wedding*, 2003 | A. J. Wilkinson, American
346. *2 Lives*, 2003 | A. Laurents, American
347. *Your Loving Simon*, 2003 | R. Colman, South African
348. *Youth*, 2003 | O. Py, French
349. *Beautiful Child*, 2004 | N. Silver, American
350. *Beauty of the Father*, 2004 | N. Cruz, American
351. *Dog Sees God*, 2004 | B. V. Royal, American
352. *Happy Endings Are Extra*, 2004 | A. Johaardien, South African
353. *The History Boys*, 2004 | A. Bennett, English
354. *Liar*, 2004 | B. Drader, Canadian
355. *Match*, 2004 | S. Belber, American
356. *The Paris Letter*, 2004 | J. R. Baitz, American
357. *Spatter Pattern*, 2004 | N. Bell, American
358. *Valhalla*, 2004 | P. Rudnick, American
359. *Blowing Whistles*, 2005 | M. Todd, English
360. *The Boy Who Fell from the Roof*, 2005 | J. Jenkin, South African
361. *Bunbury*, 2005 | T. Jacobson, American
362. *Curtsy*, 2005 | B. Drader, Canadian
363. *Questa*, 2005 | V. Bumbalo, American
364. *Rope Enough*, 2005 | S. Gilbert, Canadian
365. *Romance*, 2005 | D. Mamet, American
366. *Sir Richard Wadd, Pornographer*, 2005 | S. Postoff, Canadian
367. *A Strange and Separate People*, 2005 | J. Marans, American
368. *Strangers in Between*, 2005 | T. Murphy, Australian
369. *Telstar*, 2005 | N. Moran, English
370. *The Agony & The Agony*, 2006 | N. Silver, American
371. *Based on a Totally True Story*, 2006 | R. Aguirre-Sacasa, American
372. *Circuitry*, 2006 | A. Barrett, American
373. *Citizenship*, 2006 | M. Ravenhill, English
374. *Danny and Chantelle (Still Here)*, 2006 | P. McMahon, Irish
375. *The Drowning Room*, 2006 | V.-A. Mavenawitz, Irish
376. *Dying City*, 2006 | C. Shinn, American
377. *The Golden Thug*, 2006 | E. Roy, Canadian
378. *Holding the Man*, 2006 | T. Murphy, Australian
379. *In Gabriel's Kitchen*, 2006 | S. Antonio, Canadian
380. *The Little Dog Laughed*, 2006 | D. C. Beane, American
381. *Measure for Pleasure*, 2006 | D. Grimm, American
382. *Regrets Only*, 2006 | P. Rudnick, American
383. *Some Men*, 2006–07 | T. McNally, American
384. *Southwark Fair*, 2006 | S. Adamson, English
385. *All That I Will Ever Be*, 2007 | A. Ball, American
386. *Dalliances*, 2007 | P. Jacobs, South African
387. *The Giant*, 2007 | A. Sher, English
388. *His Greatness*, 2007 | D. MacIvor, Canadian
389. *Shadow of Himself*, 2007 | N. Bell, American
390. *Special Forces*, 2007 | J. Fisher, American
391. *Speech & Debate*, 2007 | S. Karam, American
392. *Fucking Men*, 2008 | J. DiPietro, American
393. *Now or Later*, 2008 | C. Shinn, American
394. *Octopus*, 2008 | S. Yockey, American
395. *Plague over England*, 2008 | N. de Jongh, English
396. *The Pride*, 2008 | A. K. Campbell, English
397. *Secrets of the Trade*, 2008 | J. Tolins, American
398. *Sissy*, 2008 | R. A. Bracho, American
399. *Slipping*, 2008 | D. Talbott, American
400. *Steve & Idi*, 2008 | D. Grimm, American
401. *Wig Out!*, 2008 | T. A. McCraney, American
402. *Cock*, 2009 | M. Bartlett, English
403. *The Habit of Art*, 2009 | A. Bennett, English
404. *I Have AIDS*, 2009 | S. Gilbert, Canadian
405. *The Intelligent Homosexual's Guide to Capitalism and Socialism with a Key to the Scriptures*, 2009–11 | T. Kushner, American
406. *Marcus*, 2009 | T. A. McCraney, American
407. *Me, as a Penguin*, 2009 | T. Wells, English

Overview of Entries

408. *The Miracle at Naples*, 2009 | D. Grimm, American
409. *Muscle*, 2009 | T. Wainwright, English
410. *The Muscles in Our Toes*, 2009 | S. Belber, American
411. *Myth of Andrew & Jo*, 2009 | G. van Eeden, South African
412. *Next Fall*, 2009 | G. Nauffts, American
413. *Prick Up Your Ears*, 2009 | S. Bent, English
414. *The Temperamentals*, 2009 | J. Marans, American
415. *True Love Lies*, 2009 | B. Fraser, Canadian
416. *With Bated Breath*, 2009 | B. MacDonald, Canadian
417. *Canary*, 2010 | J. Harvey, English
418. *Courageous*, 2010 | M. Healey, Canadian
419. *Mary*, 2010 | T. Bradshaw, American
420. *Banana Boys*, 2011 | E. Placey, English
421. *Bootycandy*, 2011 | R. O'Hara, American
422. *Edith Can Shoot Things and Hit Them*, 2011 | A. R. Pamatmat, American
423. *Falling in Time*, 2011 | C. E. Gatchalian, Canadian
424. *Go Back to Where You Are*, 2011 | D. Greenspan, American
425. *House of the Rising Son*, 2011 | T. Jacobson, American
426. *The Kitchen Sink*, 2011 | T. Wells, English
427. *The Lyons*, 2011 | N. Silver, American
428. *Rattigan's Nijinsky*, 2011 | N. Wright, English
429. *Sons of the Prophet*, 2011 | S. Karam, American
430. *Tom at the Farm*, 2011 | M. M. Bouchard, Canadian
431. *Trade*, 2011 | M. O'Halloran, Irish
432. *The Twentieth-Century Way*, 2011 | T. Jacobson, American
433. *Band Fags!*, 2012 / *BFs!*, 2015 | F. A. Polito, American
434. *The Best Brothers*, 2012 | D. MacIvor, Canadian
435. *From White Plains*, 2012 | M. Perlman, American
436. *Harbor*, 2012 | C. Beguelin, American
437. *Special Thanks to Guests from Afar*, 2012 | N. Spagnoletti, South African
438. *Vanya and Sonia and Masha and Spike*, 2012 | C. Durang, American
439. *The View*, 2012 | P. Rademeyer, South African
440. *The Whale*, 2012 | S. D. Hunter, American
441. *Wolves*, 2012 | S. Yockey, American
442. *Arigato, Tokyo*, 2013 | D. MacIvor, Canadian
443. *Choir Boy*, 2013 | T. A. McCraney, American
444. *Chomi*, 2013 | P. Nemakonde, South African
445. *Jumpers for Goalposts*, 2013 | T. Wells, English
446. *Late Company*, 2013 | J. Tannahill, Canadian
447. *Mothers and Sons*, 2013 | T. McNally, American
448. *The Nance*, 2013 | D. C. Beane, American
449. *Teddy Ferrara*, 2013 | C. Shinn, American
450. *Another Day on Willow St*, 2014 | F. A. Polito, American
451. *Concord Floral*, 2014 | J. Tannahill, Canadian
452. *A Hard Rain*, 2014 | J. Bradfield and M. Hooper, English
453. *Pronoun*, 2014 | E. Placey, English
454. *Riding in Cars with (Mostly Straight) Boys*, 2014 | S. Brooks, New Zealander
455. *Sextet*, 2014 | M. Panych, Canadian
456. *Versailles*, 2014 | P. Gill, Welsh

Preface

Gay (and lesbian) theater in the English-speaking world has a rich heritage. Here is proof: synopses of 456 published plays, listed in chronological order. Chosen for their aesthetic, historical, or representative value, they represent only a portion of the ones available. In deciding which scripts to consider, I concurred with William Hoffman's criteria. In his introduction to *Gay Plays: The First Collection* (ix), he defines a gay play "as one whose central figure or figures are homosexual or one in which homosexuality is a main theme." I decided not to confine myself to scripts written in English but also to accept translations. This became especially vital in examining Canadian literature since there is cross-fertilization between its French and English cultures. Hoffman goes on to define "'gay theater' as a production that implicitly or explicitly acknowledges that there are homosexuals on both sides of the footlights." He further observes that "any play can be performed gay" (x), but I stick to the ones in which the character is pretty obvious. True, before War II one must decipher that character's sexuality, but it would take a pretty obstinate reader to quarrel with the ones I have selected.

One caveat: I had always felt wary of Foucault's thesis that sexuality is a cultural/social construct. In exploring almost 2500 years of Western theatrical history, I came, however, to accept the validity of his observation. Despite the probable sameness of sexual acts across the centuries, the sexual identities of those who performed the acts obviously varied from one culture to another and from one time period to another. Marlowe could not have thought of Edward II the way I think of him. Still *Edward II* belongs to the gay repertoire even if we are projecting the term *gay* backwards upon works that could not have been so labeled on conception. Strictly speaking the parts the actors are playing in dramas written prior to the 1920s are *erastai*, sodomites, homosexuals, the first "gays" not appearing until the jazz age. But for anyone who has seen the production of *Edward II* starring Ian McKellen and James Laurenson, it is a gay play, and that's that. For actors and directors a play is not a historical document but a performative script whose meaning changes in revivals both because of the humans involved on both sides of the imaginary footlights and because of cultural events that have preceded the new production, including earlier productions and film versions.

There may be objections to some plays I omit. I leave out plays by gay playwrights in which one must search to discern a gay subtext. Thus, James Baldwin, James Barrie, Brendan Behan, Jean Cocteau, Clyde Fitch, Moss Hart, Avery Hopwood, Langston Hughes, George Kelly, Edward Martyn, Somerset Maugham, Yukio Mishima, Ivor Novello, Lynn Riggs, Saki (H. H. Munro), John Van Druten, Patrick White, Thornton Wilder, Emlyn Williams, and Oscar Wilde (just to name the ones who readily come to mind) are not present here. I do not include plays such as Lanford Wilson's *Lemon Sky* or Peter Gill's *Over Gardens Out* in which an adolescent is on the verge of discovering his sexuality. Nor do I include homosocial plays such as John Steinbeck's *Of Mice and Men* and Michael Healey's *The Drawer Boy*. I include no lesbian or transgender plays—with two exceptions, one with a gay transmale (*Pronoun*) and one with a gay intersexed person (*Curtsy*). Despite commonalities, given the way our society is structured, lesbians' and transgender persons' paths are different from those of gay males. I restrict my selection to scripts in print. A sizable number of new scripts appear as ebooks, but until someone explains to me how one will be able to obtain copies of ebooks if the publishers go out of business, I will continue to ignore them. Even so, obviously I have read only a portion of the printed scripts available. If I have missed works you consider significant, I invite you to use your blogs to add to my selection.

I am far from being a pioneer in surveying American and British gay theater. Carl Miller (*Stages of Desire*, 1996) and John Franceschina (*Homosexualities in the English Theatre*, 1997) covered the pre-twentieth-century London scene. Twentieth-century London's West End and New York's Broadway have been surveyed by Kaier Curtin (*"We Can Always Call Them Bulgarians,"* 1987), Nicholas de Jongh (*Not in Front of the Audience*, 1992), John Clum (*Acting Gay*, 1992; revised: *Still Acting Gay*, 2000); and Alan Sinfield (*Out on Stage*, 1999), plus the more specialized work by Jordan Schildcrout (*Murder Most Queer*, 2014). Introductions to anthologies serve as mini-surveys. It does not surprise me to discover that my survey is markedly different from theirs. I include many English and American plays that none of my predecessors looked at: some older works (Ronald Firbank's *The Princess Zoubaroff*), many off–Broadway experiments, and some works that they surprisingly ignored (for example, Terrence Rattigan's *Man and Boy*; Paul Zindel, *Amulets against the Dragon Forces*). But it was when I began folding in Canadian, Australian, Irish, and Scottish plays—none of which earlier surveys had regarded—that I realized how vibrant our gay theatrical heritage is. Then I found Filipino, Indian, South African, and New Zealand plays that further shaped my understanding of the gay repertoire, allowing me to see both differences and commonalities with the usual titles presented. Finally, I have the advantage that I can add the last twenty years to our evolving history.

In my summaries I have often dropped in quotations from the play so as to give some sense of the script's flavor. Note: ellipses in brackets are mine; without brackets, the author's punctuation. I sometimes use the language of the period in reference to gays even though it sounds offensive to our present ears. I list premieres whenever I could find the information, giving the names of the actors who created the gay roles. Throughout the middle sections I quote Donald Vining's impressions of plays he saw in New York. He was a theater student; his diaries offer insight into the impact productions had on a gay man at the time. In many ways, however, I think it has been an advantage that I have had to rely on texts, having seen only a few of these plays on stage, so I have not been swayed by a particular interpretation.

This guide has a personal element. Before I retired from the classroom, my books and articles were all designed to obtain tenure, promotions, and raises in salary. True, many concerned Tennessee Williams, but nowhere did I stress his gay identity. My personal reading explored gay writers, but my focus even there, like that of so many academics, was largely restricted to canonical authors. Gay pulps and Joseph Hansen's mysteries provided about the only guilty pleasures. But once retired, I felt free to explore my larger literary heritage as a gay man. So I explored mysteries, pulps, mainstream and marginalized fiction, and now plays. Throughout, I have been more interested in gay identity than in queer theory. I read Clum's admission in *Still Acting Gay* with recognition: "I overheard a graduate student say about my relationship with theory to another graduate student, 'He's read the stuff, but he just doesn't seem to care'" (xvi). I confess, my eyes glaze over when I read such a learned work as Samuele Grassi's *Looking through Gender: Post 1980 British and Irish Drama*. She seems incapable of making a statement without justifying it by reference to Foucault, Eve Sedgwick, Judith Butler, and company. I am not ready to make the leap to *queer* yet. I am still engrossed in finding out how I relate to *gay*.

I thank my friends and colleagues who have provided bits of information, encouraged me, and patiently listened to my talking about my findings. They include Dennis Bolin, Erica Bruder, Glenna Cannon, Stephen Delaney, Cathy Downs, Ron Hamm, Mike Hess, Charlie Perdue, Stephen Sabrio, Bruce Schueneman, Glenda Stewart Langley. Once again Aggie Gonzalez of the James C. Jernigan Interlibrary Loan Department at Texas A&M University–Kingsville proved to be my bloodhound angel. My play collection will join the Drewey Wayne Gunn Collection of Gay Literature at the Jernigan Library. All royalties from the sale of this volume will go to purchasing books for the Drewey Wayne Gunn Donation of Lesbian Literature. I dedicate this guide to the memory of my late partner and fellow lover of the theater Jacques Murat, whom laws forbade me to marry, and to my canine companions who have brightened my life after his passing: wise Andy, then neurotic Marsden, and now the joy named Joey.

Introduction

Theater, at least from the time it cut free from religious rites, has functioned as a haven for the marginalized, the disenfranchised, the different. It is natural to suspect that a significant number of actors and playwrights in earlier times were gay, and it is no surprise to have proof that many from the early twentieth century on were. Dissembling is natural for people who have to spend their lives concealing a major aspect of their being. When AIDS blew the closet door open, so to speak, the theater continued to be a haven for gay artists simply because it remained so supportive. A character at the beginning of David Greenspan's *Dead Mother*, 1991, parodies heterosexual discomfort: "I'm feeling a little left out. I guess I would like to see a play—more plays—with heterosexual characters." Neil Patrick Harris's ironic opening number for the 2011 Tony Awards, "It's Not Just for Gays Anymore," is a witty reflection of this same perception. Because of outside pressures, gay plays, in reality, were slow to find a home in theaters, not coming into their own until the 1960s.

The professional English stage began with the construction of a playhouse called simply the Theatre just outside London in 1576. Actors were all males; women's roles were taken by boys. Thus from the beginning the plays had a homoerotic quality, and it would not be surprising to find that many of the actors and playwrights, despite Henry VIII's 1533 buggery act, were sodomites. Certainly, theaters early on became associated with prostitution. Plays themselves were peppered with allusions to male same-sex acts. Marlowe's *Edward II*, however, is astonishing in its openness about a same-sex attraction between two men. For us today it matters not if we are viewing it with anachronistic eyes: it is the first gay play in English. There is nothing like it in Shakespeare, though his *Troilus and Cressida* has its Achilles and Patroclus, and there are two Antonios, one in *The Merchant of Venice* and the other in *Twelfth Night*, who certainly appear to modern sensibilities to be gay. These characters exist in largely solitary splendor, despite James I's reputation for sometimes acting the queen.

The playhouses were shut down by the Puritans in 1642. When they reopened in 1660 women were permitted on stage. Charles II's court became renowned for its scandalous behavior. All sorts of characters on the Restoration stage seem to verge on being gay, but in minor roles, and even then modern readers may be mistaking elegant posturing for gay camping. Curiously, it was during his reign that the Lord Chamberlain was granted the right to censor plays for political, religious, and sexual reasons. As a result, though playhouses themselves were denounced as cruising grounds, the stage could resort at best to only gay innuendo and indirection for the next three hundred years. For at least part of that time, as Rictor Norton has documented in *Mother Clap's Molly House*, sodomites created private performance spaces in which to enact parodies of marriage, birthing, and stately balls (masquerades). Norton (96) claims that these early homosexual meeting houses "bear some resemblance" to "the first music halls," but he does not indicate that more theatrical entertainment was part of their attraction. In the rest of the English-speaking world puritanism functioned as effectively as the Lord Chamberlain did in the U.K.

Oscar Wilde never wrote a gay play. That does not stop critics from looking for gay coding in his plays. All sorts of sexual meanings have been attached to words such as "Bunburying" and "Earnest." Possible homoerotic relationships have been scrutinized. The results are tantalizing, sometimes revealing. But it is wise to keep in mind Sinfield's stricture (*Out on Stage*, 33–34) that "Wilde's dandies are generally heterosexually passionate, and/or philanderers." He holds, "The closest we come to a queer scandal in Wilde's plays is in *A Woman of No Importance* (1893)" with Lord Illingworth's infatuation with his illegitimate son Gerald, but it is not spelled out whether this attraction is sexual or merely paternal. Illustrative of how subjective any reading of a gay Wilde must be, Gregory Woods (*History*, 175) uses similar language to come to a different conclusion: "the nearest Wilde comes to representing homosexual desire on the stage is in *Salomé*, in Herodias' pageboy's love for the Syrian captain of the guard." Whatever one decides about the plays, Sinfield is on target in stressing the importance of the 1895 trials to the development of a sense of gay identity, for there "the entire, vaguely disconcerting nexus of effeminacy, leisure, idleness, immorality, luxury, insouciance, decadence and aestheticism, which Wilde was perceived as instantiating, was transformed into a brilliantly precise image: the queer" (28). In taking the stand, Wilde became a character in his own personal drama and, as such, has inspired countless plays since, while *The Importance of Being Earnest* has become a trope for gay playwrights to reference repeatedly. His novel *The Picture of Dorian Gray* has been adapted for stage at least twenty-four times, according to Julian Oddy (online: doollee.com), including published scripts by John Osborne, 1975; Roberto Aguirre-Sacasa, 2009; and Neil Bartlett, 2012.

Wilde's trial came about just as the word *homosexual* was entering the English lexicon. It was coined in Germany in 1869; it came into English in 1892 via a translation of Richard von Kraft-Ebing's *Psychopathia Sexualis*. It offered a medical/psychological model to vie with the criminal/sinner model (*sodomite*). Whereas the latter prescribed punishment for social transgression, the former championed treatment. This conflict is explicitly dramatized in Mae West's *The Drag*. The psychological model also permitted affirmation of same-sex desire; homosexuals are born as such. This model is depicted fumblingly in J. R. Ackerley's *Prisoners of War*, vampirishly in Mordaunt Shairp's *The Green Bay Tree*, and positively in West's delightful *The Pleasure Man* and the Stokes brothers' *Oscar Wilde* using Wilde's own words. Despite arguments over how gay Noël Coward's *Design for Living* is, its importance as a template for latter plays involving a *ménage à trois* is clear. Such portrayals were rare, however, since during the entire interwar period the London stage had to put up with the decrees of the Lord Chamberlain and Broadway had to put up with homophobic critics (Curtin cites Brooks Atkinson, Burns Mantle, and George Jean Nathan in particular) and a hostile legal system that led to the closure of any play that took sex seriously. The so-called Wales Padlock Law, passed by the New York legislature in 1927, fairly well spelled quietus on the production of gay plays all the way through the 1950s, though a number managed to get by with introducing minor gay characters. *Gay* as a slang term for male homosexuals, by the way, is also first recorded in the 1890s. The meaning was well enough established by 1938 that Cary Grant could expect some of his audience to understand what he means in the film *Bringing Up Baby* when he says, "I just went gay."

The Second World War had a major impact on those who served. Colin Spencer writes in *Homosexuality in History*, "For the first time in their lives, many homosexuals realised they were not alone, and they could begin to articulate a homosexual identity which was shared with others" (351). Matt Cook in *A Gay History of Britain* recalls, "On the home front in World War II, the blackouts in major cities provided cover for casual sex" (149). In 1948 Alfred Kinsey published his report on male sexuality; I remember talk about it introducing the word *homosexual* into my nine-year-old vocabulary. Peace, however, brought a surge of governmental repression. Under the baleful influence of Republican Senator Joseph McCarthy, the U.S. State Department instigated a crackdown on gay federal employees. In England the number of arrests for "gross indecency" did not go up, but newspapers' decision to publicize the arrests of several prominent citizens left gays feeling they were the target of an English witch-hunt. The Lord Chamberlain's power continued to keep homosexuality off London stages. Little effort was made by the so-called kitchen sink realists to push sexual boundaries, the one striking exception being the work of a teenager: Shelagh Delaney's *A Taste of Honey*. But the general atmosphere created by the Angry Young Men encouraged gay British playwrights to attack theatrical oppression in various ways, first subtly and then increasingly more openly. The

London stage witnessed the beginnings of Peter Shaffer's enormously successful career; Joe Orton's all too short one; John Osborne's examination of a gay spy (*A Patriot for Me*); Coward's first openly homosexual play (*A Song at Twilight*); Charles Dyer's abominable caricature of a gay couple (*Staircase*), predictably admired by critics; two rather daring gay/bisexual plays by Christopher Hampton (*When Did You Last See My Mother?* and *Total Eclipse*), and the beginnings of Simon Grey's flirtation with homosexuality (*Wise Child*)—all before 1968, the year the Lord Chamberlain's office lost the right to censor theater.

Broadway likewise continued to struggle to bring homosexual themes onstage. In the 1950s the pseudo-gay plays *Tea and Sympathy* by Robert Anderson and *A View from the Bridge* by Arthur Miller teased audiences. Tennessee Williams was far more daring. The allusions to homosexuality in *The Glass Menagerie* (for those in the know), *A Streetcar Named Desire*, *Camino Real*, *Cat on a Hot Tin Roof*, and the perfectly wrought *Suddenly Last Summer* made the playwright's closet door more and more transparent. The only other truly gay play besides *Summer* was the dramatization of André Gide's *The Immoralist* by Ruth and Augustus Goetz, even in its original censored form. Hugh Wheeler launched two plays, *Big Fish, Little Fish* and *Look, We've Come Through*, in 1961. The first, in which homosexuality was so muted as to be invisible to some audience members, was a success; the second—and far more interesting work—played only five evenings, leading Marilyn Stasio to examine the reasons for its failure in her study of five flops: *Broadway's Beautiful Losers*, 1972. Sinfield (*Out on Stage*, 219) sums up her findings: "New York critics could not tolerate the thought that a sympathetic, unreformed and unpunished gay boy might hold the stage at the end." Lorraine Hansberry's *The Sign in Sidney Brustein's Window*, with its portrait of a successful gay playwright, also failed.

In 1961 the *New York Times* critic Howard Taubman began one of the more perplexing polemics to hit Broadway. Out of the blue, he published a piece headlined "Not What It Seems," in which he accused gay writers of subverting American theater by disguising their gay agenda under the cover of apparently straight situations. Less than two years later he returned to the theme with another essay, "Modern Primer," in which he provided audiences with a checklist by which to identify gay playwrights hiding behind straight facades. Ironically, he was doing pretty much the same thing gay critics do when they search out gay subtexts in the works of known gay writers, but by aiming his glare at living, practicing playwrights, his "primer" was a direct affront to the gay theater community. More insults were to follow. In 1966 Stanley Kauffman in an essay "Homosexual Drama and Its Disguises" felt called upon to announce that "three of the most successful American playwrights of the last twenty years are (reputed) homosexuals." In a follow-up essay "On the Acceptability of the Homosexual," he justified his gratuitous outing as an appeal to let writers be honest. The *Times* led the way, but pretty much all the New York critics were products of their homophobic times. In their effort to sniff out gay dishonesty, the most comical moment perhaps occurred in 1973 when Martin Gottfried swore that the seemingly incestuous brother and sister in Williams's *Out Cry* were really two men. (Two men doing it clearly aroused him more than a brother and a sister at it.) One cannot help but wonder how the careers of Williams, Inge, and Albee might have developed in a friendlier environment. John Simon became such a vile horror that I simply gave up reading any of his reviews. Following Allan Pierce's lead, Curtin (*Bulgarians*, 320–33) provides the fullest description of this sorry chapter in American theatrical history.

Off Broadway it was a different story. American gays increasingly saw themselves as an identifiable minority who could learn from the African-American and Feminist movements. Playwrights began to openly self-identify as gay. They wrote openly gay plays. And for the first time they had, especially Off Off Broadway, openly gay theaters and openly gay audiences. Joe Cino launched his Caffe Cino in 1959. It nourished the talents of Lanford Wilson (ten plays, including *The Madness of Lady Bright*), Doric Wilson (four plays), Jean-Claude van Itallie (*War*), Ronald Tavel (*Vinyl*), Robert Patrick (six plays, including *The Haunted Host*), H. M. Koutoukas (ten plays), William Hoffman (three plays), Robert Heide (two plays), John Guare (three plays), Neil Flanagan (*Candide*), and George Birimisa (*Daddy Violet*). Al Carmines (*The Faggot*) was the major force behind the Judson Poets' Theatre, 1961. La MaMa offered another vital outlet beginning 1962; Lanford Wilson and van Itallie moved there, and it gave Harvey Fierstein his start (*The International Stud*). Tavel, John Vaccaro, and Charles Ludlam formed the Playhouse of the Ridiculous in 1965, with Ludlam breaking off to start his own Ridiculous Theatrical Company in 1967. Other Off Off Broadway and Off Broadway houses were receptive to gay plays. Theater of the absurd combined with camp sensibility to produce a plethora of plays whose stories, styles, and themes are so varied as to make generalizations difficult if not impossible. The plays I include here are simply a sampling of the rich library available.

Off Broadway was responsible for the first major gay works. Both *Fortune and Men's Eyes* by the Canadian John Herbert and *Boys in the Band* by Mart Crowley were praised and reviled, especially *Boys*. The subsequent films, with *Boys* using the same cast and *Fortune* relying heavily on the Los Angeles production directed by Sal Mineo, met the same mixed reception. I have yet to see *Boys* on stage, but I hated the film when it came out. I'm not sure I even stayed until the end. I confess I had much the same reaction to Jean Poiret's still untranslated *La cage aux folles* when, dressed in my best clone attire, I saw it in Paris in 1973. Both plays presented gay images that I wanted nothing to do with. Then I saw the 1978 film of *La cage* and wondered how my younger self could have been so dense. I had the same feeling when *Boys* came out on DVD. It is now one of my favorite plays; as I type this I am hearing Leonard Frey's unmistakable voice delivering his final attack on Michael. Its historical importance is simple: for the first time we had eight men on stage who acknowledge they are gay, several of them even celebrating the fact, one pair reaffirming a committed relationship. It is not going too far to say that one can divide gay theater into before *Boys* and after *Boys*.

It was still running when the Stonewall Inn rebellion occurred in 1969. In Doric Wilson's 1982 tribute to the uprising (*Street Theater*), two characters from *Boys* (Michael and Donald) wander by as the riot is occurring. Somewhat unfairly on Wilson's part, they are appalled by the scene. (Crowley took his revenge twenty years later by revealing that Emory was one of the queens that revolted.) It took the theater three years to respond to Stonewall, but in 1972 Jonathan Katz brought his stirring documentary piece *Coming Out!* to the Gay Activists Alliance headquarters in an old NYC firehouse. The most popular gay American play during the decade was probably Terrence McNally's visit to a gay bathhouse, *The Ritz*. The most powerful was Martin Sherman's *Bent* (which first played in London), his unflinching stare at a Nazi concentration camp. The most significant, in the long run, was perhaps Lanford Wilson's *Fifth of July* in which the extraordinary thing about a gay couple is their ordinariness. Arthur Laurents wrote the first of his only two gay plays (*The Enclave*); it was the same for John Patrick (*Confession*). Alan Bowne (*Beirut, Forty-Deuce*), Victor Bumbalo (*Niagara Falls*), Christopher Durang (*Sister Mary Ignatius Explains It All for You; Beyond Therapy*), Fierstein (*Torch Song Trilogy*), and Albert Innaurato (*Gemini*) launched their careers in the 1970s. Musical comedy introduced openly gay characters (see Appendix B). *The Rocky Horror Show* premiered in London in 1973; *A Chorus Line* in New York in 1975. At the very end of the decade William Finn began his gay *Marvin* trilogy. Perhaps even more remarkable, Michael Tippett and Benjamin Britten composed gay operas: respectively, *The Knot Garden* and *Death in Venice*. As for new theaters, Doric Wilson formed TOSOS in 1972, Theatre Rhinoceros came into existence in San Francisco in 1977, the Gay Theater Alliance was created in 1978, and Atlanta's 7 Stages Theatre was established in 1979. There were also gay theaters in Chicago and Los Angeles.

In London, fringe theaters such as the Almost Free Theatre proved receptive to gay plays. The Gay Sweatshop Theatre Company was formed in 1975. It soon attracted the talents of Drew Griffiths (*Age of Consent*), Noël Greig (*The Dear Love of Comrades*), the American Sherman (*Passing By*), and later Philip Osment. Griffiths and Greig's frieze of gay history, *As Time Passes*, reminds gay audiences of the constant need for vigilance against complacency. Elsewhere playgoers had the chance to see John Hopkins's examination of a gay man trying to get out of a heterosexual marriage (*Find Your Way Home*), Peter Nichols's amusing look at military entertainment (*Privates on Parade*), Caryl Churchill's imaginative correlation of colonial and sexual oppression (*Cloud 9*), Michael Wilcox's examination of educated rent boys (*Rents*), Julian Mitchell's look at the correlation between the closet and espionage (*Another Country*), and the first of the many retellings of Joe Orton's murder (Simon Moss's *Cock-Ups*). Even Graham Greene joined in with his spoof *The Return of A. J. Raffles*.

Introduction

Dublin had its first gay play in 1968: Thomas Kilroy's *The Death and Resurrection of Mr. Roche*. Brian Friel followed with a biting attack on Irish homophobia in *The Gentle Isle*, 1971. But no gay Irish theater movement resulted. Robert David MacDonald (*Chinchilla*) put Glasgow onto the gay theater map. Australia was finally stirring. Michael Hurley in his *Guide* (263–64) credits Martin Smith's unpublished *Love Has Many Faces*, 1970, "as the first produced Australian gay play" (Smith lost his job as a consequence of the media uproar that resulted) and mentions that Stables Theater "hosted the first season of gay plays in Australia in 1976." Peter Kenna began his Cassidy trilogy with *A Hard God* and also produced *Mates*. Straight playwright Jim McNeill presented *How Does Your Garden Grow?* Steve Spears's one-man show *The Elocution of Benjamin Franklin* became the first gay Australian play to achieve international renown. But no real movement began yet. What surprised me was how vital gay Canadian theater became. Pioneer Mazo de la Roche seems to have been forgotten (both Sinfield and de Jongh discuss her without mentioning that she was Canadian). The online *Canadian Theatre Encyclopedia* credits the decriminalization of same-sex acts in 1968 as freeing playwrights. Herbert had to turn to New York to have *Fortune and Men's Eyes* produced in 1967. But now theaters in Toronto and Montreal became receptive to staging gay plays. Douglas Chambers (in C. Summers, *Reader's Companion*, 136–38) lists works by Louis Del Grande (*So Who's Goldberg?*), Larry Fineberg (*Human Remains*), Ken Gass (*The Boy Bishop*), Tom Hendry (*How Are Things with the Walking Wounded?*), Michael Hollingsworth (*Strawberry Fields*), Larry Kardish (*Brussel Sprouts*), Martin Kinch (*Me?*), John Palmer (*The End*), and David Tipe (*Diamond Cutters*). Sky Gilbert was a co-founder of Buddies in Bad Times Theatre in 1979. In Montreal there was the towering figure of Michel Tremblay, whose plays (*Hosanna, Remember Me*) were quickly translated and presented in Toronto. A Filipino play written in English appeared in 1970: Wilfrido Maria Guerrero's *The Clash of Cymbals*; but Filipino writers prefer their native tongue.

* * *

I still vividly recall picking up the *International Herald Tribune* that July morning in 1981 and reading the news item reprinted from the *New York Times*: "Rare Cancer Seen in 41 Homosexuals." I broke out in a sweat and instantly pulled up my trousers' leg to inspect the dark spot that had appeared at the edge of my left boot top. The moment was followed by a decade feeling of lymph nodes, worrying over night sweats, and watching friends waste away. It took a while for the theater to catch up to reality. David Román writes (in G. Haggerty, *Gay Histories*, 37): "The first plays to address AIDS include *One*, Jeff Hagedorn's one-person drama produced by Chicago's Lionheart Theater in 1983; *Warren*, Rebecca Ranson's multi-character play produced by Atlanta's Seven [sic] Stages Theatre in 1984; and *The A.I.D.S. Show*, a collaborative production at San Francisco's Theatre Rhinoceros in 1984. [...] The first plays produced in New York City were *Night Sweat* by Robert Chesley and *Fever of Unknown Origin* by Steven Holt. Both these plays, however, failed to galvanize New Yorkers. It was not until 1985, with the premieres of William Hoffman's *As Is* and Larry Kramer's *The Normal Heart*, that AIDS theater crossover [sic] into the mainstream." Román goes on, "Beginning in the late 1980s and continuing throughout the 1990s, emerging and established playwrights and performers began to write and produce AIDS plays for regional and national stages. Gay playwrights such as Harry Kondoleon [*Zero Positive*], David Greenspan [*Jack*], Scott McPherson [*Marvin's Room*], Terrence McNally [*Andre's Mother*], Harvey Fierstein [*Safe Sex*], and Craig Lucas [teleplay *Longtime Companion*] were among the first dramatists to address AIDS in their work." They were followed by Tony Kushner (*Angels in America*), Joe Pintauro (*Rosen's Son; Raft of the Medusa*), Doug Holsclaw (*The Baddest of Boys*), Jack Heifner (*Heartbreak*), Paul Rudnick (*Jeffrey*), Steven Dietz (*Lonely Planet*), Nicky Silver (*Pterodactyls*), Victor Bumbalo (*What Are Tuesdays Like?*), David Rabe (*A Question of Mercy*), and a host of others. AIDS was prominent in Jonathan Larson's 1990s hit musical *Rent*.

Sinfield (*Out on Stage*, 326) points out that, in contrast to the American scene, "British lesbian and gay activists tend to locate themselves within a broad-left political awareness, and therefore are more likely to present the epidemic in a wider context, rather than in 'an AIDS play' as such." He also holds (329), "We have not been writing AIDS drama because it has been done for us" (that is, by the Americans). Andy Kirby's *Compromised Immunity* and Kevin Elyot's *My Evening with Reg* stand in isolation in England, as does Geraldine Aron's *The Stanley Parkers* in Ireland. Canada was also slow to respond: Gilbert's *Theatrelife* was followed by mention of the plague in Brad Frazer's *Unidentified Human Remains*. But then we had in rapid succession Harry Rintoul's *Brave Hearts*, Colin Thomas's *Flesh and Blood*, Raymond Storey's *The Saints and Apostles*, Michael Lewis MacLennan's *Beat the Sunset*, and Gordon Armstrong's *Blue Dragons*. *Canadian Theatre Encyclopedia* (online) writes, "It is hard to determine exactly what effect the AIDS pandemic has had on writers in Canada, but it is clear that the disease has hit the theatre community especially hard. [...] perhaps that is bringing Gays and Lesbians and their concerns into focus, and encouraging an openness in the theatres that was not there before." Bruce Parr in the introduction to his anthology of Australian plays says that examples of AIDS plays there "range from one of the earliest if not the first, *Soft Targets* (1986) by the Soft Targets Company and the late Tim Conigrave, through to works of the nineties as diverse as David Paul Jobling's *Mortal Coils*, Anthony Lambert's *Bloodwork*, William Yang's *Sadness* and Richard Barrett's *Bad Poetry* [...]. Far from being 'victim art,' they are about surviving and living under the threat of death, none more so than [Alex Harding's] *Blood and Honour*" (22). To them one may add Mary Morris's *Two Weeks with the Queen*, which, like *Flesh and Blood*, was targeted for younger audiences. Even non–AIDS plays seemed haunted by death during this period. Take for examples Frank McGuinness's World War I drama, *Observe the Sons of Ulster*; Hugh Whitemore's biography of Alan Turing, *Breaking the Code*; Barry Lowe's biography of Michael Davies, *The Death of Peter Pan*; Robert Lepage and Marie Brassard's *Polygraph*.

The loss of writing and acting talent was devastating. American playwrights who died of complications due to AIDS include Reza Abdoh, Bowne, Chesley, Nicholas Dante, Richard Hall, James Kirkwood, Kondoleon, Ludlam, Terry Miller, Sidney Morris, Wheeler, Cal Yeomans. Add to them Armstrong, Conigrave, Copi, Gibson Kente, Robert Lord, Maxim Mazumdar, Manuel Puig. Symptomatic of the dark night that gay theater now entered, half the cast and many of the crew of *Boys in the Band* were struck down by the retrovirus. I began to wonder if the urgency, or lack thereof, to respond to the epidemic related to the number of cases each country was dealing with. To my surprise, it is difficult to come up with figures prior to the 1990s. The U.S. had the best reporting system. The CDC had tallied 15,527 cases by 1985, the year of *As Is* and *The Normal Heart*. (Of those, 12,529 had died.) Canada had only 648 cases, while Australia estimates that it had 4,500. A hard-to-read graph for the U.K. would indicate somewhere around 5,000 cases there. In Ireland the first case of HIV was diagnosed only in 1985. Sinfield (328) insists, "There is a different density in UK experience, chiefly because the initial transmission of HIV was slower and later. We had not developed, or been allowed to have, bath-houses and back-rooms, so knowledge about safer sex arrived in time to hinder the rate of infection."

The big blockbuster in the 1980s in New York was a musical: Harvey Fierstein and Jerry Herman's *La Cage aux Folles*, based on Poiret's play. Its rousing song "I Am What I Am" has, of course, become a gay anthem. Bernstein, who never did a gay musical, brought out a bisexual opera, *A Quiet Place*. The America stage saw the arrival of Richard Greenberg (*Eastern Standard*); Kondoleon; Kushner (*A Bright Room Called Day*), one of the few American playwrights willing to tackle political oppression; Peter Parnell (*Hyde in Hollywood*); Miguel Piñero; and Pintauro (*Snow Orchid*). Albee wrote his first gay play (*Finding the Sun*). In London Rodney Ackland felt free to recreate an earlier play into the story he wanted to tell, resulting in *Absolute Hell*. Elyot (*Coming Clean*) arrived, and Alan Bennett (*Single Spies*) began to edge out of the closet. The decade saw the start of the careers of Welsh playwrights Peter Gill (*In the Blue*) and Frank Vickery (*Easy Terms*). Throughout the U.K. gays had to cope with self-appointed moral watchdog Mary Whitehouse. Her solicitor became hysterical when he thought he glimpsed a penis during the homosexual rape scene in Howard Brenton's *The Romans in Britain*, though he finally had to admit that he had been sitting too far back in the theater to be sure. With McGuinness, gay Irish theater became a reality. Canadians Gilbert (*The Dressing Gown*), Robin Fulford (*Steel Kiss*), Frazer, Morris Panych (*7 Stories*), René-Daniel Dubois (*Being at Home with* Claude), Michael Marc Bonchard (*Lilies*), and Lepage became forces in Toronto, Calgary, Vancouver, Montreal, and Quebec. In 1986 Daniel MacIvor founded da da kamera as an adjunct to Buddies in Bad Times.

Introduction

The highly prolific Lowe, whose plays have been described by critic Stephen Dunne as "almost unintelligible to a straight audience" (in B. Parr, *Plays*, 34) achieved success on Australian stages, and David Stevens had an international hit with *The Sum of Us*, aided by its successful conversion into a film with Russell Crowe.

In reading gay dramas starting in the 1960s and on to the present, one is struck by how small casts often are. The fact reflects the growing cost of producing plays in general, fringe plays in particular. Playwrights facing economic realities became ingenious at devising two-character plays, two-handers (a term forever evoking a pornographic image in my mind), and utilizing doubling to create a multi-character play with only a few actors, often leading to visually revealing dramatic correspondences. In place of realistic sets, flexible staging became the norm. The ultimate evolution was to one-man performance pieces, either performed as one voice, often the performer's own, or as many voices channeled by the one actor to approximate a traditional cast. Some of the more outstanding examples are listed in Appendix A.

Bonnie Marranca's introduction to *Plays for the End of the Century*, 1996, sums up the point to which American theater had arrived by the 1990s: "A brief list of present conditions notably affecting Americans would have to include the new global economies and technologies transforming all manner of human exchange, the disempowerment of the middle class, changing patterns of immigration and race relations, the fall of Communism and the increased perception of fragility in democratic systems, the deterioration of urban life and civil society, AIDS and the general health care crisis, the pervasive role of media in everyday life, and influential feminist, gay, libertarian, and religious movements. All of these developments have contributed to the crisis of values and schizophrenic rhythms in American life and to the turmoil of the country's cultural and political climate. American drama has reacted to the state of affairs by making identity, sex, race, and gender its chief subjects, with such single-mindness that it seems as this cultural soap opera is the only kind of drama being written today" (xi). Twenty years later her statement needs little tweaking.

Kusner's *Angels in America* dominated the decade and beyond. It not only swept the theater awards (including the Pulitzer, the first gay play so honored), but it proved to be a hot ticket in Los Angeles, San Francisco, London, and New York. Allusions to it and parodies of its angels dot subsequent plays. Its only competitor for importance might be McNally's *Love! Valour! Compassion!* which had the good fortune to be turned into a film with its original cast minus Nathan Lane (probably for the better since Lane tends, like Ethel Merman, to be too large for the screen). New playwrights include the professionally slick Douglas Carter Beane (*As Bees in Honey Drown*), Jonathan Tolins (*The Twilight of the Golds*), and Rudnick. Charles Busch took on Ludlam's mantle. Exciting work was turned out by Silver (*The Food Chain*), Christopher Shinn (*Four*), and David Grimm (*Kit Marlowe*). Those whom Chew Yew labeled hyphenated Americans came into their own: Pomo Afro Homos (*Fierce Love, Dark Fruit*), Rez Abdoh, Iranian (*The Law of Remains*), Dwight Okita, Japanese (*The Rainy Season*), Guillermo Reyes, Chilean (*Deporting the Divas*), Ralph Peña, Filipino (*Flipzoids*), Yew himself, Chinese (*Porcelain*). Gay Puerto Ricans found their voice. Regional theater continued to be important. Tom Jacobson (*The Beloved Disciple*) is Los Angeles–based. This was the decade in which the one-man performance piece came into its own. Moisés Kaufman and his Tectonic Theater Project revitalized documentary theater, most notably with *The Laramie Project*. Hoffman's call for the "stage exploration of gay history" beyond Wilde (xxxv) was met by plays about Marlowe (*The Beloved Discipline, Kit Marlowe*), A. E. Housman (*The Invention of Love*), Benjamin Britten (*Once in a While the Odd Thing Happens*), Williams (*My Night with Tennessee*), Bayard Rustin (*Civil Sex*). In the musical theater *Rent* was one of the box office successes (it too won a Pulitzer). The other big musicals were the revised *Cabaret*, *Hedwig and the Angry Inch*, and the guilty pleasure *Naked Boys Singing*. A need for a respite from the simple act of survival led to the success of David Dillon's *Party*. On the evidence of his collection *Four Super Gay Plays*, Sean Abley's Chicago Factory Theater seems to have been a soft porn theater adventure: one of the titles is *L.A. Tool & Die: Live!*, a dramatization of Joe Gage's porn film classic.

In England in 1988 the Thatcher government passed the Local Government Act with its notorious Section 28: Prohibition on Promoting Homosexuality by Teaching or by Publishing Material.

It read: "(1) A local authority shall not (a) intentionally promote homosexuality or publish material with the intention of promoting homosexuality; (b) promote the teaching in any maintained school of the acceptability of homosexuality as a pretended family relationship. (2) Nothing in subsection (1) above shall be taken to prohibit the doing of anything for the purpose of treating or preventing the spread of disease." This was the atmosphere in which Elyot's *My Night with Reg* was produced. (It also was filmed with the same cast quite successfully.) Jonathan Harvey's *Beautiful Thing* is perhaps the most loved work of the decade, even if it is better known in its film incarnation than in its stage version. New arrivals included Philip Ridley (*The Fastest Clock in the Universe*), a leader of In-Yer-Face theater; Mark Ravenhill, who gained notoriety for his play advertised in the press as *Shopping and F**king* (allegedly, one playgoer left the theater commenting to her fellow theatergoer, "Well, there certainly wasn't much shopping"); and Samuel Adamson (*Clocks and Whistles*). Adrian Pagan's life was cut short after his one play: *The Backroom*, about rent boys. Neil Bartlett has always been a man of the theater, but his work has been largely in the form of monologues (*A Vision of Love Revealed in Sleep*) and experimental theater (such as working with puppets in *Or You Could Kiss Me*) rather than traditional dramaturgy. Ash Kotak (*Hijra*) is an English example of the hyphenated playwright (Indian, in his case).

India itself had at least two playwrights to address gay themes: R. Raj Rao (*The Wisest Fool on Earth*) and Mahesh Dattani (several plays, most notably *On a Muggy Night in Mambai*). New voices were heard in Canada. Joining the playwrights already mentioned were Jim Bartley (*Stephen and Mr. Wilde*), Steve Galluccio (*Mambo Italiano*), Greg MacArthur (*The Rise and Fall of Peter Gaveston*), Bryden MacDonald (*Whale Riding Weather*), Daniel David Moses (*The Indian Medicine Shows*), Jonathan Wilson (*Kilt*), and above all Timothy Findley, whose *Elizabeth Rex* is a masterful piece of dramaturgy. In Australia, newcomers included Michael Gow (*Furious*) and the versatile Nick Enright (*Mongrels*). In Ireland there were Gerard Stembridge (*The Gay Detective*) and Loughlin Deegan (*The Queen & Peacock*).

The millennium brought in advances that I never thought I would live to see. Thatcher's last vote was to maintain the hateful and harmful Section 28, but common sense prevailed, and the law was struck down first in Scotland, then in England and Wales. Gays were permitted to serve openly in the military and to enter civil unions. The U.S. Supreme Court by five to four, in one swoop, turned untold numbers of us from criminals to law-abiding citizens when it ruled that the government had no business in the privacy of our homes. (Of course, we had to listen to Antonio Scalia snort about the "gay agenda.") When the monumental decision permitting same-sex couples to legally bless their relationships was announced, the Chief Justice disgraced himself by congratulating us for having gained the right but assuring us that it was not the Constitution that had given it to us. (Obviously he feels his reading of the document is far superior to that of his five colleagues who granted us equal protection under the law.) How much more uplifting were New Zealand's legislator Maurice Williamson's remarks to that governing body when it was debating gay marriage; I urge you to watch his speech on YouTube if you have not already seen it. But then we have Barack Obama, who not only rid us of the ruinous "Don't Ask, Don't Tell" military policy, but cited the importance of Stonewall in his magnificent Second Inaugural Address and lit the White House in rainbow colors after SCOTUS's marriage decision. By the way, as a result of that decision, I witnessed my first gay wedding—in Texas! Both sets of divorced parents proudly walked their sons to the altar, obviously wishing them better in their marriage than they had managed in theirs.

Gay theater took on new life. The plague faded in significance. Romance, relationships, families, babies, school, music, art, sports, politics took on greater significance. A surprising number of religious plays appeared. Gay history continued to be explored, with more emphasis on pioneering activists (Alfred Kinsey in *Prok*, Harry Hay in *The Temperamentals*, Simon Nkoli in *Your Loving Simon*). Even the plays about Wilde began to stress his role as a spokesperson for love between men instead of the tragedy of his life. A new development was a growing number of gay plays for young adults by such writers as Bert Royal (*Dog Sees God*), Tommy Murphy (*Strangers in Between*), Ravenhill (*Citizenship*), Stephen Karam (*Speech & Debate*), Ricardo Bracho (*Sissy*), Daniel Talbott (*Slipping*), Tarell Alvin McCraney (*Marcus; Choir Boy*), Evan Placey (*Banana Boys; Pronoun*), Rey

Pamatmat (*Edith Can Shoot Things and Hit Them*), Tom Wells (*The Kitchen Sink*), Frank Anthony Polito (*Band Fags!*), Jordan Tannahill (*Concord Floral*). They sometimes dramatize coming out, but as often they depict teenagers already out. In the opposition between the out teenagers in Harvey's *Beautiful Thing* and the closeted ones in Patrick Wilde's *What's Wrong with Angry?* Harvey's became the norm.

South African gay playwrights for the first time gained a stage for their work. Roy Sargeant's Artscape New Writing Programme, based in Cape Town, has become instrumental in discovering and fostering LGBT voices. Already in print are plays by Robert Colman (*Your Loving Simon*), Ashraf Johaardien (*Happy Endings Are Extra*), Juliet Jenkin (*The Boy Who Fell from the Roof*), Pieter Jacobs (*Dalliances*), Gideon van Eeden (his wonderful *Myth of Andrew & Joy*), Nicholas Spagnoletti (*Special Thanks to Guests from Afar*), Pfarelo Nemakonde (*Chomi*), and Philip Rademeyer (*The View, Ashes*). The scripts weigh heavily on the dark side. Yet, though AIDS is mentioned, it does not have nearly the importance one would expect in a country still ravished by the epidemic with the number of people suffering from HIV the most of any country in the world at the moment.

Gay New Zealand plays have found homes on stages in Wellington and elsewhere, but I have been unable to find a discussion of its LGBT theater. Robert Lord produced his unpublished *Meeting Place* in 1972. Two playwrights have seen print: Ken Duncum (*Cherish*) and Sam Brooks (*Riding in Cars with [Mostly Straight] Boys*). Many others are available as mimeographed scripts or ebooks. Playmarket.org.nz supplies scripts for Susan Battye and Tim Bray (*Ponsonby Road*), Victor Bodger (*Black Faggot*), Patrick Graham (*Post Gay*), Greg McGee (*Whitemen*), Carl Nixon (*KiwiFruits*), Allen O'Leary (*Deviations*), Paul Rothwell (*Cut Out*), and Thomas Sainsbury (*Luv*). Australian playwrights also seem to have had to resort to e-publishing, Murphy being the striking exception. Australian*plays*.org lists Gary Abrahams (*Acts of Deceit [between Strangers in a Room]*, based on James Baldwin's novel *Giovanni's Room*), Robert Allan (*An Ordinary Person*), Noel Anderson (*Andy Warhol's Fifteen Minutes of Fame*), David Atfield (*Scandalous Boy*, a historical fantasy about Antinous), Kit Brookman (*Small and Tired*, a revisit of the Greek story of Orestes), David Burton and Claire Christian (*Hedonism's Second Album*), Campion Decent (*Baby X*), Justin Fleming (*The Cobra*, another dramatization of Douglas's memories of Wilde), Laura Jackson (*The Culture*), Patricia Johnson (*The White Light*), Stephen Kakavoulis (*Children of the Father*, about a pedophile priest), Tobsha Learner (*Seven Acts of Love [as Witnessed by a Cat]*), and Susan Rogers and Chris Drummond (*Night Letters*, based on the novel by Robert Dessaix).

The International Dublin Gay Theatre Festival was established in 2004 to commemorate the 150th anniversary of Wilde's birth. It has showcased works from around the world. New Irish playwrights include Deegan, Neil Watkins (one-man shows), Phillip McMahon (*Danny and Chantelle*), Patrick Kinsella (*Chalks*), and Mark O'Halloran (*Trade*). England is now producing some of its most exciting scripts, and not just in London. New arrivals include Alexi Kaye Campbell (*The Pride*), Nicholas de Jongh (*Plague over England*), Jonathan Hall (*Flamingos*), Placey, Antony Sher (*The Giant*), Matthew Todd (*Blowing Whistles*), Wells, and Nicholas Wright (*Rattigan's Nijinsky*). The biggest hit of the new century has been Bennett's *The History Boys*, which too has had the good luck to be filmed with its original cast. Canada continues to delight. Joining the continuing active scene are Brian Drader (*Liar*), Robin Fulford (*Steel Pier*), Shawn Postoff (*Sir Richard Wadd, Pornographer*), Ed Roy (*The Golden Thug*), Michael Healey (*Courageous*), C. E. Gathalian (*Falling in Time*), and Tannahill (*Late Company*). New York and American regional theaters welcomed Roberto Aguirre-Sacasa (*Say You Love Satan*), Alan Ball (*All That I Will Ever Be*), Stephen Belber (*The Muscles in Our Toes*), Chad Beguelin (*Harbor*), Nilo Cruz (*Beauty of the Father*), Samuel D. Hunter (*The Whale*), Karam (*Sons of the Prophet*), Jon Marans (*A Strange and Separate People*), McCraney (*Wig Out!*), Robert O'Hara (*Bootycandy*), Michael Perlman (*From White Plains*), and Steve Yockey (*Octopus*). Durang had his greatest success with *Vanya and Sonia and Masha and Spike*.

I cut off my selection with the year 2014. Nick Hern Books in England has devised an ingenious marketing strategy: it publishes scripts together with the theater program as plays go into rehearsal, presumably for sale during the production's run. But most publishing houses take two-three years or longer to bring a script into print. Thus the record for 2015–16 is scraggly. I could have included

Jake Brunger's *Four Play*, 2015; Robin Soans's *Crouch Touch Pause Engage*, 2015; Chris Urch's *The Rolling Stone*, 2015; Gavin Roach's *Beyond Priscilla*, 2016; a few others. It seems wiser just to hold off. Here are 456 stories (with mention of others) that have regaled us on stage or in the comfort of our armchairs: made us laugh, weep, become angry, experience puzzlement, remember, feel better about ourselves, and reaffirm our inner strengths. Despite any proclamations that gay literature is dead, gay theater is still finding an avid audience.

THE PLAYS

Pre-Modern, 5th c. BCE–18th c. CE

Probable composition of Biblical stories of Sodom and Gomorrah and of David and Jonathan, 6th c. BCE. Plato's Symposium, 4th c. BCE. Nero is Roman emperor, 54–68. Antinous becomes Hadrian's favorite, 123–30. Elagabalus reigns, 218–22. King Edward II of England murdered, 1327. Recovery of Greek literature, 14th c. "Night Officials" organize in Florence to ferret out sodomites, 1432. King Henry VIII of England decrees Buggery Act, 1533. Christopher Marlowe murdered, 1593. English theaters closed, 1642. Theaters reopen, 1660; women permitted on stage. Raid on Mother Clap's molly house, London, 1726. Lord Chamberlain given right to censor plays, 1737. Last execution for a "crime against nature" in U.S., 1785. Death penalties for sodomy repealed state by state, 1786–1873. Napoleonic Code, decriminalizes sodomy, 1791. Raid on Vere Street molly house, London, 1810. Last two men executed for sodomy in London, 1835. Repeal of U.K. death penalty for sodomy, 1861.

1 *Knights* (424 BCE) | **Aristophanes (5th c. BCE), Athenian**

[Political satire; 6M, 2W, chorus; unit set.] During the Classical Greek era, Athenian attitudes about male/male sexual relationships were so different from ours that those plays of Aristophanes in which such relationships play an important part seem alien. Since his comedies are satires, steeped in irony, there is also a problem discerning the writer's true attitudes. Often he seems to be decrying same-sex relationships, but patently some of his denouncements are actually aimed at other targets: for example, effeminacy. Universal themes keep *Birds*, *Lysistrata*, and *The Frogs* on stage, but they have few or no references to what we would label homosexuality. *Knights* does, but it would take an imaginative director to pull the play off nowadays. It is an allegory set before the house of Demos (i.e., Athens). His steward Paphlagon (i.e., the Athenian general and politician Cleon, who may well have been sitting in the first audience) has corrupted Demos through flattery and is now misusing his power for his own gains: "He's got one foot in Pylos, and the other in the Assembly. He's got his legs spread so far apart that his arsehole's smack dab over Buggerland, his hand's in Shake Downs, and his mind's on Crimea." The suffering of two slaves in Demos's household emboldens them to steal the oracles Paphlagon is forever consulting. They discover that it has been prophesied he will be replaced by a sausage seller. At that instance, such a seller passes by with his phallic wares. A commoner who has "also sold [his] arse," he is talked into taking on Paphlagon in a bizarre contest to establish which one is the more shameless—since "political leadership's no longer a job for a man of education and good character, but for the ignorant and disgusting." The slaves guarantee the sausage seller that the Knights will back him and promise him that if he wins he will be the "top dog of them all, of the market, the harbors, and the Pnyx [public assembly]! You'll trample the Council, dock the generals, put people in chains and lock them up, suck cocks in the Prytaneum [the public banqueting hall]."

So the contest begins. To prove his fitness to

govern, the sausage seller recounts how, when he was a boy, he would steal meat and hide it in his crotch, all the while swearing to his innocence—or, as Demos's slave says, "you perjured yourself about a robbery and took meat up your arse." Much such bawdiness is thrown into the exchanges. When Paphlagon brags, "I can make Demos expand and contract, thanks to my dexterity," the sausage seller responds, "Even my arsehole can do that trick!" The sausage seller tells Demos that, as a result of his listening to Paphlagon, "you're like the boys who attract lovers: you say no to the fine upstanding ones, but give yourself to lamp sellers and cobblers and shoemakers and tanners." When Demos finally comes to his senses and restores Athens's former glory, the sausage seller awards him a "split-bottom chair and a well hung boy to carry it," with the promise that if he so desires, he can also "use the boy as your split bottom too." At the same time Demos gains two girls garbed as political treaties; he is also eager to "lay them down and ratify them." *Hippeîs* was performed at the Lenaia festival in 424 BCE. § Aristophanes. *Acharnians; Knights*. Trans. by Jeffrey Henderson. Harvard Univ. Press, 1998. 219–405. Multiple translations exist.

2 Women at the Thesmophoria (411 BCE) | Aristophanes, Athenian

[Proto-feminist satire; 6M, 3W, chorus; unit set.] Buffoonery might bring *Thesmophoriazusae* alive. It is a comic attack on the tragic playwright Euripides's alleged misogyny. The stage represents briefly a section of the street outside Agathon's house and then, for the rest of the play, the site of the Thesmophoria Festival. Euripides, having gotten news that the women celebrating the festival intend to denounce him, hits upon the idea of sending a male ally disguised as a woman to infiltrate the celebrants and speak on his behalf. Who better than Agathon, his fellow playwright who has maintained a passive role in sexual relationships into adulthood? Accompanying Euripides is his Kinsmen (traditionally, his father-in-law). He professes not to know Agathon; Euripides retorts that he must have had him anally since all Athens has. Agathon appears dressed as a woman, defending his garb as his way of entering into the spirit of a female character he is creating. He rejects Euripides's scheme, out of fear that "he would make a more attractive woman than the women themselves, and so provoke their hatred" (translator's note). Thereupon, the Kinsman, with Agathon's help, agrees to shed the symbols of his masculinity and undertake the role. He enters the scheme a bit more enthusiastically than one might expect. Shaved and dressed in a woman's garment—which "has a nice scent of weenie"—he discovers he looks like Cleisthenes, another notorious passive partner in sexual relationships who maintains the appearance of a boy. The real Cleisthenes shows up later in the play to warn the women that Euripides's kinsman has penetrated their midst. When the Kinsman is unmasked, he is bound by a guard. In an attempt to rescue him, Euripides disguises himself as Perseus, whereupon the guard offers the Kinsman as "Andromeda," to be taken sexually if "Perseus" so desires. Trying a different stratagem, Euripides returns with a dancing girl, whose sexual charms distract the guard, and secures his Kinsman's release. The cross-dressing and gender transformation make the comedy an important document in a study of gender roles in Western culture. It was presented during the city's Dionysia festival in 411 BCE. A modern production appeared in New York, 1955, with David Hooks, Kelton Garwood, and Richard Longman, directed by Arthur Lithgow.

One would like to know more about the relationships among the real-life persons. Euripides in his 70s reputedly fell in love with Agathon, then in his 40s. Agathon was the host of the banquet described in Plato's *Symposium*. It took place five years before Aristophanes's play was produced. Aristophanes is one of the prominent guests; he delivers the famous creation myth of the divided souls seeking their other halves.[1] Still other Aristophanes comedies include satiric references to same-sex relationships. Thomas Hubbard's *Homosexuality in Greece and Rome: A Sourcebook of Basic Documents* (Univ. of California Press, 2003) has assembled relevant passages from them. Of particular interest is an exchange between Better Argument and Worse Argument about teaching boys, from *Clouds*, 423 BCE, a satire against Socrates's teaching methods. Although same-sex relationships were the subject of other Greek comedies and a handful of tragedies, including plays by Aeschylus and Sophocles, none of those texts has come down to us. As for Roman drama, early comedies were based on now lost Greek originals. Same-sex relationships, however, play little part in the surviving examples. Terence seems to have eschewed the subject altogether, while for Plautus (3rd c. BCE) it serves primarily as material for incidental tricks and witty barbs, mostly about masters' relationships with slaves. Hubbard's anthology assembles several examples. § Aristophanes. *Birds; Lysistrata; Women at the Thesmophoria.* Trans. by Jeffrey Henderson. Harvard Univ. Press, 2000. 443–615. Multiple translations exist.

1. The Greek philosopher Plato (4th c. BCE) perfected a literary form that has come to be known as the Socratic dialogue (since Socrates is the main figure in them). This is a discussion about a subject in which the participants try to explore all its aspects in order to arrive at a conclusion or at least to clarify the matter. They were not intended to be staged, but in modern times they have sometimes been adapted to the theater. Two of Plato's greatest dialogues explore the meaning of same-sex love: *Symposium* and *Phaedrus*. Xenophon (4th c. BCE) wrote his own *Symposium*, a response to Plato's, emphasizing heterosexual love and scorning *paiderastia*. All three works have multiple English translations. Thomas Hubbard's *Homosexuality in Greece and Rome* excerpts relevant passages.

Two Italian Renaissance texts exploring same-sex themes were modeled after the Greek Socratic dialogue. Antonio Vignale (1500?–1559) published *La Cazzaria* about 1531. Quite bawdy in language, comic in tone, it consists of a conversation between two young men about the genital area, often expressed in terms of the body politic. Though primarily heterosexual in nature, its translator Ian Frederick Moulton (9, 35) calls it "an important document for the history of homosexuality" because, "As well as being a political allegory and an erotic myth, *La Cazzaria* is also an apologia for sodomy." He also records (47) that one of the manuscripts contains an addition, not yet translated into English, in which one of the young men recounts his experience as a male prostitute. Moulton's translation—*The Book of the Prick* (Routledge, 2003)—is the third in English; two earlier ones were *La Cazzaria* (Collectors, 1968, trans. by "Sir Hotspur Dunderpate" [Samuel Putnam?]), and *The Love Academy* (Brandon House, 1968, trans. by Rudolphe Schleifer). Antonio Rocco (1586–1653) wrote *Alcibiade fanciullo a scola* in 1630 but did not publish it until the year before his death. It is also a conversation between two males, a school master and his pupil. J. C. Rawnsley translated *Alcibiades the Schoolboy* (Entimos, 2000). In an afterword (108), he addresses the question of the dialogue's intent: "Is it a satire on Machiavelli's doctrine of expediency? An historical and philosophical dissertation in the form of a dialogue? A manual for the seduction of boys? A denunciation and exposé of sodomitical schoolmasters, or perhaps 'a blow against priests'—that is to say, the earliest warning on record against Child Sexual Abuse, in particular among clergy? Or is it merely a rude jest for Carnival."

Two French writers used the dialogue form for very different purposes. The Marquis de Sade (1740–1814) published *La philosophie dans le boudoir* in 1795. Three libertines, a woman and two men, initiate a young girl into the mysteries of sexual pleasure. Dolmancé is a total sodomite, preferring men but willing to take women anally. Chevalier de Mirvel is bisexual (and engaged in an incestuous relationship with his sister). Dolmancé sums up that one must follow Nature, which means following one's impulses without regard for human laws based on fear and egotism. *Philosophy in the Bedroom* has been translated by Richard Seaver and Austryn Wainhouse (Grove, 1965). The dialogue has been the basis for some five films and was arranged for stage in 2003 as *XXX*. The last important use of the form as a means to discuss homosexuality that I have found came from André Gide (1869–1951): *Corydon*, 1911–1924. Consisting of four dialogues between a curious interviewer and Corydon, it amasses evidence that homosexuality is part of the natural order. The dialogues first appeared in English in an anonymous translation (Farrar, Straus, 1950). Richard Howard translated it anew in 1983.

3 *The Tale of Orpheus* (1480) | Poliziano (1454–1494), Tuscan

[Mythological tragedy, with songs; 6M, 4W, extras; flexible set.] A classical scholar and citizen of Florence, Angelo Ambrogina was part of the homosexual coterie there. For his play he turned to the legend, recounted by Ovid, that Orpheus introduced pederasty into Trace. *Orfeo* begins by recounting the well-known story of his descent into the underworld to retrieve his dead wife Eurydice. When he loses her again, by looking back too soon, he renounces women and announces he will "cull new flowers"—that is, young men. In a passionate outburst, he recalls Jove, who "in heaven enjoys his beautiful Ganymede" as "on earth Phoebus enjoyed Hyacinth. To this holy love Hercules surrenders, he who won the world and was won by fair Hylas." Orpheus ends by urging married men "to seek divorce, and all to flee the company of women." Outraged by his misogyny, a bacchante urges her companions to slay the singer and make a sacrifice to Bacchus. *La favola di Orfeo* was given in Mantua, probably in 1480, with Baccio Ugolino. A revised and expanded version in five acts, subtitled *Tragoedia*, was prepared for staging at Ferrara some time before 1486; traditionally it has been ascribed to Antonio Tebaldeo (1463–1537), though other names have been proposed. § *A Translation of the Orpheus of Angelo Politian and the Aminta of Torquato Tasso.* Trans. by Louis E. Lord. Oxford Univ. Press, 1931. 69–103 (both versions on facing pages).

4 *The Marescalco* (1526) | Pietro Aretino (1492–1556), Tuscan

[Sexual comedy; 16M, 5W; unit set.] The Italian Renaissance was conflicted in its attitudes toward same-sex relationship. In a sonnet Aretino, whose name became virtually synonymous with pornography, avowed he himself had been a sodomite since birth. Sixteen years before his birth, the Classical Greek scholar Marsilio Ficino introduced the concept of Platonic love; just three years after his birth, Savonarola began his vicious campaign in Florence against sodomites. Some of the greatest artists of the day were accused: Botticelli, Leonardo, Michelangelo, the aptly nicknamed Il Sodoma, Cellini. The wet nurse in Aretino's play holds that "gluttons who run after nasty pleasures [i.e., sodomites], they should all be burnt," while a pedant rages, "These insolent young fellows, these effeminate ganymedes give *istam urbam clarissimam* [this most fair city] a bad name, where the custodians of Virgilian treasures are at the mercy of *capestri sine rubore* [shameless gallowsbirds] and impudent little pansies." Yet the marescalco—a position that combines the duties of "blacksmith, stablemaster, and veterinarian" (translators' note)—is known by all to be a lover of young men, and it is pretty clear that he is having his way with a stableboy.

The stage represents a general town setting, and the greater part of the play is taken up with various exchanges among the citizens from the highest to the lowest. Its simple plot is an extended prank that the Duke of Mantua plays upon the marescalco. It is given away in a few sentences in the prologue. The duke, ordering him to take a wife, presents him a page dressed as a young woman: "When the trick was discovered, the valiant fellow was happier to find out that she was a boy than he had been sorry to believe that he was a girl." Before then, his old wet nurse, not in on the trick, has rejoiced that he will now "leave the ways of shame and sin. [...] Spruce up [his] reputation a little." When the bride is unveiled as a male, the pedant submits, "*In fine nemo sine crimine vivit* [After all, nobody lives without sinning]," while the wet nurse sighs, "Look how happy the rascal is. [...] You never get the frog out of the marsh." In their notes the translators write that "in the character of the Pedant [...] the subject of homosexuality is obviously and explicitly exploited for comic effect." They also hold that "at least one [other] character, the Cavalier, is also identified as a pederast." However, neither comes across that clearly in their translation. *Il marescalco* was performed in Mantua, 1526. Gian Francesco Malipiero converted it into an opera about misogyny in 1970. § Aretino, P. *The Marescalco*. Trans. by Leonard G. Sbrocchi and Douglas Campbell. Dovehouse, 1992. 110p. Other translations exist. David Greenspan's adaptation *A Horse's Ass*, 2008, remains unpublished.

5 *Edward II* (1593) | Christopher Marlowe (1564–1593), English

[Historical tragedy; 16M, 1W, extras; flexible set.] Louis Crompton (*Homosexuality*, 366) points out that the English Renaissance, as in Italy, "drew its inspiration from the rediscovery of Greece, whose myths and literature provided new perspectives on human behavior. Among the discoveries was the fact of Greek homosexuality, now known at first-hand rather than through the filters of Ovid and Virgil." There is amble evidence that Marlowe was personally receptive to the new learning. He opens his play *The Tragedy of Dido, Queen of Carthage*, published in 1594, with Jupiter's dallying with Ganymede, "that female wanton boy." In *The Troublesome Reign and Lamentable Death of Edward the Second, King of England, with the Tragical Fall of Proud Mortimer*, the king's wife, Isabella, complains that "never doted Jove on Ganymede / So much as he on cursed Gaveston." The elder Mortimer muses, "The mightiest kings have had their minions; / Great Alexander lov'd Hephaestion; / The conquering Hercules for Hylas wept; / And for Patroclus stern Achilles droop'd." Marlowe goes beyond Greek myth, however, in *Edward II*. Crompton observes (376) that it is "the only Elizabethan drama with a homosexual protagonist and, indeed, the only English play to touch on the theme of same-sex attraction in anything more than a peripheral way before the twentieth century." Remarkably, it is not the king's sexuality that leads to his repudiation by his nobles and thus his downfall; their objections, rather, are matters of class and economics: the king's lover is "basely born" and the cause for Edward's misuse of "the treasure of the realm." Even when Edward (1284–1327) is called "unnatural king," he is so accused for his "slaughter[ing] noble men / And cherish[ing] flatterers," not for sodomy.

Written almost entirely in blank verse, *Edward II* is a history play based on Raphael Holinshed's *Chronicles*. The play is also a romantic tragedy in which the king's affection for Piers de Gaveston (1284–1312) leads to his alienation from his queen; as a result Isabella begins an adulterous relationship with young Mortimer. The outcome is the death of all three men and her banishment to the Tower. The love Edward and Gaveston bear each other is immediately disclosed in the opening lines. Gaveston returns from exile, called back by the king's "amorous" letter. That their love is physical is hinted at when, in thinking of the entertainments he will present the king, Gaveston mentions having "a lovely boy in Dian's shape" reenact the goddess's bath, hiding "those parts which men delight to see." The king, upon joining Gaveston, "claps his cheeks and hangs about his neck [...] love-sick for his minion." When Gaveston is killed, Edward vows revenge "for the murder of my dearest friend, / To whom [...] our soul was knit, / Good Piers of Gaveston, my sweet favorite." A legend grew that Edward was killed by having a red-hot poker, a phallic symbol, inserted into his anus, clearly implying that he was a sodomite. Though Marlowe's stage directions do not explicitly describe such an ending, one of jailers calls for "a spit, and let it be red-hot." The play was presented in London, 1593, by Pembroke's Men. Modern productions include one in New York, 1958, with Robert Kidd and Neil Vipond, directed by Edward G. Greer; another in Edinburgh, 1969, with Ian McKellen and James Laurenson, directed by Toby Robertson. The latter was filmed. There have been other film adaptations, including one by Derek Jarman. It was reworked for the German stage by Bertolt Brecht. Scott Eric Smith turned the play into a chamber opera, 2001. Thomas Jonigk and Andrea Lorenzo Scartazzini premiered a grand opera in February 2017. A gay Marlowe is the subject of several modern plays. § Marlowe, C. *Complete Plays and Poems*; ed. by E. D. Pendry. Dent (Everyman), 1976. 123–90.

6 *Troilus and Cressida* (1603) | William Shakespeare (1564–1616), English

[Mythological drama; 21M, 4W, extras; flexible set.] Marlowe's contemporary has been the subject of much controversy when it comes to the subject of same-sex relationships. Many of his plays involve gender-bending (made easier by the convention that women's roles were played by boy actors), homoerotic subtexts, male bonding, and outright same-sex attractions. Two Antonios in particular allow for homosexual readings, even if the relationship is unrequited. Antonio, the title character of *The Comical History of the Merchant of Venice*, 1598, is willing to give everything he has, including his life, to make his friend Bassanio happy, knowing that success means losing Bassanio to marriage with a wealthy heiress. As one of their friends says of Antonio, "I think he only loves the world for him." A. R. Gurney read the play thus and wrote a follow-up, *Overtime*, in 1996. Paul Wagar's 2003 film version, *Shakespeare's Merchant*, leaves no doubt that the emotional bond includes a physical one. Another Antonio, a shipwrecked captain in *Twelfth Night, or What You Will*, 1602, likewise is willing to risk his life out of love for the interestingly named Sebastian: "come what may, I do adore thee so / That danger shall seem sport." He loses Sebastian to a countess. No film version of *Twelfth Night* has yet dared go so far as Wagar's does, but many stage versions do.

Shakespeare's dark take on the chaotic world of the Trojan War, *Troilus and Cressida*, presents two characters who are explicitly described in terms we today would label as homosexual. Patroclus is identified by another character as "Achilles' male varlet [...] his masculine whore." Instead of fighting the two spend their time "Upon a lazy bed the livelong day." Ulysses tries to shame Achilles into returning to battle; Patroclus joins him, emphasizing his own possible culpability: "They think my little stomach to the war / And your great love to me restrains you thus. / Sweet, rouse yourself, and the weak wanton Cupid / Shall from your neck unloose his amorous fold." Patroclus is killed by Hector. Following the classical plot, Achilles returns to battle to avenge his death. The two men have limited time on stage, however, and their relationship is more an homage to Greek sources than an examination of love. The play was registered in 1603 as having been presented by the King's Men.

There are other plays by Shakespeare for which directors have produced gay interpretations: *Richard II* (the king), *Romeo and Juliet* (Mercutio), *The Merry Wives of Windsor* (Slender), *Much Ado about Nothing* (Don John), *Othello* (Iago), *Coriolanus* (Coriolanus and Aufidius), and *The Two Noble Kinsmen* (Arcite and Palamon). Meanwhile, the arguments about Shakespeare's own sexuality continue to be debated. Stanley Wells's *Looking for Sex in Shakespeare* (Cambridge Univ. Press, 2004) and *Shakespeare, Sex, & Love* (Oxford Univ. Press, 2010) take the most common-sense approach to the whole topic. Shakespeare becomes a character in a number of modern gay plays, often in connection with Marlowe, but his sexuality generally remains ambiguous in them. § Shakespeare, W. *The Complete Works*; ed. by Stanley Wells and Gary Taylor. Clarendon, 2005. 743–76.

7 *Sodom, or The Quintessence of Debauchery* (1671?) | John Wilmot, Second Earl of Rochester (1647–1680), English

[Pornographic satire; 9M, 6F, extras; 4 sets.] It seems fitting that the bisexual writer—his poems speak openly of sex with both mistresses and boys—pays homage to Aretino by calling for the setting of Act 1 to be "hung round with Aretine's Postures." A satire on the libertine court of Charles II, the play is basically one extended smutty joke. Tired of sex with women, Bolloxinion, King of Sodom, announces: "I do proclaim, that Buggery may be us'd / Thrô all the Land." His unhappy queen and her maids of honor are reduced to using dildos. Their daughter persuades her brother to take her sexually; the mother tries to enter the incestuous game but loses out, instead masturbating her son to ejaculation. Not even threats from hell sway Bolloxinion to return to the old ways. General Buggeranthos is quite happy with the edict since his soldiers now "Each buggers with content his own comrade." Written in heroic couplets around 1671, the play was not published until 1684. It is generally classified as a closet drama. However, it was allegedly staged by Rochester, and it was performed in Madison, Wis., 1986, and in Edinburgh, 2011. Hal Duncan adapted it as *Sodom: The Musical*, 2013. § Wilmot, J., Earl of Rochester. *Sodom, or The Quintessence of Debauchery.* Brandon House, 1966. 47–123.

8 *The Relapse, or Virtue in Danger* (1696) | John Vanbrugh (1664–1726), English

[Social comedy; 10M, 4W; flexible set.] Male characters in post–Commonwealth plays can confuse present-day readers/viewers. Examples of strong male bonding present the same interpretative problems as they do in Renaissance drama, but construing the campiness of the effeminate fops (beaux, dandies, mollies, macaronis) that populate the period's comedies poses a new problem. One needs to keep in mind that such behavior was considered a mark of elegance and that such characters are in fact generally womanizers. Still quite a list of plays exists that have been singled out as having if not an explicit homosexual character, at least one that seems highly possible. Franceschina's extensive survey *Homosexualities in the English Theatre* seems exhaustive, yet Miller's *Stages of Desire* adds yet other titles. Especially interesting is the latter's mention of Mary Pix's *The Adventures in Madrid*, 1706. According to Miller, a young girl disguised as a boy is "pursued by Gaylove who calls her his little Ganymede and fairy. This may be the first recorded use of 'gay' and 'fairy' in the context of male homosexuality" (220).

One character all critics agree on is Coupler, the matchmaker (or pimp) Vanbrugh created for *The Relapse*, his sequel to a play by Colley Cibber. Young Fashion turns to Coupler for help in murdering his older brother. Upon their meeting, Coupler begs Young Fashion to let him "put my hand in your bosom." Fashion parries, "Stand off, old Sodom!" But when he learns that Coupler will help him, he does not object that Coupler wants his "warm body" as payment: "take possession as soon as thou wilt," he says. Coupler purrs, "Sayest thou so, my Hephestion?" The play opened in London, 1696, with Benjamin Johnson and Mary Kent in a trousers role. Franceschina comments how "the same-sex encounter [...] is somewhat softened by the fact that a woman [...] played the character of Young Fashion"; he goes on to note that, significantly, "when the play was performed in the eighteenth century with a man playing the role of Young Fashion, the lines suggesting same-sex behavior were omitted" (148). § Vanbrugh, J. *The Relapse, or Virtue in Danger*; ed. by Bernard Harris. Norton (New Mermaid), 1971. 130p.

Early Modern, 1891–1943

Walt Whitman's Leaves of Grass, *1855. Gilgamesh tablets translated into English, 1871. Germany's Paragraph 175 criminalizes homosexual acts, 1871. Paul Verlaine imprisoned for wounding Arthur Rimbaud, 1873. "Dublin Castle scandals," 1884. U.K.'s Criminal Law Amendment Act ("the blackmailer's charter"), 1886. Krafft-Ebing's* Psychopathia Sexualis, *1886. Cleveland Street scandal, London, 1889. Pyotr Ilyich Tchaikovsky commits suicide, 1893. Oscar Wilde sentenced to prison, 1895. Magnus Hirschfeld in Germany and George Ives in England push for equal rights for homosexuals, 1897. Havelock Ellis and John Addington Symonds's* Sexual Inversion, *1897. Edward Prime-Stevenson's* The Intersexes *(by "Xavier Mayne"), 1908. Sergei Diaghilev's Ballets Russes in Paris, 1909. Edward Carpenter's* The Intermediate Sex, *1912. Herbert Gerber founds Society for Human Rights in Chicago, 1924. Leopold and Loeb case, 1924. New York State passes "Wales Padlock Law," 1927. Nazis destroy Hirschfeld's Institute, 1933. Federico García Lorca assassinated in Spain, 1936. Nazis use pink triangle to distinguish homosexuals in concentration camps, 1937.*

9   *Spring's Awakening* (1891) | **Frank Wedekind (1864–1918), German**

[Sexual tragedy; 16M, 7W; flexible set.] For Wedekind, sex is the driving force behind all our actions. This forerunner of expressionism and of epic theater, subtitled *A Children's Tragedy*, was published in 1891. It is a savage indictment of the ignorance in which adults keep adolescents about what is happening to their bodies and the potentially tragic results thereof. Homosexuality plays a relatively minor part in the intertwined stories, but its very presence, portrayed sympathetically, is revolutionary. The term *homosexual* first appeared in print in Germany in 1869; *heterosexual* did not appear until 1880. So Wedekind would have known both. The main plot follows the grievous consequences of heterosexual explorations. But the scenario also includes two boys discussing the arrival of puberty, a circle jerk, a scene with Hans Rilow masturbating to a reproduction of a nude female, and Hans's seduction of Ernst Roebel in a vineyard. Hans muses, "Thirty years from now, when we think back on an evening like this, it might seem beautiful beyond words." Ernst declares, "I could never have been happy if I hadn't met you. I love you, Hans, like I've never loved anyone before." Hans then slightly modifies his earlier statement: "When we think back on this in thirty years, we might even make fun of it all. But right now it's so beautiful." Their passionate kiss may well be the first envisioned on stage between two males since Edward II and Gaveston's. All three scenes, however, were cut from the 1906 premiere of *Frühlings Erwachent* in Berlin. The first uncensored English production appeared, in a translation by Edward Bond, in London, 1974, with Dai Bradley and Gerard Ryder, directed by Bill Bryden. Of the several film adaptations, Arthur Allan Seidelman's 2008 version retains the gay subplot. The homoeroticism also remains in Steven Sater and Duncan Sheik's 2006 adaptation of the drama as a rock musical. Thomas Kilroy used the story to critique Irish culture in his *Christ Deliver Us!*, 2010. § Wedekind, F. *Four Major Plays*. Trans. by Carl R. Mueller. Smith & Kraus, 2000. 1–51. Other translations exist.

10 *The Blackmailers* (1894) | John Gray (1866–1934) and Marc-André Raffalovich (FRA 1864–1934), English

[Crime drama; 6M, 7W; 4 sets.] The partners were part of Wilde's circle. Thus, it is not surprising that their play has a Wildean flavor (*An Ideal Husband* especially seems to hover in the background), though without Wilde's linguistic brilliance. The text provides no hard evidence that Claud Price and the younger Hal (Hyacinth) Dangar are in a sexual relationship, but one certainly gains the impression that they are (the very name "Hyacinth" recalls the Greek myth). The two engage in blackmailing members of their own class whose secrets they learn through various forms of indiscretion. It becomes easy to read many of their speeches as code, with *blackmailer* standing for *homosexual*: "Take off your mask, Mr. Dangar," Price says, "and show the face of the blackmailer." When caught out, Dangar throws up to his kinfolks, "The only intelligent affection ever wasted on me was the affection of a scoundrel like myself," whereupon his mother melodramatically announces, "He is not my son. I have *no* son." But according to Dangar, when he was a child she took pride in the fact, "My boy is not like other boys." Laurence Senelick notes "the irony of turning deviants—usually the target of blackmail—into perpetrators, who use extortion as a weapon against an unsympathetic society." By turning everything topsy-turvy, the authors dramatized the shallowness and the hypocrisy of London society just a year before Wilde's trial. Near the end of the play, Dangar contemplates suicide, but when he receives a letter from Price summoning him to Paris—"Come. We understand one another now and the World"—Dangar accepts with alacrity: "I am still so young and I could be so happy. At any rate I could enjoy myself." According to Senelick, the play was presented in London, 1894, for one evening only and was not published until the present collection. § In Senelick, L., ed. *Lovesick*. 15–53.

11 *At Saint Judas's* (1896) | Henry Blake Fuller (1857–1929), American

[Tragedy; 4M, 1W, extras; 1 set.] Fuller published one of the earliest American novels with a homosexual protagonist, *Bertram Cope's Year*, 1919. His closet drama, written in the symbolist mode, is set in the sacristy of the aptly named church of St. Judas. It calls for eight stained glass windows representing aspects of traditional Christianity to become progressively animated so as to underscore the conflict on stage. A bridegroom and his best man, both former military officers, discuss the calumny that has followed the bridegroom from the moment he declared his love for Angela. It quickly becomes obvious to the reader, though not to the groom, that Oliver, his best man, driven by jealousy and thwarted love, has been the source of the slanders. Finally, Oliver bursts out, "I shall not let you go. Our friendship has been too long, too close, too intimate. It shall not be destroyed; it shall not be broken. No one shall come between us. […] No one loves you more than I." The play ends with the best man lying on the floor in a pool of blood, the bride triumphant. It first appeared in *The Puppet-Booth: Twelve Plays*, 1896. § In Senelick, L., ed. *Lovesick*. 59–71.

12 *When the King Comes He Is Welcome* (1896) | Lord Alfred Douglas (1870–1945), English

[Tragedy; 2M; 1 set.] Wilde's lover and bad angel wrote his blank verse play about 1892, the same year he wrote his much quoted poem "Two Loves." Set in 16th-century Padua, the closet drama has only two characters: Giovanni and Francisco. At age 12 the two "Did vow each other love eternally" and then, "Four years agone when I told eighteen winters, / And thou one summer less, we did regraft / Our souls the one to the other." Francisco that day was symbolically wounded by a boar. Afterwards, as they wandered "hand in hand," a dove visited them; in a bit of Victorian camp, a passing gentleman observed, "There are more queens than one / That favour doves, methinks the Cyprian / May well have amorous words for these two toys." But now Giovanni must break the news that his father has commanded him to marry. Under Francisco's influence he welcomes Death the King, "a friend to Love," and drinks from a poisoned cup. Francisco follows suit, and together the two die, Francisco bestowing a final kiss on his friend's lips. It was published in *Poems*, 1896 (Paris), and collected in *Lyrics*, 1935. § Douglas, A. *Lyrics*. Richards, 1943. 92–111.

13 *Saul* (1903) | André Gide (1869–1951), French

[Biblical drama; 11M, 2W, extras; flexible set.]

Though writing the play in 1896, shortly after his sexual liberation in Africa, Gide did not publish it until 1903, the year after *L'immoraliste*, his autobiographical novel recording that liberation, appeared. Following the Biblical story, Daoud (as he is called here) pledges, "Jonathan, my brother! My soul has sobbed with love. [...] More than my soul—ah, Jonathan, more than my soul." But in Gide's dramatization, Daoud's beauty and strength bedazzle not only Jonathan but also Saul and his queen, to the downfall of all three. Beset by his personal demons, Saul yields to them even as he fears their consequence. When he overhears his son and Daoud declare their love for each other, he is wracked with jealousy. He goes so far as to shave off his beard, a symbol of authority, in the hopes of appearing younger in order to attract Daoud. But nothing will appease "the burning in my soul—my soul stirred by your songs—and leaping—from my lips—toward you—Daoud—my delight." Daoud, however, loves "Saul [only] as my King, [but] Jonathan more than myself." In the end, Daoud mourns the deaths of his lover and his would-be lover but, realist that he is, prepares to wear the crown in Saul's stead. The play explores a variety of themes, not least the need for restraint and self-control, but also such matters as predestination versus free will. *Saül* was not performed until 1922, in Paris. § Gide, A. *My Theater: Five Plays and an Essay*. Trans. by Jackson Matthews. Knopf, 1952. 1–107. Also translated by Dorothy Bussy, 1953.

14 *"Mistakes"* (1906) | **Herbert Hirschberg (1881–unknown), German**

[Crime drama; 5M, 1W; 1 set.] Obviously influenced by the German homosexual emancipation movement under the leadership of Dr. Magnus Hirschfeld, this *Dramatic Study* exposes many of the problems that the infamous Paragraph 175 created but lacks any true resolution. The plot centers on a lawyer, Edmund Manhardt, 28. He is being blackmailed by his good-looking manservant, Gerhard, for his indiscretions with him. Edmund is delighted by the return of his school friend Kurt Kleefeld, now a physician. Edmund is still in love with him, though he recognizes that his emotions are not reciprocated. To his credit, Edmund accepts his "nature" and realizes that marriage would make any bride miserable. The father knows the truth, but emotionally blackmails his son into wedding a heiress in order to save his bank, which he has led into bad investments. The chosen bride is the woman Kurt loves but has not been allowed to marry because of class snobbery. She fires Gerhard, and the disgruntled manservant brings matters to a head. As a result, Edmund kills himself, to his widow's relief. In the course of the play, Kurt recognizes that Edmund's nature cannot be changed, though he thinks he can help him cope better; he sums up: "Edmund is completely normal except for his emotional proclivities." He labels "the law which punishes such unhappy men [...] a legislative mistake, a disastrous mistake, a gap in the education of the legislators." Edmund's wife, however, argues that it would "be better if such ... people were harmlessly interned in madhouses," and she has the last word before the final curtain. "*Fehler*" was published in 1906. § In Senelick, L., ed. *Lovesick*. 77–96.

15 *The Dangerous Precaution* (1907) | **Mikhail Kuzmin (1872–1936), Russian**

[Romantic comedy, with songs; 6M, 1W, extras; 1 set.] During the brief period of Russian liberalism, Kuzmin wrote the important novel *Wings* (*Kryl'ya*, 1907), stories, poems, and several plays with gay themes. This bagatelle recounts young Floridal's culminating discomfort with his father's unexplained decree that he pose as his daughter Dorita disguised as his son Floridal. This convoluted masquerade is unpleasant not least because René has fallen in love with "Dorita." Floridal on his part confesses, "I feel a certain agitation, which cannot be explained merely as pity for René." In a song a courtier argues, "You'll find the difference not so very great" between "a woman and a man of tender years," for "Heads or tails, in this game / Top or bottom's all the same." And, in fact, when Floridal reveals the truth, René declares that his feelings remain unchanged. The two kiss, and René calls for a jig to be danced: "My grief has fermented, and its cork has popped. I want to be absurdly merry, because today I am insanely happy!" *Opasnaya predostorozhnost* was published in 1907. Though Walter Nouvel wrote the music for the songs, there is no record of a production at the time. § In Senelick, L., ed. *Lovesick*. 101–10.

16 *The Gentleman of the Chrysanthemums* (1908) | **Armory (1877–unknown), French**

[Social drama; 8M, 6W; 2 sets.] Wilde's spirit

hovers over this campy work. Its title character, Gill Norvège, is a Parisian writer and media darling, whose flamboyant dress, effete manners, and extraordinary statements titillate his public: "I handed my private life over to them. Better, I live in a glass cage so that everyone can see me. Better yet, I live entirely for them, my tastes are entirely for them, my vices are entirely for them, they may not care for them but in the end they find them as thrilling as those of a spoiled child." The play reveals how he works society to his advantage. Gill successively displays a white, a mauve, and a yellow chrysanthemum, the equivalent of Wilde's green carnation, though the significance of Gill's natural colors is never clear. Friends of his who are also homosexual appear. Gill has had numerous amours, at least one of which led to blackmail; he is willing to feign love to a woman to suit his purposes. But he shows no regrets about his nature— his "aesthetics." He takes comfort in the painters Leonardo and Il Sodoma and lashes out at those who are "trying to impose laws on Beauty and prescribe what gender it's to be." He fails to obtain the admiration of a young poet, Jacques Romagne, to whom he takes a fancy, but it is clearly only a temporary setback for him. *Le monsieur aux chrysanthèmes* opened in Paris, 1908. Armory also published under his birth name Carle Dauriac. § In Senelick, L., ed. *Lovesick*. 117–53.

17 *The Madras House* (1910) | Harley Granville-Barker (1877–1946), English

[Problem play; 8M, 14W; 4 sets.] Granville-Barker, who was the original John Tanner in Shaw's *Man and Superman*, follows the Irish playwright's lead in bringing onstage social issues. Here it is "the woman's problem" as seen via a decisive moment when two families must determine whether or not to sell their fashion emporium for women, with one of the families having six daughters to provide for. Mr. Windlesham, the store's manager, enters in Act 3 with "the gait of a water-wagtail." He is all surface, all artifice, and provides a comic interlude by his mannerisms and the way he "speaks English as much like French as his French is like English." He shows off sketches and then the clothes on models to the amusement of the prospective buyer. The entry on gay theater in *The Cambridge Guide to Theatre* (414), claims that it is the first modern play "to feature a character whom the audience is invited to identify as homosexual," the beginning of "a long history of stage representations of homosexuality as effeminacy." His role is short, however, and he plays no part in the unfolding plot. The play opened in London, 1910, with Charles Maude, no director listed. § Granville Barker, H. *The Madras House: A Comedy in Four Acts*; ed. by William-Alan Landes. Players, 1999. 87p.

18 *The Venetian Madcaps* (1914) | Mikhail Kuzmin, Russian

[Masque; 5M, 3W, extras; 3 sets.] A spin on commedia dell'arte, the play is set "in eighteenth century Venice, the Venice of Goldoni, Gozzi and Longhi." It opens with Count Stello and Narcisetto "embracing" before a mirror. To her lover Harlequin's complete indifference, the actress Finette decides on a whim to seduce Stello. She fails; instead she entices Narcisetto, even though she insists that he still loves Stello. In another bizarre twist, Stello proposes that he and Narcisetto attend the carnival disguised as Finette and Harlequin. As the procession crosses a bridge, "Narcisetto silently stabs his friend, kisses him and throws the body noiselessly into the canal." When Finette asks if he did it out of love for her, he responds, "I love nobody but the Count. I never loved anyone but him." Finette and Harlequin plan their hasty departure for Verona. The play, with music, was composed in 1912. *Venetsianskie bezumtsy* was first performed in a private home, 1914. § Kuzmin, M. *Selected Prose & Poetry*. Trans. by Michael Green. Ardis, 1980. 364–416. See also *The Death of Nero*. In *Selected Writings*. Trans. by Michael A. Green and Stanislav A. Shvabrin. Bucknell Univ. Press, 2005. 131–91.

19 *The Princess Zoubaroff* (1920) | Ronald Firbank (1886–1926), English

[Sexual comedy; 7M, 8W, extras; 1 set.] Wilde served as a model for Firbank, both his life and his writing. Where Wilde was discreet, however, Firbank, though often coy, is fairly direct. Marriage is only a social convention in his world. So Eric Tresilian really did not expect Enid to take his proposal seriously. They both soon regret the union; Enid says, "His Hellenism once captivated me. But [...] the *Attic* to him means nothing now *but Servants' bedrooms*. [...] *Closets*." They accept Adrian and Nadine Sheil-Meyer's invitation to spend their honeymoon at their home outside Florence. There they meet other English expatriates, including two modeled on Wilde and Douglas: Lord Henry Orkish, who enjoys watching naked Italian boys cavort in the Arno, and his protégé Reggie Quintus ("too good-looking for a man"), who adores bananas (surely a double entendre) and who suggests to Eric that they "might frivol round together one evening." Also present is the servant Angelo, born in *bella* Taromina but a resident for some time in Naples, where he posed as "a model." Almost immediately Eric and Adrian disappear for an extended tour lasting half a year. They return to find their wives have joined the Princess Zoubaroff's (lesbian) convent, leaving behind Nadine's baby boy who was born while they were away. As the curtain falls Eric and Adrian seem ready to set up house together, serving as joint fathers. Published in 1920, the campy play was not produced until 1951 in a London theater club. It received its first public staging in London in 1975 with Michael Nation, Peter Cox, James Horne, Nigel Martin, and John Pople, directed by Edgar Davies. § *The Complete Ronald Firbank*. Duckworth, 1961. 699–765.

20   *Baal* (1922–26) | Bertolt Brecht (1898–1956), German

[Psychological drama; 12M, 8W, extras; flexible set.] Inspired by the relationship between the French poets Arthur Rimbaud and Paul Verlaine, Brecht began *Baal* in 1918. As the plot evolved it came to depict the life of excess led by his amoral title character. Baal is an itinerant entertainer who is compared to Whitman and Verlaine; there may also be an allusion to Wilde in the lines "His best retreat / On earth had always been the toilet seat. / For there a man can sit, content to know / That stars are overhead, and dung below" (compare Wilde's "We are all in the gutter, but some of us are looking at the stars"). Baal's guiding principle is, "Don't say no to any vice as such." (Compare Wilde's, "I can resist everything except temptation.") With no compunction, he seduces women and then drops them. But for the greater part of the play he is with Ekart, who has invited Baal to join him on the road. Baal repeatedly declares his love. Hugging Ekart, he says, "Now I've got you close. I've got you. Can you smell me? It's better than women! [...] Look, Ekart, you can see stars over the woods." Later, he says, "I don't care for women any more." When he discovers Ekart holding a tavern waitress on his lap, in a rage of jealousy, Baal stabs him. Lost, Baal declines into death. His last words are, "Stars. Hm." Published in 1922, *Baal* premiered in Leipzig, 1923. Brecht revised it with Elisabeth Hauptmann (1897–1973) for its Berlin premiere, 1926. It was produced in New York, 1965, with Michell Ryan and James Earl Jones, directed by Gladys Vaughan, the explicit relationship between the two characters leaving the *New York Times* critic uneasy. The story has been filmed several times, once with Rainer Werner Fassbinder, 1970; once in English with David Bowie, 1982. During the same period as *Baal*, Brecht began working on the script that ultimately became *In the Jungle of Cities* (*Im Dickicht der Städte*, 1927). Likewise inspired by Rimbaud, it depicts a struggle between two men that has often been read as homoerotic. § Brecht, B. *Collected Plays*, v1. Trans. by William E. Smith and Ralph Manheim. Pantheon, 1970. 1–58. Includes *In the Jungle of Cities*. Trans. by Gerhard Nellhaus. 107–63. Other translations for both exist.

21   *Mustn't Do It!* (1922) | Johanna Maria Goedhart-Becker (1885–1979), Dutch

[Domestic drama; 3M, 2W; 1 set.] The play comes down on the side of homosexuality as innate to a person, neither criminal, nor sinful, nor mentally aberrant. If it is a "horror," it is the heterosexual world that has made it so. Young Walt finally comes out to his mother, after the family becomes concerned why his sister's fiancé seems to be avoiding the house. Walt and Charles were formerly fast friends; Walt suspects Charles is avoiding him because they are both gay. Indeed, he is right. When the two finally confront each other, Walt argues, "You can't just consider yourself.— You're sacrificing someone else." Charles breaks off the engagement. Walt's parents vacillate: one moment accepting, the next ranting. When Walt turns to his pastor, "He was outraged and called it a sin and a shame. A person like me is dangerous…. A little understanding—or even a bit of tolerance—not a word of that." But Charles feels liberated: "ever since I've stopped lying, I feel freer, healthier." Charles prepares to leave, to find "Somewhere where I can be free." *Wat niet Mag…* opened for two nights in Rotterdam, 1922. § Van Ijssel de Schepper Becker, J. M. *Mustn't Do It! (Wat niet Mag…)*. Trans. by Laurence Senelick. Broadway Play, 2010. 62p.

22 Spring Cleaning (1923) | Frederick Lonsdale (JEY 1881–1954), English

[Moral comedy; 6M, 5W; 2 sets.] By presenting his play as a warning against the new decadence, Lonsdale escaped censorship even as he titillated audiences with his portraits of roués and loose women, including a working prostitute. His plot centers on Margaret Sones, who has gotten in with a "cursed lot of degenerates" and is on the verge of having an affair with one of them. Her husband, a writer, fights to regain her. Drawing a deliberate parallel with the pretentious bunch she has invited for dinner, he invites a prostitute to join them. Among her guests is Bobby Williams, 22, a fairy, a "powder puff," a "caricature of a human being." The women (save one who slights him) depend on his sense of fashion, but he is rudely mocked by all the other men. Bobby stoically says, "I never mind what anybody says—I never have." His final word, aimed at the husband, is "Beast!" De Jongh (*Not in Front*, 31), ignoring *The Madras House*, claims him as "the first of the flamboyant homosexuals to take the modern stage." He also argues that "Lonsdale has a strange, equivocal admiration for the chap" who "unlike the rest of the posturers, has the courage to be unconventional, to be effeminate" (32). The play premiered in New York, 1923, with Robert Noble. It opened in London, 1925, with Denys Blakelock. § Lonsdale, F. *Spring Cleaning*. Collins, 1925. 168p.

23 The Life of Edward the Second of England (1924) | Bertolt Brecht, German

[Historical tragedy; 18M, 1W, extras; flexible set.] Written in verse and prose in collaboration with Lion Feuchtwanger (1884–1958), Brecht's *Leben Eduards des Zweiten von England (nach Marlowe)* is a radical adaption of Marlowe's drama, colored by what was happening in Germany post–World War I. For some reason Piers becomes Daniel, and Queen Isabella becomes Queen Anne. The phallic poker disappears; Edward is smothered to death. But the homosexuality is more candidly addressed. Here, the public ridicules Edward's sexuality: "The other day Ned puked on Tanner Street." "How so?" "A woman crossed his path." A peer sneers, "People of London, come and feast your eyes: / Behold King Edward with his pair of wives." But, if anything, Edward's fidelity to Gaveston seems nobler than in Marlowe. Towards the end, Edward says to one of the faithful: "There's nothing left amid such deafness but bodily / Contact between men. And even that is very / Little. All is vanity." The literal foulness to which he is submitted as a prisoner does not befoul his spirit. The premiere was in Munich, 1924. It was given in London, 1968, with John Stride and Charles Kay, directed by Frank Dunlop. After this adaptation, Brecht's fascination with homosexuality largely disappeared. § Brecht, B. *Collected Plays*, v1. Trans. by William E. Smith and Ralph Manheim. Pantheon, 1970. 165–255. Other translations exist.

24 The Prisoners of War (1925) | J. R. Ackerley (1896–1967), English

[Military drama; 7M, 3W; 1 set.] Ackerley penned the first play with a gay protagonist in a contemporary setting. He based it on his own experiences as a prisoner of war. Five soldiers have been captured by the Germans near the end of World War I and placed in an internment camp in neutral Switzerland. Tensions between the men grow out of their boredom from inaction. The sexual tension between two of them was largely missed by the first audiences but seems almost blatant to present-day viewers. The author's alter-ego, Captain Jim Conrad, 24, who "doesn't like women," obviously has a crush on Second Lieutenant Allan Grayle, 19. The mercenary Grayle, "*educated at a good public school*" and thus presumably savvy to male/male affection, uses Conrad. He deliberately sets out to make Conrad jealous by palling with Captain Eric Rickman, flaunting their friendship by calling him Eric instead of Captain. Grayle has no idea that Rickman is setting him up in order to fleece him. Lieutenant Harry Tetford moves to break up the new pair. It becomes clear that he feels about Rickman the same way Conrad feels about Grayle, with the difference that their relationship seems to have a future after the war. In describing the prisoners, Conrad might well be describing the popular view of homosexuals at the time: "we're a race apart. Temperamentally unsound. I know all my weaknesses and I cherish them. I value them more than my strength. A race [a]part." The play is largely a psychological study, with relatively little action and no sharp resolution. It was performed privately in London, 1925, with George Hayes, Robert Harris, Carleton Hobbs, and Raymond Massey, directed by Frank Birch. § In Wilcox, M., ed. *Gay Plays*, v3. 89–135.

25 *Semi-Monde* (w. 1926) | Noël Coward (1899–1973), English

[Social satire; 9M, 9W, extras; 6 sets.] Though the closeted playwright attempted to find a producer, his light-hearted portrayal of promiscuity, adultery, homosexuality, and generally aimless behavior precluded any production of the play at the time it was written in 1926. Inspired by an evening he spent bar-hopping in New York, Coward moved his comedy to Paris during the years 1924–1926. The stage is populated almost entirely with expatriates: British, American, and Russian. A married couple is involved in an adulterous relationship, she with a writer, he with the writer's daughter. The daughter also has her eyes on Cyril Hardacre. He first appears in the company of Beverley Ford, with whom he is obviously in a relationship. But she is convinced that Cyril is "on the wrong track," and at play's end they are married. A number of lesbians and five other gay men pop in and out of scenes, but despite a number of lengthy exchanges they serve mostly as stage dressing. Albert Hennick knows the gay Parisian scene intimately; he also alludes to an attempted gay mugging. Luke Bellows is an American actor of some renown. The others are barely described. All in all, the play has too many characters (more than thirty-seven, though doubling allows for fewer actors) and too little plot. It was not staged until 1977, in Glasgow, with Rory Edwards, Robin Hooper, Paul Geoffrey, and Garry Cooper, under the direction of Philip Prowse, and remained unpublished until 1999. § Coward, N. *Semi-Monde*, Methuen, 2001. 91p.

26 *The Drag* (1927) | Mae West (1893–1980), American

[Sexual drama; 13M, 4W, extras; 2 sets.] West was one of the earliest Americans to try to speak out for gay rights in a public setting. The New York police thwarted her attempt to take her play from tryouts to the Broadway stage in 1927, and her *Homosexual Comedy* was not published until 1997. The message she tried to get out is astounding for its time. In an exchange between Dr. James Richmond and Judge Robert Kingsbury, the doctor (who has been reading the work of the German pioneer for sexual reform Karl Ulrich) argues that "a man is what he is born to be." Therefore, he asks, "are we going to declare as outcast and criminal these unfortunates who through no fault of their own have been born with instincts and desires different from ours? [...] are we going to force them into secrecy and shame, for being what they cannot help being, by branding them as criminals and so lead them into the depths of misery and suicide?" The judge cites "there are approximately five million homosexuals in the United States" (this at the time when the U.S. population was around 19.04 million). Currently, the doctor is seeing David Caldwell, who is distraught when his lover falls in love with another man. What neither Richmond nor Kingsbury—nor the playgoer for quite a while—suspects is that this lover is the judge's son, Rolly Kingsbury, husband to the doctor's daughter. The play implicitly critiques a society that forces homosexuals into sham marriages that leaves the spouse unhappy. Admittedly, Rolly is callous, showing no remorse that his wife "is the same today as the day I married her, if you know what I mean." Rolly has fallen in love with a civil engineer, Allen Grayson, who in turn is in love with Rolly's wife. The play ends melodramatically with David murdering Rolly. But West uses the moment to critique yet another of society's misplaced values. The judge convinces the police to label the death a suicide: it is more honorable to die by one's own hand than to be murdered because of a homosexual entanglement.

The present-day viewer may wince at some of the outdated psychology, such as David's ready acceptance that "I was born a male, but my mind has been that of a female." But the play seems ahead of its time in many respects. West's most audacious move was to turn Act 3 into a recreation of the era's popular drag balls, the actors being gay men that she recruited specifically for this scene. According to George Chauncey (*Gay New York*, 313), it "lasted twenty minutes and allowed thirty of its performers to put on a 'show'" with songs and dances. The scene is filled with gay slang, campy references, and double entendres. One exchange goes like this: Duchess says, "I don't mind a little drink once in a while" (this is during prohibition). Clem answers, "Why you big Swede. You'd take it through a funnel if anybody would give it to you." Duchess replies, no doubt with a wink and a leer, "Funnel? That's nothing. I'd take it through a hose. Whoops." Clem also mentions how he's found a taxi driver who's "been riding me ever since." Previews were held in Bridgeport, Conn., and Paterson, N.J., with Jay Sheridan, Allan Campbell, and Leo Howe, directed by Edward Elsner; the author's name was listed as "Jane Mast." § West, M. *Three Plays*; ed. by Lillian Schlissel. Routledge, 1997. 95–140.

27 *Oscar Wilde* (1928) | **Lester Cohen (1901–1963), American**

[Biographical study; 10M, 5W; 5 sets.] This pioneering play established the classical pattern for subsequent dramas about Wilde: pre-trial events, the trial and prison, and the aftermath in Paris. It is unusual in presenting Wilde as a bisexual fatally enthralled by Douglas. Only a hint of other homosexual relationships crops up. Wilde's own words are used, including excerpts from *The Ballad of Reading Gaol* during a phantasmagoric scene set in Wilde's cell. At the end Douglas has definitively quit him, and Wilde accepts his status as an outcast. Several characters are invented; many real life ones are missing or presented under pseudonyms; the painter James Whistler has an unexpected turn. Cohen expressed regret in his foreword that "production is no longer advisable in our saintly metropolis," owing to recent crackdowns by police on Broadway. § Cohen, L. *Oscar Wilde: A Play*. Boni & Liveright, 1928. 179p.

28 *The Pleasure Man* (1928) | **Mae West, American**

[Theater drama; 23M, 11W, extras; 3 sets.] Homosexuality is not central to West's campy story of a day and an evening in a Midwestern vaudeville theater, but many of the players are openly gay. In many ways it is a more interesting play than *The Drag*. Paradise Dupont, his four Boys, Peaches, and Bunny are all female impersonators. The chatter of the Boys becomes too much at times, but they all, especially Paradise, are respected by everyone save two pretentious "dramatic actors." For them the impersonators are "queer [...] extraordinarily queer. [...] They lack perception [...] of the finer qualities which go to make up the true artist of the legitimate drama." More typical is the good-natured gibe aimed at Paradise's troupe when they are told their dressing room is next to the acrobats': "don't push the chewing gum out of the knot-hole." The gays give as well as take. When Stanley Smith, one of the theater's personnel, warns Paradise, "And don't you annoy the boys, Violet," Paradise pertly responds, "Lavender, maybe, but violet never." Such campy dialogue and innuendoes enliven the text. Peaches asks, "Paradise, did you ever have a platonic love affair?" Paradise replies, "Oh yes, but his wife found it out." This exchange also works dramatically as a direct gibe at Rodney Terrill, the title character who tries to seduce every woman he meets, claiming he is providing them pleasure. Paradise calls him out: "if you're a man, thank God, I'm a female impersonator." Rodney's callous disregard for the women's feelings catches up with him this day. The story ends melodramatically with his castration and accidental death at the hands of the man whose sister Rodney impregnated and then pushed aside. This occurs during a drag ball at the home of a retired female impersonator who has invited the entire troupe over for an evening of fun. Of the large cast, Stanley and Paradise emerge as the most admirable. The play opened in New York, 1928, with Leo Howe, Charles Ordway, and Gene Drew, directed by West. The police closed the production and arrested the entire cast; the trial resulted in a hung jury. West cut all gays from her novel version in 1975. § West, M. *Three Plays*; ed. by Lillian Schlissel. Routledge, 1997. 143–200.

29 *Strange Interlude* (1928) | **Eugene O'Neill (1888–1953), American**

[Psychological drama; 6M, 3W; 6 sets.] Little in the script indicates that the novelist Charles Marsden, the heroine's best friend, is gay, but O'Neill clearly intended him to come across as such. He is a composite of the gay artists Charles Demuth and Marsden Hartley. In *O'Neill* (Little, Brown, 1973) Louis Sheaffer quotes the playwright as saying, "I've known many Marsdens on many different levels of life and it has always seemed to me that they've never been done in literature with any sympathy or real insight" (242). The script describes Charles as having "*an indefinable feminine quality about him, but it is nothing apparent in either appearance or act.*" In one of Charles's interior monologues, he himself claims that he is a sexless creature. Never once does he show any interest in or sexual awareness of other men. Another character calls him "one of those poor devils who spend their lives trying not to discover which sex they belong to." Influenced by Freudian psychology, the play covers a quarter of a century in the life of Nina Leeds. Having lost her fiancé in World War I, she suffers remorse that she never allowed him to consummate their love sexually. Seeking to establish some sense of wholeness in her life, she fashions different relationships with three men. Charles emerges as the most stable constant in her search. She reflects, "Charlie has always loved me in some queer way of his own." He has the last words in the play; summing up his relationship with Nina, he thinks how he, having "passed beyond desire, has all the luck at last." It is O'Neill's only play with an obviously gay character, but other works of his have been read appreciatively through gay lens (the early shipboard plays, *The Great God Brown*). The nine-act play opened in New York, 1928, with Tom Powers, directed by Philip Moeller. It has been filmed several times. § O'Neill, E. *Strange Interlude*. Boni & Liveright, 1928. 352p.

30 *Rope* (1929) | Patrick Hamilton (1904–1962), English

[Crime drama; 6M, 2W; 1 set.] Although Hamilton denied it, the play is almost certainly based on the 1924 Leopold-Loeb murder case. Here two Oxford students conspire to commit the perfect crime. They then flaunt moral codes further by inviting the victim's father to have a meal served off a chest concealing his dead son's body. The two youths have an emotional S/M relationship, Wyndham Brandon dominating the Spaniard Charles Granillo. Is theirs also a physical relationship? The script provides at least one indirect clue: in describing their male servant, the playwright notes, "*He is an almost perfect servant [...] but not, perhaps, completely impersonal—his employers being in the habit of making the occasional advances towards him.*" More interesting is their older friend and mentor, the poet Rupert Cadell. The script describes him as "*a little foppish in dress and appearance [...] enormously affected in speech and carriage. [...] His affection almost verges on effeminacy.*" He has a game leg as a souvenir of his participation in World War I; he therefore uses a "*very exquisite walking stick,*" a phallic symbol that proves to be a swordstick. Whatever level of intimacy he has had with the two youths, he intuits the truth and defends himself with that sword. For Arthur Laurents (*Original Story By*, Knopf, 2000), when he adapted the play for Alfred Hitchcock's 1948 film, there was no doubt that "Homosexuality was at the center of *Rope*, its three main characters were homosexuals" (124). Unfortunately the miscasting of Rupert muddled this interpretation. The play opened in London, 1929, with Robert Holmes, Sebastian Shaw, and Anthony Ireland, directed by Reginald Denham. The New York production was titled *Rope's End*. The play has been telecast several times. Schildcrout devotes Chapter 2 of *Murder Most Queer* to plays (and some films) inspired by the two Chicago killers. § Hamilton, P. *Rope*. French, 2003. 65p.

31 *The Public* (w. 1930?) | Federico García Lorca (1898–1936), Spanish

[Theater drama; 6M, 2W, extras; flexible set.] At the time of his assassination (perhaps for political reasons, perhaps because of his sexuality), Lorca left behind drafts of his only gay drama, an incomplete work in six scenes. Only one manuscript, minus the fourth scene, survives. Rafael Martínez Nadal traces its history in *Lorca's The Public: A Study of His Unfinished Play* (Calder & Boyars,1974). Surrealistic, its plot (if that is the right word) is impossible to convey in a few sentences. Lorca's familiar symbols show up: horses, blood, sand, the color green, the moon, ruins, masks. Theater is a major theme, tied into the story of Romeo and Juliet. Homosexuality is another: one of the Horses says, "On the shores of the Dead Sea grow some lovely apples composed of ash, but the ash is good." The two themes intertwine. When the Director labels his stage "Theater in the open air," a Horse says, "No. Now we've inaugurated the true theater, the theater beneath the sand." Gonzalo tells the Director, "I love you in front of others because I abhor the mask, and because now I've succeeded in ripping it off you." The Director tells a visitor, however, not to "assume I'm capable of bringing the mask out on stage" because of questions of "morals [...]. And the spectators' stomachs." The play is at times scatological: two men engage in a profane litany. The first says, "If I turned into caca?" The second responds: "I'd turn into a fly." "If I turned into an apple?" "I'd turn into a kiss." A man says, "the anus is man's curse. The anus is man's failure, it's his shame and his death." In a final call for liberation, the converted Director answers the Conjurer's lament—"Taking things away is easy. What's difficult is putting them back"—by saying, "It's much more difficult to replace them with other things." Lorca's family refused to allow the play's publication until 1976; *El público* received its world premiere in 1978 at the Universidad de Puerto Rico. An English version was presented in London, 1988, with Gerard Murphy,

Phillip Joseph, and Nigel Cooke, directed by Ultz. The play became the basis for an opera with libretto by Andrés Ibáñez and music by Mauricio Sotelo in 2015. § García Lorca, F. *The Public and Play without a Title: Two Posthumous Plays.* Trans. by Carlos Bauer. New Directions, 1983. 1–48. Also translated by Henry Livings, 1988. A more accurate English title is *The Audience.*

32   *But It Still Goes On* (1931) | **Robert Graves (1895–1985), English**

[Psychological drama; 6M, 4W; flexible set.] The play was apparently kindled by the poet's 1929 memoirs in which Graves wrote freely about gay attractions between schoolboys before moving on to describe his part in World War I. The straight Dick Tompion, alienated by his sense that some undefined catastrophe overtook the world before that war, wreaks havoc on his family and friends. The gay David Casselis is in love with him. Realizing there is no hope, he decides to "try to be in love with Dorothy because she's Dick's sister." His perfidies go further. He enjoyed the power he had over other boys in school and gloried in the way a gay officer in war "becomes a sort of military queen-bee." He lies when he says he has never acted on his "obsession." We get a fleeting view of one of his pickups in a London oyster bar. He feels repulsed by Dorothy's body and contrives to remain in "his office at night to work" when he is in fact "doing things so disgusting and so horrible" that she recoils when she finds out. Dorothy melodramatically kills him on Hampstead Heath; Dick and a friend of hers abet Dorothy in covering up her culpability. This friend and her lesbian sister also try to gain Dick's affections, but he spurns them, angrily demanding of the lesbian, "Why the Devil aren't you content to remain as God made you?" More melodrama ensues, including two suicides for which Dick is indirectly responsible. The play was collected with other materials in 1931. § Graves, R. *But It Still Goes On: An Accumulation.* Cape & Smith, 1931. 207–318.

33   *Vile Bodies* (1931) | **H. Dennis Bradley (1878–1934), English**

[Social satire; 14M, 14W; flexible set.] It is a pity that this relatively faithful dramatization of Evelyn Waugh's novel has been largely forgotten. Though the main plot line remains whether or not Adam Fenwick-Symes will marry Nina Blount, several of the characters are unmistakably gay. Even before we meet him, Adam's friend Miles Malpractice is identified by his aunt as "terribly *tapette*," while his mother acknowledges that nothing is likely to be going on between him and a young woman in whose company he is seen: "In that direction, at least, I think we may hold him above suspicion." A customs official mistakes the contents of his luggage for that of a woman. We meet his current boyfriend, a racecar driver. An Italian waiter also has a part in the drama, flirting unsuccessfully with Adam. The proprietress of the hotel at which the waiter works refers to him as a "queen," "Fairy Prince," and "Pansy" and accuses him of powdering his nose. The comedy was given a private performance in London, 1931, with Ernest Thesiger, Leslie Holland, and Dennis Val-Norton, directed by Lionel Barton and the author listed as "Arthur Boscastle." It was revised for a 1932 production. § Bradley, H. D. *Vile Bodies: A Play in Twelve Episodes Adapted from Evelyn Waugh's Novel.* Chapman & Hall, 1931. 177 pp.

34   *Dangerous Corner* (1932) | **J. B. Priestley (1894–1984), English**

[Psychological drama; 3M, 4W; 1 set.] Priestley sets his play up as a mystery: why did Martin Caplan kill himself? Was it because he had stolen money from the publishing firm in which he was a partner? But the attempt on the part of his surviving family, friends, and lovers to find the truth turns into a psychological study not only of Martin but of them. It emerges that Martin was bisexual: "He seemed to think that everybody young, male or female, ought to be falling in love with him." And indeed "the Whitehouse family—father, daughter and son—[...] all fell in love with him." The son, Gordon Whitehouse, holds that Martin "didn't really care for women at all," at the same time that he admits, "Martin was the only person on earth I really cared about." He finishes his confession by defiantly saying, "And now you can call me any name you like, I don't care." His brother-in-law chooses to label him "some sort of hysterical young pervert." Priestly undercut just how daring his drama was by ending it with a gimmick: he contrives to restart the action from the beginning; this time the characters avoid the dangerous corner that started them off on their series of revelations, leaving the sham of the characters' lives unruffled and Gordon's sexuality concealed. The play opened in London, 1932. with William Fox, directed by Tyrone Guthrie. (Cecil Holm took over the role in New York.) The drama has been telecast several times. § Priestley, J. B. *My Six Favorite Plays.* Stein & Day, 1979. 351–406.

35 *Queer People* (1932) / *Tragedy in Jermyn Street* (1934) | Michael Hill (unknown), English

[Sexual melodrama; 3M, 4W; 3 sets.] Given when it was published (by a seemingly otherwise unknown writer), the play's explicitness startles. There was no way it could be produced, other than privately. Jim Marlowe is expelled from prep school for corrupting the morals of Clifford Terry. For ten years the headstrong Jim carries the torch for the younger boy: "I cannot get away from you, Clif, and no matter what happens I can't stop wanting you. [...] And it is not only the physical side of things that count." They meet up again by coincidence at Jim's cousin's home; Clif is engaged, but it does not take Jim long to scuttle those plans. Still Clif wavers about running off with Jim. He comes to Jim's flat in Jermyn Street to renounce their plans. Jim's cousin shows up on the fiancée's behalf, sending Clif into hiding in the bedroom. Mavis has already discerned the truth, for she is a lesbian: "I always have been, but as you will have noticed, I live alone. Queer people should." Giving up on Clif, Jim proposes that he and Mavis carve out a celebate life together. Clif presumably overhears them; he shoots himself. Hill published his play in 1932. He returned to it in 1934, revising it under the title *Tragedy in Jermyn Street,* apparently to make the gay argument stronger. I have not seen this text. § Hill, M. *Queer People: A Play in a Prologue & Three Acts.* Cranley & Day, 1932. 59p.

36 *Design for Living* (1933) | Noël Coward, English

[Sexual comedy; 6M, 4W; 3 sets.] Written as a vehicle for the playwright and his friends Alfred Lunt and Lynn Fontanne, the comedy has become a prototype for numerous gay plays since then. Covering some four years, it depicts an evolving *ménage à trois* between a woman, Gilda, and two bisexual men, Otto and Leo. The latter, speaking to Gilda, sums up their relationship: "The actual facts are so simple. I love you. You love me. You love Otto. I love Otto. Otto loves you. Otto loves me." Otto defends their unorthodox arrangement: "A gay, ironic chance threw the three of us together and tied our lives into a tight knot at the outset. To deny it would be ridiculous, and to unravel it impossible. Therefore, the only thing left is to enjoy it thoroughly, every rich moment of it, every thrilling second." Not that that is so easily achieved. Each man asserts his sexual claim on Gilda, but she bolts and marries high-minded Ernest Friedman, leaving Otto and Leo to fall back upon themselves. The play wittily uses three leaving-the-bedroom scenes to make the physical relationships clear: first with Gilda and Leo, second with Gilda and Otto, and third with Leo and Otto. By then Leo has achieved success as a playwright, Otto as a painter, and Gilda as an interior decorator. She is now ready to accept their unorthodox arrangement. The non-creative Earnest (he is an art dealer) recoils from their "disgusting three-sided erotic hotch-potch" and leaves the three collapsed in laughter. The play opened in New York, 1933, directed by Coward; it did not appear in London until 1939. There have been several telecast versions. § Coward, N. *Play Parade.* Doubleday, 1933. 1–111. Also includes *The Vortex,* 1924, whose protagonist has often been labeled a closet case.

37 *The Green Bay Tree* (1933) | Mordaunt Shairp (1887–1939), English

[Psychological melodrama; 4M, 1W; 2 sets.] Although heavily indebted to theories of Sigmund Freud and Havelock Ellis, the play is relatively circumspect. De Jongh (*Not in Front,* 35) attacks it as "the most dishonest and morally disreputable play about homosexuality to reach the stages of London and Broadway between the wars. It was also the most commercially successful and critically applauded." Certainly, it fuels the myth that homosexuals recruit young boys. Over a decade before, Mr. Dulcimer, a stereotypical fairy, bought David Owen, 11, from his drunken father and adopted him as Julian Dulcimer. He then shaped the youth into his own image. A crisis arises when Julian's terrier brings him into contact with veterinarian Leonora Yale. He proposes marriage to her, whereupon Dulcie informs Julian that he will have to provide for her out of his own resources; his allowance will be terminated. Meanwhile, religion has changed the father; Mr. Owen invites Julian to return home while he trains to become a veterinarian himself. But David discovers that he prefers the pleasant life of Julian to the austere life of David. He returns to Dulcie. Trying to save his son, Owen shoots Dulcimer. Even dead, Dulcie triumphs. The play ends with Julian recreating the flower arranging scene with which Dulcie opens the play. It premiered in London, 1933, with Frank Vosper and Hugh Williams, directed by Milton Rosmer. Laurence Olivier appeared in the New York production. Curtin (*Bulgarians*, 181) reports that the unpublished New York script ended slightly differently from the one used in London. § In Wilcox, M., ed. *Gay Plays*, [v1]. 51–97.

38 The Rats of Norway (1933) | Keith Winter (1906–1983), Welsh

[Sexual drama; 7M, 2W; 3 sets.] Winter, who at the time was Noël Coward's lover, published a novel with the same title in 1932; the novel so resembles the play that it is possible the latter was written first. Despite (or perhaps because of) all the psychological theories being bandied about between the world wars, sexualities seem to have been ill-defined. Stevan Beringer and Hugh Sebastian are fellow teachers in a Northumberland public school. The two are obviously attracted to each other. But Stevan declares his love for Tilly, and Sebastian is having an affair with the headmaster's wife. Stevan has never been with Tilly sexually (and may well be a virgin), while Sebastian admits, "Love is sex to me these days." Sebastian also says, "I couldn't live without Jane, and yet as far as contentment goes I'm far happier with you." He begs Stevan to emigrate with him to Canada. Stevan is too weak to accept the offer, though Sebastian thinks he will come around. It is too late, however. Sebastian has become an alcoholic as a result of his service in the war. His heart weakened, he dies in Jane's bed. Stevan knows something is wrong and appears at the crucial moment; together he and Jane take Sebastian's body to his own room. Jane observes, "You loved him too, didn't you?" "Yes," he answers. "More than Tilly?" "Yes." Chetwood, another teacher, is a stereotypical gay: *"slim, effeminate-looking,"* given to powdering his face. The rest put up with his silly ways, but Stevan is rude to him on every occasion. Perhaps Chetwood represents something he fears? The play opened in London, 1933, with Laurence Olivier, Raymond Massey, and Tony Bruce, directed by Massey. § Winter, K. *The Rats of Norway: A Play in Three Acts*. Heinemann, 1933. 104p.

39 Oscar Wilde (1936) | Leslie Stokes (unknown) and Sewell Stokes (1902–1979), English

[Biographical study; 17M, 1W; 6 sets.] Though a solid piece of work, staged with the approval of Lord Alfred Douglas (who had stopped the London staging of Maurice Rostand's *Le procès d'Oscar Wilde*), the greater part of the brothers' play now seems a historical curiosity, only Act 3 bringing something fresh to the legend. As with Cohen's earlier play, Act 1 provides glimpses of the events leading up to the trials; Act 2 concerns the trials; Act 3 depicts Wilde upon his release from prison. The dialogue contains many of the writer's *bons mots*. The central thesis of the work, as voiced by him, is, "One must be in harmony with one's self. One's own life, that is the important thing." The play was produced privately in London, 1936, with Robert Morley, John Bryning, and John Carol, directed by Norman Marshall. It opened in New York, 1938. It made its lead actor a star, but critics were still uneasy about Wilde himself. Vining (*Diary*, v1, 121) wrote that the matinee performance provided him one of his "happiest moments." The tragedy became a basis for the 1960 film *Oscar Wilde*. (A second 1960 film, *The Trials of Oscar Wilde*, derives partly from the closet drama by John Furnell: *The Stringed Lute: An Evocation in Dialogue of Oscar Wilde*, Rider, 1955.) § In Hodges, B., ed. *Forbidden Acts*. 239–302.

40 Whiteoaks (1936) | Mazo de la Roche (1879–1961), Canadian

[Domestic drama; 7M, 4W; 1 set.] De la Roche based her character Finch, 18, on the Canadian poet Robert Finch (1900–1995), who in fact was gay. In the play he is "musical" (often a code word), "very sensitive and nervy." He accidentally drops a letter from a friend who, he says, "helps me with my music." The letter begins, "Darling Finch." His brother reacts angrily: "My God! That this sort of muck should be written to a brother of mine!" Finch rereads the letter, "his face [...] illuminated by understanding," and "wildly" rips it to shreds. He then melodramatically picks up a towel and chokes himself, before dropping it in "horror at what he is doing." His grandmother is the one family member to sympathize with his aspirations. All her large family is jostling to be her heir; she chooses to leave her large fortune to Finch. De Jongh (*Not in Front*, 45) remarks on the fact that

Finch "is the first—the only—homosexual character in pre-war Anglo-American theatre to be specifically 'rewarded' although he is gay." But homosexuality plays no direct part in the plot; Finch wants to get away from his oppressive family in order to study and perform music, with no hint that he also longs to explore his sexuality. The play is a dramatization of her novel *Whiteoaks of Jalna*, 1929. It opened in London, 1936, with Patrick Boxill, directed by Nancy Price. § De la Roche, M. *Whiteoaks: A Play*. Little, Brown, 1936. 124p.

41 *Outrageous Fortune* (1943) | Rose Franken (1895–1988), American

[Domestic melodrama; 4M, 7W; 1 set.] Julian Harris is a composer; at the moment he is collaborating with his lover, the never-seen Russel Train, on a musical comedy. He is also engaged and is dismayed to discover that his fiancée may be in love with him; he has assumed she sees him as simply a "stepping stone to what [she wants] out of life. [...] Security and glamour." His mother says, "I do not know what it is in Julian, but I know he cannot make a woman happy." Barry Hamilton, his niece's music teacher, seems uncertain whether he himself is gay or straight. He recalls, "The boys on the block used to call me sissy. Maybe I was. Maybe I am." Later he confesses to having had a crush on a neighboring boy. Crystal, an older woman, tells him, "You were born with a few too many F cells in your body," and in good *Tea and Sympathy* fashion beds him and saves him. Before then, Julian makes a sexual overture and is rebuffed. Julian gives out that he is the innocent one, that Barry made the advance, but his fiancée tries to kill herself. His older brother, for the first time, recognizes that Julian is gay. He reacts typically: "I'd rather see him dead than the thing that he has become." The more enlightened Crystal asks, "If he were ill or crippled, would you turn against him?" The brother confronts Barry, who "*realizes that he has the chance to clear himself of Julian's implications. He makes his choice.*" That is, to say nothing. To the brother's credit he does not withdraw a job offer he has earlier made to Barry. There are other intertwined plots in this complex drama, including one in which the family doctor does not get a position simply because he is Jewish. The play opened in New York, 1943, with Brent Sargent and Dean Norton, directed by Franken. According to Sinfield (*Out on Stage*, 178) it was banned in the U.K. Curtin in discussing the play at some length asserts (*Bulgarians*, 263) that Julian, its "guilt-ridden yet defiant American Jew, was the only unmistakably and admittedly gay male character seen in a serious drama produced on the Broadway stage in the 1940s." § Franken, R. *Outrageous Fortune: A Drama in Three Acts*. French, 1944. 198p.

Post–World War II, 1945–1969

Alfred Kinsey's Sexual Behavior in the Human Male, *1948. Lavender Scare begins in Washington, 1950. Mattachine Society founded in Los Angeles, 1950. Guy Burgess and Donald Maclean flee U.K. to Russia, 1951. Series of arrests in England, 1953–54, including Sir John Gielgud's, lead to creation of Wolfenden Committee. Alan Turing commits suicide, 1954. Wolfenden report published, 1957. Evelyn Hooker's report questioning the idea that gays are mentally unhealthy, 1957. U.S. Supreme Court applies First Amendment rights to a gay magazine, 1958. José Sarria of San Francisco becomes first openly gay candidate for a public office, 1961. Illinois becomes first state to decriminalize same-sex acts, 1961. Limited decriminalization of homosexual acts in England and Wales, 1967. Ken Halliwell murders Joe Orton, 1967. Decriminalization of homosexual acts in Canada, 1968. Paragraph 175 modified in East Germany, 1968; in West Germany, 1969. U.K.'s Lord Chamberlain stripped of power to censor plays, 1968. Campaign for Homosexual Equality founded in U.K, 1969. Stonewall Inn riots, 1969 (June 28).*

42   *Auto-da-Fé* (1945) | Tennessee Williams (1911–1983), American

[Sexual tragedy; 1M, 1W, 1 set.] Given New York authorities' and critics' general hostility towards gays, Williams felt correctly that homosexuality was not a subject he could openly broach at the beginning of his career. Still, any gay playgoer recognizes that Tom Wingfield's closing lines in *The Glass Menagerie*, 1944, allude to his cruising the streets. In *A Streetcar Named Desire*, 1947, Blanche's young husband, Allan Grey, committed suicide after she threw up to him that she witnessed his sexual encounter with an older male friend. Between these two plays he published the haunting short play *Auto-da-Fé*. Eloi Duvenet is a paranoid New Orleans postal worker. By chance a photograph "Of two naked figures," obviously both men, falls out of an unsealed letter. The letter was sent by a university student to "One of those—opulent—antique dealers on—Royal." Eloi called upon the student, 19, for obscure reasons, and was rebuffed. The information is dragged out of him by his sanctimonious mother. When she finds out that all this happened a week earlier, she tells him it is too late to go to authorities, that he must burn the letter and its contents. Becoming hysterical upon seeing the photograph again, Eloi rushes into the house and sets it on fire, immolating himself. The play received a professional production in New York (*Ten by Tennessee*, 1986) with Richard Howard, directed by Michael Kahn. § Williams, T. 27 *Wagons Full of Cotton and Other One-Act Plays*. New Directions, 1945. 105–20.

43   *Deathwatch* (1947) | Jean Genet (1910–1986), French

[Prison drama; 4M; 1 set.] The play crackles with sexual tensions between prison inmates, but is it a gay play? For the object is power, not sexual favors. The dandified Maurice and the macho Lefranc vie for the attention of Green Eyes, the prison's second most brutal murderer (the unseen but often mentioned Snowball is first) and therefore the acknowledged center of potency in their four walls. However, their attraction to the man is sublimated as a pretense to be interested in Green Eyes's girlfriend, whose portrait he has tattooed on his chest. In an act of desperation to gain Green Eyes, Lefranc strangles Maurice, but Green Eyes denounces him to the leering guard. An early example of Theater of the Absurd, *Haute surveillance* was published in 1947; it opened in Paris, 1949. It was produced in Cambridge, Mass., 1957, with Harold Scott, directed by Stephen Aaron. Genet revised the script in 1985; this version was produced in New York, 1988. Vic Morrow and Barbara Turner adapted the story as an English-language film, 1966. Genet also wrote and directed the gay film *Un chant d'amour*, 1950, and prepared the unpublished script for the unfilmed *Le Bagne*, 1952, both set in prisons. § Genet, J. *The Maids / Deathwatch: Two Plays*. Trans. by Bernard Frechtman. Grove, 1954. 101–63. Also translated by David Rudkin, 1987.

44 *"Now Barabbas..."* (1947) | William Douglas Home (1912–1992), Scot

[Prison drama; 17M, 4W; unit set.] Home based his play on his own prison experience (he was court-martialed for refusing to obey an illegal military command). It takes place during the weeks just before one of the inmates is to be hanged for shooting a policeman. Three of the prisoners are homosexual. The newly arrived Evelyn Richards is stereotypically effeminate: overly long hair, theatrical gestures; he is a chorus boy who dislikes women. Medworth is not so obvious. He is a 60-year-old former teacher who has committed some unspecified transgression, almost certainly having improper relations with one of his pupils. When young Jock Roberts, another newbie arrives, Medworth immediately puts the make on him. He alludes to the story of David and Jonathan, who "loved each other very much. [...] And Jonathan was much, much older than his friend." Paddy O'Brien, 33, takes offense at Medworth's attentions to the youth. Since he has already reacted negatively to Richards's campiness, saying, "They ought to hang the likes of you," one initially thinks that he is simply being protective. It becomes clear, however, that he and Richards are in some sort of a mutual relationship. To spite Paddy, Medworth denounces Richards to the governor, with the result that Richards is transferred to another prison. Roberts's girlfriend leaves him for another man, but before Medworth can take advantage of his vulnerable state, he himself is paroled. The last we see of the prison, Paddy *"stands behind Roberts, looking down at his hair. His hand steals out towards it, but he checks himself."* Paddy suggests they take a walk together and *"puts his arm through Roberts's."* Officer King has been the most lenient of the guards, but he now warns, "Break it up, this ain't 'Yde Park on Sunday night. [...] O'Brien! Roberts! If yer likes it arm-in-arm, I've got a pair of bracelets here. (*He swings his handcuffs in his hand.*)" After opening privately in 1947, the script somehow received the Lord Chancellor's approval and was performed publicly in London with Peter Doughty, Basil Gordon, and Julian Somers, directed by Colin Chandler. § Home, W. D. *"Now Barabbas..."* Longmans, Green, 1947. 105p.

45 *The Fire That Consumes* (1951) | Henry de Montherlant (1895–1972), French

[School drama; 6M; 1 set.] Set in a Catholic school for boys in the Parisian suburbs, the play demonstrates the baneful power the priesthood can have over impressionable youths. Father de Pradts takes a more than pedantic interest in Serge Souplier, 14, and becomes quite jealous of the boy's relationship with the slightly older day student Andre Sevrais. Buffeted by the emotional turmoil the priest creates, the boys question the nature of their "special friendship." They pledge a blood brotherhood based on purity. Overcome, Souplier moves to kiss Sevrais, who checks the impulse. Finding the two in what appears to be a compromising situation, Father de Pradts has Sevrais expelled. A tutor tells Sevrais that Father de Pradts deliberately led the two boys into a trap "to get you expelled, and leave the field clear for himself." But the priest is checked by his superior, who recognizes that de Pradts loved Souplier "for his human carnality [...] not because of his spiritual beauty" and expels the second boy also. *La ville don't le prince est un enfant* was published in 1951, but Montherlant would not permit a performance until 1963, in Paris. The English version opened in London, 1977, with Nigel Hawthorne and Dai Bradley, directed by Bernard Miles. A 1997 French film was released in English-speaking countries under the title *The Fire That Burns*. § Montherland, H. de. *The Fire That Consumes*. Trans. by Vivian Cox and Bernard Miles. Ritchie, 1980. 73p.

46   *Third Person* (1951) | Andrew Rosenthal (1917–1979), American

[Domestic drama; 3M, 3W; 1 set.] According to Sinfield (*Out on Stage*, 16), no New York theater would take the play, so Rosenthal turned to London. The printed script comes with notes detailing the cuts and rewrites that the Lord Chamberlain demanded, offering fascinating insight into the vagaries of British censorship. In the last days of 1947, tensions in the Moreland household come to a head. Hank is back from the war in the Pacific, but things are not going well. His wife Jean reveals that they have not slept together for six months. Hank's wartime friend Kip, at loose ends, has settled in with the family. He obviously worships Hank, to Jean's discomfort and Hank's obliviousness. Hank's old college friend, the ironically named Felix, is intensely jealous of Hank and Kip's closeness and initiates a showdown between husband and wife. Speaking cattily to Jean, he says, "So you three are just going to grow old gracefully, together? If I were bi-lingual I'd call that quite a 'ménage à trois.'" On a "little F.B.I. expedition," he uncovers that before the war Kip had lived with the painter Eric Lowman. The implication is that they were lovers. Felix also discloses that Kip has a troubled background and twice attempted suicide. When Jean pours out what Felix has said, Hank reacts: "Christ, one of these seconds you're going to come right out and accuse me of having something to do with him! I've done a lot of things in my life, Jean, but that doesn't happen to be one of them." He accosts Kip and, in a moment of intense emotion, strikes him. Kip leaves. Finally Hank looks objectively at Felix and has it out with him. Felix's wife, who clearly understands his nature, tells Hank he is better off not being friends with her husband. Presumably Hank and Jean's marriage will endure, but in the revised script he does say that Kip "may be gone—but my *feeling* for him isn't. It's right *here* ... and at last, thank God, I can say it!" The play opened in London, 1951, with Denholm Elliott, Kenneth Hyde, and Roger Livesey. Rosenthal later turned it into a novel *The Extra Man*, 1977. § *Plays of the Year*, v7; ed. by J. C. Trewin. Elek, 1953. 339–441.

47   *Camino Real* (1953) | Tennessee Williams, American

[Symbolic drama; 26M, 10W; unit set.] Williams borrowed Baron de Charlus from Marcel Proust's *À la recherche du temps perdu* for *Ten Blocks on the Camino Real*, published in *American Blues* in 1948. Then in a relatively bold move for a playwright of his stature, he expanded the role to create a significant scene, Block Four, in his highly innovative, full-length *Camino Real*. Different from both the romantic dreamers and the clueless fools who have stumbled onto the nameless plaza, the baron is seeking sensation and atonement. Kilroy, the play's hero, greets him as "A normal American. In a clean white suit." The baron responds, "My suit is pale yellow. My nationality is French, and my normality has been often subject to question." He remarks, "Once upon a time [...] I used to wonder. Now I simply wander. I stroll about the fountain and hope to be followed. Some people call it corruption. I call it—simplification." In an in-joke about New York gay bars he names the "hot-spots, [...] the Bird Circuit." Kilroy sums up, "A very unusual type character." At scene's end, however, the baron's body has been deposited into the street cleaners' barrel. Jacques Casanova and Lord Byron are also among the characters, but Williams does not reveal their bisexuality. The play opened in New York, 1953, with David J. Stewart, directed by Elia Kazan. The short version was telecast in 1966 with Tom Aldredge, directed by Jack Landau. § Williams, T. *Camino Real*. New Directions, 2008. 156p. Includes *Ten Blocks on the Camino Real*.

48   *One Foot to the Sea* (1953) | Harold Levitt (1920–2013), American

[Ship romance; 8M, 1W; flexible set.] Levitt presumably based his play on his service in the U.S. Navy. The main plot follows a battle between a man and a woman over a youth. Steve Montvidas, 45, the cargo ship's cook, assumes a proprietary hold on his mess boy, Allen Gode, 20: "The boy [...] belongs to me [...]! The kid is more to me than any woman could be!" He resents his shipmates who try to set the virginal Allen up with a woman while they are moored at a New York dock and is furious when he discovers him with a prostitute. Then Steve confuses the situation by pretending that he has been with all sorts of women himself. Allen fights back, declaring his freedom. He returns to the woman, who implores him not to return to "the filth of what that man is." But when she offers herself to Allen, he becomes ill and flees back to the ship. Steve awaits him with a knife, planning to kill him. Allen begs, "Do whatever ye want to me." Steve having won, the two end up laughing *with such abandon, such finality, with so much affection, holding each other's arms ... what else is there to do but ring the curtain down."* The play opened in New York, 1953, with Donald Stuart and Gene Remington, directed by Tom Hill. § Levitt, H. *One Foot to the Sea: A Play in Three Acts.* Burdge, 1954. 114p.

49 *South* (1953) | Julian Green (FRA 1900–1998), American

[Psychological drama; 8M, 6W; 1 set.] Green was openly gay. But talk about the love that dare not speak its name! It is so silent in *South* that many a playgoer must have wondered what all the fuss was about. Set on a plantation near Charleston during the twenty-four hours before the bombardment of Fort Sumter, the central character is an American soldier of Polish descent, Lieutenant Jan Wicziewsky. He is in love. Is it with his host's niece? No, that is ruled out. Is it perhaps the host's daughter? The lieutenant leads her to think so momentarily, and "who knows," he says. "She might have been salvation." Or could it be the owner of a nearby plantation, a Southern abolitionist named Eric MacClure? If so, that is equally hopeless. Jan challenges Eric to a duel and then goads him into killing him. Before then, as the English director points out, there has also been much talk about the South and the North, whites and blacks, American and European differences—and heterosexuality, but not its opposite. Nevertheless, the play was not licensed for public performance in England. *Sud* opened in Paris, 1953. Green did his own translation for the 1955 private London production with Denholm Elliott, directed by Peter Hall. It was telecast in 1959, perhaps the earliest gay television drama. The script became the basis of a 1973 opera by Kenneth Coe. § Green, J. *South: A Play.* Boyars, 1991. 128p.

50 *Tea and Sympathy* (1953) | Robert Anderson (1917–2009), American

[Sexual melodrama; 9M; 2W; 1set.] Anderson scripted one of the most talked about plays (and movies) of the decade. Because he is effeminate, prep schoolboy Tom Lee, 17, is suspected of being homosexual. His fellow students and even his super-macho housemaster Bill Reynolds bully him. Reynolds's wife lashes out at her husband: "An innocent boy goes swimming with an instructor ... an instructor whom he likes because this instructor is one of the few who encourage him, who don't ride him .... And because he's an off-horse, you and the rest of them are only too glad to put two and two together and get a false answer ... anything which will let you go on and persecute a boy whom you basically don't like." Goaded by her husband, she gets at a possible, and quite different, truth: "Did it ever occur to you that you persecute in Tom [...] the thing you fear in yourself?" The play ends with her saving Tom's heterosexuality by seducing him, voicing its often quoted, and often parodied, curtain line: "Years from now ... when you talk about this ... and you will ... be kind." The play opened in New York, 1953, with John Kerr (later Anthony Perkins) and Leif Erickson, directed by Elia Kazan. Vining (*Diary*, v2, 470) recorded that he "got thoroly [*sic*] lost in the play, was completely convinced by it while seeing it, but later felt that matters were exaggerated." Anderson wrote the screenplay for the 1956 film. I hated it. § Anderson, R. *Tea and Sympathy.* Random House, 1953. 182p.

51 *The Immoralist* (1954) | Ruth Goetz (1912–2001) and Augustus Goetz (1897–1957), American

[Psychological drama; 6M, 2W; 3 sets.] The play opened at the height of McCarthyism, but, in the words of Curtin (*Bulgarians*, 291), "Surprisingly enough there were no repercussions from the public, the police or the politicians." Surprising, since the drama, though censored, was still pretty explicit about the dangers of sexual repression to a gay man and even more so to his wife. Presumably the fact that the husband-wife team adapted the play from Nobelist André Gide's autobiographical novel protected it. Michel's father and his future brother-in-law suspect that he is homosexual. When he was 11, he was expelled from boarding school after he was caught with another boy. But Marcelline pays no heed to their warnings. She and Michel marry. They flee to Algeria, where the playgoer finds them two months later, Marcelline still a virgin. Through his houseboy, Bachir, Michel discovers the world of Arab boys willing to prostitute themselves. He also meets Moktir, a former university professor who has accepted that "the keenest pleasures are not intellectual." Moktir, however, retains a moral censor; he reproves Michel for his dishonesty with his wife. Marcelline sinks into alcoholism. When Bachir goads him about her condition, Michel tries to prove himself by finally having sex with her. At the same time, attempting to gain Moktir's respect, he announces that from now on, "I will say what I am like! This one thing I can do! I can speak out!" He sends Marcelline back to Normandy, not knowing she is pregnant. There she regains her strength. Michel unexpectedly shows up and confesses the depths of loneliness to which he has sunk—letting "those who are like me" use him and being shunned "by those who are not." But he begs her, "Marcelline, punish me for what I did, but not for what I am." The play ends with the possibility they will carve out some kind of life together. It opened in New York, 1954, with Louis Jourdan and James Dean, directed by Daniel Mann. Vining (*Diary*, v2, 482) recorded his pleasure in seeing it: "The tolerance of homosexuality as a subject in two successful plays this year should finally silence the self-pitying. In the case of *Tea and Sympathy* there is no real foundation for the suspicions leveled at the boy but in this there are no less than three characters who avow themselves to be just what they are." § In Hodges, B., ed. *Forbidden Acts*. 303–60.

52 *Cat on a Hot Tin Roof* (1955) | Tennessee Williams, American

[Psychological drama; 5M, 6W, extras; 1 set.] Is Brick Pollitt a closet case or not? What was the nature of his relationship with his best friend Skipper? Is it symbolic that the previous owners of their Mississippi plantation were a gay couple whose bedroom is now Brick and Maggie's? He refuses to bed her after she and Skipper, in her words, "made love, if love you could call it, because it made both of us feel a little bit closer to you." She also confesses that she confronted Skipper about his feelings, whereupon "he made that pitiful, ineffectual little attempt to prove that what I had said wasn't true." And then he began to drink himself to death, and Brick became an alcoholic as well. Maggie insists she does not mind that "It was one of those beautiful, ideal things they tell about in the Greek legends"—if Brick will only be honest. But Brick shies so violently from the notion that his and Skipper's relationship could have been anything but "a clean, true thing" that when his father brings the matter up, he turns on him and reveals Big Daddy's cancer has not been cured as his family has led him to believe. Before then he has also confessed that Skipper called him and "made a drunken confession to me on which I hung up." Williams in an authorial note says "*the inadmissible thing that Skipper died to disavow between them* [...] *may be at the heart of the 'mendacity' that Brick drinks to kill his disgust with. It may be the root of his collapse. Or maybe it is only a single manifestation of it, not even the most important.*" The play opened in New York, 1955, with Ben Gazzara, directed by Elia Kazan. The third act was not the one Williams gave the director. Kazan cajoled him into changing it. Williams made the mistake of publishing both versions. In 1974 he returned to the play and combined the two scripts for a definitive final version. It opened in New York with Keir Dullea, directed by Michael Kahn. James Poe and Richard Brooks wrote the screenplay for the highly successful 1958 film. The play has been telecast twice. § Williams, T. *Cat on a Hot Tin Roof*. New Directions, 1975. 173p.

53 *Game of Fools* (1955) | James Barr Fugaté (1922–1995), American

[Political drama; 15M, 4W, extras; 7 sets.] By the gay activist and author of *Quatrefoil*, the play is a psychological study of four Midwestern friends arrested for political reasons and imprisoned on trumped-up charges of sodomy. The differing reactions of each of them and of their respective families provide a powerful indictment of American homophobia and religious hypocrisy. Unable to take his father's disdain after his release from prison, Jasher Pureson slashes his own throat. Paddy O'Reiley allows himself to be sequestered by his fanatical mother in a monastery. Frenchy English, who has been struggling with accepting his sexuality, embraces celibacy and proposes marriage to a woman willing to accept his past. Only Johnnie Babton has the strength to fight the varying kinds of injustice through sheer will of personality and the support of his parents. Johnnie's vitality makes Frenchy face up to the fact that he is again running away, and they join forces. Published in 1955, the play was performed in Los Angeles. The Mattachine Society in their first meetings called themselves the Society of Fools. § Fugaté, J. B. *Game of Fools: A Play of Those Fools, by Those Fools, and for Those Fools Who Stubbornly Refuse to Perish from This Earth*. ONE, 1955. 100p.

54   *Quaint Honour* (1958) | **Roger Gellert (1927–2013), English**

[School drama; 5M; 2 sets.] John Holmstrom set his only play in a public school. Unlike earlier schoolboy plays, it does not duck the question of sexuality in an all-male environment. Rather, the script gives voice to the more enlightened arguments of the time about the nature of homosexuality, including a defense of adolescent sexual experimentation. On a dare from his former fag, house prefect John Tully sets out to seduce the younger Tim Hamilton, to find that the boy blooms as a result of his attention and that he himself begins to have feelings for the lad. Unfortunately, they are caught by the priggish (and homophobic) head of house and reported to the housemaster. The latter prides himself on his enlightened attitude but reveals how outmoded his thoughts are. Tully is expelled; Hamilton decides to leave on his own to sort out his thoughts. The playgoer gains the impression that he is the strongest of the lot. The play was given a private showing in London, 1958, with John Charlesworth and Michael Caridia, directed by Frank Dunlop. § In Wilcox, M., ed. *Gay Plays*, v2. 9–49.

55   *Suddenly Last Summer* (1958) | **Tennessee Williams, American**

[Gothic drama; 2M, 5W; 1 set.] From the perspective of liberation politics, the play is highly suspect for its portrait of a predatory homosexual. It is also Williams's most perfectly wrought gem: a vision of the world as Darwin's jungle, *red in tooth and claw*, "a hideous story but [...] a true story of our time and the world we live in." Sebastian Venable, the gay character, never appears. He was murdered last summer in Cabeza de Lobo, an event that has traumatized his cousin Catherine. Sebastian's mother Violet wants to stop her from reporting what she witnessed. Violet calls in a psychiatrist Dr. Cukrowicz, unashamedly offering to subsidize his work with mental illnesses if he will perform a lobotomy on Catherine. Violet's jungle-like conservatory in her Garden District home becomes the setting for an evaluation. Catherine is brought in to recount her story. Her mother and her brother, also present, beg her to keep quiet for fear of losing Violet's money. But Catherine is compelled to tell what happened when she was chosen to accompany Sebastian abroad last summer to attract young men after Violet lost her looks. At Cabeza de Lobo he had turned "from the evenings to the beach," near where "bands of homeless young people [...] lived [...] like scavenger dogs, hungry children." One day a "band of naked children pursued [him] up the steep white street in the sun that was like a great white bone of a giant beast that had caught on fire in the sky." And when they caught him, brought him down, "he was lying naked as they had been naked against a white wall, and [...] They had *devoured* parts of him." Sebastian had completed the "*image!*—he had of himself as a sort of!—*sacrifice* to a!—*terrible* sort of a—[...] God." The play opened in New York, 1958, as the second part of *Garden District*, directed by Herbert Machiz, and was telecast in 1993. Gore Vidal wrote the screenplay for the 1959 film.

An out-and-out gay play also set in New Orleans, *And Tell Sad Stories of the Deaths of Queens*, was begun about this time but not completed until the late 1960s. It tells a story of a drag queen who picks up a straight sailor and lets him abuse her. There followed the ambiguous case of Lot in *Kingdom of Earth*, 1967–68, before Williams created his next gay characters in *Confessional*. § Williams, T. *Suddenly Last Summer*. New Directions, 1958. 90p.

56   *A Taste of Honey* (1958) | **Shelagh Delaney (1938–2011), English**

[Domestic drama; 3M, 2W; 1 set.] Delaney was associated with the so-called kitchen sink realism which revitalized British theater in the 1950s. Her play traces the continuing war between Helen and her daughter Jo. Act 2 finds the unwed Jo pregnant and alone. Her mother has married a younger man, who will leave her, but, in Helen's words, Jo has a "pansified little freak to lean on." This is Geoffrey Ingram, a Manchester working class student whom Jo befriends when he is thrown out of his rented room, probably because he is gay. De Jongh (*Not in Front*, 92) points out that in him Jo "has discovered a surrogate mother-figure, whose domestic skills and maternal compassion help her through a lonely pregnancy." But, without Jo's knowledge, Helen throws him out. From a present-day perspective Geof seems contrived. Not the slightest evidence is produced that he has any interest in other men; Geof, nevertheless, seemed a breakthrough at the time. De Jongh (93) goes on to emphasize how he "emerges from the play [...] as the one authentically good person within it [....]

Delaney had thus written the first major British play in which a gay and effeminate man is both ridiculed and approved, derided and accepted." It opened in London, 1958, with Murray Melvin, directed by Joan Littlewood. Delaney and director Tony Richardson co-wrote the 1961 screenplay. § Delaney, S. *A Taste of Honey: A Play*. Grove, 1959. 87p.

57 *Big Fish, Little Fish* (1961) | **Hugh Wheeler (GBR 1912–1987), American**

[Psychological drama; 5M, 2W; 1 set.] The closeted playwright leaves it largely to his actors to convey the gay nuances in the play; the text barely sidles up to the idea that two of William Baker's friends are in love with him. Of snobbish Basil Smythe, William's married mistress says, "Sometimes I can't understand. I mean, one man being so fond of another man. But it's sweet." After William in essence spurns Basil's offer of a two-week all-paid vacation in Miami, he changes his will once again and, instead of leaving his money to William, bequeaths it to the good-looking young author Ronnie Johnson. Of recovering alcoholic Jimmie Luton, William himself says, "Jimmie, do you think I didn't know? [...] Who am I to mind. People are the way they are. And that's how it ought to be." Wheeler informs readers that the moment for Jimmie *"is probably the happiest in his life."* The play opened in New York, 1961, with Martin Gable and Hume Cronyn, directed by John Gielgud. Vining (*Diary*, v3, 246) wrote that it was "chock full of funny lines and very real people. Hume Cronyn gave a wonderful performance of an ugly little bug of a man who's a repressed homosexual." § Wheeler, H. *Big Fish, Little Fish: A New Comedy*. Random House, 1961. 115p.

58 *Look: We've Come Through* (1961) | **Hugh Wheeler, American**

[Sexual drama; 4M, 2W; 1 set.] Sex is alluded to constantly in Wheeler's second play of the year. For wannabe actress Jennifer it is a tool to get what she wants. For her flatmate Belle it is mental, an ideal; when she loses her virginity to Jennifer's husband, she is disappointed that she feels no different. For Jennifer's agent sex is a commodity, something you trade for other benefits. The hustler Bobby pegs him as essentially a "queer." Bobby's friend Skip, on shore leave from the Navy, sees sex as power. Whether he has actually been with all the women he claims cannot be known, but we see him try to force Bobby into giving him a blowjob. Bobby is the most complicated. Is he gay, bisexual, or gay for pay? He does not hide the fact that he is a hustler and receives compensation for his services from the unseen Arthur Millington. But he breaks with the man, to his avaricious mother's dismay. And he fights off Skip's advances, literally. Bobby dislikes that the agent treats him like "a cheap hustler or something." Skip calls him a "little son-of-a-bitch faggot" when Bobby resists. Does a hurt ego turn Bobby to Belle? Or has he truly fallen for her? The play ends with his questions: "You and me? *(He takes her in his arms. He kisses her.)* Wow! What you know? Live and learn, don't you?" The play opened for a brief run in New York, 1961, with Ralph Williams, Burt Reynolds, and Zack Matalon, directed by José Quintero. § Wheeler, H. *Look: We've Come Through: A Play*. Dramatists, 1963. 67p.

59 *Now She Dances!* (1961–2003) | **Doric Wilson (1939–2011), American**

[Absurdist drama; 4M, 3W; flexible set.] Wilson was one of America's first playwrights to make gay experiences his almost exclusive subject. The original one-act version of *Now She Dances! A Fantasia on the Trial of Oscar Wilde* exists as a manuscript in the New York Public Library; the present text was published in 2003. In a note Wilson informs readers that the play is his "most fiercely autobiographical," its immediate inspiration having been his entrapment and arrest by a New York policeman. A wildly inventive work, filled with literary, political, and cultural allusions, it is a loose retelling of Wilde's *Salome* intercut with flitting references to Wilde's trial. The play opens with Lane the butler, "the quintessential closet queen" imported from *The Importance of Being Earnest*, and Bill, Lane's very macho and very heterosexual helper, setting up the stage. Lady Herodias arrives with a tale about how she was accosted by someone handing out flyers for the Gay Defensive Front. Bill is puzzled: "If they're so happy, why run around protesting?" To Lady Herodias's consternation, Lane explains that the circular came from one of Wilde's progeny: "Mr. Oscar Wilde is not a fit subject for conversation. Certainly not in a family entertainment," she exclaims. Herod sets out to apprehend the miscreant: "He'll be charged with perversity! With playing footsy with the wrong feet. With … with mimeography!" In Act 2, a Prisoner—a part originally played by Wilson—is led in: "an attractive, personable, contemporary gay male, dressed for Saturday night on West Street." When asked his name, he responds, "Jokanaan," followed by a list of outstanding gays in history, ending with Alfred Taylor, the man tried with Wilde. Lane and Prisoner recognize a kinship, and Lane feels called upon to defend the closet. Like the young Syrian in *Salome*, Bill inexplicably kills himself. Salome, who has attacked homosexuality throughout the play, obtains Jokanaan's head. The 1961 version opened in New York with Wilson and Thomas Lawrence, directed by William Ashley. § In Susoyev, S., and Birimisa, G., eds. *Return to the Caffe Cino.* 405–62.

60 *The Boy in the Basement* (1962) | **William Inge (1913–1973), American**

[Sexual tragedy; 3M, 1W; 2 sets.] Though written in the early 1950s, the play, the closeted playwright's first with an openly homosexual character, did not appear until a 1962 collection of one-acts. Another from the same time, *The Tiny Closet*, may be read as the portrait of a closeted homosexual or as a study of gender defiance. Set in a mining town close to Pittsburgh, *Boy* has as its protagonist Spencer, 46, a mortician who escapes his domineering mother and nearly mute father with trips to Pittsburgh for gay weekends. The mother's suspicions about her son redouble after he calls her in the middle of the night asking her to wire him money. Her fears are confirmed during a meeting of do-gooders, where she discovers her son was one of those arrested in a police raid on a gay bar. Incapable of escaping her emasculating domination, Spencer's misery worsens when the body of a teenage boy he has altruistically befriended is brought in, a drowning victim, and deposited on the embalming table in the basement—a symbol of his own life. The play was presented in New York (*Tiny Closets*, 1995) with Robert Buckley, directed by Dan Wackerman. § Inge, W. *Eleven Short Plays*. Dramatists, 1990. 37–54. Includes *The Tiny Closet*. 56–65.

61 *Man and Boy* (1963) | **Terence Rattigan (1911–1977), English**

[Social melodrama; 5M, 2W; 1 set.] The closeted Rattigan had high hopes for his play; its implausible plot dooms it. The setting is an apartment in Greenwich Village on July 13, 1934. A crooked father schemes to use his (straight) son to lure an extremely closeted businessman into shoring up the father's latest financial scam. To achieve this end, Gregor Antonescu does not tell his dandyish son what he is up to, but dresses him appropriately and warns him not to call him "father." When Mark Herris arrives in Act 2, Gregor leads him to believe the apartment is his love nest and his son is his lover. He also hints that he would be pleased if Mark would take an interest in the boy while Gregor is away on business trips. The son is willing to play his father's game, but time runs out for Gregor, and his scheme falls through. The play opened in 1963, first in London and then in New York, with Austin Willis, directed by Michael Benthall. § Rattigan, T. *Man and Boy: A Drama in Three Acts*. French, 1963. 90p.

62 *The Toilet* (1963) | **Leroi Jones (1934–2014), American**

[School tragedy; 11M; 1 set.] In this brutally realistic drama, a gang plots a fight between Jimmy Karolis and Ray Foots in a high school boys' restroom after Karolis sends Foots a letter "telling him he thought he was 'beautiful' … and that he wanted to blow him." One of the gang members cannot resist beating up Karolis first, causing Foots to abort their plan. But Karolis demands the two meet in combat. It comes out that they have earlier had a very different encounter in the same restroom, one in which, Karolis says, "You put your hand on me" and "said your name was Ray." He denounces the other boys: "You stupid bastards. I love somebody you don't even know." Both Foots and Karolis injured, all but Karolis leave. Foots returns and cradles Karolis's head. Published in 1963 in *Kulchur* magazine, the play opened in New York in 1964 with Jaime Sanchez, directed by Leo Garen. § Jones, L. *The Baptism & The Toilet*. Grove, 1966. 33–62.

63 *The Baptism* (1964) | **Leroi Jones, American**

[Absurdist farce; 4M, 1W, extras; 1 set.] The play calls into question accepted social and religious values. A Minister prepares to welcome a Boy into the church. A Homosexual sneers that the teenager looks like rough trade. Some of the congregation, however, are ready to greet the Boy as the Son of God reincarnated, especially after they discover he ejaculates three times a day while praying to God. A Messenger arrives on his motorcycle to announce that God intends to destroy the world this evening and to take the Boy away. The Boy protests that he "was sent here to save man" and will "not leave" until he has accomplished his mission: "Nothing will make me forsake this flesh" (31). The Messenger prevails, and the Homosexual, the most rational of the lot, departs to cruise Bickford's, a popular gay bar of the era. The play opened in New York, 1964, with Taylor Mead, directed by Jerry Benjamin. Jones later took the name Amiri Baraka and shied away from his early experiences with homosexuality. § Jones, L. *The Baptism & The Toilet*. Grove, 1966. 7–32.

64   *Entertaining Mr. Sloane* (1964) | Joe Orton (1933–1967), English

[Dark comedy; 3M, 1W; 1 set.] Orton has become almost as much a gay icon as his literary forebear Wilde. In this, his gayest play, a brother and a sister compete to gain the favors of the new roomer. Mr. Sloane, 20, is an opportunist ready to do anything and anyone. He did have second thoughts about letting a photographer take nude photos of him, resulting in his accidentally killing the man. Now he has taken a room in Kath's and her father's home, unaware that the father can identify him as the murderer. Seduced by Kath, Sloane impregnates the 41-year-old. He is hired by Ed, the gay brother, to be his chauffeur (and probably to perform other duties). When the father realizes who Sloane is, he threatens to go to the police. Sloane kills him too. Ed and Kath are so smitten with the young man that they agree, in return for Sloane's favors, to fabricate a story about how their father died. The two siblings work out a deal whereby they will share Sloane, each having him six months at a time. There is nothing overtly homosexual in the text; the closest we get are lines such as the father's memory of the then 17-year-old Ed and presumably another boy "committing some kind of felony in the bedroom." The action is another matter. John Lahr in his introduction records that Orton wrote his director: "Eddie [is] the central pivot of the play. His stalking of the boy's arse [should be] as funny and wildly alarming as Kath's stalking of his cock." The play opened in London, 1964, with Dudley Sutton and Peter Vaughan, directed by Patrick Dromgoole. Clive Exton wrote the script for the 1970 film. § In Hoffman, W., ed. *Gay Plays*. 199–279.

65   *The Haunted Host* (1964) | Robert Patrick (1937–), American

[Psychological drama; 2M; 1 set.] Patrick has taken gay life as his almost exclusive subject. In this, his first play, Jay cannot shake off the ghost of his ex-lover Ed, who killed himself. Jay realizes, "The minute you try to live someone else's life for him, or let him live yours—it's suicide. And that's what we both wanted: to give up our lives to each other so we wouldn't have to live them ourselves." Their self-destructive common ground was writing. Now, just as Jay is trying to exorcize the ghost, a Village friend asks him to put up a former college classmate for the evening. Frank turns out to be a straight would-be writer hoping to get tips from Jay. He looks uncannily like Ed. The two men's campy confrontation mysteriously dispels Ed's lingering spirit. The script gets off a number of barbs ironically parodying straights' mentality. Jay says: "Tell me, Frank, how long have you been heterosexual? [...] Started as a kid, huh? Tsk-tsk. Tell me, do you think one of your teachers, or possibly even one of your parents might have been heterosexual? Do you think that might have been the reason you—" Later Jay asks, "What do straight boys *do* together?" The play opened in New York, 1964, with Patrick and William Hoffman, directed by Marshall W. Mason. § In Susoyev, S., and Birimisa, G., eds. *Return to the Caffe Cino*. 123–62. In Berman, E., ed. *Homosexual Acts*. 83–136.

66   *The Madness of Lady Bright* (1964) | Lanford Wilson (1937–2011), American

[Psychological drama; 2M, 1W; 1 set.] Now dated, the play is a virtual monologue revealing the growing loneliness and despair of an aging queen, Leslie Bright. A boy and a girl provide a nonrealistic counterpoint to what is going on in his mind. At one point the boy says, "Some pansies live a sane life and some don't. Like anyone else, I suppose." A *tour de force* for the actor, it builds to Leslie's total breakdown as he roves through his memories and tries unsuccessfully to establish telephone contacts with old tricks. As Clum (*Still Acting*, 200) says, "Like many gay protagonists, he romanticizes the role of victim and outcast, thus making his isolation both bearable and inevitable."

Clum (201) quotes Robert Patrick from his preface to *Untold Decades*, about how in the Village he finally met "the kind of brave and brazen gay men I longed for, but half the time they were so crippled by identity crises and simple self-hatred that they couldn't maintain an affectionate erection, must less a relationship." Wilson's play opened in 1964 with Neil Flanagan, directed by Denis Deegan. William Hoffman records, "It was one of off-off-Broadway's first big hits, and a landmark in gay plays." The next year Wilson produced his first full-length play, the almost plotless *Balm in Gilead*. It is set in an all-night New York coffee shop whose regulars include gays, gay-for-pay hustlers, transwomen, and lesbians. Needing a cast of twenty-four, Wilson turned to Cafe La MaMa to stage it and began his long career with director Marshall W. Mason. § In Hoffman, W., ed. *Gay Plays*. 177–97.

67 *The Sign in Sidney Brustein's Window* (1964) | **Lorraine Hansberry (1930–1965), American**

[Social drama; 6M, 3W; 1 set.] Gay playwright David Ragin is a secondary character, but the remarkable thing is how little is made of his sexuality by the others. An African American activist does react negatively: "I'm sorry if it makes me unsophisticated in your eyes; but after a while, hanging out with queers gets on my nerves!" Sidney Brustein tells David simply, "If somebody insults you—sock 'em in the jaw. If you don't like the sex laws, attack 'em. I think they're silly. You wanna get up a petition? I'll sign one. [...] *But*, David, please get over the notion that your particular sexuality is something that only the deepest, saddest, the most nobly tortured can know about. It ain't— [...] it's just one kind of sex—that's all. And, in my opinion [...] the universe turns regardless." Sidney attacks David instead for his attraction to the avant-garde, but David's play turns out to be a success. In contrast, the world of the idealistic Sidney tumbles around him as he becomes involved in a political campaign that proves to be as corrupt as the candidate it defeats, his life further complicated by his relationships with his wife and her two sisters. The play opened in New York, 1964, with John Alderman, directed by Peter Kass. § Hansberry, L. *The Sign in Sidney Brustein's Window: A Drama in Three Acts*. Random House, 1965. 143p.

68 *The Bed* (1965) | **Robert Heide (1939–), American**

[Absurdist drama; 2M; 1 set.] In 1961 Heide wrote the unpublished *West of the Moon*; Wendell Stone (in B. Harbin, *Legacy*, 187, 189) cites it as "One of the first plays to deal openly and positively with gay sexuality." It "concerns a hustler who attempts to seduce a religious young man whom he meets when the two seek shelter in a Christopher Street doorway during a sudden rainstorm." Joe Cino liked it so much he invited Heide to write his "existentialist play." The result was *The Bed*. Two men are lying in bed, where they may have been for two (sexless) days: Jack, a trust fund baby, supports Jim. The latter is bored with existence: "With you. With me. With both of us together. Something's *not* working. I can't go on. I've just about passed the point of endurance. I am not up to this. I'm thinking of maybe pushing off. Out." He contemplates jumping out of the fourth-floor window, but finally just walks out. Jack regards the clock and then the audience. The play opened in 1965 with Jim Jennings and Larry Burns, directed by Robert Dahdah. It was filmed by Andy Warhol. The Caffe Cinco also premiered Heide's *Moon*, 1967, in which a gay man, half of a gay couple from upstairs, offers bread to another man, half of a straight couple whose marriage has reached a dead end. § In Susoyev, S., and Birimisa, G., eds. *Return to the Caffe Cino*. 328–36. Includes *Moon*. 338–53.

69 *A Patriot for Me* (1965) | **John Osborne (1929–1994), English**

[Historical tragedy; 31M, 7W; flexible set.] Inspired by Robert Asprey's fictionalized biography *Feasting with Panthers*, the closeted playwright created a seemingly sprawling work, but it is actually an intricately structured dramatization of key points in the life of Colonel Alfred Redl (1864–1913), head of counter-intelligence for the Austro-Hungarian empire and arch traitor, working as an agent for the Russian empire. In the world of espionage that unfolds, as one character says: "We all play parts, *are* doing so now, *will* continue to do so." The play opens with a duel to the death resulting from one officer's calling another "Fräulein Rothschild." Not until Act 2 do we find out that the offending officer, Max von Kupfer, is himself gay. Redl's sexuality is not disclosed until the very end of Act 1. Act 2 begins with an opulent drag ball. Various characters are thus simultaneously outed yet hidden behind flamboyant costumes. Here we have the play's most serious discussion of homosexuality, followed immediately by a short scene depicting a Viennese neurologist with an absurd theory about its origin and nature. The act ends with Russian intelligence officers' entrapment of Redl. Act 3 is composed of short scenes showing his pull towards younger men, his long deferred revenge against Kupfer, effected by his sending him to Russia as a spy and then betraying him, and his own unmasking and subsequent suicide. The play opened in London, 1965, with Maximilian Schell, Frederick Jaeger, John Castle, and Douglas Sheldon, directed by Anthony Page. It became the basis for a 1985 German-language film *Oberst Redl*. § Osborne, J. *A Patriot for Me*. Faber, 1995. 103p.

70   *Degrees* (1966) | **George Birimisa (1924-2012), American**

[Romance; 2M, 1W; 1 set.] In 1966 the play was broadcast on WBAI, a New York listener-sponsored radio station, "complete and uncut," according to Birimisa, "despite its very gay content, a first for radio in America." Its male leads are an early odd couple. Robert Ginsberg, a physician, is tidy, ordered, politically conservative; his lover Louie, an aspiring novelist whom he is supporting financially, is his polar opposite in every way. It is not clear whether Robert knows that Louie has been with a woman while he was in Boston seeing his mother. Robert has not come out to her, but via a telephone call during which she speaks to Louie it would seem that she knows the truth about their relationship and even depends on Louie to give Robert direction. Like some old couple the two quarrel, in this case over the Vietnam conflict, and Louie offers to leave. Robert cannot bring himself to apologize; instead, like a parody of the ending of *My Fair Lady*, he asks, "Do you know where I put the TV Guide?" As the lights dim, the two are contentedly watching a Disney program. The play was produced onstage in New York, 1966, with Patrick Sullivan and Dan Leech, directed by Murray Paskin. § *Birimisa: Portraits, Plays, Perversions*; ed. by Lanny Baugniet and Paul Sagan. Sweetheart, 2009. 27–41.

71   *A Song at Twilight* (1966) | **Noël Coward, English**

[Psychological drama; 2M, 2W; 1 set.] Coward was supposedly inspired by the closeted life of Somerset Maugham for his portrait of writer Sir Hugo Latymer. Married now for twenty years to his German translator, he receives a visit from his former mistress, the actress Carlotta Gray, at his hotel suite in Switzerland. Ostensibly she is seeking permission to quote from his letters in her forthcoming autobiography. After caustically dissecting her acting abilities, he refuses, whereupon she drops a bombshell for the Act 1 curtain by telling him that she has in her possession the letters he wrote to the now deceased Perry Sheldon, "the only true love of your life." Hugo accuses her of blackmail for her "threat to expose to the world the fact that I have had, in the past, homosexual tendencies." She ripostes, "Tendencies in the past! What nonsense! You've been a homosexual all your life and you know it." Though Hugo's wife, upon her return, expresses her sympathy that the "conflict within him between his natural instincts and the laws of society has been for the most of his life a perpetual problem that he has had to grapple with alone," Carlotta's judgment that he has been guilty of "vitiating [his] considerable talent by dishonesty" retains its validity. Coward labeled his play a comedy, and indeed it is witty. But the portrait of Hugo will probably leave most playgoers with a sense of the sad waste of his life. The play was one of a trio presented in London in 1966 under the collective title *Suite in Three Keys* with Coward, directed by Vivian Matalon. It has been telecast twice. § Coward, N. *A Song at Twilight: A Comedy in Two Acts*. French, 1966. 68p.

72   *Staircase* (1966) | **Charles Dyer (1928–), English**

[Domestic drama; 2M; 1 set.] Since Dyer was careful to include in the program and book publication the information that he was married and had three children, one must wonder what he was up to in giving one of the two characters his name and providing an anagram, Harry C. Leeds, for the other. For that matter, seven other names dropped in the course of the play are also anagrams. In an end note he allows that perhaps "Charlie is alone. Nobody else!" Brixton barbers, the two men have been in a relationship for twenty years, interrupted by a two-year hiatus during which Charlie served time in prison. He has been arrested again for propositioning Ed Chrysler (another anagram) while dressed in drag, and the chief constable

Rychard Lees (ditto) has summoned him to appear in court. The two lovers bicker the duration of the play. A former actor, Charlie was briefly married and is expecting the arrival of his daughter momentarily. Both men are in love/hate relationships with their mothers; fathers are never mentioned. The play (based on a novel not published until 1969) opened in London in 1966 with Paul Scofield and Patrick Magee, directed by Peter Hall. Dyer wrote the screenplay for the miserable 1969 film. § Dyer, C. *Staircase.* Grove, 1969. 89p.

73 *When Did You Last See My Mother?* **(1966) | Christopher Hampton (1946–), English**

[Sexual drama; 3M, 2W; 1 set.] Sinfield (*Out on Stage*, 247) sees the play as a "challenge" to "the notion that public-school boys grow out of same-sex interests as they leave." Though Hampton's plot is straightforward, he was influenced by the Theater of the Absurd in his dramaturgy. Now between school and university, Ian and Jimmy share a bedsit. Though they have both had homosexual adventures, Jimmy professes to be straight. The sexual tension between them leads to bickering, fights, and walkouts on Jimmy's part. Jimmy beds Linda. Ian fails with Dennis—who has disappointed Jimmy because of "an anatomical deficiency"—but unexpectedly scores with Jimmy's mother. She returns a second time, supposedly to apologize to him. On her way home she dies in a car accident. Sinfield notes, "As in *Tea and Sympathy*, Ian has the benefit of [a] loving sexual experience with an older woman, but now it proves fatal to her and doesn't straighten him out" (248). Jimmy returns to inform Ian, who feels guilty. Not knowing what has occurred between Ian and his mother, Jimmy feels equally guilty and invites Ian to stay with him and his father. After Jimmy leaves, Ian consoles himself: "And before long, doubtless I shall be back to go to bed with you." Sinfield neatly supplies the moral: "Gays are here to stay [...], and repression is dangerous." The play opened in London, 1966, with Victor Henry and Julian Holloway, directed by Robert Kidd. § Hampton, C. *When Did You Last See My Mother? A Play in Six Acts.* French, 1967. 66p.

74 *Where's Daddy?* **(1966) | William Inge, American**

[Social satire; 3M, 3W; 1 set.] In a sendup of 1960s youth culture, Tom Keen spouts psychobabble and an existential mishmash to browbeat his pregnant wife Teena (whom he has illogically married in order to legitimize the baby) into agreeing that they should put the child immediately up for adoption and then divorce in order to be free to pursue their acting careers. The couple in the apartment across the hall and Teena's mother acquiesce to his hair-brained ideas. The only person with integrity is Tom's surrogate father "Pinky" Pinkerton. An old queen, he saved the 15-year-old Tom from prostituting himself on the New York streets. Though Pinky admits to pretending to be "the Baron de Charlus strolling through the bois," he asserts his belief "in God, and love, and the sanctity of the home, and all those comforting mores that everyone today considers terribly reactionary." In *A Life of William Inge* (Univ. of Kansas Press, 1989) Ralph Voss claims, "Pinkerton is the most personally revealing character that William Inge ever put on the stage" (226). Pinky chastises Tom, and the play ends with the couple keeping the baby and remaining married. Missing from the script is any explanation why Tom turned out the way he has, given the education he received from Pinky. Performed on Cape Cod the year before, the play opened in New York in 1966 with Hiram Sherman, directed by Harold Clurman. Vining (*Diary*, v3, 429) wrote, "From practically the first line this was the worst play I've seen in years." Inge tried to address homosexuality more directly in his last play, *The Disposal*, 1968. Set in a prison, it was expanded as the unpublished *The Last Pad*, 1970, but it was an even bigger failure when produced. § W. Inge. *Where's Daddy?* Dramatists, 1994. 73p.

75 *Fortune and Men's Eyes* **(1967) | John Herbert (1926–2001), Canadian**

[Prison drama; 5M; 1 set.] Herbert based his play in part on his incarceration in 1947–48 as the result of being caught dressed in drag. Set in a reformatory for teenage felons, this character study depicts the change in young Smith, who goes from being a dazed innocent to a hardened punk whose final words, said with sadistic pleasure, are, "I'm going to pay them back. [...] I'll pay you all back." The play begins with his arrival in the cell shared by the deeply closeted Rocky, a hardened criminal though he is not yet 20; the flamboyant Queenie, a cat burglar; and the fragile Mona, who was mugged and then suffered the indignity of her attackers insisting that he had made a pass at them, a lie easily accepted by the policeman arriving on the scene. Smitty himself has been sold out by his abusive sire after he stole a car to try to get his mother out of his father's reach. Smitty is straight, but quickly learns that sex is power in the reformatory. He initially accepts Rocky's protection, but as he gains strength and knowledge of how the system works, he breaks free and offers, in turn, to take Mona under his protection. He thereby gains Rocky's and Queenie's enmity, but he is now prepared to fight. Act 2 opens with Queenie's drag number ("A Hard Man Is Good to Find"), followed by Mona's emotional delivery of Portia's defense before the judge from *The Merchant of Venice*—both in preparation for the Christmas show. Mona's act rejected, he and Smitty remain behind, whereupon Mona shares Shakespeare's Sonnet 29 with Smitty. Their cell-mates return for the final showdown, triggering a guard's appearance. The latter's vicious treatment of Mona, egged on by Rocky and Queenie, leads directly to Smitty's vow.

The play received a workshop production in Stratford, Ont., in 1965, but no Canadian company would take it on. Its first full production had to wait until its 1967 New York opening with Bill Moor, directed by Harvey Hart. Vining's description (*Diary*, v3, 470) is worth quoting at some length: "The audience gathering for the play was almost exclusively male, tho there were perhaps twenty women in the audience of about 200 in the little basement theatre. It was also a rather furtive and sniggering audience and I suppose I felt just as self-conscious going to a play about homosexuality in prison. As it turned out, it was a quite well constructed play. [...] The language was forthright and the campy part of the queen was predictably effective with the audience, including me." The 1969 Los Angeles production had Michael Greer, directed by Sal Mineo. Herbert wrote the screenplay for the 1971 film. He went on to write other gay plays, none quite so successful as this one. § Herbert, J. *Fortune and Men's Eyes*. Grove, 1967. 96p.

76 *White Lies* **(1967) /** *White Liars* **(1968) | Peter Shaffer (1926–2016), English**

[Psychological drama; 2M, 1W; 1 set.] In almost all his major plays Shaffer created a homoerotic subtext: *Five Finger Exercise*, 1958; *The Royal Hunt of the Sun*, 1964; *Equus*, 1973; *Amadeus*, 1979. Harold Gorringe, the antiques dealer in *Black Comedy*, 1965, is obviously gay. But Frank of *White Liars* is the only character in Shaffer's works to actually admit he is in love with another man. He is the business manager for a rock singer, Tom. The latter is superstitious and wants to consult a fortune teller at an English seaside resort during the off-season. Bit by bit the playgoer finds out that she and both men have concocted fake biographies. Frank bribes her to warn Tom off the woman that he presents as his girlfriend. When Tom exposes the ruse, Frank breaks down and confesses, "I wanted him to leave her alone! ... And to stay with me. In—my—bed. [...] He'd been there six months." He leaves. Speaking to the empty room, the fortune teller sums up: "Your lover? What lover? There never *was* one! [...] go home and find someone *real!*" Paired with *Black Comedy* (with Donald Madden playing the antique dealer), *White Lies* opened in New York in 1967 with Madden and Michael Crawford, directed by John Dexter. Shaffer was unhappy with the script and revised it twice for London productions, each time slightly modifying its title. James Boham and Ian McKellen appeared in the 1968 production. § *The Collected Plays of Peter Shaffer*. Harmony, 1982. 149–79. Includes *Black Comedy*. 181–238.

77 *Wise Child* **(1967) | Simon Gray (1936–2008), English**

[Crime farce; 3M, 1W; 1 set.] Presumably the program, if not the actor's mannerisms, would give away that Gray is playing gender games in a major way. As reconstructed by the audience by the end of the play, Jock Masters was an accessory to the brutal beating of a postman. To escape the police, he dressed as a woman, Mrs. Artminister, but the teenager Jerry saw through his disguise, and the two hooked up, Jock posing as his mother and Jerry now playing the role of Garfield and performing con acts to make money for the two. They end up in a hotel run by the homosexual Simon Booker. His lover was a priest who was forced out of the church and fled to Canada. He has taken to seducing young boys under the guise of teaching them to pray while he fellates them. He immediately sets his eyes on the young Garfield. Jerry's own position is unclear. He nestles against his mother (whom he knows, of course, is a man) and manages to turn the game of rock-paper-scissors into a sadomasochistic ritual. He hates the very "smell" of women, but dresses in drag. Jock meanwhile has become tired of the drag act; in one scene he attempts to seduce the maid, creating for the audience at that point what appears to be a lesbian encounter. Jock pushes Jerry to lead Booker along, but Jerry resists and in the end kills Booker. Jock takes Booker's clothes and leaves to meet his fate dressed as a man. Jerry dons the maid's clothes (which she left behind when Jerry interrupted the scene), in essence taking on his "mother's" role: "It's a wise boy that knows its own," Jock has said. The script's racism jars; there seems no real reason for the slurs even in the context of its time. The dark comedy opened in London, 1967, with Alex Guinness, Gordon Jackson, and Simon Ward, directed by John Dexter. § Gray, S. *Plays One*. Faber & Faber, 2010. 97–202.

78 *Boys in the Band* (1968) | Mart Crowley (1935–), American

[Dark comedy; 9M; 1 set.] From the play's first appearance, Off Broadway, it was understood that it had made a major breakthrough in the portrayal of gays on stage. As such it met wide acclaim. It was equally denounced for its depiction of narcissistic, back-biting, self-loathing homosexuals, especially the following year in the wake of the Stonewall Inn riots. In a recent interview Edward Albee (whose *Virginia Woolf* was a major influence on the second act) admitted that he still hated the play. But almost fifty years after its debut, one can see more clearly how the pathos of the piece is balanced with witty repartee. Many of the lines have entered the gay treasury of quotations. And, like it or not, its depiction of gays quite accurately reflects one segment of society at the time (and, for that matter, later). Michael, who would give anything not to be gay, hosts a birthday party for Harold, to which he invites five of their friends. Harold's opening speech, when Michael chides him for arriving late to his own party, is unforgettable: "What I *am*, Michael, is a thirty-two-year-old, ugly, pockmarked Jew fairy—and if it takes me a while to pull myself together and if I smoke a little grass before I can get up the nerve to show this face to the world, it's nobody's goddamn business but my own."

The evening is complicated by the unexpected arrival of Alan, Michael's college friend, with whom he has always tried to pass as straight. He begs his friends to butch it up. But the presence of Cowboy, Emory's birthday present, and Emory's irrepressible campiness quickly blow any facade to pieces. The suspicion grows that Alan may in fact be a super closet case; he has just left his wife, and his reaction to Emory is extreme. The evening is also complicated by a simmering quarrel between Hank, who has left his wife for Larry but expects to move into a similar marriage with him, and Larry, who refuses to embrace monogamy, seeing it as a parody of straight ideals. Michael proposes they all play a game in which they get points by calling up "the *one* person we truly believe we have loved" and telling him so. Emory and Bernard (the one African American at the party) hang up the phone, both desolated; Hank and Larry begin working towards reconciliation with a new definition of the meaning of a relationship; Alan returns to his wife. The party breaks up. Before he leaves, Harold delivers his final verdict on Michael: "You are a sad and pathetic man. You're a homosexual and you don't want to be. But there is nothing you can do to change it. Not all your prayers to your God, not all the analysis you can buy in all the years you've got left to live." Alan leaves as much an enigma as he was when he arrived; the self-hating Bernard and Michael depend on the kindness of friends more than ever. But abrasive Harold, stereotypical Emory, the couple in progress Hank and Larry, and book-reading Norman, Michael's closest friend, emerge as relatively strong characters, greeting life in their distinctive ways in relatively positive terms.

Boys opened in New York in 1968 with Leonard Frey, Kenneth Nelson, Robert La Tourneaux, Cliff Gorman, Laurence Luckinbill, Keith Prentice, Reuben Greene, and Frederick Combs, directed by Robert Moore. Vining (*Diary*, v4, 37) described the evening he saw it: "In the first act we screamed with laughter as the gay party got under way but the second act, as they got drunker and nastier, was much more sober. Fortunately, only one of the characters was terribly campy, one was mildly so, and the rest were allowed some dignity and masculinity despite their sexual proclivities. The scene where they played a game in which each man phones the one person he loved best to tell him so was a bit unbelievable but very well done and touching. At least one couple was allowed some happiness together and despite jealous scenes, chose to call each other during the game and eventually retired to the bedroom to make love." Thereafter Vining refers several times to the play's effect on his friends. Crowley wrote the screenplay for the 1970 film, in which all the original cast reprised their roles. Crayton Robey put together an informative documentary film *Making the Boys*, 2011, about its incarnation as both play and film. In 2002 Crowley produced a sequel, *The Men from the Boys*. § In Hodges, B., ed. *Forbidden Acts*. 443–517. In Hodges, B., ed. *Out Plays*. 3–83.

79   *The Death and Resurrection of Mr. Roche* (1968) | **Thomas Kilroy (1934–), Irish**

[Psychological drama; 6M; 1 set.] Kilroy created what is probably Ireland's first gay play. Six boozers end up at Kelly's flat in Dublin. One of them is Mr. Roche—no first name, though Myles calls him Agatha. Although they label him a queer, "The Queen of Dunleary," only Kelly seems bothered by his presence. He announces loudly, "We don't want him and the type he goes around with. Perverts!" Myles counters, "I don't give a tuppenny curse how people like it. You know? I mean sex. It takes all kinds. 'Course I'm broadminded [...]. I mean, this is the twentieth century. We've all gotta live together." But even Myles joins in when they take it into their drunken heads to thrust Roche into a narrow passage, knowing that he suffers from extreme claustrophobia. When they realize what they have done, they check: Jeremy, a failed medical student, announces that Roche is dead. In a panic Kelly pushes them to deposit the body on a park bench somewhere. Left with his best friend Seamus, he confesses how he let Roche spend the night with him once, and "God forgive me. I let him handle me." Almost certainly Kelly is a closet case and does not know how to deal with the fact. When Roche reappears, very much alive, and begs to be allowed to stay while the rest go to mass, Kelly accuses him, to his apparent bewilderment, of "trying to blackmail me." Left alone, Roche answers the telephone. It is Seamus, who hangs up when Roche identifies himself. The play opened in Dublin, 1968, with Ronnie Walsh and Niall Toibin, directed by Jim Fitzgerald. § Kilroy, T. *The Death and Resurrection of Mr Roche*. Gallery, 2002. 81p.

80   *Total Eclipse* (1968) | **Christopher Hampton, English**

[Biographical study; 9M, 4W, extras; flexible set.] The play distills the tumultuous encounter between the French poets Paul Verlaine (1844–1896) and Arthur Rimbaud (1854–1891). It focuses on the emotional and, to some extent, physical sides of the relationship, but completely ignores the poetic impact, the only poem recited being one by a now obscure French writer. The play opens in late summer 1871 with Rimbaud's response to Verlaine's invitation to join him and his wife in Paris. Verlaine is instantly smitten with the crude teenager, so different from the refined life that imprisons him in his in-laws' home. Following facts closely, the scenes portray his flight with Rimbaud, the wife's attempt to recapture her abusive husband, the decisive moment in 1873 when Verlaine fires a gun at Rimbaud, his subsequent trial, and their last meeting in 1875 after his release from prison. The play concludes with an epilogue set in 1892 revealing Verlaine's effort to publish all of Rimbaud's poetry. Rimbaud returns in his reveries and kisses the drunken Verlaine. The play is a fascinating portrait of the two men, even though it adds little to our understanding of their complex influence on each other as writers. The play opened in London, 1968, with John Grillo and Victor Henry, directed by Robert Kidd. It was telecast in 1973. Hampton wrote the screenplay for the 1995 film; it too has been published. § Hampton, C. *Total Eclipse*. Faber & Faber, 1981. 72p.

81   *Change* (1969) | **Wolfgang Bauer (1941–2005), Austrian**

[Absurdist drama; 6M, 4W, extras; 7 sets.] Hugh Rorrison (in M. Banham, *Cambridge Guide*, 84) in summing up Bauer says that his "characters inhabit an escapist, self-destructive world of drugs, dreams, pop music, promiscuity and role-playing into which violence occasionally intrudes." Here, Antoine, an art dealer who has "changed horses" and become "Ambidextrous," gets caught up in a bizarre scheme concocted by the painter Frank Swann and the art critic Hugh Richards. They have come upon Basil O'Malley, a locksmith who aspires to be a painter. They decide to build up Basil's reputation and then drive him to kill himself. Antoine is more than happy to assist them in their "diabolical plan." A caricature of a gay man, he wears "a purple velvet smoking jacket" and is listening to "our private national anthem [...] The

'Pathétique'" in his first appearance on stage. Basil proves more wily than they anticipate. He gratuitously assaults Antoine with a broken goblet. Later, having gotten them all high, he proposes a game in which everyone will change identities. Antoine is to exchange identities with his wife, to the dealer's delight. Basil and Frank will exchange theirs. Frank goes into the bathroom and hangs himself. *Change* was performed in Vienna in 1969. There have been three film versions, all in German. (Bauer also wrote *Magic Afternoon*, 1967, in which two males bond homoerotically through their intense misogyny and violent behavior. In addition to German film versions, it was filmed in English as *The Young Unknowns*, 2000.) § Bauer, W. *Change and Other Plays*. Trans. by Renata Esslin and Martin Esslin. Hill & Wang (Mermaid), 1973. 1–133. Includes *Magic Afternoon*. Trans. by Herb Greer. 135–215.

82 *Enemy!* (1969) | **Robin Maugham (1916–1981), English**

[Military drama; 3M; 1 set.] Maugham based his play on his own service in World War II. He shows how the struggle to survive can create unusual friendships, even make unexpected bedmates. The scene is North Africa in spring 1942. Ken Preston, an English soldier who has survived an attack, comes upon a destroyed tank in the desert. A German soldier, Paul Seidler, has taken refuge beside it. Gradually it emerges that Ken has served prison time for having sex with an underage girl. Paul's Jewish lover died in a concentration camp. Even though Ken says that they're "on different tracks," apparently they share a common sleeping bag. When an English officer shows up, Ken tries to hide Paul's presence. There are too many clues in sight, though, that someone else is present. The officer immediately pegs Paul for a homosexual, or at least a pretty boy: "They'll be queueing up for him in the prison camp." Ken snaps and accuses the officer of being "what we're fighting against." Obtaining his weapon, Ken forces him to leave. He and Paul prepare to march southward to find sympathetic Bedouins. After first being staged in Guilford in 1969, the play came to London with Dennis Waterman and Tony Selby, directed by Ronald Eyre. In 1981 Maugham converted it into a novel called *The Deserters* (though its American title was *Enemy*). It ends with Paul's death at the officer's hand. § *Plays of the Year*, v39; ed. by J. C. Trewin. Elek, 1971. 311–96.

Post-Stonewall, 1970–1981

First Gay Pride march in New York, 1970, in London, 1972. APA removes homosexuality from list of mental disorders, 1973. Anita Bryant begins fear campaign in Florida, 1977. Mary Whitehouse brings charges of blasphemy against U.K.'s Gay News, 1977. Harvey Milk assassinated in San Francisco; rainbow flag unfurled, 1978. Sir Anthony Blunt exposed as former Russian spy, 1979. Scotland decriminalizes homosexual acts, 1980. U.S. "Moral Majority" begins hate campaign, 1981. Police raids on Toronto bathhouses launches Canadian Pride movement, 1981. "Gay cancer" reported in New York Times, *1981 (July 3).*

83 *The Clash of Cymbals* (**1970**) | **Wilfrido Maria Guerrero (1911–1995), Filipino**
[Adolescent romance; 13M, 2W; 2 sets.] Neil Garcia in Philippine Gay Cullure (Hong Kong Univ. Press, 2009) faults Guerrero for making his play "heavily derivative of Western homosexual theater," irrelevant to "the situation of local homosexuals at this specific time" (92). Unlike the traditional Filipino relationship, the gay couple here are both "masculine" and "equally" in love as symbolized by the equality of cymbals. Edwin, 19, and Butch, 17, meet and fall in love. Both mothers acquiesce to the relationship at the same time they try to get help from the absent fathers and a psychiatrist. For the fathers the boys are simply "sick and—depraved." For the psychiatrist, homosexuality is more complex. There is much talk about the nature of love between men, and even more talk about the causes, reviewing all the theories of the day before essentially settling on a medical explanation. Butch's father kidnaps him twice, but he escapes both times. After Edwin's father melodramatically dies during his confrontation with his son, Edwin threatens suicide if his mother does not give him enough money to join Butch. The play ends with a "deafening" clash of cymbals. It was presented by the U.P. Ichthyophilic Society in Manila in 1970 with Edwin Abreu and J. Ong, directed by Guerrero. § Guerrero, W. M. 12 New Plays. Regal, 1971. 267–327.

84 *Confessional* (**1970**) / *Small Craft Warnings* (**1972**) | **Tennessee Williams, American**
[Barroom drama; 7M, 2W; 1 set.] In 1970 Williams came out on national television. The same year he published *Confessional* with its two openly homosexual characters. Directed by William Hunt, the play premiered in 1971 at the Maine Theatre Arts Festival. Williams revised and expanded the script to become *Small Craft Warnings*. Habitués are gathered at a small bar somewhere on the coast between Los Angeles and San Diego to drink and bicker. In their midst briefly appears Quentin, a screenplay doctor, and Bobby, a teenage cyclist from Iowa whom he has picked up, mistakenly thinking the boy is straight trade. Leona, one of the regulars, latches onto them. She announces that she is "practically what they call a faggot's moll," having learned about gay life from her deceased brother. She holds that the gay scene is filled with "sickness and sadness." Quentin agrees: "There's a coarseness, a deadening coarseness, in the experience of most homosexuals." He abandons Bobby, who decides to bike on into Mexico. The evening ends with changes in everyone's life but without any real epiphany. The expanded version opened in New York in 1972 with Alan Mixon and

David Huffman, directed by Richard Altman. Vining (*Diary*, v4, 252) complained, "It's a very flawed play but not without interest. [...] The really excruciating scene, badly written and badly played, was the speech of the older homosexual who explains at much too great length how homosexuals are scarred." § Williams, T. *Dragon Country: A Book of Plays*. New Directions, 1970. 151–96. *Small Craft Warnings*. New Directions, 1972. 86p.

85 *Find Your Way Home* (1970) | **John Hopkins (1931–1998), English**

[Domestic drama; 3M, 1W; 1 set.] Hopkins earlier wrote a BBC telefilm *Horror of Darkness*, 1965, with a gay character. This new play brings freshness to the familiar motif of a married man facing up to the fact that he is gay. Having chosen his wife and two children over Julian Weston a year previously, Alan Harrison unexpectedly shows up at Julian's flat and announces that he wants to return. He finds "Julie" with David Powell, whom Julie is tired of. Alan apologizes for his earlier action, pleading that he ran away "mostly from myself." They have sex between acts. Act 2 begins with Alan's wife Jackie showing up, surprised to discover that Julie is not a woman, as in other extramarital affairs he has had. Recriminations follow before Jackie accepts that Alan will not return home. In Act 3 David pops back in and reveals unsavory aspects of Julie's character. Facing up to their shortcomings, Alan and Julie, however, want to try to make a real go of it this time with "no lies." Though overwritten, the drama makes a sincere attempt to show all sides, both the woman's and the men's. The premiere was in London, 1970, with Anthony Bate, directed by Kevin Billington. Vining wrote of the 1974 New York production (*Diary*, v4, 367): "Since the apex of the triangle was so personally unsexy and so shallowly written, the play couldn't make much effect. The language was forthright but it won't advance homosexuality one bit even tho it ends with the males setting up house together." § In Hodges, B., ed. *Out Plays*. 85–147.

86 *Norman, Is That You?* (1970) | **Ron Clark (CAN 1933–) and Sam Bobrick (1932–), American**

[Domestic comedy; 3M, 2W; 1 set.] Though the authors fill their script with dated clichés of every sort, it manages to be funny and finally affirmative in its own way. Ben Chambers, his wife having run off with his brother, pays an unexpected call on his son Norman (a New York store window dresser). Norman has not had the courage to come out to his parents, but now his father discovers he is living with another man, Garson Hobart. He tries to heterosexualize his son by hiring a female prostitute, then he tries to get rid of Garson (becoming even more upset when the latter outs Ben's favorite composer Stephen Foster). Mrs. Chambers shows up in the last scene, having realized she does not really love her brother-in-law. She is more accepting of the fact that "it's a new world now. It's all out in the open. There's a sexual revolution going on in this country." Norman himself finally finds the courage to announce, "I have no guilt and if you want to be miserable about the way I am, well, that's up to you. But whether you're miserable or not I can't let it affect my life." The play ends with his parents scheming how to set Norman up with a doctor or a lawyer. It opened in New York, 1970, with Martin Huston and Walter Willison, directed by George Abbott. Vining wrote (*Diary*, v4, 121), "I laughed a great deal, [...] even as I deplored so much of the play." The playwrights also wrote the script for the 1976 film in which the Jewish family becomes an African American family. They went on to create *The Paul Lynde Show*. § Clark, R., and Bobrick, S. *Norman, Is That You? A Comedy in Two Acts*. French, 1977. 73p.

87 *Blow Job* (1971) | **Snoo Wilson (1948–2013), English**

[Crime drama; 3M, 1W; 1 set.] Wilson portrays a nightmarish world inhabited by two gay victims, two skinheads, and a mentally disturbed woman. The skinheads plan to rob a safe in Cottrell's home. One comes up with the idea to pose as a straight couple in order to deflect attention. Both are implicated in Cottrell's murder, the transvestite hitting him over the head with a hammer and the other mutilating him with a screwdriver. McVittie is a gay security officer patrolling the area. He is accidentally injured when his dog seizes a stick of gelignite and it explodes. The woman finishes him by cutting his jugular. The first reviewers found political significance; present-day audiences more likely will experience only its shock value (the dog's death is rendered graphically). Gays could well ask why the victims must be gay, and what does it mean that Wilson wants both played by one actor? And what gives with the deliberately misleading title? (It comes from a song by Nick and Tony Bicat.) The play opened in Edinburgh, 1971, with Constantin de Goguel, directed by David Hare. § Wilson, S. *Pignight & Blowjob*. Calder, 1975. 46–86.

88   *Butley* (1971) | Simon Gray, English

[Dark comedy; 4M, 3W; 1 set.] The playgoer may feel guilty for laughing at the title character's antics. Cruel and manipulative, university lecturer Ben Butley has failed in his relationships with both women and men. He enjoys making clandestine trouble for other people—"fun," he calls it. His infantilism is symbolized by his love of nursery rhymes. Ben's wife Anne has left him for "the most boring man in London." Joey, his former tutee whom he has finagled into sharing an office, a flat, and his clothes, is moving out of both the flat and the office today—though, spineless, he keeps postponing his announcement until the arrival of his boyfriend Reg forces him into the open. Ben thinks he has found Joey's replacement in another young tutee, but at the play's end Ben faces up to his failures. There is no promise, however, that self-recognition will effect any change, and the playgoer leaves uncertain even about Joey and Reg's future. The play opened in London, 1971, with Alan Bates, Richard O'Callaghan, and Michael Byrne, directed by Harold Pinter. Gray also wrote the screenplay for the 1974 film. § Gray, S. *Plays One*. Faber & Faber, 2010. 1–96.

89   *The Gentle Island* (1971) | Brian Friel (1929–2015), Irish

[Domestic/social drama; 5M, 1W, extras; unit set.] Friel skewers Irish romanticism. When Dubliners Peter Quinn and Shane Harrison arrive at Inishkeen (Irish for "gentle island"), Peter declares that "it's heavenly." In truth, it is hellish. All the families save one have abandoned it. The Sweeneys, behind their veneer of respectability, are vicious, cruel, dangerous bunglers. During World War II they were scavengers, living off the spoils of the dead floated their way. They continue to show no respect for life, exemplified by the father's maiming a hapless dog left behind. Shane, 32, may see through their facade, but Peter, twice his age, seems oblivious to the peril he has put them in. The Sweeney daughter-in-law is not satisfied sexually by her husband Philly. She proposes to Shane that they have sex. When he refuses, she turns into an avenging fury. She tells her father-in-law that she caught Shane and Philly naked in the boathouse, with Philly "doing for the tramp what he couldn't do for me." Perhaps her story is true; it may be a lie. But she uses it to egg on her father-in-law to shoot Shane. When he finds himself incapable of killing Shane in cold blood, she grabs the rifle. Instead of killing him, the bullet severs Shane's spinal cord so that he will never walk again. The younger son has had enough: he leaves the island to his father, Philly, and the wife. The play opened in Dublin, 1971, with Edward Byrne and Shane Connaughton, directed by Vincent Dowling. § Friel, B. *The Gentle Island*. Davis-Poynter, 1973. 81p.

90   *Coming Out!* (1972) | Jonathan Katz (1938–), American

[Docudrama; 5M, 5W; no set.] Since Katz is a historian, it is not surprising that the script comes with forty-five endnotes. An appendix has photocopies of fifteen newspaper reviews since the performance itself was historical. What may be surprising is how relevant the play remains forty years later. It is the first example of gay documentary theater. Written in free verse, it opens with a celebration of the Stonewall Inn riots. It then moves back in history, beginning with colonial cases of sodomy and continuing forward with stories of gays who have come out and the words of repressive hatemongers. The spirit of Walt Whitman and the presence of Allen Ginsberg and Judy Grahn are particularly important. At times the actors' voices are filled with anger, as when recounting the Boise, Idaho, witch hunt of 1955; more often they are liberating and celebratory, proclaiming in clarion tones, "Coming out is not asking for trouble, / it sets a cornerstone / for a fuller self-respect." The play end with an exhilarating chorale lifted during "the Annual Anniversary / March and Celebration / of the new Gay Liberation Movement / commemorating the Great Battle of 1969." The play opened at the GAA Firehouse in New York, 1972, with gay and lesbian nonprofessional actors, including Blake Berggren, Charlie Brown, Bruce Buchy, Steve Krotz, and Michael Lee, directed by David Roggensack. § Katz, J. *Coming Out! A Documentary Play about Gay Life & Liberation in the U.S.A.* Arno, 1975. 70p.

91 *The End* (1972) | **John Palmer** (1943–), **Canadian**

[Sexual farce; 4M, 3W; 1 set.] Palmer is one of the founders of the Toronto gay theater scene though his plays seem rather minor pieces. *The End* is a shapeless satire whose sense of the ridiculous comes from its characters. It opens with Belinda and Webster's preparation for a party celebrating their anniversary. Their plans are quickly derailed with the arrival of five uninvited guests. First is Ju-Jube, whom Webster had a sexual fling with at college and who is still infatuated with him. Just back from Cairo, Ju-Jube has moved to sex with adolescent boys; with him is a student he picked up at the airport. A suicidal psychiatrist who badly needs to see a psychiatrist tracks Belinda down, having talked to her on a helpline. Finally, one of Belinda's office mates, who refuses to admit she is lesbian, and the woman from next door, clutching a gun and claiming to have shot her boyfriend, show up. There ensue much coming and going, slamming of doors, stage business (particularly with flowers), along with some nudity and generally bizarre behavior before the guests depart the following morning, having arrived at some degree of resolution in their messed-up lives. The play opened in Toronto, 1972, with George Dawson and Peter Jobin, directed by Martin Kinch. § Palmer, J. *The End / A Day at the Beach*. Coach House, 1991. 19–108.

92 *Satyricon* (1972) | **Paul Foster** (1931–), **American**

[Absurdist drama; 12M, 6W, extras; unit set.] As is evident here, Foster was grounded in the Theater of the Ridiculous movement. Petronius Arbiter, using characters from his novel *Satyricon*, concocts one divertissement after another to amuse the Roman emperor Nero. Simultaneously, Nero plays out all the ways he tries to kill his mother Agrippina. The play is stuffed with innuendoes. For example, the Bacchants chant about how they want meat, including such lines as "I wanna suck those Roman bones / And tongue that Roman meat." A Spanish character named Penetracion, in answer to Agrippina's question about his stock in trade, replies, "Nine inches. Every inch a piece of gold." Nero and Tigellinus have an exchange: Nero says, "Everybody experiments when they're young. Didn't you?" Tiggy answers, "I tried it once. I didn't like it." Nero responds, "I tried it once. I liked it." There is even an extended reference to fisting. The play ends with Petronius's suicide and Nero's departure. One of at least five plays inspired by the Roman novel, it opened in New York in 1972 with David Lucas and Charles Stanley, directed by John Vaccaro. § *The Off Off Broadway Book*; ed. by Albert Poland and Bruce Mailman. Bobbs-Merrill, 1972. 510–28.

93 *Elagabalus* (1973) | **Martin Duberman** (1930–), **American**

[Psychological drama; 4M, 4W; 1 set.] Duberman is essentially a gay historian. His collection *Radical Acts* (New Press, 2008) contains *Visions of Kerouac*, 1976, a loosely connected series of vignettes about the Beats, and *Posing Naked*, 1998, a play about Professor Newton Arvin. *Elagabalus* is far more interesting. Adrian, a young man of the present, self-identifies with the Roman emperor. Martijn Icks in his study *The Crimes of* Elagabalus (Harvard Univ. Press, 2012) writes, "In Duberman's interpretation, both Elagabalus and Adrian are tragic victims of their conservative surroundings, in which there is no room for those who deviate from conventional standards" (211). Adrian endangers his uncle's political ambitions by acting out Elagabalus's exploits, going so far as to plan a double wedding to a male stablehand whom he has taken in ("Hierocles") and the female Puerto Rican housekeeper, Faustina. Adrian is visited by his grandmother and mother. The grandmother tries to persuade him to give up his folly; his mother defends him to the family doctor who accompanies them: "Adrian is not delusional. It is a calculated conceit. The boy wants more than one life. So should we all." Besides defending her son, she also poses a different kind of danger to the family's reputation by having an S/M affair with her chauffeur. In the end Adrian castrates himself and dies. The play was tried out in 1973 in a workshop. § Duberman, M. *Male Armor: Selected Plays, 1968–1974*. Dutton, 1975. 279–352. Also includes *Payments*. 127–278.

94 *The Enclave* (1973) | **Arthur Laurents** (1917–2011), **American**

[Domestic drama; 6M, 3W; 1 set.] Laurents surprisingly wrote only two gay plays, both quasi-autobiographical. Ben, 40, has convinced his friends to join him in creating a series of adjoining townhouses, their own enclave where they can live safely. Before the project is finished, he falls in love with Wyman, a brash, self-assured man fifteen years younger than he with whom he proposes to share his place. All the friends, including his brother and sister-in-law, know he is gay; they can accept the fact—but only as long as he keeps silent: "You waited this long, why did you have to rub our faces in it now?" For a moment it appears that they will drive Wyman away, but he has more backbone than any of them, including Ben. Meanwhile, one of the friends, Donnie, gets so turned on by Wyman that he makes contact again with a hustler and takes him to Ben's place; when he doesn't pay up, the hustler badly beats Donnie up. Ben's gay doctor friend patches up the wounds; Donnie's wife confesses she has always known, but she too accepts silence as virtue. A contrast is set up between the way the group treats Ben and Wyman and the way they treat a couple consisting of a black man married to a much younger white woman. The playwright rushes the play's resolution, but Ben finally gains the courage to say, "This is what I am. And even to my surprise, I like it." The play opened in New York, 1973, with Barton Heyman and Tom Happer, directed by Laurents. § Laurents, A. *Selected Plays*. Backstage, 2004. 99–167.

95   *Hosanna* (1973) | Michel Tremblay (1942–), Canadian

[Domestic drama; 2M; 1 set.] Tremblay, in the words of Leonard Doucette (in M. Banham, *Cambridge Guide*, 1122), takes as his domain a world of "social and economic despair, peopled by transvestites, homosexuals and misfits." *Hosanna* is a study of the traps that gender/role-playing games hold for participants in forging identity. Claude Lemieux (aka Hosanna) returns, distraught, to his flat dressed as Elizabeth Taylor in *Cleopatra*. Soon after, Raymond Bolduc (aka Cuirette), dressed in full leather drag, appears. Both are past their prime but dress as if they are still young, slender, and attractive: as Cuirette says, "I don't want things to change!" But something devastating has happened to Hosanna. As they bicker about a variety of matters—including Cuirette's dependence on Hosanna's income as a hairdresser, an impending visit from Hosanna's supposedly ignorant mother, and Cuirette's threat to hitch up with one Reynald—it comes out that Cuirette was in on a brutal joke played on Hosanna. The gay scene, tired of the latter's bitchiness, rigged a drag party at which everyone showed up as Cleopatra, outshining the pathetic costume Hosanna created. As a result of their stripping away their facades, Hosanna and Cuirette reaffirm their love for each other. Cuirette says, "The important thing is that you be yourself, that's all. [...] Claude ... it's not Hosanna that I love." Hosanna removes his drag; naked, he turns to Cuirette: "Look, Raymond, I'm a man.... I'm a man, Raymond." *Hosanna* premiered in Montreal, 1973. The English version opened in Toronto, 1974, with Richard Monette and Richard Donat, directed by Bill Glassco. It became one part of the 1974 film *Il était une fois dans l'est*. § Tremblay, M. *Hosanna*. Trans. by John Van Burek and B. Glassco. Talonbooks, 1991. 87p.

96   *Kennedy's Children* (1973–75) | Robert Patrick, American

[Psychological drama; 3M, 3W; 1 set.] This play probably is Patrick's most widely known. The setting is a New York bar on February 14, 1974. The action consists entirely of a series of self-absorbed monologues by five characters who have been influenced by the legacy of President Kennedy. (A bartender is also present, but he is mute.) One of the two men is gay. An actor, Sparger, unlike the other four characters, seems unaffected by the political and cultural changes that took place during the 1960s. He was caught up totally in the Off Broadway theater movement. All five now register a sense of futility. One of the women laments, "The men don't understand Women's Lib and the women can't dig Gay Power. The blacks don't need us and the Indians don't want us. And the new kids are no use." But she clings to the hope that "we did *some* good. We did." The Vietnam war has driven the other male character literally insane. Even apolitical Sparger feels disillusioned: "The Buffo [Caffe Cino?] had been started by rejects, nomads, exiles, rebels, outcasts. [...] And now more and more we attracted not the real rebels, or the real dropouts, but failures and phonies from uptown who just wanted to do whatever had been original and daring the year before." The play opened in New York, 1973, with Don Parker, directed by J. Kevin Hanlon. It was subsequently revised. It was telecast in 1982. § Patrick, R. *Kennedy's Children: A Play in Two Acts*. French, 1976. 47p.

97   *How Does Your Garden Grow* (1973) | Jim McNeil (1935–1982), Australian

[Prison drama; 8M, 1W; flexible set.] Largely ignored by Australian gay literary histories, presumably because McNeil was straight, the play indeed seems mostly a historical curiosity. The setting is the prison where the playwright himself was an inmate. To appeal to his cell mate, Mick Harrison, George converts himself into the very feminine Brenda. Another prisoner, Sam Jenkins, is also appreciative of the transformation and inherits Brenda when Mick is paroled. Ironically, Mrs. Harrison, when we meet her, exudes masculine strength to the point that another prisoner remarks, "No wonder so many blokes are all turning poof these days." (In reporting back to George and Sam, Mick conceals that when he leaves, he will be very much under her thumb.) Nothing physical happens between the men, and the actors remain demurely clothed even when taking baths. Instead of sexual games, they play checkers. It opened in Sydney, 1974, with Darrel Hilton, Martin Harris, and Max Cullen, directed by John Bell. § McNeil, J. *How Does Your Garden Grow: A Play*. Currency, 1974. 139p.

98   *The Ritz* (1974–75) | Terrence McNally (1938–), American

[Farce; 8M, 3W, extras; unit set.] Set in a gay bathhouse in New York, the play offered heterosexuals at the time a tour of an unknown world while winking at the gays in the audience; it now provides a slice of pre–AIDS history. One of the patrons, in explaining why he has chosen the Ritz this evening, names the principal bathhouses catering to gays at the time: "I didn't have much choice," he says. "I don't speak Spanish, so the Continental is out. The Club Baths are just too far downtown. I'm boycotting the Beacon. Man's Country's had it and I've been barred from the Everard." His listener exclaims, "Nobody gets barred from the Everard. How'd you manage that?" Though a period piece, the play still generates laughter. After his dying Mafia father-in-law calls for a hit on him, Gaetano Proclo is tricked into hiding in the family-owned bathhouse. His brother-in-law is counting on the idea that no one will blame an "enraged brother catching his dear sweet sister's balding fat slob husband in an unnatural act with one of these fruitcakes" for dispatching him. Since, however, Proclo signs in under the brother-in-law's name (Carmine Vespucci), the detective hired by the family as a last minute replacement knows none of them (and is himself mistakenly assumed to be gay because of his high-pitched voice), and as the patrons are used to playing roles, melodrama quickly become farce. Googie Gomez, a Puerto Rican entertainer hoping to gain her big break, having been misled into thinking a major producer will be in the audience, contributes further mayhem. Having obviously never heard of Bette Midler, Vespucci assumes she is another patron in drag.

One of the regulars is Claude Perkins, a chubby-chaser who turns out to have been Proclo's friend in the army. They even had an act with a third buddy, lip-syncing the songs of the Andrew Sisters. The flamboyantly out ("If you just saw me walking down the street, you'd think I was a queen") and sexually insatiable Chris ("The thing that no one understands about me is that sex is just my way of saying hello") stirs up further mischief. Tiger and Duffy, the two bath attendants, look so much alike that they confuse Proclo. To his surprise, he learns that they have been lovers for three years. Hints are dropped that Proclo may be less straight than he himself thinks. He admits that at Catholic school he "was the butt of every sissy joke played." Among other madcap activities this evening we see him and Claude, along with Chris, reprise their Andrew Sisters act: "We're three caballeros, three gay caballeros, / They say we are birds of a feather." At the end he leaves with his wife, but the smile on his face may be interpreted in all sorts of ways. An earlier version in which Proclo is gay opened in New Haven in 1974 under the title *The Tubs*, directed by Anthony Holland. The revised play premiered in New York, 1975, with Paul B. Price, F. Murray Abraham, John Everson, and Christopher J. Brown, directed by Robert Drivas. Vining (*Diary*, v4, 428) wrote, "The play is immaculately crafted, very funny, and [...] I admired the talent of McNally inordinately. Gay Task Force will probably hate his caricatures of a chubby chaser and a screaming queen but in this case I'm not inclined to be supersensitive." McNally also wrote the screenplay for the 1976 Richard Lester film. § In Hodges, B., ed. *Out Plays*. 148–207.

99   Human Remains 1975) | Larry Fineberg (1945–), Canadian

[Absurdist drama; 2M, 1W; 1 set.] Fineberg uses bisexuality for comic effect. No sooner has

Billy slashed his wrists in the bathtub, than his former lovers Jeremy and Olive—now a couple—show up to bandage his wounds. They have come to tell him that his mother has committed suicide and to take him to the funeral. In a comical anticipation of *Angels in America*, Billy is besieged by a giant bird who defecates on his skylight; at a crucial point it breaks through the glass and tumbles, dead, into the room. The men fight. The three of them recall their skewed relationships with each other and with others, including Billy's brief affair with Louie, who has been arrested by the police in Queen's Park "naked, and bumping into trees" with "a leaf tied around his penis." The memory seems to rekindle the spark between Billy and Jeremy. Olive tries to kill herself by taking too many tranquilizers but succeeds only in throwing up. Finally, Billy is convinced to leave. But he has the final word: "Maybe." The play opened in Toronto, 1975, with Richard Moffatt and Thomas Hauff, directed by Stephen Katz. (Fineberg also wrote the unpublished *Devotion*, 1985, about a bisexual artist leaving a psychiatric hospital upon the suicide of his mother.) § Fineberg, L. *Four Plays*. Playwrights Co-op, 1978. 101–44.

100   *Mates* (1975) | **Peter Kenna (1930–1987), Australian**

[Sports drama; 3M, 1W; 1 set.] *Mates* provides another instance how transvestism and machismo can equally function as forms of drag imprisonment. Neil plays the part of Sylvia in a Sydney drag cabaret. Gary, a footballer, has fallen in love with him, but is frightened that he will be found out, destroying his career. On this particular evening, he again fails to show up to take Neil home. Neil calls Gary up and threatens to kill himself—after outing Gary. Gary swiftly shows up in a panic. Neil points out, "I'm a man too, you know, and it's as important to me as it is to you." A second plot involves an elderly busher who wanders in after hours seeking the heterosexual brothel that used to be here. A cleaning woman appears; she reveals that she worked as one of the prostitutes. The play ends inconclusively: Gary takes Neil to the hospital after his botched suicide attempt; the busher leaves with the cleaning woman for breakfast. The play opened in Sydney, 1975, with Jon Ewing and Peter Fisher, directed by John Bell. § In Parr, B., ed. *Australian Gay and Lesbian Plays*. 41–70.

101   *Passing By* (1975) | **Martin Sherman (1938–), American**

[Sexual comedy; 2M; unit set.] Sherman cancelled a 1983 New York production "for fear that [it might] fan some of the misconceived and prejudiced linkage of homosexuality and physical illness that was then popular in the American press." But lately the play has proved its resiliency. Toby and Simon meet at a Manhattan movie theater in 1972. They spend an enjoyable night together and tell the usual lies, mixed in with some truth, about their backgrounds and all. Toby proves to be something of a hypochondriac. Simon can't shake him out of his head and, picking up a clue Toby dropped, tracks him down to the wine store where he works. Looking into Toby's eyes, Simon comments how they are yellow. This time the illness is real: Toby has hepatitis. A week later Simon is diagnosed with the same. They end up sharing Toby's apartment while convalescing—bickering, taking care of each other, playing with their dreams of the future. Even though Toby says, "Look, we don't even know each other. We've just been sick together," they do come to know each other. Still, Toby takes up the grant he has received to go to France to paint; Simon will take care of the house while he is gone. What will happen when Toby returns? A hint comes from Toby: "I had a wonderful hepatitis." The play opened in London, 1975, with Simon Callow and Michael Dickinson, directed by Drew Griffiths. It had its American debut in Hartford, Conn., in 1979 under Rob Logamarsino's direction. § In Wilcox, M. ed. *Gay Plays*, [v1]. 99–120.

102   *P.S. Your Cat Is Dead* (1975–78) | **James Kirkwood (1924–1989), American**

[Social comedy; 3M, 1W; 1 set.] The closeted playwright came closest here to writing a gay play. For the third time a petty thief, Vito Antonucci, breaks into actor Jimmy Zoole's highly vulnerable top floor apartment through the skylight. This time the robbery is interrupted: first by the arrival of Jimmy's girlfriend, second by Jimmy himself, to receive the news that not only is Kate leaving him but his beloved cat has died at the vet's. Jimmy's life is already a mess, chiefly—according to Kate—because he always plays it safe. When he discovers Vito hiding under his bed, he knocks him out momentarily and ties him up over the kitchen sink—for no good reason save that the playwright can justify Jimmy's removing Vito's pants and underwear when he needs to urinate. That action also permits the possibility to arise that the hitherto straight Jimmy might be aroused by the naked man. Certainly Vito's dissection of Jimmy's character as they share a joint leads to a reevaluation of his goals. At play's end there arises the distinct possibility that Vito, who is hungry for affection of any kind, may move in with Jimmy. Whether they will share the bed remains unknown. It opened in New York, 1975, with Keir Dullea and Tony Musante, directed by Vivian Matalon. Vining (*Diary*, v4, 438) wrote, "Too much of the humor depended on scatological language [...] but there was some wit, too. I enjoyed it but still don't think it will be a success." A revised version, which eliminated three characters, opened in 1978. The play became the basis for a novel (which was published first, in 1972) and for a 2002 film. § Kirkwood, J. *P.S. Your Cat Is Dead: A Comedy in Two Acts*. French, 2004. 84p.

103   *The Return of A. J. Raffles* (1975) | Graham Greene (1904–1991), English

[Crime caper; 8M, 2W; 2 sets.] Greene flirted with homosexuality throughout his writing career. Here he makes his one foray into a period piece: "*An Edwardian Comedy Based somewhat Loosely on E. W. Hornung's Characters in* The Amateur Cracksman." It is late summer 1900, a few months before Wilde's death. Lord Alfred Douglas has become friends with Bunny, Raffles's lover. He is present to witness Raffles's return from the dead, the crack burglar having faked his death. Seeing an opportunity to strike at his father again, Douglas persuades Raffles to rob his father's home in the country. They find the Marquess of Queensberry's bed chamber being used by the Prince of Wales and one of his mistresses. A German agent is after indiscreet letters that he has written her. This catches Scotland Yard's attention, but they nab Raffles instead. Bunny is willing to do whatever it takes to save him, but the Prince comes to the rescue. The play ends with Douglas off to Paris to join Wilde, and Raffles and Bunny off to the Loire Valley to try their skills there. The play opened in London, 1975, with Denholm Elliott, Clive Francis, and Peter Blythe, directed by David Jones. § Greene, G. *Collected Plays*. Penguin, 1985. 263–325. Two 1980 plays hold gay interest: *Yes and No* and *For Whom the Bell Chimes*. 355–414.

104   *The Shadow Box* (1975) | Michael Cristofer (1945–), American

[Psychological drama; 5M, 4W; unit set.] Years before gay plays had to deal with the reality of death from AIDS, Cristofer focused on the simple fact that we all—gay, straight, bi, and asexual—are going to die: "it's the one thing in this world you can be sure of!" What differs in each case is how the dying person and friends and family react. Here we have two straight people and a gay, or perhaps bisexual, man facing death. The gay man's ex-wife and his lover rise to the occasion better, stronger than do the straight man's wife and the straight woman's daughter. Brian and his former wife, Beverly, have continued to be friends. His lover Mark is tortured but remains steadfastly with him. We discover that they met in San Francisco when Mark was selling his body just to keep alive. Beverly and Mark confront each other, and she forces Mark to face his unrealistic hopes. There follows a tender moment when Brian wets himself. He says, "I am truly disgusting." Mark replies, "No, you're not. Just wet." The dying Brian hides behind a barrage of words, but he has the last words in the play: "This moment." That's what we all have. The premiere was in Los Angeles, 1975, with Laurence Luckinbill, directed by Gordon Davidson. It was telecast in 1980. § Cristofer, M. *The Shadow Box: A Drama in Two Acts*. French, 1977. 87p.

105   *Caprice, or Fashion Bound* (1976) | Charles Ludlam (1943–1987), American

[Fashion satire; 6M, 5W; flexible set.] In his biography, *Ridiculous!* (Applause, 2002), David Kaufman writes that the play, though "Basically a parody of the fashion industry and—less directly—of the art world, [...] is also a mockery of homosexuality." But he goes on, "While making fun of homosexual stereotypes, the play also set out to defend and celebrate them." He notes that "this was the first time that Ludlam played a specifically gay character" (231). Claude Caprice and Twyfford Adamant are rival couturiers. Caprice has the higher reputation; his clothes are deliberately ugly, thereby heightening the beauty of the wearer. His inspiration comes from his lover Adrian. His chief supporter is the rich Baroness Zuni Feinschmecker. Fashion spies add to the intrigue, further complicated by the baroness's husband and Caprice's landlord as the complete pervert. With lots of scatological humor, the plot twists and turns, ending with Adamant mistakenly poisoning himself. The loss grieves Caprice: "I need you. I need an adversary." The farce was performed by Ludlam's Ridiculous Theatrical Company in 1976 with Ludlam, John Brockmeyer, and Bill Vehr, directed by Ludlam. Kaufman records that Ludlam "alienated a portion of his large gay audience with this play" (231). It certainly has neither the power nor the campy humor inherent in his better-known drag works. § *The Complete Plays of Charles Ludlam*. Perennial Library, 1989. 357–95.

106 *Confession* (1976) | **John Patrick (1905–1995), American**

[Domestic farce; 2M, 1W; 1 set.] This is a rare moment in which the discreet Patrick tackled a gay theme. Chuck, according to his lover Chandler, "can't accept the fact that he's leading a perfectly normal life—for someone of his persuasion." He threatens for the umpteenth time to return to his New England father suffering from a spastic colon. When their neighbor Rita asks, "Isn't it time he decided which way to jump," Chandler recites his lover's troubled childhood: Chuck's mother was raped and murdered when he was three, he was kidnapped by a sex maniac when he was eight, and his minister's wife seduced him in a canoe when he was 14. Rita suggests that Chandler commit suicide to prove how much he loves Chuck. She provides the sugar pills. Waiting to die, Chuck confesses that he made up his entire childhood in an attempt to appear glamorous: "Let's face it, Chan. I'm a hypocritical, pathological, homosexual fabricator." Chandler is shocked when Chuck—having spilled much of the bottle in an attempt to block Chandler's gulping them down—swallows all he can find on the floor. But when Chuck discovers that the pills are fakes, he tries to kill Chandler for real. They end up forgiving each other, of course, and turn on Rita when she reappears. The comedy was third in an evening of plays entitled *Suicide—Anyone?* given in St. Thomas, V.I., 1976. Patrick wrote another gay farce, *The Gay Deceiver*, 1987. A revamped *Charley's Aunt*, it was strangely irrelevant to the time at which it appeared and was staged only in regional theater. § Patrick, J. *Suicide—Anyone? Three One Act Plays*. Dramatists, 1976. 43–64.

107 *Conpersonas* (1976) | **Paul Steven Lim (PHL 1944–), American**

[Psychological drama; 2M, 2W; 1 set.] The play is a kind of mystery. Miles Zeigler invites his fiancée Shelagh, her daughter Rhoda, and his former lover Jesse Jugenheimer to a Thanksgiving meal. Just before they are to arrive, he steps into the bathroom. His twin brother Mark, a Jesuit priest, arrives and discovers that Miles has shot himself. Because the twins are identical, both Jesse and Shelagh are drawn to him. The rest of the first act is a long encounter between Mark and Jesse in which practically every comment Jesse makes is a sexual innuendo. Mark gets drunk and disappears into the bedroom. Jesse follows, but all we know is that Mark throws up in the bathroom. Act 2 is given to Mark and Shelagh. More verbal games ensue. Shelagh lists the people she imagines seek him out for confession as fags, fag hags, and the daughters of fag hags who "compete with their own mothers." She recounts how she met Miles in a gay bar; he was pointed out as someone "very *accommodating*" who "*tricks* with anyone who wants him. Anyone, anytime, anywhere—even in public johns." Miles impregnated her, but she got an abortion because he also infected her with gonorrhea. She reveals that the pistol Miles used was one of a pair. She and Mark end up in the bedroom, where Rhoda joins them. At play's end, Mark invites all three to return that evening for the never-eaten meal. We last see him disappearing into the bedroom with the pistol. After an earlier college production, the play was given in Washington, D.C., 1976, with Peter Miner and Paul Hough, directed by David Cook. § Lim, P. S. *Conpersonas: A Recreation in Two Acts*. French, 1977. 77p.

108 *Gemini* (1976) | **Albert Innaurato (1947–), American**

[Ethnic comedy; 4M, 3W; 1 set.] Innaurato first collected *Gemini* in the aptly named *Bizarre Behavior* (Bard/Avon, 1980), all six of which have gay interest. The Italian-American family has become almost as much a staple for gay humor as the Jewish-American family. Judith Hastings and her younger brother, Randy, show up unexpectedly in the Geminianis' backyard in Philadelphia to celebrate their friend Francis's 21st birthday. They find an eccentric assortment of characters: Francis's father and his girlfriend Lucille and, next door, the divorced and quite sexual Bunny Weinberger and her probably autistic son Herschel. Having had sex with him, Judith is unprepared for Francis's announcement, "I think I'm queer." She is even more taken aback when she realizes that Francis has an unrequited crush on her brother: "Perhaps I have sensed it all along and I was attracted to Francis because he was …." (Gay? Safe?) Randy takes the news more lightly. As he says while undressing, "Well, there's only one way to find out," followed by a deliberate misquotation from *Tea and Sympathy*: "When you think of this, and you will, be kind." But nothing happens. Both Francis's father and Lucille have already intuited that he is gay; all they're concerned about is his happiness. Herschel develops his own peculiar crush on Randy. The play opened in New York, 1976, with Robert Picardo, directed by Peter Mark Schifter. Richard Benner adapted it to the screen as *Happy Birthday, Gemini*, 1980. It became a musical in 2006. § In Hodges, B., ed. *Out Plays*. 211–75.

109 *Pogey Bait* (1976) | **George Birimisa, American**

[Military comedy; 6M; unit set.] "Pogey bait" is slang for candy sexual predators use to lure boys. Apprentice Seaman Frankie Borkovich, 18, is naive but intuitively smart. When he discovers his World War II destroyer is shelling the French rather than the Germans whom he volunteered to fight, he is disgusted. Wanting out of the war, he decides to tell the captain the truth, that he is homosexual. He has not counted on the captain's having a personal vendetta against Frankie's sexual partner Chief Petty Officer Lefty Lefko. The captain tries to coerce Frankie into confessing Lefty has sodomized him. Hoping to curry the captain's favor, a yeoman second class fabricates a confession from Frankie. A psychology student interviews Frankie and turns in a report that is a parody of the warped way gays were viewed at the time. The captain lets drop a story about Lefty's affair with another seaman in hopes of making Frankie jealous and thus vindictive. Throughout all these manipulations, the black gallery cook (Dubois Garvey Lambert, who himself confesses to being "double-gated") acts as Frankie guardian and warns him what the captain is up to. Frankie turns the tables on his accusers, accusing them of having homosexual relations with him and others. In order to avert a scandal, he will receive his "yellow discharge […] for queers" as soon as the ship arrives back at home port, making him a free man again. The play opened in Los Angeles, 1976, with Quentin Yeager, John Stefano, and Anthony Sweeting, directed by Birimisa. The script was subsequently extensively rewritten. § *Birimisa: Portraits, Plays, Perversions*; ed. by Lanny Baugniet and Paul Sagan. Sweetheart, 2009. 137–74.

110 *Streamers* (1976) | **David Rabe (1940–), American**

[Military drama; 10M; 1 set.] Rabe has created gay characters in a number of his plays. A lost go-go dancer in *In the Boom Boom Room*, 1972, is befriended by her gay neighbor. In *Streamers* three soldiers in 1965 share a room in a camp close to the District of Columbia, waiting to be shipped out to Vietnam. Billy Wilson is highly educated but adopts a hick's persona in an attempt to fit in. Roger Moore is a middle class African American who has more or less assimilated to the white world. Richie Douglas is an affluent New Yorker who goes from concealing his homosexuality to becoming aggressively open about it, taunting Billy, whom he reads as a closet case. Into their midst comes another African American, the streetwise Carlyle. He assumes all three are gay. When Richie makes an advance, he responds, leading Richie to beg Roger and Billy to leave them alone for a while. Upon their refusal, Carlyle is prepared to have sex with Richie in front of them. Disproportionately outraged, Billy starts a verbal fight with Carlyle that escalates into a knife/razor fight. Billy is fatally stabbed, as is a drunken sergeant who wanders in at the wrong moment. The play's final scene brings on the dead sergeant's best friend. Informed that Richie is "queer," he shrugs off the information: "There's a lotta worse gonorrhea in this world than bein' a queer." The play seemed daring at the time; it now rings hollow even as a period piece, its emotions fake. It opened in New York, 1976, with Peter Evans, directed by Mike Nichols. Rabe also wrote the screenplay for the 1983 film. § Rabe, D. *Streamers*. French, 2009. 99p.

111 *As Time Goes By* (1977) | **Noël Greig (1944–2009) and Drew Griffiths (1947–1984), English**

[Historical polemic; 7M; flexible set.] The collaborators early joined the Gay Sweatshop Theatre Company and relished its political bent. Through a series of pageant-like scenes with songs (both popular numbers and some written especially for the play), the audience is presented three key moments in gay history: the raid on London's Cleveland Street brothel in 1889, with a brief glimpse of Edward Carpenter and his lover George Merrill; the Nazis' attack on gays in Berlin, 1929–34, both their nightclubs and Magnus Herschfield's Institut für Sexualwissenschaft; and the police infiltration of New York's Stonewall Inn, 1969. Historical and fictional characters interact, presenting varying thoughts about sexuality and the oppressive political systems in which gays find themselves. Allusions are dropped to key figures from Wilde through Williams (especially for *Menagerie* and *Streetcar*) and to such icons as Marlene Dietrich and Judy Garland. A romantic nostalgia for classical Greece pops up in some speeches. It is noted how political movements from Communism through Black Power have been hostile to gay rights: "We're not part of the world, you and I, not as far as they are concerned." The implicit message is that gays must be vigilant and never let down their guard; whatever meager rights we gain can be snatched away in a moment by zealots from both extremes of the political spectrum. It premiered in Nottingham, 1977, with Philip Osment, Alan Pope, Gordon McDonald, Bruce Bayley, Philip Timmins, Pete Charles, and Griffiths, directed by Greig. § *Two Gay Sweatshop Plays*. GMP, 1981. 5–70. Includes Greig's *The Dear Love of Comrades*, 1979, about Carpenter and Merrill.

112 *Chinchilla: Figures in a Classical Landscape with Ruins* (1977) | **Robert David MacDonald (1929–2004), Scot**

[Historical drama; 11M, 4W; unit set.] In his introduction, MacDonald acknowledges that the play is "clearly based on Diaghilev [1872–1929], his company, his career," but insists that the characters are "amalgams of various people." After reading the playwright's obituary, one might suspect there is a strong autobiographical element. The results are not entirely satisfying. Though the play offers glimpses of some of the reasons Sergei Diaghilev's company was so revolutionary, by erecting a fictional facade the audience is left uncertain what is documentary and what is invented. A question one of the characters poses is never answered: "the theatre dates so quickly and so badly: what is left of a superstitious Russian faggot with a white streak, eternally wrapped against the cold?" Anchored to one day in June 1914 in Venice, the story moves often to the past, but also looks to the future and even includes dreams. Though the company will suffer from the decision, the ballet impresario Chinchilla renounces his principal dancer, choreographer, and lover Vatza when the latter marries a woman who has been pursuing him. He looks to replace his errant star as he ogles the barely clad boys on the Lido (in homage to Thomas Mann's *Der Tod in Venedig*). Wilde is also invoked. It opened in MacDonald's Glasgow theater, 1977, with Gerard Murphy, David Hayman, Garry Cooper, Mark Lewis, and Douglas Heard, directed by Philip Prowse. § MacDonald, R. D. *Plays One*. Oberon, 1991. 131–200.

113 *A Day after the Fair* (1977) | **James Purdy (1914–2009), American**

[Absurdist drama; 4M, 1W; flexible set.] Purdy is an acquired taste. I find no record of a production of this play, first published in 1977 in a limited edition, but I wonder whether such would induce the *frisson* of *Grand-Guignol* or cause the playgoer to collapse in a fit of giggles. The clown Arnold hires a former professional assassin, Oswin, to avenge his and his brother Neil's being fired by the Clown Master. Everyone wants Neil. He is "Arnold's only love." Oswin has loved him since the day he "saw his pink flesh"; he demands Neil as his payment for killing the Clown Master so he can continue, in Arnold's words, "making filthy love" to him. Oswin's wife, Elga, has had an affair with Neil, lying "naked" with him all afternoon. And the Clown Master proclaims, "Neil belongs with me." Neil poisons the pregnant Elga. The dying Elga urges Oswin to kill the Clown Master and cut out his lying tongue. Oswin murders both him and his servant. Neil kills his brother and cuts out *his* tongue, urging Oswin to share in making a meal of it. Oswin urges Neil to murder him. The curtain falls before there can be further mayhem. § Purdy, J. *Two Plays*. New London, 1979. 1–40.

114 *Privates on Parade* (1977) | **Peter Nichols (1927–), English**

[Military drama, with songs; 10M, 1W; flexible set.] Nichols based his play on his own military experiences. During World War II and the opening years of the Cold War, drag shows became a British military staple. Young, naive, and straight, Steve

Flowers reports for duty with a troupe of British soldiers recruited to entertain the men stationed in Malaya in 1948. He falls in love with the one woman in the show, Sylvia Morgan, a Eurasian who teaches him about sex. He also gains a sort of education from a flaming queen, Terri Dennis (who in production generally steals the show), and more subtly by a couple, the campy Charles Bishop and his mate Len Bonny. The fluffy series of sketches turns darker at the end of Act 1 when Steve learns from Sylvia that the sergeant-major is a traitor, engaged in gun-running with the Communists among a number of unsavory schemes. In a showdown in Act 2 most of the troupe's members are wounded, Len murdered. The plays ends with the survivors embarking on a ship to return to England; Terri suffers the indignity of being escorted aboard by police as the result of being caught having sex with a sailor. The play's premiere, with music by Denis King, was in Stratford, 1977, with Denis Quilley, Tim Wylton, and Joe Melia, directed by Michael Blakemore. Nichols wrote the screenplay for the 1983 film; it too has been published. § Nichols, P. *Privates on Parade: A Play with Songs*. French, 1977. 67p.

115 *Vieux Carré* (1977) | **Tennessee Williams, American**

[Memory play; 5M, 5W, extras; unit set.] This autobiographical play recalls aspects of Williams's first sojourn in New Orleans, 1938–39. An unnamed writer summons up memories of the inhabitants of the rooming house in which he lived, in particular his demented landlady; a mismatched, constantly quarreling couple, Tye and Jane; and the tubercular painter Nightingale; as well as his younger self. Nightingale and another man, a well known photographer, are openly gay. The writer, still struggling to understand his sexuality, confesses to one experience: "I couldn't have consciously, deliberately, selected a better place than here to discover—to encounter—my true nature." Nightingale propositions him: "Little man, you are sensual, but I, I—am rapacious," but the writer is put off by his state of health. A young jazz musician named Sky magically appears and invites the writer to join him on a trip to the West Coast. At play's end the writer prepares to join him and escape all the loneliness that has filled the house. It opened in New York, 1977, with Karl Johnson, Richard Kane, Robin McDonald, and Jack Elliott, directed by Keith Hack. § Williams, T. *Vieux Carré*. New Directions, 1979. 116p.

116 *Fifth of July* (1978) | **Lanford Wilson, American**

[Domestic drama; 4M, 4W; 1 set.] Almost nothing is made of the fact that the play's main character is not only gay but in a stable, loving relationship. He is also a paraplegic, as a result of the Vietnam war, but that too is just a fact, not a symbol of any kind. The setting is an old farmhouse outside Lebanon, Missouri, on July 4–5, 1977. Ken Talley has returned with his lover Jed to take a teaching position in his old high school. Jed is a botanist, interested in turning the homestead into a floral showplace. When faced, however, with the reality of a classroom full of adolescents, Ken freaks out. Without consulting Jed, his sister June, or his aunt Sally, he decides to sell the place to the couple with whom he and June spent their hippy years in Berkeley. John is an old high school mate whom Ken had an affair with before John fled to Europe with Gwen. When Sally, who has finally spread her husband's ashes around Jed's rose bushes, finds out about Ken's scheme, she outbids John and offers the place to Jed. Gwen, who has seemed to this point to be an airhead, confronts Ken: "You think you don't need Jed, you don't need to be useful—you'll sell the damn roof over your head to get out of facing yourself. You're on the edge of nowhere, baby, and you listen to me 'cause I *been* nowhere. Now are you gonna get to work or are you gonna lose it all?"

Ken thinks of the ending to a science fiction story a troubled youth he is trying to help has written in which space explorers realize that "they were alone. And they were very happy, because then they knew it was up to them to become all the things they had imagined they would find." He thinks about what he needs to do to prepare for classes. In the final lines of the play he evokes both Jed's garden and the student's story. It opened in New York, 1978, with William Hurt and Jeff Daniels, directed by Marshall W. Mason. Vining (*Diary*, v5, 334) was most taken by the gay couple's open display of affection: "The play started right off with one male lover coming in from gardening and kissing the lead. [...] The love between the two men was handled very tenderly, with more than one embrace, one very prolonged in an emotional crisis and some nice touching. In fact the botanist lover was the nicest character in it." The play was telecast in 1982. § In Hodges, B., ed. *Out Plays*. 276–347.

117   *Furtive Love* (1978) | Peter Kenna, Australian

[Theater drama; 4M, 2W; 2 sets.] This is the second play in Kenna's Cassidy Trilogy, Joe Cassidy being the one character common to all. In the first play, *A Hard God*, 1973, we meet Joe in 1946 at age 16. Through his friendship with another boy, he becomes aware of his budding sexuality. Though they never progress beyond mutual masturbation, Joe finds himself in conflict with his Irish-Catholic upbringing. *Furtive Love*, set in 1955, finds Joe a playwright and an actor in his own play. He remains a virgin despite his stage manager George Cooper trying to talk him into acting on his desires. George is carrying on an affair with another actor, the bisexual Tom Parkinson (who gives a cogent explanation of his attraction to both sexes), but Tom has tired of George's clinginess. Too, he is becoming interested in Joe. Joe finally accepts Tom's invitation. George tells him, "Now you won't feel obliged to raise your eyebrows at anybody else's behaviour. You can lie and steal and cheat with as clear a conscience as any of us. I don't think you were ever really afraid of the consequences of sin, Joe. You were only in some doubt as to whether it was worth it. Well, now you know it is I expect you'll be better at it than most. Converts always are." The third play, *An Eager Hope*, 1978, has yet to be published. Set in 1966, it intertwines Joe's homosexuality, Catholic faith, and his family's influence on him. *Furtive Love* opened in Adelaide, 1978, with Tony Sheldon (who also played Joe in *A Hard God*), Alan Wilson, and Ray Meagher, directed by John Tasker. § Kenna, P. *Furtive Love*. Currency, 1980. 58p.

118   *Lord Alfred's Lover* (1978–80) | Eric Bentley (GBR 1916–), American

[Biographical study; 12M, 1W; flexible set.] Though going over familiar ground in his retelling of Wilde's fall, Bentley makes his take seem fresh. He gives greater space to Douglas (Bosie), who serves as narrator of the piece from his perspective in 1945, the year of his death. Bentley pairs Robbie Ross and Bosie as Wilde's good and bad angels, Bosie pushing him to his downfall, Robbie trying to save him. The full nature of Wilde's bisexuality is addressed; Constance has her scene. Prominence is given to the rent boys Wilde hires, stressing their importance to his sexual life before and after Redding Gaol. The political significance of the trial is given weight, particularly the desire of the government to hush up any hint about homosexuals in political power; memory lingers of Bosie's brother who committed suicide as a result of his affair with Lord Rosebery, the British prime minister 1894–95. Lines given to Constance about her husband apply to the play: "You make a person rethink everything, even a person who doesn't think at all very often." Daniel-Raymond Nadon (in B. Harbin, *Legacy*, 54) writes that the playwright saw his play "as a coming out story [. . .]. For Bentley, the most important line of the play is when Wilde says, 'Posing as a sodomite'—the fateful phrase *is* libel now. I do not *pose* as a sodomite. I *am* a sodomite.'" The twice-married Bentley clearly identified with Wilde; he himself only came out when he was 53. An early version of the play was published in 1978 in *Canadian Theatre Review*. It received its first production in Gainesville, Fla., 1979, directed by Kerry McKenney. Bentley directed the 1980 Buffalo, N.Y., production with Maxim Mazumdar, Philip Nye, and John Emmert. § Bentley, E. *Lord Alfred's Lover: A Play*. Personal Library, 1981. 18–124.

119   *The Man with Straight Hair* (1978–94) | George Birimisa, American

[Sexual drama; 2M, 2W; unit set.] Adrian, a self-described "nellie queen," is in love with Joey. Joey has no idea who he is, or perhaps more accurately is afraid to face the truth. Since it is the McCarthy era, it is not surprising that he insists he is not "queer"—"that all I am is trade." Comforting the older Dinah after she has a backroom abortion, Joey invites her to move in with the two of them without consulting Adrian and introduces Adrian as merely his roommate. (Simultaneously, Adrian invites his sister, in flight from her abusive husband, to take over their spare room, but she quickly hooks up with a cab driver.) Adrian goes along with the charade until he discovers Joey and Dinah having sex. He is ready to move out. So is Dinah, her GI Joe having shown up. Lost, convinced sex is the solution to his problems, Joey tries to rape Dinah. After she leaves, he pulls the same trick on Adrian. At the end of the play the super-macho Joey is alone, his body shaking with fear. The premiere, under the title *A Rainbow in the Night*, took place in Los Angeles, 1978, with Peter Lazer and Grainger Hines, directed by James Monroe Stinson. It was revised and produced in 1994 under its new title. Much of the material in the early Birimisa plays reappears in his final, autobiographical drama *Viagra Falls*, 2006, with new information about the years in which he was writing the plays. § *Birimisa: Portraits, Plays, Perversions*; ed. by Lanny Baugniet and Paul Sagan. Sweetheart, 2009. 176–216.

120 *A Perfect Relationship* (1978) | Doric Wilson, American

[Sexual comedy; 4M, 1W; 1 set.] Though some of the barbs in this satiric piece, subtitled *A Domestic Comedy*, seem passé, perhaps we have achieved the right distance to enjoy its campiness in much the same way we take pleasure in Coward's early work. Greg and Ward have been housemates for eleven years. Though they have never had sex, they act like an old married couple with their routines, their bickering, and their understanding of each other. Their friend Muriel, who has sublet the Christopher Street apartment to them, provides the only disruption in their lives as she pops in with no warning, dragging her newest boyfriend along with her. Then Ward picks up Barry as his trick for the night, and their ordered life threatens to shatter. Barry warns Ward that whenever he tries for a one-night stand, it turns instead into a relationship: "I wish I knew what I do wrong. Other people seem to have no problem being promiscuous." But then he meets Greg and is all ready to become his lover. Ward does not take the suggestion that he should vacate the apartment well and tries to finagle the lease in his name, only to discover that the moneyed Barry has beaten him to it. Muriel points out how stupidly both Ward and Greg are behaving, but it takes Barry's falling in love with her latest boyfriend to resolve the situation. The play opened in New York, 1978, with Bob Lowe and Paul Morreale, directed by Michael O'Brien. § Wilson, D. *Two Plays*. Sea Horse, 1979. 16–137. Includes *The West Street Gang*.

121 *A Prayer for My Daughter* (1978) | Thomas Babe (1941–2000), American

[Crime drama; 4M; 1 set.] Babe has created a play that should work better than it does. The middle-aged Sean and his young accomplice and probable lover Jimmy are pulled in, in the early hours of July 4, for questioning about the murder of an old woman. The two investigating officers are just as corrupt. Jack is a junkie, like Jimmy; the two shoot up together. Kelly removes himself emotionally from his family, including his suicidal daughter—who in fact kills herself before dawn. Sean, who calls Jimmy his daughter at times, lets him take the rap. There is confused discussion about what it means to be a man. Sean theorizes, "There's a woman inside me [...] and she aches for the men she has known." He recalls an incident during the Vietnam conflict when another soldier he was attracted to was killed, and he spent twelve hours cradling the dead man. Jimmy questions, "Who said to be a man was easy?" Ordered to strip naked, he cradles himself in Kelly's lap, forming a momentary pieta, sexually exciting the homophobic officer. Jimmy takes advantage of the position to seize Kelly's gun and accidentally shoots him, but the bullet lodges in his wallet. Then all four revert to their expected roles. The play opened in New York, 1978, with Laurence Luckinbill and Alan Rosenberg, directed by Robert Allan Ackerman. Babe and playwright Neal Bell were partners. § Babe, T. *A Prayer for My Daughter: A Drama*. French, 1978. 63p.

122 *A Tower near Paris* (1978) | Copi (ARG 1939–1987), French

[Absurdist farce; 5M, 1W; 1 set.] Copi (né Raúl Damonte Botana) was also a cartoonist, a quality that decidedly marks his plays. In *Tower* a group of friends are welcoming in 1977 in Luc and Jean's high-rise apartment in a Paris suburb. Daphnee is an American acidhead who has killed her daughter and plans to smuggle her body back to the States. During moments of lucidity she tries to persuade Luc of her love for him. Micheline, a myopic man during the day and an expansive drag queen at night, brings a gay Arab he has picked up. Ahmed kills a boa constrictor that shows up in a toilet and prepares a meal from it and the rat it has swallowed; he also tries to revive a frightened sea gull that flies through an open window while they watch the next tower over burn as a result of a helicopter crashing into it. Luc and Jean spend a lot of time bickering, but they do not hesitate to have shower sex with the door open for everyone to listen to their antics. In the end Jean agrees to drive everyone to the police station to support Daphnee as she turns herself in, but he inexplicably drives the car into the burning structure, killing everyone save Micheline and Ahmed, who have remained behind and who discover they have apartments in the same building in Paris. *La tour de la Défense* was published in 1978; its premiere was in Paris, 1981. The English translation was given a public reading in New York, 1987. § In Kourilsky, F., and Temerson, C., eds. *Gay Plays.* Trans. Mark O'Donnell. 85–187. (The translator missed that the play ends with a quotation from *A Streetcar Named Desire.*) Also includes Copi's AIDS play *Grand Finale.* Trans. Michael Feingold. 189–248.

123   *T-Shirts* (1978) | **Robert Patrick, American**

[Sexual comedy; 3M; 1 set.] On the evidence presented here, not much had changed in New York gay life since *The Boys in the Band*. If anything gays are more cynical; as one character says, "Gay life is okay if you're very pretty or if you're rich and inhuman." Marvin, 40, a successful playwright, and Kink, 30, a craftsman, are roommates, not lovers. This rainy night their doorbell is rung by young Tom seeking shelter since his sexual partner, the landlord, is not yet in. What follows is a lot of banter, much wordplay, and sexual tension. The talk is almost entirely about bars and baths and sex. Politics, liberation, personal goals are entirely missing from the conversation. Marvin says to Tom, "I can't do anything about the way gay life is and I don't want to sour it for anybody that gets along in it." The play opened in Minneapolis, 1978, with Vic Campbell, Gray Tuel, and Charles W. Pashon, directed by Richard E. Rehse. § In Hoffman, W. ed. *Gay Plays*. 1–46.

124   *Bent* (1979) | **Martin Sherman, American**

[Historical drama; 11M; flexible set.] While working with the Gay Sweatshop, Sherman was inspired by Greig and Griffiths's *As Time Goes By* to address the presence of the pink triangle in gay history. The resulting play—as Ray Schultz writes (in E. Nelson, *Encyclopedia*, 569)—is "an important milestone in gay theatrical and cultural history. Sherman cast a spotlight on a chapter of gay history that had largely been ignored by both society and Holocaust historians. Indeed, *Bent* helped to popularize the pink triangle, the Nazis' signifier for homosexuals, as a symbol of contemporary gay pride." Unlike the earlier play, there is no indication that Sherman meant his stand as a warning. His emphasis instead is on the nature of love under hostile circumstances. Act 1 takes place in Berlin in 1934 as the Night of Long Knives begins the Nazi purge of gays. Drunken, Maximilian Berber has the mischance to pick up one of the storm troopers and bring him back to his and Rudolf Hennings's apartment. The owner of the nightclub where the pickup happened rats on Max, and the storm trooper is killed. Max and Rudy flee. For a time they live by their wits, but the authorities catch up with them. Max has always taken care of the fragile Rudy, but he is powerless to act when the sadistic guards on the train taking them to Dachau torture and murder him, forcing Max to join in. Deciding to survive at all costs, and having learned from Horst, another prisoner, that the pink triangle is "the lowest," he is willing to engage in necrophilia with a dead teenage girl to prove that he is "not bent" and receive instead a yellow star.

Act 2 is set entirely in the prison yard where the prisoners are forced to move a pile of rocks from one place to another, and then back again. Knowing that it is the least degrading of all the tasks the Nazis assign prisoners, Max finagles getting Horst assigned to work with him. Horst accuses Max of confusing pain and love: "You don't make love to hurt." But the two men fall in love and manage through language alone to have a joint orgasm. Horst exclaims, "We made love. We were real. We were human." Horst comes down with a persistent cough; Max fellates an SS captain to get medicine, pretending that it is for himself. The sadistic captain discovers the truth and kills Horst before Max's eyes. Earlier Horst has said, "There are queer Nazis. And queer saints. And queer mediocrities. Just people. I really believe that. That's why I signed Hirschfeld's petition. That's why I ended up here. That's why I'm wearing this triangle. That's why you should be wearing it." Max removes Horst's jacket with the pink triangle and dons it, then deliberately walks into the electric fence surrounding the enclosure. The London premiere, 1978, starred Ian McKellen, Jeff Rawle, and Tom Bell, directed by Robert Chetwyn; the New York production starred Richard Gere, David Marshall Grant, and David Dukes, directed by Robert Allan Ackerman. Vining (*Diary*, v5, 241) had surprising little to say, merely noting that it attracted "many women and many gays" and that "It was a rather harrowing account of Germany's persecution of gays." Sherman also wrote the script for the 1997 film. § In Hodges, B., ed. *Forbidden Acts*. 519–92. In Shewey, D., ed. *Out Front*. 79–147.

125   *Cloud 9* (1979) | Caryl Churchill (1938–), English

[Political satire; 4M, 3W; flexible set.] Churchill has stated that the major theme of her play is "the parallel between colonial and sexual oppression," including gender expectations. To achieve her end she calls for specific gender and racial reversals. But in the process she builds on very politically incorrect gay stereotypes. The actor who plays Edward in the first act must be a woman, she decrees, going along "with the stage convention of having boys played by women," also "highlighting the way [his father] tries to impose traditional male behaviour on him" (iv). She does not acknowledge how this casting also reinforces the notion that gay men are effeminate, really women at heart. In Act 2, set in 1979 (a hundred years have gone by, though the characters have aged only twenty-five years), Edward is played by a man, but the impression is deepened that he is a nelly queen—although the possibility is briefly considered that he could in fact be a transwoman: "I think I'm a lesbian," he says. Harry Bagley, a colonial character (who also makes a brief appearance at the end of Act 2), reinforces a second stereotype: that gay men are child molesters and homosexual recruiters. Edward says to him: "You know what we did when you were here before. I want to do it again. I think about it all the time." Gerry, Edward's lover, plays yet a third stereotype: the promiscuous gay male endlessly cruising in dangerous situations. He becomes disturbed when he feels that he and Edward have fallen into the heterosexual model: he snaps, "I'm not the husband so you can't be the wife." When they split, Gerry misses Edward, but that does not stop him from picking up Harry when he wanders into the scene. There is equal play with lesbianism in both acts, though it is less laden with caricatures. The play opened in London, 1979, with Jim Hooper and Tony Rohr, directed by Max Stafford-Clark. Vining (*Diary*, v5, 372) wrote enthusiastically about its 1981 New York opening, calling it "a terribly funny, very ingenious sex comedy" yet one that "could also be touching." § Churchill, C. *Cloud 9*. Theatre Communications, 1994. 87p.

126   *Latin! or Tobacco and Boys* (1979) | Stephen Fry (1957–), English

[School satire; 2M; no set.] In a note for a production of his absurdist comedy, subtitled *A Play in Two Unnatural Acts*, Fry writes that it was "an experiment in the techniques of theatre and comedy, combined with a not entirely disgraceful undergraduate desire to shock." Two schoolmasters—Dominic Clarke, 26, the Latin teacher, and Herbert Brookshaw, 50s—are the only seen characters. The playgoers fill in as the students, including supposedly Rupert Cartwright, 13. Brookshaw becomes suspicious why Cartwright is getting so many merit points and corners the boy. He finds out that Clarke, under the pretext of tutoring him, has "carnally violated that boy in ways too vile, too diverse, for the sane mind to grasp." Clarke admits the truth and inquires what Brookshaw intends to do with the information. The latter agrees to keep his silence in return for twice-weekly administrated humiliation involving a clothes hanger or wet towel and crunchy peanut butter. Unfortunately, Clarke can't resist making a few corrections on Cartwright's final before it is sent to the examiners and is stupid enough to use a different colored ink. Longing to be the perpetual boy with his perpetual mate, Clarke disappears with Cartwright into Morocco. The play premiered at Cambridge, 1979; it received a professional production in Edinburgh, 1980, with Fry and John Davies, directed by Simon Cherry. § Fry, S. *Paperweight*. Heinemann, 1992. 428–70.

127   *News Boy* (1979) | Arch Brown (1936–2012), American

[Political drama; 6M, 1W; 1 set.] Brown turned from a successful career as a director of porn films to the theater. *News Boy* dramatizes how right-wing politicians use homosexuals as scapegoats. Tim Johnstin, facing marriage, arrives at Hank Farelli's apartment seeking confirmation whether he is gay, straight, or bi; he and Hank "used to fool around" when they were roommates in prep school. But Hank is out on another of his wild adventures. His housemate, Bill Morrissey, listens reluctantly. He rejects the role of "bringing people out." Regardless, he and Tim fall in love. Complications arise when Tim's mother decides to run for New York state senator against the incumbent, who has become mired in scandal. To Tim's shock she denounces homosexuals as "An undesirable segment of our society that disgusts sensible citizens and corrupts and violates our children." By then Tim has been seen often enough in the company of gays for a reporter to out him as "an alleged homosexual." The mother summons Tim to attend a news conference to affirm his heterosexuality. After careful consideration, he refuses to show, and the mother publicly disowns her son. At their next meeting Tim treats her affably: "I think you did the wise thing. It solved both of our problems instantaneously." He and Bill prepare to move in together. The play opened in New York, 1979, with Lynn Miller, L. B. Rosser, and Robert Redding, directed by J. Kevin Hanlon. Sixteen of Brown's plays have been published; none of the others has received the same attention. § Brown, A. *News Boy*. JH, 1980. 84p.

128 *Rents* (1979) | **Michael Wilcox (1945–), English**

[Sexual drama; 5M; flexible set.] The playwright delights in exploding gay stereotypes. Here he depicts socially stigmatized rent boys as very ordinary persons. In de Jongh's words (*Homosexuality*, 168), "The amateur rent boy of the Edinburgh 1970s emerges, in terms neither sentimental nor glamorising, as a student speculator no more dangerously on the make than an average city financier or property dealer." Richard Ridley, whom Wilcox admits is autobiographical, is called in at the last minute to fill in for a lecturer at an Edinburgh school. There he meets Phil MacFerson, a young actor preparing for his exams with the opening scene of Beckett's *Waiting for Godot*. Phil's roommate Robert, 18, has a poorly paid job in a clothing store. With no sense of guilt, both of them work as hustlers for extra money. Robert is also a master at ripping off the clothing store, supermarkets, and Richard's credit card. In the playwright's own words, the play is all "about money and survival." De Jongh goes on, "All that Robert can achieve is the dogged devotion of a middle-aged lecturer, who comes from an earlier gay generation in whom guilt has been inculcated. He is unassertive, reticent, polite and soft" (170). As to Phil and Robert's relationship, even they aren't sure what it is. The play is composed of short vignettes revealing slices of the characters' lives. It opened in Edinburgh, 1979, with David Whitaker, David Bannerman, and Jimmy Chisholm, directed by Chris Parr. § Wilcox, M. *Plays 1*. Methuen Drama, 1997. 1–62. Also includes *Accounts*. 63–137.

129 *Richmond Jim* (1979) | **Cal Yeomans (1938–2001), American**

[Sexual drama; 3M; 1 set.] In all his plays Yeomans stresses the importance of sexual acts, from simple kissing to fetishes, as the foundation of a gay identity and the establishment of meaningful personal relationships. Jim, 20, of Richmond, Va., takes a holiday in New York to check out the gay scene in the hope of finding out more about himself. He is picked up by Mike, 35, a leatherman. Their sexual evening is momentarily interrupted by a talisman figure, Biddy, who advises Jim, "Don't be afraid to experiment. You might discover an infinity of new heavens." After he leaves, Mike begins Jim's initiation into "The S&M leather life." The first step is to dress him appropriately. This includes Mike's placing a cock ring around Jim's penis and testicles. Yeomans writes, "It would be natural if Jim began to get an erection." Jim says, "I don't feel like I'm me." When Mike asks, "Is that bad?" he replies, "No, not really. I guess I'm discovering more of me I didn't know existed." Yeomans sums up, "The metamorphosis is complete and remarkable. No trace remains of Richmond Jim." The play opened in San Francisco, 1979, with Randy Bennett, Joe Cappetta, and Charlie Hufford, directed by Guy Bishop. § *Folsom Magazine*, 1981. Currently available online. Also available online: *Sunsets: 3 Acts on a Beach*, 1980–1981.

130 *Beer and Rhubarb Pie* (1980–90) | **Daniel Curzon (1938–), American**

[Domestic comedy; 3M, 1W; 3 sets.] Having established himself as an important liberation novelist, Curson turned to theater. The present play began as a short story, then a one-act play, before finally lengthening to three acts. Two couples, one straight and one gay, are having sexual problems. Rosa and Fernando have come to an impasse in their marriage. Fernando claims that they have not "grown apart," that their problem is they've "grown together," that they've "been together for too long." Len and Bob have shifted from being lovers to being roommates. Now Len is having second thoughts, but Bob emphatically rejects any possibility of their again having a sex life. Len reacts so viciously that Bob decides to move out. While he and Rosa (with whom he works) commiserate, Fernando arrives at Len's to undertake some carpentry work. He begins deliberately flirting with him. The play ends with the macho

Cuban-American rather improbably being taken anally: "Welcome to the other side," Len says. The short version opened in San Francisco, 1980, with Richard Staven and Thomas Mark. The three-act version was not produced until 1990, in New York. § Curson, D. *Collected Plays*, v1. IGNA, 2003. 316–63.

131 *Forever After* (1980) | **Doric Wilson, American**

[Domestic satire; 4M; 1 set.] A post-modern exercise, the play sets out to examine, in the words of Emmanuel Nelson (*Contemporary*, 448), two questions: "Is it possible for two men to be genuinely in love with each other forever? If so, is it possible for an artist to represent convincingly such a relationship on stage without slipping into soap operatic triviality, melodrama, sentimentality, or defensive polemics?" David and Tom are our lovers/actors, playing under the watchful eyes of the muses of tragedy and comedy (two male actors in drag). The lovers, "Christopher Street Clones," discuss their relationship, their hopes for the future, their emotional limitations. Melpomene, the cynical muse of tragedy, says, "You can spot the lovers in any crowd—they're the ones being nasty to each other." But David and Tom plow on, determined to make their romance work. As actors they insist they are really straight: "All actors in gay plays are." They parody recent work of "Robert Sherman" with his "'bent' for rocks," "Sam Patrick's" "naked bodies on the TV screen" (*T-Shirts*), and "Martin Shepard's" "child" (*Buried Child*). The audience is involved in other inside jokes. The play opened in New York, 1980, with Hunt Block and Anthony Errinson, directed by Wilson. § Wilson, D. *Forever After: A Vivisection of Gaymale Love without Intermission*. JH, 1980. 76p.

132 *Another Country* (1981) | **Julian Mitchell (1935–), English**

[School drama; 10M; 5 sets.] Influenced by the story of Guy Burgess, one of the Cambridge spies, the play, in Clum's words (*Still Acting*, 173), shows "how the brutality and hypocrisy of a closed, privileged, masculine society, when turned against a homosexual member of that society, creates a traitor." It is set in an English public school in the 1930s. Tommy Judd is an ardent Leninist. Guy Bennett, the main character and a master of innuendo and double entendre, becomes by degrees more openly homosexual: "It doesn't come as any great revelation. It's more like admitting to yourself—what you've always known." Thoughts of another student, Martineau, who hangs himself after he is discovered having sex with another boy, is never far from the minds of several of the students. In the midst of the boys' jockeying for power, an old school boy Vaughan Cunningham pays a visit and has tea with a select few. It is obvious from his allusions that he is gay. He and Bennett establish a tenuous connection. Bennett is caught out when he bribes a young fag to take a note to the boy he is having a clandestine affair with; as a result he is subjected to corporal punishment from the house prefect. In the aftermath he vows to become a career diplomat in order to undermine the system: "What better cover for a secret agent than apparent total indiscretion?" The play opened in London, 1981, with Rupert Everett and David William, directed by Stuart Burge. Mitchell wrote the script for the 1984 film. § Mitchell, J. *Another Country*. Amber Lane, 1982. 95p.

133 *Beyond Therapy* (1981) | **Christopher Durang (1949–), American**

[Sexual farce; 4M, 2W; 4 sets.] Gay themes found their way into Durang's plays from the beginning. In his first great success, *Sister Mary Ignatius Explains It All for You*, 1979, one of the nun's former students is gay. In the present play, a gay, or bisexual, character is the lead. With the approval of his therapist, Bruce places two ads seeking female companionship. Prudence answers both, to the dismay of her incompetent and unethical therapist, who is having an affair with her. She is taken aback when she discovers that Bruce was married but his wife divorced him when she found him having sex with the gas meter reader. He is now living with Bob, but assures her Bob will move into an apartment over the garage when he and Prudence marry and the two men will only occasionally have sex. Bob is not happy about the plan (nor is his unseen mother). He threatens suicide; Bruce rushes him to see his equally incompetent therapist. Everyone ends up in a restaurant, where Bob picks up the waiter, to discover too late that he is a sociopath released from reform school. The absurdist comedy ends inconclusively, though it leaves the impression that Bruce and Prudence may well marry. It opened in New York, 1981, with Stephen Collins and Jack Gilpin, directed by Jerry

Zaks. Vining (*Diary*, v5, 448) wrote of its 1982 reprisal: "*Beyond Therapy* proved to be more suitable to a gay group than any of us had known since it is a cartoon sort of play about a man who is answering ads in the personal columns of New York Review, wanting to marry while yet retaining his male lover. The scenes involving the male lover's jealousy when the woman comes to the apartment were terribly funny." Robert Altman and Durang co-wrote the script for the so-so 1987 film. § Durang, C. *Complete Full-Length Plays 1975–1995*. Smith & Kraus, 1997. 205–60.

134   *Cock-Ups* (1981–83) | **Simon Moss (1959–), English**

[Biographical study; 7M, 1W; unit set.] Moss was the earliest to realize how fascinating the life and death of Joe Orton might be on stage. Detective Inspector Truscott, the bumbling police officer in *Loot*, investigates the murder-suicide. Homophobic, he misreads every clue about what happened. Also present on the scene are a psychiatrist and his mate who want to interview Ken Halliwell, the gay chauffeur who was assigned to pick Orton up that morning, and two neighbors. Via ghostly apparitions, the playgoer witnesses Joe and Ken's troubled life together. Ken emerges as a pathetic mess who nevertheless garners sympathy for the brutal way Joe treats him before Ken snaps and kills him and then takes his own life. The play's tone shifts constantly between tragical, comical, and farcical. Its premiere was in Edinburgh, 1981. Moss revised it for its Manchester and London openings, 1983. § Moss, S. *Cock-Ups*. Faber & Faber, 1984. 92p.

135   *Forty-Deuce* (1981) | **Alan Bowne (1945–1989), American**

[Sexual drama; 8M; 1 set.] Bowne conjures up a gritty slice of life that still packs a punch. It covers half a day in a Time Square room used as a flophouse by teenage male hustlers. This was the era when the area was given to prostitution and pornography. (Forty-deuce is slang for 42nd Street.) They are under the care of an older man, Augie, who himself must pay for protection from a never-seen Mike. Wanting to pull off a big drug deal, Ricky, one of the hustlers, picks up a runaway, 12, at the bus terminal and brings him to the room, planning to pimp him out to a pederast, 50. The kid overdoses on drugs and dies. His naked body remains on stage for the duration of the play. Desperate for the money, Ricky goes on with his plan, hoping to get the predator he has contacted high enough that he will not realize he is sodomizing a dead boy. The play delivers a range of emotions. A scene where the boys try to explain how to get to Harlem by subway is out-and-out comedy. A virtuoso monologue by the pederast provides riveting insight into the mind of a man intelligent enough to know he has become a sadistic monster and to understand that "treating you kids as 'product' is our way of keeping you at arm's length. […] the vocabulary of commodities." But there is no epiphany for any of the characters. The play opened in New York, 1981, with Kevin Bacon, Orson Bean, Ahvi Spindell, Tommy Citera, Mark Keyloun, and John Noonan, directed by Tony Tanner. Browne wrote the script for the 1982 Paul Morrissey film. § Bowne, A. *Plays*. Broadway Play, 1997. 35–90. Includes *Beirut*, 1986, his most commercially successful play.

136   *Kiss of the Spider Woman* (1981) | **Manuel Puig (1932–1990), Argentine**

[Prison drama; 2M; 1 set.] The now mythical story began in 1976 as a novel consisting entirely of dialogue: *El beso de la mujer araña*. Stage adaptations by others soon appeared in Mexico City and Milan. Puig's own version premiered in 1981 in Madrid. Strictly speaking, it may not be part of a gay repertoire, for Molina, the putative gay character, speaks of himself as if he is a transwoman. He says of himself and his friends: "We're normal women; *we* only go to bed with men." One could question his assertion, however; he is in prison "for gross indecency," a charge that would seem to go beyond transvestism, and once released, he is warned by his godfather "not to dally with minors again." He may be trying to ingratiate himself in his straight cellmate's eyes by stressing that he is a woman. Valentin has been arrested for his political activities. Unknown to him, Molina has been bribed by the authorities to elicit information about Valentine's comrades. They have not counted on Molina's falling in love with Valentin. To pass the time Molina recounts the plot of films. Valentin slowly grows to respect Molina as a friend, a respect maintained even when Molina offers him sexual release. In a flash forward at the end the playgoer learns that Molina will try to get a message to Valentin's comrades, only to be arrested

and killed, while Valentin will die as a result of torture. The play had its English-language premiere in London, 1985, with Simon Callow, directed by Simon Stokes. Leonard Schrader wrote the script for the 1985 film version; a musical version opened in New York in 1993. Both have been published.
§ Puig, M. *Kiss of the Spider Woman and Two Other Plays*. Trans. by Allan Baker. Norton, 1994. 7–73.

137 *Niagara Falls: A Comedy in Two Parts* (1981) | Victor Bumbalo (1948–), American

[Ethnic comedy; 3M, 2W; 2 sets.] This two-part play shows how a never-seen gay couple acts as a catalyst to change an Italian-American family's lives, especially the women's. In the first part, *American Coffee*, the mother informs her husband that their gay son and his lover have flown in for their daughter's wedding. Though insisting that he loves his son, the father becomes frantic imaging all the embarrassing things they could do at the reception, until finally, for the first time in her life, the mother rebels. The second part, *The Shangri-La Motor Inn*, finds the newlywed daughter camped out in the lobby of a motel in conversation with the night man, Fred Heneberry. Having apparently taken a crash course on the gay scene from her brother, she discerns at once that Fred is gay—to his great delight, his having had problems being believed on a trip to New York and now preparing to head to San Francisco. The daughter, thinking of her brother and wary of the predicable life she sees as her future, laments, "How did he end up with the wonderful life?" Her husband, whose only role models have been Italian-American men like his father-in-law, comes looking for her. As they talk, he begins to heed his wife's call to adventure and accepts that his new brother-in-law provides a good role model for a meaningful marriage. With no sense of irony, he says, "There's something relaxing about coming out." The play opened in New York, 1981, with William Castleman, directed by Bumbalo. § Bumbalo, V. *Niagara Falls and Other Plays*. Calamus, 1984. 3–86. Includes *Kitchen Duty*, 1979, and *After Eleven*, 1983.

138 *Pines '79* (1981) | Terry Miller (1948–1995), American

[Romantic comedy; 8M, 1W; 1 set.] In his afterword Miller attacks a recently published unnamed novel (Kramer's *Faggots*?), "an alleged satire of contemporary gay life." He questions, "How did we go from silly stereotypes to self-vivisection without nurturing our lives with positive, healthy romantic fantasies?" He insists that not only are gays entitled to theatrical romances as much as straights are, but that "Gay Romantic Comedy may become our most subversive form of theatre." The present play gives us snapshots of six weekends in a home on Fire Island across the summer of 1979. The music of disco plays throughout. The owner, John, is a drug dealer who rents out rooms to long-term escapees from Manhattan. Jeff comes out of his shell of innocence and finds a lover in, of all people, his office mate, all inhibitions broken down by smoking too much pot. Curt and Hank go through a really rough stretch—Curt wanting total commitment, Hank fearful of letting go—and almost break up, reconciling only after Hank brings a rather ludicrous porn star back to the house. In a running joke across the summer, Anita has escaped the watchful eye of their next-door neighbor Brenda. There is nothing to suggest that she is not a real woman, but when Anita finally shows up and is recaptured, she turns out to be a boa constrictor. We then learn that Brenda's son killed himself. She confesses, "Ever since then, I have tried to understand. Maybe that's why I'm out here each summer." But for her, as for the others, the time has come to move on beyond Fire Island. The play opened in New York, 1981, with Terry Helbing, Clarke Evans, Walter Dietrich, Mark Carson, Archie Harrison, and Kent Wells, directed by Richard Northcutt. § Miller, T. *Pines '79: A Romantic Comedy*. JH, 1982. 131p.

139 *Remember Me* (1981) | Michel Tremblay, Canadian

[Psychological drama; 2M; 1 set.] As in *Hosanna*, two men feel trapped by their personas. Ex-lovers, still friends, they meet in the home they once shared. Luc needs comforting: his father is dying, and he feels he himself has been taken over by the banal but much loved character he plays in a television series. The older Jean-Marc, a French teacher and aspiring novelist, recognizes that his writing is mediocre and that he is tired of serving as an emblem of the openly gay schoolteacher. They bare their souls. Luc was the one to walk out, feeling stifled by Jean-Marc's possessiveness. (Jean-Marc discovered that Luc was actively tricking on the side, though Luc insists that he never cheated, always keeping his physical needs separate from the love he felt, and still feels, for Jean-Marc.) He is thinking of coming out just to get away from the character the public confuses with him. Jean-Marc does not argue against the decision, but he begs him to do it for the right reason: "If you declare to the world that you're gay, at the risk of losing your job, your friends, your allies, it strikes me you should be doing it out of solidarity, not just to exorcise some character that's taking over your life." Jean-Marc has a new (never seen) partner, but the play ends with him leaving to visit the dying father. Luc stays behind. His final line, unknown to him, is the same as that with which Jean-Marc opens the play. *Les anciennes odeurs* premiered in Montreal, 1981; the English version first played in Manitoba, 1984, with Allan Gray and John Moffat, directed by Peter Brask. § Tremblay, M. *Remember Me: A Play*. Trans. by John Stowe. Talonbooks, 1984. 58p.

140 *Something Cloudy, Something Clear* **(1981) | Tennessee Williams, American**

[Memory play; 5M, 3W, extras; 1 set.] At the end of Williams's life he began to introduce gay characters into his plays with more frequency. He published *Steps Must Be Gentle* (about Hart Crane) in 1980, *Now the Cats with Jewelled Claws* and *The Traveling Companion* in 1981, and in 1982 he offered *The Remarkable Rooming-House of Mme Le Monde*, to be published posthumously (1984) as it turned out. He reworked Chekhov's *The Sea Gull* as *The Notebook of Trigorin* for performance in Vancouver in 1981 (pub. 1997), bringing Trigorin more to the fore and making him bisexual. And he continued to mine his autobiography. Returning to an earlier short play *The Parade, or Approaching the End of Summer*, he conjured up his 1940 Provincetown romance with the Canadian dancer Kip. The results are an evocation of the past as seen from the present, "a sort of double exposure." Williams names his alter-ego August, but the details correspond closely to the playwright's life. Kip is straight; he meets August's sexual demands reluctantly. August justifies his actions: "He could have easily broken away, but he didn't." Their mutual friend Claire asserts, however, "I'll not have you use him again like a whore." Other Williams memories surface: his early infatuation with Hazel Kramer; his recall of Frank Merlo's last days; a mixed tribute to Tallulah Bankhead. August ends the play with the thought that, "while this memory lives, the lovely ones remain here, undisfigured, uncorrupted by the years that have removed me from their summer." It opened in New York, 1981, with Craig Smith, directed by Eve Adamson. § Williams, T. *The Traveling Companion and Other Plays*. New Directions, 2008. 165–92. *Something Cloudy, Something Clear*. New Directions, 1995. 85p.

141 *Torch Song Trilogy* **(1981) | Harvey Fierstein (1954–), American**

[Domestic comedies; 4M, 2W; flexible set.] The three plays remain funny, but at this distance they seem more than a little clichéd, passé. Each affects a different style to represent Arnold Beckoff at three different points in his life. First produced in 1978, *The International Stud*, the name of the gay bar in which Arnold works as a female impersonator, alternates between his monologues and dialogues between him and a fan, Ed Reiss. The two fall in love, but Ed is bisexual and torn between Arnold and a woman named Laurel. *Fugue in a Nursery*, 1979, occurs a year later. Ed and Laurel are together; Arnold has a new boyfriend Alan. Laurel, who is enamored of gays, invites the two for a visit. The play is structured as a series of constantly shifting and overlapping duos. There is talk about marriage, open relationships, the idea that one person always loves more than the other. Ed seduces Alan, but in an epilogue Laurel visits Arnold to say that she and Ed are getting married. *Widows and Children First!*, also 1979, is conventionally structured. Five years have passed. Alan has been killed in a gay-bashing. Arnold is in the process of adopting a gay teenager David. Ed has left Laurel and is staying with Arnold. Arnold's mother, who is in denial that her son is gay, flies in for a visit. There is the expected confrontation between mother and son, with her grudging acceptance of him, and another between Arnold and Ed, with the possibility that they may try again. Streetwise David seems the most well-adjusted of them all.

The trio were presented together in 1981 with Joel Crothers, Paul Joynt, Matthew Broderick, and Fierstein, directed by Peter Pope. Vining (*Diary*, v5, 416) recorded his impressions: "Feirstein [*sic*] is without doubt a fat and to me unappealing camp and I can't believe that the three attractive characters would love him as they did in the play because he was also a screaming type, but let him have his fantasies. He acts well, if quite broadly, and he writes very well indeed. In scenes with the mother he didn't stack the deck but let the mother state her case very forcefully. In many scenes, such as the one in a dark back room of a backroom bar, I laughed uproariously." Fierstein wrote the screenplay for the 1988 film. He went on to write a second, much looser trilogy, *Safe Sex*, 1987. § In Hodges, B., ed. *Out Plays.* 406–527.

AIDS, 1982–1989

AIDS acronym adopted, 1982. Northern Ireland forced to decriminalize homosexual acts, 1982. New Zealand legalizes same-sex acts, 1986. U.S. Supreme Court upholds sodomy laws, 1986. Cardinal Joseph Ratzinger (future Pope Benedict) issues On the Pastoral Care of Homosexual Persons, *1986. ACT-UP founded, 1987. AIDS Memorial Quilt displayed in Washington, 1987. Section 28, forbidding promotion of homosexuality, becomes law in U.K., 1988.*

142 *Coming Clean* (1982) | **Kevin Elyot (1951–2014), English**

[Sexual drama; 5M; 1 set.] Elyot originally called his play "Cosy," an allusion to Mozart's *Cosi fan tutti*. It raises the question: when does an open relationship become infidelity? Tony, an apprentice writer, and Greg, an American teacher, have been living together for five years, but their relationship is fraying. It unravels completely when Tony discovers Greg has been in a four-month affair with Robert, an actor working for them as a house cleaner, and faces that his high-minded acceptance of an open relationship without jealousy is empty rhetoric. Greg tries to convince him that "just because [things] are changing, it does not mean they're coming to an end. We can't chuck the whole thing out!" But Tony wants domestic comfort or nothing. (Ironically, Robert feels the same way.) In the last scene Tony brings in a German trick he has picked up. Via their conversation, we discover that Greg has returned to New York to visit his parents, and Tony is moving in with a friend. Elyot wrote in the foreword that, at the time, "AIDS was a barely credible rumour filtering from across the Atlantic. The play's final scene has an elegiac quality—in retrospect, almost a sense of foreboding." It opened in London, 1982, with Eamon Boland, Philip Donaghy, and Ian McCurrach, directed by David Hayman. § Elyot, K. *Four Plays.* Nick Hern, 2004. 1–72.

143 *Easy Terms* (1982) | **Frank Vickery (1951–), Welsh**

[Domestic comedy; 2M, 2W; flexible set.] In his introduction to the *Selected Plays* (xii–xiii), Phil Clark says that Vickery is "obsessed with the 'taboos' of life. The issues that people found hard to talk about in public life but had strong opinions about in private. That, for him, was where the drama/theatre of his plays existed." Vi Davies is another in the line of manipulative mothers who use their supposed fragility to get their way and then don innocent faces when caught out. When Vi has a stroke, her son Howard quits college and returns home to take care of her. She gives him no breathing space. Then he falls in love with Bernard. This is Mr. Fowler, her insurance man. Faced with her certain incomprehension, Howard cannot bring himself to tell her, but of course the truth leaks out. She reacts predictably. While on vacation (in Bernard's caravan, unbeknownst to her), a neighboring woman shakes Vi by planting the seed in her mind that all her neighbors probably blame her for keeping Howard from pursuing his own life. Then when Bernard shows up, the same woman blurts out his name, revealing to Vi for the first time that Bernard and Mr. Fowler are one and the same. But Vi is resilient, and she does love her son. He returns to school, training to be a teacher. In the final scene, in her new assisted-living apartment, she recounts to Bernard over tea how she is helping one of the aides whose son has just revealed he is gay. Then she uses her well-honed technique to manipulate Bernard into buying his proposed new caravan in a town she wants to visit. The play premiered in Swansea, 1982, with Bill Lynn and Richard Locke, directed by Joan Mills. § Vickery, F. *Easy Terms: A Comedy*. French, 1997. 71p.

144 *Happy Birthday, Daddy* (1982) | **Richard Hall (1926–1992), American**

[Domestic drama; 4M, 1W; 1 set.] Hall worked hard to champion gay literature. Perhaps too hard. All three of his plays retain interest, but they are marred by chunks of unintegrated propaganda. Here he returns to the classic plot of the closeted male finally accepting himself. After seventeen years of marriage, Nick has moved in with Deke, whom he met at the Everard Baths. Tensions have been growing between the two men, however, as the result of Deke's insistence on an open marriage. All comes to a head at the birthday party Deke throws for Nick, to which he invites Nick's ex-wife Jean and their son Joey. Jean turns out to be less hostile than might be expected; all Joey wants is for his father to return and life to go back to the way it was. In a tense moment, he reveals that he went along with his school chums in beating up "a queer," and then disappears. Nick and Deke quarrel about how Joey should be handled, and Nick walks out on him to return to his wife. In Act 2 Deke picks up Ernie, who wants to intellectualize gay sex. Jean pops in long enough to beg Deke to take Nick back before he drives her crazy. She and Ernie leave together. Nick returns from having spent a week at Fire Island (where he also apparently met Ernie). Jean and Joey show up again. This time Deke confronts the teenager: "Your father is gay and he loves you. Do you understand that?" Joey again walks out, but one senses that he may consider Deke's words. At play's end, Deke offers to serve up the uneaten birthday cake which he has frozen. The play opened in New York, 1982, with Larry Maxwell, Kerry Ashton, and Nole Cohen, directed by J. Kevin Hanlon. § Hall, R. *Three Plays for a Gay Theater & Three Essays*. Grey Fox, 1983. 1–46. Includes *Love Match*, 1977, and *Prisoner of Love*, 1978.

145 *If This Isn't Love!* (1982) | **Sidney Morris (1929–2002), American**

[Domestic drama; 2M; 3 sets.] Morris reflected on his own life in writing this play. Three scenes, each set in a different decade, distill the ties that keep two men together for twenty years. Aspiring actor Adam (Jewish) and future teacher Eric (Irish-Catholic) meet as teenagers in night school during the 1950s. It is love at first sight set against the backdrop of McCarthyism. Entrapped by police, Adam is found guilty of "Solicitation for sodomy." Eric is more innocent, but that changes. In the 1960s as they prepare for the march on Washington, in the act of emptying pockets to raise bail for a friend caught in a raid on gay bars, Adam discovers that Eric has been having sex with another man. They break up, but in Act 3 we learn that they reconciled during the march. In the 1970s the two men are on their terrace overlooking the route the Gay Pride parade will take. Eric has his own school for special-needs students; Adam has made money off television commercials and become a successful actor. Adam has also suffered a stroke that left him wheelchair-bound, but he manages to stand when Eric spots his mother marching under the Parents of Gays banner. The play opened in New York, 1982, with Adam Caparell and Paul Malec, directed by Leslie Irons. § Morris, S. *If This Isn't Love! (Two Men—Twenty Years—Three Acts)*. JH, 1982. 101p.

146 *Snow Orchid* (1982–93) | **Joe Pintauro (1930–), American**

[Ethnic drama; 4M, 1W; unit set.] In his afterword to the 1992 publication, Pintauro writes, "Gay male existence does not begin with parades and bars. The most difficult years of gay life take place early, in the home, where homophobia can make life hell and where the gay person faces the first, tortuous separations of his life." Sebbie Lazarra, 21, wants out of his dysfunctional family. Sexuality is not really the problem. They know he is gay: his younger brother is uncomfortable with the fact, but his mother and father's chief concern is that his lover is Irish-American instead of a good Italian-American boy. Rather the problem is the psychological disorders both his parents suffer from. The father suffers from bipolar disorder. He has just returned from a mental institution where he was committed after trying to kill himself in New York's Holland Tunnel. The mother suffers from intense agoraphobia. And she smothers Sebbie. He says, "I'm the sonofabitch they named

Sebastiano. I caught the arrows." When Vinnie Doogan invites him to join him at his uncle's in Fort Worth, Texas, Sebbie hesitates because of the mother's dependence on him. But with the return of the father (bearing a stalk of orchids, that flower named for the male testicles), he agrees to join Vinnie. Vinnie promises the father that he will "be with [Sebbie] for the rest of his life, even if he goes off with a woman, or another one like [me], or becomes a drunk." Shocked by his departure, the mother makes another effort to leave the house, whereupon the back wall opens to reveal a magical snow scene, whose meaning is left for the audience to decipher. The play opened in New York, 1982, with Robert Lupone, directed by Tony Giordano. Pintauro heavily revised the script for its 1993 London production, in which Vinnie (played by Adam Magnani) appears on stage. § In Wilcox, M., ed. *Gay Plays Five*. 213–69.

147 *Street Theater* (1982) | **Doric Wilson, American**

[Historical drama; 12M, 2W; flexible set.] The play is a light-hearted, often satiric, still serious meditation on the Stonewall Inn riots. Through the figures of Murfino, the bar owner, and two vice cops, one an S/M closet case, the point is made that gays are exploited for all kinds of unethical reasons. Michael and Donald from *The Boys in the Band* wander onto the scene but don't want to get involved. A closet case is so appalled by their refusal that he comes out to join the cause. Tribute is paid to both the leather and the drag communities for their willingness to fight. Two radical gays foreshadow the political savvy and destructive infighting that will emerge in the riots' aftermath. Also present are a butch lesbian, a flower child, and a youth escaping the hinterlands. Many of the clichés and stereotypes about gays are scrutinized and made fun of. The play opened in San Francisco, 1982, with Harvey Hand, Duane Cropper, Steev'n Lloyd, and David Williston, directed by Allan Estes. The cast of the New York production included Vito Russo. In 1983 the play opened at the Mineshaft sex club with Terry Helbing replacing Russo. § In Shewey, D., ed. *Out Front*. 1–77.

148 *Auto-Erotic Misadventure* (1983) | **F. J. Hartland (1958?–), American**

[Character study; 2M, 1W; unit set.] The play demonstrates again how difficult it is to achieve E. M. Forster's admonishment "Only connect." Three characters sharing a Washington, D.C., apartment try but fail miserably. Chris is an uptight maître d' (so he says; he may be a waiter) who has just been dumped by his boyfriend. Brandon is an aging callboy ("with a B.F.A. in English literature, what else could I do for a living?"). Norma is a frumpy secretary whom males ignore. Chris copes by turning to macramé. Norma tries all the single bars. Brandon does "what I do best. And I'm proud of a job well done. It's the Puritan work ethic." Depressed, Norma begs Cliff just to hold her; he refuses. Brandon becomes depressed about his work; he and Norma end up embracing, then going to bed together, to Cliff's great discomfort. Norma gets her hopes up, but Brandon has no desire to give up his profession. Cliff confesses he loves Brandon. Brandon makes like he is going to embrace Cliff and knees him in his testicles. The apartment empties. Cliff goes to Myrtle Beach to manage his own restaurant, still alone, addicted now to soap operas. Norma ends up in Minneapolis seeing a shrink. And Brandon accepts being kept by an older man who promises him a modeling job. The play opened in New York, 1983, with Paul Zappala and Jon Wool, directed by Peter Gordon. § *Off-Off Broadway Festival Plays*, 8th series. French, 1984. 33–58. Includes Ross M. Levine's bathhouse drama *A Change from Routine*. 63–76.

149 *Finding the Sun* (1983) | **Edward Albee (1928–2016), American**

[Domestic drama; 4M, 4W; 1 set.] From the time of *Who's Afraid of Virginia Woolf?* Albee had to put up with innuendos that his females are really gay men *en travesti*, but the playwright showed little interest in exploring gay lives. Here for the first time he created men who self-identify as gay. Even so, both are married. Cordelia takes a worldly view of her husband: "I *know* Daniel sleeps around; well, I'm pretty sure I know it, and I suspect it's with guys. I *hope* it is." Abigail is not so suave. She attacks Benjamin: "You and your sidelong glances, your letters you won't let me read, your odd phone calls, your feeble excuses for getting home late." She tries unsuccessfully to drown herself (the setting is a beach). Benjamin begs Daniel and Cordelia to create a *ménage à trois*. When he begs for someone to hold him, it is Cordelia who responds. Also present on the beach is Fergus, 16, who seems both more innocent and wiser than his years.

Warned to beware of the two men, he is fascinated by the revelations about them. Near the end of the play he mysteriously disappears. The play is set in no particular time, but two years into the plague, it seems curiously outdated (or in denial) when Daniel says of sex, "Herpes is about the only thing you can catch—apparently." It was first performed in Greeley, Colo., 1983. Gay sons appear in two later Albee plays. The one in *Three Tall Women*, 1991, is present on stage but mute. The teenager in *The Goat, or Who Is Sylvia? (Notes toward a Definition of Tragedy)*, 2002, discovers that his father is carrying on an adulterous relationship with a farm animal; as the story unfolds, young Billy (note the name) feels a certain sexual interest in his sire, but his sexuality plays little part in the evolving farce. § Albee, E. *Finding the Sun*. Dramatists, 1994. 39p.

150 *Webster* (1983) | **Robert David MacDonald, Scot**

[Historical drama; 10M, 4W; flexible set.] In a rare look at someone other than Marlowe and Shakespeare, MacDonald portrays a Jacobean troupe having problems with its principal playwright John Webster (1580?–1634?). Though married and the father of a spastic son who seems to exist in a state of perpetual sexual excitement, Webster is not above using his bed as a casting couch for boy actors. Harry is the current favorite, having succeeded Luke, though neither seems to have much going for him save looks. The intrigue leads to Luke's twin brother Mark trying to kill Webster but managing only to destroy his mouth and jaw. The manuscript of *The Guise* on which Webster has been working is destroyed, though a poem is salvaged for *The Devil's Law-Case*. Michael Coveney wrote in *The Citz*, 1993 (online): "It is much the most autobiographical of MacDonald's plays and portrays the stress on the dramatist's stable domestic life by his weakness for passing homosexual attractions." The play opened in MacDonald's Glasgow theater, 1983, with Ciaran Hinds, Rupert Farley, and John Breck, directed by Philip Prowse. § MacDonald, R. D. *Plays One*. Oberon, 1991. 17–80.

151 *Bearclaw* (1984) | **Timothy Mason (1950s–), American**

[Ethnic drama; 3M, 1W; 1 set.] Two plays that Mason premiered in 1984 both deal with death. *Bearclaw* is set in a St. Paul nursing home where Paul Bearclaw is one of the orderlies. He gets through his days with cigarettes, an infectious sense of humor, and a genuine interest in his patients. He is gay, in an unsatisfactory relationship with a journalist. Newly arrived Peter Asgard, having suffered a debilitating stroke, is in his care. Peter was a high school history teacher driven to change the lives of all losers he met for the better, never noticing that he was ignoring the needs of his own son. Now he tries to convince Paul that he should better himself. His lawyer son discovers that Paul is half Chippewa; his father is a drunkard whom he is ashamed of. Peter tries to instill a sense of pride. Any number of questions arise as a result of the complex welter of emotions Peter unleashes. He himself comes to understand how he has failed Peter Jr., and Paul seems to come to some peace with himself and his future. Peter Jr., invites Paul to join him and his wife after Peter's funeral and begins to give him directions for finding his home. Paul's final line takes on symbolic meaning: "Hey, I'll find my way." The play opened in Westport, Conn., with Bruce McCarty, directed by B. Rodney Marriott. The script was subsequently revised § In Wilcox, M., ed. *Gay Plays*, v2. 71–101.

152 *The Dressing Gown* (1984) | **Sky Gilbert (USA 1952–), Canadian**

[Sexual drama; 7M, 1W; flexible set.] *A Faery Tale for Adults Only*, the play uses the age-old device of following an object as it passes from one person to another, in this case a magical dressing gown. As it goes from male to male, the audience is presented a panel of gay stereotypes of the period. There are Jim, a boy just discovering his sexuality; David, who will not admit he is gay; Steven, who is saving up to get a trans-op procedure; Barry, a clone who is in an open relationship with Larry, a leatherman (professionally they are respectively a teacher and a banker); Jim, a drug punk who almost ODs while using a dirty needle; and Elliot, an aging comic actor. Elliot completes the circle by returning the gown to an older Jim. Between Jim and Elliot the gown passes through the hands of Martha, a would-be actor, in love with Jim, trying to understand why men are sometimes so self-destructive. Elliot tells her: "For some reason, in our particular society, to be a man is to be hard, is to win; it's to be a fighter and quite often, a killer." The play opened in Toronto, 1984, with David

Sereda, Alan Powell, Bill Gentile, David MacLean, Christopher Thomas, Joe-Norman Shaw, and Grant Cowan, directed by Gilbert. He subsequently revised the play. § Gilbert, S. *The Dressing Gown*. Playwrights Canada, 1989. 80p.

153 *Levitation* (1984) | **Timothy Mason, American**

[Domestic drama; 6M, 3W; 1 set.] What begins as a seemingly realistic play peopled with many characters turns slowly, almost imperceptibly, into a memory play in which there is actually only one character confronting loss and death. Joe Dahl returns to his parents' home in Minneapolis. There he engages with his dead mother and father, who not only accepted his sexuality but remained close to his first partner after the latter, for undisclosed reasons, moved out. The ghosts of his father's favorite teacher and Orville Wright (who died in 1948) appear. Joe's sister, who was not so accepting, and two of her children (one of whom thinks he is probably gay) show up, along with a mysterious visit from Ira, Joe's (current?) partner. Ira reveals that Joe has locked him out of his apartment: "He locked everybody out, no one could get through." Joe half-heartedly defends himself: "suddenly everyone I saw was so unmistakably doomed and everything I had I was going to lose, one way or the other." Earlier he says, "I just ... didn't want to die alone." His father holds, "You don't have to throw away a thing. [...] But you're gonna have to let go." The last person Joe sees as everyone drifts away from him is his gay nephew. The meeting seems symbolically affirmative. Joe is able to enter the empty house. It opened in New York with Ben Siegler and Bruce McCarty, directed by B. Rodney Marriott. § In Wilcox, M., ed. *Gay Plays*, v3. 59–88.

154 *Night Sweat* (1984) | **Robert Chesley (1943–1990), American**

[AIDS fantasy; 12M; unit set.] Chesley was writing from an intensely personal perspective even though it would be several years before he was diagnosed as HIV-positive. Still, unlike his later *Jerker*, this play has mostly historical interest. Though subtitled *A Romantic Comedy*, Chesley described it as "a gay nightmare about a fantasy suicide club" dreamed up by "a community which based a significant part of its identity—and economy—on a celebration of sex now facing a lethal sexually-transmitted disease." Diagnosed with HIV, Richard decides to join the Coup de Grâce Club to end his life. As he witnesses others with the virus playing out their sometimes raunchy death fantasies, it becomes clear that he actually wants to live but is blaming himself for having caught the virus. He is rescued by a man to whom he has been drawn, who insists that he "think about what a beautiful thing it is that one man can love another" and "how hard we've fought together so that can be so! [...] meanwhile you're going to live! Live until the very *moment* you die! [...] And make love! Make love in every possible, safe and sensible way!" Clum (*Still Acting*, 37) writes of the play, "It celebrates the possibility of a present ecstasy, and it does so through vivid enactment of sexual acts that begin as manifestations of both Eros and Thanatos but later are expressions of love. The play ends with a celebratory dance that defies sexual norms and gender definitions as it defies death." It opened in New York, 1984, with Guy Bishop, directed by Nicholas Deutsch. § *Hard Plays / Stiff Parts: The Homoerotic Plays of Robert Chesley*. Alamo Square, 1990. 9–69.

155 *Progress* (1984) | **Doug Lucie (1953–), English**

[Sexual drama; 6M, 2W; 1 set.] Looking back on his play in a 2013 online blog for *What's on Stage*, Lucie wrote that it "dissected and ridiculed the human impulses behind identity politics and shone a light on the hypocrisy of many who spouted progressive ideals while behaving in a conventionally reactionary way." Will and Ronee, husband and wife, pride themselves on being liberal activists. She has provided refuge to an abused wife; he has joined a men's group that is "trying to change our attitudes by being open and supportive without resorting to traditional hierarchical structures." Two of the members, Oliver and Martin, pose as a couple, but it comes out that their relationship is sexless—by Oliver's choice despite his neediness for Martin's emotional support. Martin has turned to the fourth member, Bruce, but he wants only sex and pushes Martin away when he in turn becomes needy. Everything falls apart when the three men confront each other. Simultaneously, Will and Ronee's marriage comes to an end, precipitated by Will's seduction of the abused wife. Ronee leaves to join a lesbian friend. The play ends either upbeat or ironically, depending upon how one takes the closing lines, heard from an earlier tape Will has made of a group meeting: "I really think we're getting somewhere here. Let's keep going." It opened in London, 1984, with David Bamber, Struan Rodger, and Kevin Elyot, directed by David Hayman. § Lucie, D. *Progress.* Dramatists, 1985. 66p.

156   *As Is* (1985) | William M. Hoffman (1939–2017), American

[AIDS drama; 6M, 2W; flexible set.] "Every morning I examine my body for swellings, marks. I'm terrified of every pimple, every rash. [...] I feel the disease closing in on me." These lines still reverberate for gay men who survived the 1980s. Hoffman gives a human dimension to AIDS by focusing his play on one couple. When their story begins, they are trying to settle up their common property, Rich having left Saul for Chet. When it is disclosed that Rich is HIV-positive, Chet flees— too late, it turns out, for he dies of AIDS. Saul, who is HIV-negative, reconnects and remains faithful to Rich in sickness as in health. Rich goes through the stages of dying: raging against the world, thinking about trying to infect as many men as he can before he dies, begging Saul to obtain enough pills to kill himself. The jokes with which gays tried to retain sanity are made. As the play progresses the two men mention more and more friends who have died. Clum (*Still Acting*, 58) sums up, "*As Is* is not only a play about coming to terms with disease and with one's love for a partner but also a play about coming to terms with one's past without guilt or regret. Sexual promiscuity is not lamented as a probable cause of Rich's contracting AIDS but is celebrated, its loss lamented. [...] The play is also about proving depth of commitment and concern, thus confounding notions of superficiality and fecklessness." Rich's brother refuses to turn his back on him, though after all these years he still blocks Saul's name from his memory. Another prominent character is a female hospice worker who functions as chorus. Her curtain speech resonates with love: "The other night Jean-Jacques— he's this real queen, there's no other word for it— he told me what he misses most in the hospital is his corset and high heels. I mean he weighs all of ninety pounds and he's half-dead. But I admire his spirit. [...] Last night I painted his nails for him. [...] Flaming red. He loved it." The play opened in New York, 1985, with Jonathan Hogan, Jonathan Hadary, and Steven Gregan, directed by Marshall W. Mason. It was telecast in 1986. The play was later revised. § In Shewey, D., ed. *Out Front.* 493–551. In Osborn, M. E., ed. *The Way We Live Now.* 3–61.

157   *Being at Home with Claude* (1985) | René-Daniel Dubois (1955–), Canadian

[Crime drama; 4M; 1 set.] A criminal interrogation moves into its final hour. It is the morning of July 5, 1967, at the time of the Montreal Expo. A hustler Yves has confessed to killing Claude, 22, the university student he has been meeting for a month. Even after thirty-six hours of grilling the motive remains unknown. Finally, Yves describes their last meeting in a twenty-five minute monologue. He and Claude had their most intense sexual experience ever, achieving simultaneous orgasms. In order to freeze the moment forever, Yves had instinctively seized a knife that had fallen beside them and slit Claude's throat. Yves tries to return to hustling, but nothing is now meaningful. The plot is thin, but with virtuoso acting the play could be mesmerizing. *Being at Home with Claude* premiered in Montreal in 1985. The English-language version opened in Toronto in 1987 with Stephen Ouimette, directed by Duncan McIntosh. Dubois wrote the screenplay for the 1992 film. § *The* CTR *Anthology: Fifteen Plays from* Canadian Theatre Review; ed. by Alan Filewod. Trans. by Linda Gaboriau. Univ. of Toronto Press, 1993. 389–433.

158   *Coming of Age in Soho* (1985) | Albert Innaurato, American

[Ethnic drama; 6M, 1W; 1 set.] The failed writer Bartholomew ("Beatrice") Dante, 36, leaves his wife once again, claiming, "I am not bisexual! I am a homosexual who suffers temporary amnesia in the presence of strong-willed ladies." His objective: "to try and grow up." But he has scarcely moved into his new loft when two adolescents show up at his door: Odysseus (Dy) MacDowell, 16, a runaway from affluence, and Puer Schlussnuss Dante, 13, his illegitimate son by a German terrorist whom he abandoned. Beatrice is uncomfortable with both: Dy, because he recognizes that he is sexually attracted to the teenager; Puer, because he knows that he does not love his own son.

His wife continues to argue for her right to maintain the marriage since she is running for Congress and "in America you can't run for higher office with a fag for a husband." She shows up with her Mafia brother, but in the end she renounces her claims. In an ironic switch on the *Commedia*, Mrs. Dante guides Beatrice to understanding. He must disavow any sexual feelings he has for Dy and accept his role as father for Puer. The play's tone is mixed. The scene with Danny, the brother's 18-year-old henchman guarding the teenagers, is close to farce. Danny, rather unexpectedly, admits to being straight but with "aberrations." After a Seattle workshop, the play went into rehearsal in New York but was rewritten before its 1985 opening with John Procaccino and Evan Miranda, directed by Innaurato. As a result of bad reviews, he revised it again and then wrote the autobiographical *Gus and Al*, 1987. § *Best Plays of Albert Innaurato*. Gay Presses of New York, 1987. 1–78.

159 *In the Blue* (1985) / *Certain Young Men* (1999) | Peter Gill (1939–), Welsh

[Romance; 8M; unit set.] In 1985, Gill directed a sketch with Ewan Stewart and Michael Maloney, *In the Blue*, in which the middle-class Michael becomes intrigued by the lower-class Stewart. Gill returned to the script in 1999, expanding their story and adding those of six other men. *Certain Young Men* continues to look at attractions across class divisions, but the men are individuals, not representative types. Still, their lives are fashioned to some degree by the stereotypes handed them. Must one attend Pride parades and hire only gay workmen? Is it basically all about sex based on the fact that "blokes suck cock better"? "Why shouldn't being queer be an axe to grind [...]? It's not something it's easy to avoid." Robert argues that the word "partner" smacks of "the market place. [...] We're just another niche in the market." For that reason "gay culture" is pretty much the "make of your underwear." He sums up, "I don't see pair bonding as some predetermined absolute." The couples are alternately tender and violent, involved in others' lives and secretive. Plot is minimal. The expanded version opened in London with Alex Newman, John Light, Jeremy Northam, Andrew Woodall, Andrew Lancel, Peter Sullivan, Robert Sean Chapman, and Danny Dyer, directed by Gill. § Gill, P. *Plays One*. Faber & Faber, 2002. 251–81. *Plays Two*. Faber & Faber, 2008. 123–216.

160 *It's All Due to Leprechauns* (1985) | Greg Branson (AUS unknown), English

[Political drama; 4M; flexible set.] Ralph is pulled between his sexual attraction to Sean, a young Irish-born actor having his first success (probably in Churchill's *Cloud 9*), and the promise of power offered by Mervyn, his MI-6 chief. The setting is London during the winter 1978–79, climaxing with the car-bombing death of Alrey Neave, M.P., at the hands of INLA on March 30. Sean's brother is a member of the Irish group; Ralph sells him out. Having savored the taste of success, he then breaks with Sean. The similarity between gay liberation and Irish insurgency is never spelled out, though Sean's remark—"Underneath, just ordinary people, most of them, struggling to survive"—might apply to both groups. The script is innovative in staging different times and places simultaneously to bring out the sharp disjunctions in Ralph's life. It had a special showing in New York, 1985. § Branson, G. *It's All Due to Leprechauns*. Playwrights, 1986. 64p.

161 *The Lisbon Traviata* (1985–90) | Terrence McNally, American

[Psychological tragedy; 4M; 2 sets.] Stephen describes opera: "Love and death. That's all they're ever singing about. [...] Opera is about us, our life and death passions—we all love, we're all going to die." Unfortunately, as Mike, his lover of eight years, tells him, "You live in some opera no one's ever heard of. It's hard loving someone like that." Theirs is supposed to be an open relationship even in the time of plague. Stephen and his friend Mendy spend Act 1 dishing about Maria Callas and other greats in Mendy's apartment so that Mike can be with his pickup Paul. Save for the fanaticism of the two opera queens, there is no indication that Stephen has lost control of his life. Act 2 is a showdown between him and Mike over Paul. After pulling every low trick possible with Paul, Stephen carries out his threat to kill Mike "before I let you run off and the two of you laugh at me." There are three published versions. In the first, which opened in New York, 1985, with Benjamin Hendrickson, Seth Allen, Stephen Schnetzer, and Steven Culp, directed by John Tillinger, Stephen murders Mike. In the second, which opened in New York, 1989 (with Nathan Lane), Stephen threatens Mike but does not kill him. For the third, McNally folded the two versions together and returned to the original ending. Schildcrout devotes much of Chapter 5 of *Murder Most Queer* to the changes. § In Shewey, D., ed. *Out Front*. 355–418. McNally, T. *The Lisbon Traviata*. Firestone Theatre, 1990. 128p. *Selected Works*. Grove, 2015. 83–167.

162 *Never the Sinner: The Leopold and Loeb Story* (1985–94) | **John Logan (1961–), American**

[Crime drama; 6M, 1W; flexible set.] The play follows the real-life case so closely as to be a docudrama, but Logan insists it should be viewed as a romance. Nathan Leopold (1904–1971) and Richard Loeb (1905–1936) become entranced by Nietzsche's concept of the *übermenschlich*. For Loeb committing the perfect crime would be one way to obtain superman status. He works out the plot; only the victim remains to be chosen. Leopold is willing to go along as part of the pact they have made for "an even exchange of sexual activity for criminal activity. Leopold would take part in crimes primarily to accommodate Loeb and Loeb would take part in sexual acts primarily to accommodate Leopold." After the murder of Bobby Franks, Leopold exalts, "We're together now. Forever." At the trial the prosecutor argues, "They killed *him because they were made that way*. Because somewhere ... somehow ... in the infinite processes that go into the making of a boy or man something ... *slipped*." Following a college production, the play opened in Chicago, 1985, with Denis O'Hare and Bryan Stillman, directed by Terry McCabe. Logan continued to refine the script, the final version appearing in 1994. § Logan, J. *Never the Sinner: The Leopold and Loeb Story*. Overlook, 1999. 142p.

163 *The Normal Heart* (1985) | **Larry Kramer (1935–), American**

[AIDS drama; 8M, 1W; flexible set.] The play is an autobiographical work that serves as a documentary of the first years of the AIDS crisis. Dr. Emma Brookner (modeled after Dr. Linda Laubenstein) is one of the first to articulate the gravity of the situation. Ned Weeks is the Kramer stand-in: angry, loud, demanding that something be done as he loses friend after friend. His lover Felix Turner, a journalist with the *New York Times*, is temperamentally his opposite: closeted, trying not to antagonize the political bigwigs. The plague eventually catches up with Felix (who, Clum [*Still Acting*, 63] notes, has "a death scene that Dumas or Giuseppe Verdi would have admired"), leaving Ned lamenting that he did not do more. The play was a success in New York and London and in its recent television reincarnation, perhaps to a large degree because of the actors it attracted for the starring roles. Sinfield (*Out on Stage*, 321–22) recapitulates its fundamental flaws: "Ned's analysis is undermined by his inability to endorse gay men as they currently are. He is obsessed with the approval of straight society—the mayor, the *New York Times*, his brother Ben. He colludes in the notion that straight-acting role models should spearhead the campaign [...]. He fails to notice that his movement is dominated by white and upper-middle-class men. [...] What passes for politics here [...] is little more than casting round for someone to blame." Clum (63–64) adds, "Kramer has trapped himself in his own rhetoric. There is no space for resolution of the crisis that obsesses him, no space for the love that could be a counter to the promiscuity he excoriates as not only exploitative and destructive—as he presented it in his novel *Faggots* (1978)—but now also deadly." The play opened in New York, 1985, with Brad Davis and D. W. Moffett, directed by Michael Lindsay-Hogg. It was televised in 2014. A 1992 sequel, *The Destiny of Me*, delves into Ned's background. Kramer also wrote a satirical play about public indifference to the crisis: *Just Say No: A Play about a Farce*, 1988. § Kramer, L. *The Normal Heart and The Destiny of Me: Two Plays*. Grove, 2000. 1–118.

164 *Observe the Sons of Ulster Marching towards the Somme* (1985) | **Frank McGuinness (1953–), Irish**

[Military drama; 9M; flexible set.] With this play the Irish playwright began interlinking the difficulties of forging a gay sexual identity with that of creating an Irish cultural identity out of the political and religious muddle of Northern Ireland. Set in World War I, the play is permeated by death. It is narrated by the elderly Kenneth Pyper, the only member of his outfit to survive the deadly battle of the Somme. A sculptor, he lived in Paris before the war. He recounts a confusing story about his experience there with a whore who "had three legs. The middle one shorter than the normal two," and claims to have murdered her (him?). David Craig does not believe the story at all. The two men have an instant attraction to each other.

Almost as soon as they meet, Kenneth cuts his thumb peeling an apple (which quickly takes on sexual significance) and begs David, "Kiss it better." Later, during a battle, David saves Kenneth's life. One of their fellow soldiers says, "I saw Craig, what he did. He blew his own breath into Pyper's mouth. It was a kiss." Depending upon the director, the men's relationship can become totally sensual, especially in one scene on an island to which the two, on leave, escape. The other six men also arrange themselves into couples with some degree of intimacy playing out for each pair. The play opened in Dublin, 1985, with Bosco Hogan and Lorcan Cranitch, directed by Patrick Mason. § McGuinness, F. *Plays One*. Faber & Faber, 1996. 91–197.

165 *Raw Youth* (1985) | **Neal Bell (1950?–), American**

[Political drama; 3M; 3 sets.] A closeted Congressman who has "voted down fruitcake rights for the last fifteen mean-spirited years," a father who has cut a deal with the FBI to get him out of prison in return for his entrapping the Congressman, and a bisexual son whom the father proposes to use for that purpose are the unlikely characters the playwright assembles. No explanation is offered why the FBI wants to expose "Congressional homos." The son goes along with the scheme to save his father, but no one, including him, anticipates his feeling sorry for his target and sabotaging the evidence. What should have been either a trenchant exposé of hypocrisy or a tender reconciliation of father and son becomes an implausible muddle. It is the type of dramaturgical problem repeated throughout Bell's writing career. The play opened in New York, 1985, with Ben Siegler and James Ray, directed by Amy Saltz. § Bell, N. *Raw Youth: A Play*. Dramatists, 1986. 48p.

166 *When She Danced* (1985) | **Martin Sherman, American**

[Biographical study; 3M, 5W; 1 set.] The dancer Isadora Duncan presides over a 1923 Tower of Babel in Paris (six different languages are spoken). This particular evening she has invited Italian diplomat Luchiano Zavani to dinner, hoping that his government will provide her a school in Italy. A Greek pianist, Alexandros Duncan Eliopolos, 19, his second name in honor of her, is there to play Chopin. Isadora's husband, the Russian poet Sergei Esenin, becomes irrationally jealous. She quickly claims that Alexandros is a pederast (a usual French term for a homosexual) and then apologizes. Alexandros boasts, "It's all right. It is true. [...] Elliopolos is great pederast. Best pederast in all Europe. It is very Greek." Luchiano is more interested in him than in Isadora. Alexandros is agreeable: "For you—Isadora—for you—I perhaps sacrifice myself." But then it comes out that Luchiano is not a diplomat; he is merely a worker in the Italian embassy, whose dress misled Isadora. Alexandros laughs, "I almost give my pee-pee to file-clerk." Sherman barely alludes to Sergei's bisexuality; Isadora mentions only in passing, "He powders his face. He wears make-up." Stirred into the farcical incidents are serious discussions of art and its relationship to the spirit. The audience is also reminded of the tragedies of Isadora's life. The play opened in Guildford, Eng., 1985. Its American premiere was in New York, 1990, with Robert Sean Leonard and Robert Dorfman, directed by Tim Luscombe. § Sherman, M. *When She Danced*. Samuel French, 1988. 88p.

167 *Breaking the Code* (1986) | **Hugh Whitemore (1936–), English**

[Biographical study; 7M, 2W; 2 sets.] Based on the biography by Andrew Hodges, the play recounts how the mathematician Alan Turing (1912–1954) broke two very different codes: he solved the mystery of the Nazis' Enigma code and he broke the social code of his day by being open about his homosexuality. Moving back and forth in time, the play records both his interest in artificial intelligence and his disdain for conventional morality. Dillwyn Knox, his administrative officer, warns Alan about his behavior, but Alan is so enclosed in his world that he does not have a clue Knox is also gay. When Alan is robbed as a result of one of his pickups, he calls the police and, under questioning, admits that he has committed "a Gross Indecency." As a result he is placed on probation and subjected to hormone therapy. The day he first meets Knox he has attended a showing of Disney's *Snow White and the Seven Dwarfs*. When Knox asks if it doesn't have a sad ending, Alan replies, "No, she wakes up in the arms of a handsome prince." Under stress from the treatment he receives, Alan decides to kill himself with a poisoned apple. The play's final words are those of the wicked queen. By now, Alan is consumed by the question whether the mind can exist outside the body, but there is no indication he hopes to find his prince in death. The play opened in London, 1986, with Derek Jacobi, directed by Clifford Williams. It was telecast in 1996. Snoo Wilson will dramatize the same events. § Whitemore, H. *Breaking the Code*. French, 1988. 105p.

168 *Diary of a Somebody* (1986) | John Lahr (1941–), American

[Biographical study; 3M, 2W; 1 set.] Lahr published his edition of *The Orton Diaries* in 1986; the same year he staged this dramatization of the journal, the second play to try to make sense of Ken Halliwell's rage against Joe Orton. Many of the lines are Orton's; just as many do not appear in the fatal diary. After a brief prologue, the play covers the period from November 20, 1966, to August 2, 1967, seven days before Halliwell murdered Orton. All the familiar facts are presented: Joe's growing theatrical success, his promiscuity and apparent cruelty to Ken, the growing strain between the two men, the mystery of why they stayed together in such cramped quarters. Lahr provides no real insights anymore than he did in his biography *Prick Up Your Ears*. Many of the references in the play are meaningful only to someone who know that biography: for example, Joe's fleeting allusion to prison. It opened in London, 1986, with John Sessions, Bruce Alexander, and Richard Denning, directed by Jonathan Myerson (whom Lahr credits in his introduction as co-writer). It was subsequently revised. § Lahr, J. *Diary of a Somebody: Based on The Orton Diaries*. Limelight, 1989. 70p.

169 *Innocence: The Life and Death of Michelangelo Merisi, Caravaggio* (1986) | Frank McGuinness, Irish

[Biographical study; 6M, 3W; 3 sets.] Written in modern idiom, the play treats its audience to glimpses of the Italian painter Caravaggio (1571–1610) and members of his entourage. He lives in a world where all men are gay and all women are prostitutes. Prominent are his sometimes mistress Lena and street hustlers/lovers Antonio and Lucio, the subjects of his *Bacchus, Boy with Basket of Fruit, Boy Bitten by a Lizard*, etc. Caravaggio accepts his companions easily at the same time that he tries to defend himself to his disapproving family: his straight, uptight brother, a priest, and the ghosts of his dead parents and sister. The Cardinal to whom he pimps the two street boys tells him: "You remind us of unpleasant truths, Caravaggio. For that you may be hated. Your sins may be condemned. But you will be forgiven, for you are needed. Forgiven everything eventually. Dangerous words. A dangerous man. Saving himself by the power of his seeing. And by his need to tell what he sees." Having killed a man while in the company of Lucio, he flees to Naples. But Lena affirms that "somehow we'd won, we turned the world upside-down, the goat and the whore, the queer and his woman." Her final act is to transform a nude Antonio into the composition for *John the Baptist*. The play opened in Dublin, 1986, with Garrett Keogh, Peter Holmes, and Joe Savino, directed by Patrick Mason. § McGuinness, F. *Plays One*. Faber & Faber, 1996. 199–289.

170 *Irving* (1986) | Miguel Piñero (1946–1988), Puerto Rican

[Ethnic comedy; 5M, 2W; 1 set.] Piñero published the play in his 1986 collection *Outrageous: One Act Plays*, which contains four other plays with gay characters. Irving Horowitz decides to come out of the closet to his Jewish family. He invites them to his apartment for the grand announcement. His sister Mimi surprises him with her African American boyfriend Butcher Castleton, who is his sexual partner. Neither sibling has realized s/he is sharing the same man. Irving's parents react predictably to his announcement. His brother Richard knows just a bit too much about gay life. His uncle could not care less "whether you're a faggot or not," all he wants to know is whether "it'll keep you from making money." Irving answers that "it all depends on how far gay liberation goes." Butch is not happy about being inadvertently outed along with Irving, but when Mimi leaves, he remains with Irving. § *Outlaw: The Collected Works of Miguel Piñero*. Arte Público, 2010. 133–57. The other gay plays are *Paper Toilet*; *Cold Beer*; *Sideshow*; and *Tap Dancing and Bruce Lee Kicks*.

171 *Jerker, or The Helping Hand* (1986) | Robert Chesley, American

[AIDS drama; 3M; unit set.] *A Pornographic Elegy with Redeeming Social Value and a Hymn to the Queer Men of San Francisco in Twenty Telephone Calls, Many of Them Dirty*, the play affirms the right of men to love despite the plague decimating their number. J.R. is a paraplegic Vietnam veteran.

Having gotten Bert's phone number while the latter was drunk at the Badlands bar celebrating his birthday (February 14, 1985), J.R. calls and initiates phone sex with him. Clum (*Still Acting*, 59) observes, "While the physical isolation and separateness of the characters and the solitary practice of masturbation are poignant reminders of the reduction of eroticism in the age of AIDS, the scenes celebrate the power of sexual fantasy to join these men." They move from mutual orgasms to discussions of their lives and their terrible moment in history. In response to the attacks being leveled against gay promiscuity as the cause for the spread of AIDS, Bert affirms, "For me, for a lot of guys, it was ... *living*; and it was *loving*." Throughout, J.R. retains his anonymity, but he asserts that it was in Vietnam "I learned what 'immoral' means. And that's why nobody but nobody tells me I'm immoral if I love a man, if I love a hundred men in one night." In their last conversation Bert lets drop that he has a touch of flu. J.R. must leave for a short trip to New York. When he returns, he places a series of calls, only to get Bert's answering machine. The last time he gets a recording: "The number you have reached [...] Has been disconnected." It opened in Los Angeles, 1986, with David Stebbins and Joe Fraser, directed by Michael Kearns. A radio station aired excerpts, leading to FCC repression. The play was adapted for film in 1991. § In Shewey, D. ed. *Out Front*. 449–91.

172 *A Quiet End* (1986) | **Robin Swados** (1953–), American

[AIDS drama; 5M; 1 set.] Three gay men—Max, Tony, and Billy—share an apartment set up by an AIDS charity: "Every morning we wake up. Every night we check our vital signs. Or vice versa." Tony survived Vietnam, but, suffering from guilt for all the men he may have infected, he is the first of the three to die. Billy, who "can count the number of men I've slept with on one hand," decides to return to his Midwestern family and finally be open with them. Before he dies, Max makes an uneasy truce with his former lover Jason. They split because Jason wanted commitment; Max argued for "holding on to your personal freedom, about having an 'open relationship,' about how it would keep things from going stale." Max admits, "Maybe a lot of the stuff we said *was* stupid. Maybe a lot of the advice *was* foolish. But not intentionally." The play opened in Long Beach, Calif., 1986, with Fred Bishop, Thomas Jackson, Randolph Powell, and Bruce Wieland, directed by Jules AaronIt. § In Helbing, T., ed. *Gay and Lesbian Plays Today*. 149–212.

173 *Touch* (1986) | **David Demchuk** (unknown), Canadian

[Sexual drama; 2M; 1 set.] The play explores how difficult, if not impossible, it is for lovers to know one another. Gary and Ken are naked in bed, looking through a stack of porn magazines. Ken muses how "two people, in a relationship, they have such different perspectives on each other, on what they have together, you'd think that making love they'd ... *meet*, but even then each one of them is still [...] alone." Gary likes to make up stories about what led to the sexual acts depicted in the magazines to aid his arousal. Ken objects that too many of the images show one male dominating the other. Gary counters, "We're all raised to hate and be afraid of gays, and then things have to change when we understand we're gay ourselves. [...] I have to hurt myself, a little, to feel anything at all." He tries to begin a story in which the two men are Ken and Gary. Robert Wallace in his introduction notes, "The central irony of this very ironic play is that the characters' ideological positions are overshadowed by the actors' physical positions in bed. In effect, the actors perform for the audience an example of the erotics at issue. If the audience agrees with Ken [...] it must question its voyeuristic position in the theatre. If it agrees with Gary [...] where does it draw the line? Would the audience watch these two nude men do more than talk?" The play opened in Toronto, 1986, with Daniel MacIvor and Ron Jenkins, directed by Sky Gilbert. § In Wallace, R. ed. *Making, Out*. 41–57.

174 *A Bright Room Called Day* (1987) | **Tony Kushner** (1956–), American

[Political polemic; 5M, 6W; 1 set.] One of our few gay political writers, Kushner turns to Hitler's rise to power for a play filled with polemics against the Reagan era. However, it has none of the intensity of Greig and Griffiths's *As Time Goes By* or Sherman's *Bent*. The central focus is on a group of friends around a German actress in 1932–33. Scenes are regularly interspersed with a running commentary by a woman contemporary to the play's presentation drawing parallels between events then and now. Gregor Bazwald, a gay worker for Hirschfeld's Institut, says the portentous things one would expect him to say, somewhat humanized by his rejection of the Communist party on the grounds "They won't let me wear mascara." When Hitler comes to power and the Institut is burned, he thinks of killing himself but, after a lusty encounter with a Silesian in the bushes, he decides his depression was occasioned by "Too much pent-up energy" caused by lack of sex. He prepares, instead, to head for Paris. Two years before its official premiere Kushner workshopped the play (with Stephen Spinella as Baz). It opened in San Francisco, 1987, with Jeff King, directed by Oskar Eustis. In the London production the commentator railed against Thatcher. § Kushner, T. *Plays*. Broadway Play, 1999. 1–73.

175 *Burn This* (1987) | Lanford Wilson, American

[Domestic drama; 3M, 1W; 1 set.] It's almost as though Wilson tried too hard here to write a commercial success. Choreographer Anna, advertising agent Larry, and dancer Robbie shared a loft apartment in Manhattan. Robbie and his lover Dominique have just been killed in a freak boating accident; Larry and Anna return from the funeral in Texas. They have discovered that Robbie's family not only pretended not to know he was gay but had never seen him dance. His homophobic brother Jimmie (aka Pale) shows up to collect his things. He makes the obligatory derogatory comments about faggots to Larry, but clearly feels some guilt for the way he treated his brother. His marriage has fallen apart, and he is attracted to Anna. She in turn finds him more exciting than her boyfriend Burton, a talented script writer. Larry gets his share of witty lines about opera queens, gay New Year's Eve parties, and homophobic seat mates in airplanes, and he is the one who sets up Anna and Pale, but it is ultimately a pretty thin role. The play opened in New York, 1987, with Lou Liberatore, directed by Marshall W. Mason. § Wilson, L. *Burn This*. Dramatists, 1998. 66p.

176 *Compromised Immunity* (1987) | Andy Kirby (unknown), English

[AIDS drama; 5M, 2W; unit set.] In his introduction to the play, Philip Osment records Gay Sweatshop's distaste for Kramer's puritanical reaction to the era of promiscuity and casual sex. Kirby provided them with an antidote to *The Normal Heart*. Set primarily in a London isolation ward during the last weeks of Gerry Grimond's life, Britain's first AIDS play has some political/economical content. Gerry 36, denounces the researchers' greater interest in getting the Nobel Prize than in finding a cure. He notes that "it's tests that bring the money in [...], not a vaccine," and continues, "They found cures for Lassa Fever and Legionnaire's disease soon enough, and with millions of government money. But this is different, AIDS is associated with junkies and queers so the first priority is a test so that the rest of you are safe." The play's dramatic focus, however, is on the surprising friendship that develops between him and his young, straight nurse Peter Dennett. Peter must learn not to be afraid of the virus, and he must convince his girlfriend to feel the same way. Disturbed that no one is visiting the often abrasive Gerry, Peter wants to convince Gerry's former lover to drop by. In trying to track Hugh down, Peter meets young Ian Edwards. Ian stands for the generation that may be knocked about by the plague but remains unbowed. Even after Ian realizes that Peter is straight, he continues to flirt with him. Accused of being "bloody persistent," he cheekily responds, "That's how I'm still gay after eighteen years in Ammanford [his hometown]." Though Gerry dies, Ian will explore this new, if compromised world that lies before him, and Peter now knows that sexuality does not stand in the way of friendship. The play opened in Leicester, 1987, with Peter Shorey and Duncan Alexander, directed by Osment. § In Osment, P., ed. *Gay Sweatshop*. 51–79.

177 *Lilies, or The Revival of a Romantic Drama* (1987) | Michel Marc Bouchard (1958–), Canadian

[Sexual drama; 9M; 1 set.] Bouchard dramatizes the social, religious, and personal evils of homophobia, repression, and jealousy. In 1952 ex-prisoner Simon Doucet requests a meeting with Bishop Jean Bilodeau. When he shows, Doucet forces him to watch a re-enactment of events that occurred in 1912 when the two were Roberval School students. While rehearsing a school production of d'Annunzio's *Le Martyre de saint Sébastien*, Doucet and another actor, Vallier, fell in love. Bilodeau repressed his sexuality. Vallier's mother supported her son; Simon's father savagely beat him when Bilodeau disclosed their secret. Hating the town, Simon began setting fires. He entered an unloving marriage and prepared to depart for

France. To keep him there Bilodeau blew up the balloon that was to serve as their first transport. He tried to persuade Simon to run away with him, promising he would get along with Vallier. Simon rejected the idea and returned to Vallier. The two attempted suicide by immolation. Bilodeau saved Simon but left Vallier to die; the bishop says, "It was Sodom and Gomorrah that was burning, and I was God, punishing you both by saving you and letting him die." But he admits, "I wanted you to remember me. [...] I loved you so much I wanted to destroy your soul." The bishop now begs to be stabbed much as St. Sebastian was shot with arrows. Simon is tempted, but concludes, "I hate you so much.... I'm gonna let you live." *Les feluettes, ou La répétition d'un drame romantique* premiered in Montreal, 1987. It had its English-language premiere in 1991 with John Dolan and John Gilbert, directed by Brian Richmond. Bouchard and Linda Gaboriau wrote the screenplay for the 1996 film. An opera version with music by Kevin March premiered in Montreal, 2016. § Bouchard, M. M. *Lilies, or The Revival of a Romantic Drama*. Trans. by L. Gaboriau. Playwrights Canada, 1990. 69p.

178   *Mean Tears* (1987) | Peter Gill, Welsh

[Sexual drama; 3M, 2W; flexible set.] This bleak work portrays unrequited, foolish love. Steven, as his friend Paul says, is "addicted" to Julian. Julian is narcissistic, totally unreliable, incapable of commitment, and bisexual. In Act 1 he pursues Celia; in Act 2, Nell. Between times with them, he returns to Stephen. Julian identifies with the amoral Shelley, reciting lines from "Epipsychidion." Steven, in a discussion of opera, reveals his intimate knowledge of *Der Rosenkavalier*, but he has not the Marschalin's wisdom to recognize the futility of his love for Julian. Paul seems to be the one stable character, though one wonders why he puts up with such losers. In a final gesture Steven threatens the vain Julian with a knife, to "scar [him] in the only way that would matter," but ends by taunting him with a rewritten nursery rhyme. The premiere was in London, 1987, with Karl Johnson, Bill Nighy, and Garry Cooper, directed by Gill. § In Clum, J., ed. *Staging Gay Lives*. 163–213.

179   *Mr. Universe* (1987) | Jim Grimsley (1955–), American

[Sexual drama; 4M, 3W; 3 sets.] Frustrated at not finding a publisher for his first novel, Grimsley turned to drama. *Mr. Universe* seems heavily indebted to others' works. Dodging the plague by setting it in New Orleans in 1979, Grimsley has the requisite drag queens, Vick and the vicious "Judy." It has a female hooker who has just murdered one of her clients. There is a bag lady who remains convinced that her husband is still alive. And there is a muscle man who appears to have walked over from Albee's *Sandbox*, though this angel of death (or violence) is mute. Judy tries to seduce the muscle man, but in an altercation with him she is killed with her own knife. The hooker makes it appear that she is the guilty party. The play ends with Vick's pondering what will become of him and the muscle man, now covered in blood. The premiere was in Atlanta, 1987, with Jeff Lewis, directed by Steve Kent. Grimsley went on to write other, less derivative, plays, including the enigmatic *Math and Aftermath*, 1988, about the making of a gay porn film on the beach at Bikini Atoll the day before the hydrogen bomb test occurs there. § Grimsley, J. *Mr. Universe and Other Plays*. Algonquin, 1998. 5–66. Includes *Math and Aftermath*. 201–54.

180   *Nasty Little Secrets* (1987) | Lanie Robertson (1936–), American

[Biographical study; 4M; 1 set.] In his retelling of Orton and Halliwell's relationship, the third such, Robertson emphasizes Ken's side of the emotional turmoil. Act 1 stresses his frustrated attempts to write publishable fiction, the collages that he creates including the defaced library books, and the pair's arrest and incarceration for their crime. Act 2 sketches Joe's meteoric rise to fame against the accumulating evidence of Ken's descent into psychosis. The play ends on a fanciful note: Joe and Ken, still in love, still able to laugh, ascend on a rope through the ceiling like the ending of *What the Butler Saw*. Two characters have been invented for the play: a police officer who hounds them constantly and a literary agent who eyes Joe as a prize to be guarded from Ken. Save for a music hall turn midway through the play, it is fairly straightforward in its retelling of the story. The play opened in Philadelphia, 1987, with Simon Brooking and Craig Fols, directed by Stuart Ross. § Robertson, L. *Nasty Little Secrets: A Play in Two Acts*. French, 1989. 100p.

181 *Round 2, or New York in the 70s* (1987) | Eric Bentley, American

[Sexual drama; 9M; flexible set.] The play is one of at least five gay (or quasi-gay) adaptations of Arthur Schnitzler's *Reigen* (often called *La Ronde*). Others are Michael John LaChiusa's musical *Hello Again*, 1993; Michael Kearns's *Complications*, 2002 (the basis for the 2004 film *Nine Lives*); Jack Heifner's *Seduction*, 2004; and Joe DiPietro's *Fucking Men*, 2008. In order to remain faithful to the spirit of the original, Bentley set his play in New York at the end of the 1970s, before AIDS. There are ten pairings between nine men, forming a complete circle. He chose as his characters, in the order in which they hook up, a hustler, a soldier, an art student, a lawyer, a businessman, his lover, a teenager, a playwright, a female impersonator, and a nameless person in the limelight. The picture painted of gay life is pretty depressing. The businessman and his lover, for example, have pledged to be monogamous, yet each has a string of affairs he hides from the other. The lover justifies himself: "Gay people always lie. Fabricate. Fantasize." The playwright sums up, "Sex isn't sex unless someone's being deceived." In the context of the encounters the hustler and the teenager emerge as the more honest of the nine. Bentley himself says (according to Daniel-Raymond Nadon, in Harbin, *Legacy*, 55) that a "point often missed in production" is that "the soldier is the only one that seeks purely physical sex. The others are searching, unsuccessfully, for love through the sexual act." The premiere was in Silver Lake, Calif., 1987. § In Wilcox, M., ed. *Gay Plays*, v4. 1–43.

182 *Steel Kiss* (1987) | Robin Fulford (unknown), Canadian

[Crime drama; 4M; flexible set.] On the evening of June 21–22, 1985, a popular high school teacher and librarian, Kenneth Zeller, 40, was brutally murdered in Toronto's High Park, a popular cruising place, by five teenagers, 15 to 18 years of age. Fulford was moved to write his play. It is a challenge for the actors: each must play multiple roles: the teenagers, their girlfriends, their families, the victim (all four actors give voice to his inner thoughts at various points), his pick-up, members of the community, including a homophobic preacher, and members of the judicial system. The teenagers engage in mindless pranks; their gay-bashing is very much a product of their culture. The play opened in Toronto, 1987, with Jack Nicholsen, David Kinsman, Ron Jenkins, and Greg Morrison, directed by Ken McDougall. In 1996 Fulford followed with a sequel, *Gulag*. It shows the four in prison and on parole. Billy, the weakest of the four in the first play (and the leader of the charge that kills the man), predictably turns out to be a "fag." Surprisingly, however, he and Neil had sex in prison. In a drunken stag party Billy now kills him the same way the original victim is killed. § Fulford, R. *Faggot! Steel Kiss and Gulag*. Blizzard, 1999. 74p.

183 *Straight and Narrow* (1987) | Jimmie Chinn (1940–2011), English

[Domestic comedy; 4M, 3W; 1 set.] As Sinfield points out (*Out on Stage*, 343–44), the play is written for straight audiences and therefore accommodates "mainstream ideas about gays." It tries to have it both ways, by stressing that its protagonists "are almost like a straight couple" but at the same time holding "that they can never quite be 'normal.'" For untold years Bob Swift and Jeff Shotter have been partners at work (they design and install kitchens) and at home. The family-less Jeff has been willing to put up with Bob's larger-than-life mother and his dithering sisters. But Jeff's increasing desire to have children of his own provoked a holiday to Malta to sort out matters away from them all. There Jeff met Terri and ratcheted up the tensions between the two. They return to find their home filled with Bob's people. The sisters and their husbands approve of the pair's life; the mother acts as if she is clueless. Matters seem to be coming to a head, with Bob, who serves as narrator, finally ready to out himself to her. But he ducks the subject once again. The last we see of the couple they have moved back into their usual routines, leaving the larger issues (which, after all, do not interest the play's straight audience) unresolved. It opened in London, 1987, with Peter Rose and Mick Cawson, directed by Joanne Burnett. § Chinn, J. *Straight and Narrow: A Comedy*. French, 1992. 51p.

184 *Theatrelife* (1987) | Sky Gilbert, Canadian

[AIDS romance; 3M, 3W; 2 sets.] The play moves away from the sense of paralysis AIDS first introduced to a feel for developing ways to cope. Director Geoffrey Gregson has assembled a cast to revive an old-fashioned play very similar to Sutton

Vane's *Outward Bound*, about a voyage of the dead. The ingénue's role is filled by Tom Delaney, to whom Geoffrey is attracted sexually. Straight Lorenzo Chironi, apparently with the best intentions, discloses to Geoffrey that Tom is HIV-positive. Geoffrey asks Tom whether he is "inflicted with [...] the disease." Tom, after asserting that he has no regrets ("I've always known what I wanted to do and then I've done it"), circles the question: "It is painful but sometimes it is also very beautiful for it makes me conscious of my own mortality. This disease, it repels; but in a strange way, it attracts. It bewitches, it alarms, it keeps us in suspense." When Geoffrey refuses to let up, Tom finally answers: "My disease is—[...] Love!" Lorenzo, in the play within the play, has the final words: "Wots a body to do!" But earlier he and Geoffrey have laughed over his flub in dress rehearsal when he'd said instead, "Wots a body to die." The play opened in Toronto, 1987, with Graham Harley and Steven Walker, directed by Gilbert. § Gilbert, S. *This Unknown Flesh: A Selection of Plays*. Coach House, 1995. 65–123.

185 *Absolute Hell* (1988) | Rodney Ackland (1908–1991), English

[Barroom drama; 11M, 10W; 1 set.] *The Pink Room, or The Escapists* opened in London, 1952. Explicit references to homosexuality were banished from the script. It still was roundly criticized for going against the postwar mood: instead of depicting the heroic side of the British character, the stage was populated with various failures, most notably characters guilty of self-deception. Ackland, however, refused to give up on his unpublished play and rewrote it as *Absolute Hell*. He could now be open that several of the characters were gay. The setting is a club bar, La Vie en Rose; the time is June–July 1945 with new elections taking place. The cast is large, and each has his own story. Much of what plot there is centers around Hugh Marriner, a failed writer, a drunkard, and a pathological liar. He cheats on his partner of nine years, Nigel Childs. The latter cannot stomach Hugh's failings longer; he walks out of their relationship, taking up with a woman who has promised to back his career as a dress designer. Hugh clings to the idea that Maurice Hussey, another gay, will back his script at the film studio where he works. Maurice relies entirely on the opinions of his flunkey and sex partner, Cyril Clatworthy, passing them on as his own. In an ironic turn Hugh ends up playing a similar scenario with one of the returning soldiers, with the difference that Sam is straight. Hugh also toys with the idea of starting a new life with the club's proprietress. It does not take long for both Hugh and Nigel to realize they have made a mistake, and there is a possibility that they will renew their life together. But at play's end Hugh is preparing to move back in with his mother as the club literally falls apart. This second version opened in London, 1987, with David Rintoul and Vincent Brimble, directed by Sam Walters and John Gardyne. It was telecast in 1991. § Ackland, R. *Absolute Hell*. Oberon, 1990. 142p.

186 *Carthaginians* (1988) | Frank McGuinness, Irish

[Political drama; 4M, 3W; 1 set.] The play has been seen as a companion piece to *Observe the Sons of Ulster*. It commemorates Bloody Sunday, the January 30, 1972, murders of thirteen civil rights marchers in Derry, Northern Ireland. The setting is a Derry graveyard, where three women keep vigil, expecting a resurrection. They are aided by four men. Johnny Harkin has spent time in prison as a result of his joining the IRA; Seph, who became an informer, is now virtually mute; Paul has been driven mad by events. Dido Martin, "patriot and poof," is the most healthy of the seven, a caretaker who looks after the others. Hark is divided in his emotions between one of the women and Dido. He early tells Dido, "You are known as a queer in this town. I do not like being seen with queers. I do not like queers. I do not like you." Dido jokes, "He's just playing hard to get." Indeed, later Hark kisses Dido and grabs his crotch. But here every gesture is also political: "Is the united Ireland between your legs? What happens when cocks unite? Disease, boy, disease. The united Ireland's your disease." In Scene 4 Dido enters in drag and leads them in a play he has written, *The Burning Balaclava*. It is a campy sendup of the Troubles, challenging sectarian and gender roles. Hark observes the parallel between Dido, Queen of Carthage, and Dido, queen of Derry. After the names of the thirteen murdered men are recited, a kind of epiphany is reached. As the others sleep, Dido delivers the final speech in the play. It opened in Dublin, 1988, with David Healihey, directed by Sarah Pia Anderson. § McGuinness, F. *Plays One*. Faber & Faber, 1996. 291–379.

187   *Eastern Standard* (1988) | **Richard Greenberg (1958–), American**

[Romance; 3M, 3W; 2 sets.] Clum (*Still Acting*, 54) writes: "In the world of *Eastern Standard*, gay men and straight men and women are united by education and class in ways that make their differences in sexual orientation relatively unimportant." Two couples—one gay, the other straight—conclude that they can manage "all the disappointments, which are inevitable, and compromises, which are legion, and lies, which are our daily bread" by acknowledging "the sadly infrequent—accidental—happinesses of all the rest of our lives." But their path to this point of acceptance and laughter has taken various turns. The four meet at a restaurant as the result of an altercation caused by a bag lady. Drew, a painter, and Stephen, an architect, have remained fast friends, even after Drew realized he has no chance with the straight Stephen. Phoebe, a financial advisor mixed up emotionally with a crook, and Peter, a television writer who has just learned he is HIV-positive, are siblings. The idealistic Stephen is entranced by Phoebe, who is attracted to him but incapable of committing. The acerbic Drew is equally entranced by Peter, who feels in his situation that he is unable to commit. Nonetheless, the four end up at Stephen's beach house. He also invites the waitress, who has a crush on him, and at her instigation, the bag lady. She again acts as a kind of catalyst, urging them, "ya can't weigh yourself down with backward philosophies. Ya just gotta assess the situation and *travel*." Peter accepts Drew's proposal to grab what happiness they can while they have the chance, and Stephen accepts Phoebe's proposal of marriage. The play opened in 1988 under Michael Engler's direction, first in Seattle with Tom Hulce and then in New York with Peter Frechette. § Greenberg, R. *Eastern Standard*. Dramatists, 1989. 82p.

188   *The Heidi Chronicles* (1988) | **Wendy Wasserstein (1950–2006), American**

[Feminist drama; 3M, 5W; flexible set.] The play follows the life of Heidi Holland across a quarter of a century. She moves from being an idealistic art history student through her growing feeling of disillusionment even as she adopts a child. She maintains two enduring male friendships: one with the man she could have married but doesn't, and the other with gay pediatrician Peter Patrone: dedicated, cynical, charming. It takes her nearly nine years to come out to her, but he becomes increasingly outspoken. During the years that follow he has a number of partners (all played by the same actor). The 1980s are hard on him. He deals professionally with children with immune deficiencies. Personally, he faces a decreasing number of friends as AIDS ravishes the community: "my world gets narrower and narrower. A person only has so many close friends. And in our lives, our friends are our families." His first partner, another pediatrician with whom he split years before, "isn't very well." The last we hear of Peter, he is living with a "nice anesthesiologist [...]. He still runs that ward and on weekends they garden at their home in Bucks County." The play opened in New York, 1988, with Boyd Gaines and Drew McVety, directed by Daniel Sullivan. It was telecast in 1995. § Wasserstein, W. *The Heidi Chronicles*. Dramatists, 1990. 75p.

189   *Polygraph* (1988) | **Robert Lepage (1957–) and Marie Brassard (unknown), Canadian**

[Crime drama; 2M, 1W; unit set.] Basing their play on a true experience that Lepage endured (in which he was for a while a murder suspect), the co-authors/actors developed the script through improvisions with the third actor, Pierre Phillipe Guay, so that it constantly went through revisions. The play utilizes film techniques to look at the triangular relationship of François Tremblay, a gay political science student turned waiter, Lucie Champagne, an actress who lives next door to him, and David Haussmann, a criminologist originally from East Berlin. David and Lucie meet when she witnesses a suicide in the subway. She is an actress set to play the role of a murder victim in a film, not knowing her character is based upon a friend of François. More, it turns out that David is the one who administered the polygraph test that upheld his innocence, a fact, however, that was not disclosed. Probably as a result of his ordeal, François sought satisfaction through S/M games. Now finding out that Lucie is reenacting his friend, he sinks into depression. The highly stylized play ends with his throwing himself in front of a subway train. *La polygraphe* opened in Quebec, 1988. The second version was translated for its English premiere in London, 1989, with the same cast (Guay playing François), directed by Page. It was adapted as a film in 1996. § Lepage, R., and Brassard, M. *Polygraph*.

Trans. by Gyllian Raby. Methuen Drama, 1997. 44p.

190 *Single Spies* (1988) | **Alan Bennett (1934–), English**

[Biographical studies; 8M, 1W; 3 sets.] The evening consists of two short plays about the gay Cambridge spies Guy Burgess (1911–1963) and Anthony Blunt (1907–1983). *An Englishman Abroad* was based on an incident related to Bennett by the Australian actor Coral Browne about her meeting Burgess in Moscow in 1958. It is a wry comedy centered on Burgess's request that she purchase him a new suit and some pajamas when she returns to London. The irrepressible Guy is quite open about his sexuality, introducing her to his Communist-supplied Russian boyfriend. He is a virtual prisoner, but he admits no regrets save that he misses English gossip. Coral muses, "it occurs to me that we have sat here all afternoon pretending that spying, which is what you did, darling, was just a minor social misdemeanour, no worse—and I'm sure in certain people's minds much better—than being caught in a public lavatory the way gentlemen in profession constantly are, and that is just something one shouldn't mention. Out of politeness."

More interesting is the second play, *A Question of Attribution*. Blunt was an art historian and Surveyor of the Queen's Pictures. He is fascinated by a painting attributed to Titian. Cleaning revealed portraits of three, not just two men; then x-rays uncovered a fourth and a fifth, just as the spy ring was uncovered a man at a time after Burgess's and Maclean's flight. At the time of the play, the late 1960s, Blunt has confessed but been granted immunity; his activities are still unknown to the public. He and the Queen have a long discussion about the Titian. He sums up, "Because something is not what it is said to be, Ma'am, does not mean it is a fake. It may just have been wrongly attributed." Blunt's homosexuality is barely hinted at, though he clearly has an eye for good-looking males. Bennett and Simon Callow directed and starred in the London production, 1988. *An Englishman Abroad* began as a teleplay in 1982; *A Question of Attribution* was adapted as a teleplay in 1991. § Bennett, A. *Plays Two*. Faber & Faber, 1998. 273–351.

191 *This Island's Mine* (1988) | **Philip Osment (unknown), English**

[Political drama; 4M, 3W; unit set.] In a series of thirty-four poems that form a dramatic narrative, the actors speaking often in the third person about themselves, Osment reflects on the ordeals of sexual and ethnic refugees reeling from the economic and homophobic blows of the Thatcher government, the AIDS epidemic, and the ethnic violence of the period. Shakespeare's *Tempest* provides an ironic counterpoint to the action: Caliban, whose island it is, is treated as an outcast. Young Luke flees the narrowness of his hometown to join his gay uncle Martin in London. There he encounters an intertwined community of other bruised souls. Mark is fired from his job as a waiter because he is gay and his fellow workers fear contacting AIDS from him. Mark's lover Selwyn is beaten up by the police because he is black. A Russian refugee warns, "They want someone to blame." Prospero will not act responsibly. The narratives, particularly Martin's, refer to America's earlier witch hunts and to the aftermath of the Stonewall Inn riots, but no parallel is drawn between Thatcher and Reagan. The audience does learn of an American father of one of the U.S. refugees who feels no guilt about sending possibly tainted blood to third world countries; the profit motive reigns paramount. The evening still ends affirmatively. Luke's heart is broken by his first love, but he is ready to set off into the "unknown future." The play opened in London, 1988, with Paul Cowling, Robert Ray, Richard Sandells, and Peter Shorey, directed by Osment. § In Osment, P. ed. *Gay Sweatshop*. 81–120.

192 *Zero Positive* (1988) | **Harry Kondoleon (1955–1994), American**

[AIDS drama; 4M, 2W; 1 set.] This play is more straightforward than many of the works Kondoleon wrote, but his sense of absurdity crops up not only in a pseudo–Greek play in Act 2 with all its parallels to the present situation but also in the model trains that endlessly circle the tracks in an apartment. Himmer and Samantha both test seropositive, which Himmer hears as zero positive: "The zero for the infinite nothingness and the plus sign like a cross on the grave." Their friend Prentice is against the tests. He laments that "the whole romance angle of life has been drained out of everyday experience. Everyone meets everyone else and suspects they're meeting their executioner, it makes the most casual overtures seem [...] extinctive."

Other frustrated lives intertwine theirs. Himmer's father has retreated to the time he and Himmer's mother were married and happy. Patrick is so distraught over his failed acting career that he attempts suicide: "I want to make a difference. I want to know when I go off it makes sense that I came on in the first place." Deborah just wants to find something worthwhile to support with all her money. To this end she agrees to back Himmer's mother's play *The Ruins of Athens*, using proceeds to inaugurate a research center. Himmer proposes making Socrates's potion of hemlock a true poison for anyone so inclined to drink. But he begins to have second thoughts, and instead his father is the one who drinks the fatal brew. The play opened in New York, 1988, with David Hyde Pierce, directed by Ken Elliott. § In Osborn, M. E., ed. *The Way We Live Now*. 205–79.

193 *Adam and the Experts* (1989) | Victor Bumbalo, American

[AIDS drama; 5M, 2W; flexible set.] Bumbalo manages to find humor in the AIDS crisis even as his play chronicles one man's struggle with the virus and his ultimate death. Adam is the central character. Though they are not lovers, he loves Eddie and tries, often overbearingly, to help him. To this end Adam drags Eddie to quack healers, and himself consults a priest (who fears he has contacted the virus). Eddie says to Adam, "I'm not a person to you anymore. I'm a [...] disease." Eddie takes a more rational approach, marrying their friend Sarah for her health insurance benefits. He inadvertently messes up by requesting a helper from the Gay Men's Health Crisis Center, whom he ends up having to comfort when the would-be buddy breaks down in sobs. Another friend also becomes a burden while Eddie is in the hospital: "Between the nurses waking you up for no reason and Jim's endless phone calls, if I don't get home soon, I'm going to drop dead of exhaustion." Under the stress of denial, Adam's psyche splits; since he persists in talking to his alter ego as if it is really present, he leaves confusion in his wake, especially when a conversation with his unseen other dovetails with the conversation he is having with an actual person. But after Eddie's death, Adam affirms, "There are too many dead. Too, too many. [...] I don't want to forget. Not anymore. We have to remember what they were like to hold, touch, and love. If we do that, we won't be like a tribe that vanishes forever." The premiere was in New York, 1989, with John Finch and Benjamin Evett, directed by Nicholas Deutsch. § Bumbalo, V. *Adam and the Experts*. Broadway Play, 1990. 78p.

194 *Amulets Against the Dragon Forces* (1989) | Paul Zindel (1936–2003), American

[Adolescent drama; 5M, 2W; unit set.] The setting is Staten Island, 1955. The characters seem marginalized in much the same way the borough is from the rest of the city. In a time before hospice, young Chris's mother specializes in caring for the terminally ill. They end up in Floyd DiPardi's home looking after his dying mother. They find also teenager Harold Farley, a former street hustler who shares Floyd's bed. Neither particularly tries to hide the relationship. Chris creates an imaginative world that seems inspired by Joseph Campbell's description of the heroic journey. He shares it with Harold and convinces him that the two should leave for Florida to join Chris's father. Chris's father rejects the idea; Floyd fights to keep Harold with him. They reveal that they know Chris has fooled around with two night employees he encountered during a former assignment his mother had. Chris reveals that a drunken Floyd picked him up and passed out without doing anything. He tells Floyd, "I want to learn how to love ... whoever I love.... I don't want to be ashamed and angry like you." Floyd begs Chris not to be afraid of "that part of you you don't like so much [...]. Someday it may fit you more kindly." The play opened in New York, 1989, with Matt McGrath, Loren Dean, and John Spencer, directed by B. Rodney Marriott. § Zindel, P. *Amulets Against the Dragon Forces*. Dramatists, 1989. 69p.

195 *Ancient Boys: A Requiem* (1989–90) | Jean-Claude van Itallie (BEL 1936–), American

[AIDS drama; 4M, 1W; unit set.] Four friends gather in August 1984 to remember their friend Reuben, a conceptual artist who died of AIDS. These memories of their interactions with him are reenacted on stage. Slides that he has assembled as part of his art montage appear on screen along with the music he chose to accompany them. All the time the dead Reuben is constructing a giant pyramid made out of found pieces, into which he retreats. The play differs from most AIDS plays in projecting a rather negative outlook on gayness. Talking to a psychotherapist, Reuben muses, "AIDS is like one of the Biblical plagues [...]. Alzheimer's is another. They're warnings. [...] Something to do with the planet. We are the earth [...]. We're her consciousness. When we're sick, she's sick. If the earth dies because of our pollution, it'll be earth suicide. The hole in her ozone is the biggest cancer of all. And it's there because we just can't stop ourselves [...]. We're out of control, like a wild, horny teenager in the cockpit of spaceship earth." He goes on, "We may not find a physical cure for AIDS until we learn what AIDS energy means. And why it's happening now." The play was van Itallie's response to the death of his friend, puppeteer Robert Anton. He revised the printed version for its first performance, 1990, in Boulder, Colo., directed by Joel Fink. § In Kourilsky, F., and Temerson, C., eds. *Gay Plays*. 329–93.

196   *The Death of Peter Pan* (1989) | **Barry Lowe (1947–), Australian**

[Biographical study; 7M, 2W; flexible set.] Lowe bases his play on the known facts about the last years of Michael Davies (1900–1921), one of the boys who inspired their guardian James Barrie's *Peter Pan*. It begins on November 11, 1918, while Michael is still at Eton. He meets Rupert Buxton, a Harrow boy, and is immediately attracted to him. But Michael has trouble accepting the fact, even though his friend Roger Senhouse is quite open in his comments about other men, openly flirting with a waiter while they are in Paris. A third Eton friend, Arthur Basset, represents England's puritanism; he becomes apprehensive about Rupert's growing influence on Michael. Rupert wins by deliberately stripping naked to pose for Michael's sketchbook. The four lads end up at Oxford; nearby is Sandford Pool, where a monument commemorates two students who drowned in 1843. Roger borrows a copy of E. M. Forster's *Maurice*. Michael is moved by the novel: "It has a happy ending. No one commits suicide." He wonders, "had there been a book like this available would those two poor friends have drowned themselves [...]?" Arthur brings news of a friend who killed himself after being caught with a man in Kensington Gardens and smugly informs Michael and Rupert that everyone, including their dean, knows they are having sex "at Sandford Pool. At night." Feeling trapped, Michael and Rupert return to their Edenic bower and strip, preparatory to drowning themselves, Michael says wistfully, "Obviously it is still too soon for happy endings."

There are other homosexual ties. Nico, the youngest of the Davies boys, develops a special friendship with a younger boy at his school; when Barrie (1860–1937) is informed, he irritably observes, "It seems your tutor cannot distinguish the joys of boyhood friendships from the squalor of his imagination." Rupert calls attention to Barrie's fondness of Michael: "You do realise, don't you, that he loves you the way I do?" When Michael assures him that Barrie has never touched him, Rupert says, "That's his tragedy." The play opened in Carlton (Melbourne), 1989, with David Tredinnick, Sam Sejavka, and Kevin Hopkins, directed by Robert Chuter. The script was subsequently revised. Lowe is one of Australia's most prolific gay writers; he also did the screenplay for the 1997 film *Violet's Visit*. § Lowe, B. *The Death of Peter Pan*. Playscript, n.d. 111p.

197   *Hyde in Hollywood* (1989) | **Peter Parnell (1953–), American**

[Hollywood satire; 10M, 3W, extras; flexible set.] In a reflection of the vagaries of gaining a critical reputation, whereas D. S. Lawson (in E. Nelson, *Contemporary* [...] *Playwrights*, 354) calls Parnell "one of the most imaginative and inventive theatrical voices in American literature since Edward Albee," neither Sinfield nor Clum even mentions him. This play "features the first major character in Parnell's mature work to be overtly depicted as gay" (Lawson, 351–52). More implicitly than explicitly, it judges Hollywood, particularly MGM, for not having the courage to stand up to America's political, religious, and sexual hatemongers: "Why is a business so in love with courage so frightened itself?" Herman Buss, aka Hollywood Confidential, unleashes a campaign against degenerates. Inevitably Hyde, a gay Jewish actor and director, becomes one of his targets, not least because he has entered into a sham marriage with a starlet whom Herman is in love with and whom he kills. Recognizing what a danger Herman is to democracy, without yet knowing the full truth of Herman's culpability, Hyde begins a film *Harry Babylon: His Rise and Fall* in which he plays the title role. It turns out to be his last film, an acclaimed masterpiece. Hyde discovers the truth about Herman's guilt. The two fight atop one of the giant Hollywoodland letters. Both fall, Herman to his death. Twenty years later Hyde is interviewed by his scriptwriter's son. He is now wheelchair bound because of his "wooden, hollow" legs. A postmodern exercise, the play is set in 1939, but the action seems more appropriate to the 1950s, the heyday of *Confidential* magazine and McCarthyism. The interview is dated 1959, the year Kenneth Anger published *Hollywood Babylon*. All sorts of allusions and veiled historical references dot the script. The premiere was in New York, 1989, with Robert Joy, directed by Gerald Gutierrez. It was telecast in 1991. § Parnell, P. *Hyde in Hollywood*. Broadway Play, 1991. 101p.

198   *Saint Oscar* (1989) | **Terry Eagleton (1943–), English**

[Biographical study; 6M, 1W, chorus; flexible set.] Eagleton, a literary theorist of Irish descent, sees Wilde as a subversive whole: Irish colonial, *déraciné*, radical, socialist, homosexual, perverse, a man of the theater, and a precursor of Roland Barthes. "I'm a fifth columnist [...], a spy, a changeling, an alien smuggled into the upper class to corrupt their offspring. Or do I mean a double agent? I dine with dukes and prowl the slums at night. Sometimes I get a bit confused about which side I'm on," Wilde tells a friend. The play consists of five set pieces: an interview with his mother, a conversation with his friend Richard Wallace (an imaginary character), the trial with the prosecution undertaken by Irish barrister Edward Carson, Douglas's visit to him in prison, and Wallace's and then Carson's encounter with him in Paris. The play is filled with quips, all but one invented by Eagleton. Among others, at his trial he throws out the very Irish charge against the English system, "You subjugate whole races, you condemn the mass of your own people to wretched toil, you have reduced my own nation to misery and despair, and all you can think about is which sexual organ goes in where." The play opened in Derry, N.I., 1989, with Stephen Rea and Peter Hanly, directed by Trevor Griffiths. It was telecast in 1991. Eagleton was one of the co-authors of the screenplay for Derek Jarman's *Wittgenstein*, 1993. § Eagleton, T. *Saint Oscar*. Field Day, 1989. 66p.

199   *The Sum of Us* (1989) | **David Stevens (PSE 1940–), Australian**

[Domestic comedy; 3M, 1W; 2 sets.] Stevens earlier directed a pre–AIDS comedy set in an Australian STD medical facility (*The Clinic*, 1982). This *Comedy of Love* remains his biggest theatrical hit. Ironically, a father's complete acceptance of his gay son creates problems. Single father Harry Mitchell has tried to understand and back up Jeff ever since he discovered him at age "fourteen [...] up Willy Jones's bum." When Jeff brings Greg home from a bar, Greg is startled by the way Harry treats his appearance as perfectly ordinary: "It hurts a bit, makes me feel guilty about—about what we do. Maybe it's too domestic. Sort of makes the atmosphere—I dunno—not very sexy." He flees. So does the woman Harry meets via a dating service; she cannot accept sharing a home with an openly gay stepson. Harry suffers a debilitating stroke, rendering him incapable of speaking. In the final scene he and Jeff are in the park when Greg reappears. He has finally come out to his parents and been kicked out of the house. There is a clear possibility that the two young men will get back together. The play is set in a Melbourne blue-collar milieu: Jeff is a plumber; Greg a gardener. Its premiere was in Williamstown, Mass., 1989. It came to New York, 1990, with Tony Goldwyn and Neil Maffinand, directed by Kevin Dowling; it opened in Sydney, 1992. Stevens wrote the script for the 1994 film. § Stevens, D. *The Sum of Us: A Comedy of Love*. Fireside Theatre, 1990. 110p.

200   *Unidentified Human Remains and the True Nature of Love* (1989) | **Brad Fraser (1959–), Canadian**

[Crime drama; 4M, 3W; flexible set.] Ric Knowles (in E.-M. Kröller, *Canadian Literature*, 126) sums up Frazer: his "plays revel in clever lines, shallow characterization, sex, violence, comic-book captions, and the production of Beaumont-and-Fletcheresque *frisson*." Here, a serial killer is attacking women in Edmonton. The gay community is facing inroads being made by AIDS. David, the main character, in talking unknowingly to the serial killer, says, "It kills you, Bernie. It doesn't matter who you are." When asked if he thinks about it "that much," David responds, "All the time." It is left up to the playgoer, however, to infer parallels between murderer and virus; the play is more interested in presenting variations on urban legends. Benita, a psychic, recounts several throughout the evening. The play touches on various troublesome issues without analyzing them. What does it mean that a closeted homosexual is the serial killer? David, who works as a waiter after an unhappy experience as a television actor in Toronto, toys with his 17-year-old busboy for no good reason. David's apartment mate Candy seems a more sympathetic character, but she mistreats a lesbian with whom she has a one-night fling and behaves irresponsibly with a man who turns out to be married. (He also acts as a momentary red herring, leading the audience to think he might be the serial killer.) The premiere was in Calgary, 1989, with John Moffat and Peter Smith, directed by Fraser, Bob White, and Susan Ferley. Fraser wrote the screenplay for the 1993 film version, *Love and Human Remains*. *Poor Superman*, 1993, is something of a sequel, about David's involvement with a married man. Fraser wrote the script for its film version, *Leaving Metropolis*, 2002. § Fraser, B. *Unidentified Human Remains and the True Nature of Love*. NeWest, 1996. 123p. Bound with *Love and Human Remains*.

Early Nineties, 1990–1994

Jeffrey Dahmer arrested, 1991. Australia and Canada permit gays to serve in military, 1992. U.S. adopts disastrous "Don't Ask, Don't Tell" policy for military, 1993. Ireland decriminalizes homosexuality, 1993. AMA removes homosexuality from list of illnesses, 1994.

201 *Advice from a Caterpillar* (1990–91) | **Douglas Carter Beane (1959–), American**

[Sexual comedy; 3M, 1W; 2 sets.] The play in many ways remains Beane's most honest. It maps out the interactions of a straight woman (Missy) with a straight (Suit), a bisexual (Brat), and a gay (Spaz) man. A conceptual artist beginning to break into the big time, she is "the other woman" in the married Suit's life, with mixed feelings about her status. Spaz, her best friend, is a performance artist/caterer. Brat is his lover, an actor with a fixation on Bertolt Brecht. Spaz becomes aware that Brat is paying a bit too much attention to Missy. Indeed, they end up having sex and falling in love. The two decide to commit, even after Brat acknowledges the truth of what Suit says to Missy: that she is contemplating changing her life for "a guy who has no job right now, no hints of jobs in the future, no security, is an admitted bisexual, at any minute may just desert you for a senate page or an Olympic skater or even another woman. And who knows? Is perhaps carrying a deadly virus that there is no known cure for." But Spaz observes, "Love, in whatever combination, is what matters." Perhaps they have fallen down the rabbit hole, but so what? Following a college production, the play was revised extensively before its debut in New York, 1990, with Eric Swanson and Michael Ornstein, directed by Edgar Lansbury. The script was further revised for its second New York production the next year. Beane also wrote the screenplay for the 1999 film. His first screenplay was for the dismal *To Wong Foo Thanks for Everything, Julie Newmar*, 1995. § Beane, D. C. *Advice from a Caterpillar: A Comedy in Two Acts*. French, 1991. 79p.

202 *The American Plan* (1990) | **Richard Greenberg, American**

[Domestic drama; 2M, 3W; 2 sets.] Set in the late 1960s, with a coda dated ten years afterwards, the play has a Jamesian quality, at the same time it is Williams-like. Lili Adler is a desperately unhappy young heiress anxious to get away from her overbearing mother, a German refugee. They are passing the summer at their opulent vacation home in the Catskills. Nick Lockridge, a gigolo on the make, shows up on their beach, pretending to think it's part of the nearby hotel property. The mother in effect buys Nick for her daughter. But then she catches him kissing Gil Harbison, who has tracked Nick down. Gil proposes they both marry: "We become excellent husbands. We prosper. We sire wonderful children. Our families become best friends. And we're … us … our whole lives. That's my plan." The mother stops the plan before it can unfold. After her death, Nick visits Lili in her New York home. Nothing is said specifically, but perhaps he is hoping for a second chance at her or her fortune. Lili tells him he should have been more steadfast before: "Do you really think I didn't know? […] I would have gone with you anyway—Anything to get out of this place! […] I would have let you have your life." It is too late. The play opened in New York, 1990, with Tate Donovan and Eric Stoltz, directed by Lynne Meadow.

§ Greenberg, R. *Three Days of Rain and Other Plays* [cover]. Grove, 1999. 87–167.

203 *The Baltimore Waltz* (1990) | **Paula Vogel (1951–), American**

[AIDS fantasy; 2M, 1W; flexible set.] Vogel takes a highly idiosyncratic approach to dramatizing the AIDS crisis. Her elegy is dedicated "*To the memory of Carl—because I cannot sew*" (a panel for the AIDS quilt). Carl, her brother, died in 1988. When the curtain falls, the audience realizes that the opening and closing scenes recall his struggle and death, while all the other scenes are a fantasia in which Vogel's alter ego Anna suffers from ATD, Acquired Toilet Disease, which unmarried elementary school teachers are particularly vulnerable to. Carl persuades her to seek an unorthodox cure prescribed by a Viennese doctor. He assures her, "It's not a crime. It's an illness." While Carl is cruising with his stuffed bunny prominently displayed, Anna goes through Kübler-Ross's six stages—to which an anonymous character adds a seventh: Lust. A student activist holds, "There is something radical in two complete strangers committing biological necessity without having to give into bourgeois conventions of love, without breeding to produce workers for a capitalist system, without the benediction of the church, the family, the bosses." In the last scene Anna crashes back into John Waters's Baltimore, where Carl dies. The premiere was in Douglas, Alaska, 1990, with Rick Bundy, directed by Annie Stokes-Hutchinson. § In Hodges, B., ed. *Out Plays*. 528–66. In Lane, E., and Shengold, N., eds. *Actor's Book*. 491–536.

204 *Blood and Honour* (1990) | **Alex Harding (GBR 1949–), Australian**

[AIDS drama; 2M, 1W; unit set.] Harding dedicated his play to his partner, who died of AIDS. It is fueled by anger, naming names and calling out political homophobes; it likewise attacks racism, seeking a common union among all marginalized persons. The mother says, "Again it's being done by men: old politicians; young politicians with an eye for the main chance; yabba, yabba, [Michael] Yabsley clones, all lacking in any imagination. No sense of the richness of diversity. Insisting that we must *all* be the same, pure!" Colin Peters, a television journalist, has contacted the virus. His lover, Michael Yang, of Asian descent, is HIV-negative, but some suspect he has infected Colin just because of his ethnicity. Colin's mother has grown from being a stereotypical wife of a career diplomat to a feminist and now a proud supporter of her son and his partner. The actors also play other characters, including the virus itself, to provide a rich density to the text. In their own voice they vow to take control, and both Colin and Michael come out publicly. The play opened in Sidney, 1990, with John Turnbull and Anthony Wong, directed by Margaret Davis. § In Parr, B., ed. *Australian Gay and Lesbian Plays*. 237–76.

205 *La Maison Suspendue* (1990) | **Michel Tremblay, Canadian**

[Domestic drama; 5M, 3W; 1 set.] The lives of three generations intertwine through their occupancy of the family home in 1910, 1950, and 1990, moments from one year echoing across the other years. A couple—Jean-Marc, a former professor, and Mathieu, an actor, the father of an 11-year-old boy—arrive toward evening. Mathieu never had a family before his marriage; Jean-Marc is trying to come to terms with the ghosts of his. His great-uncle was also his grandfather. In order to provide an accepted family unit for Jean-Marc's father, his grandmother enters a marriage of convenience, vowing never to see her beloved brother again. Jean-Marc's aunt is homophobic, perpetually angry with her gay brother Édouard, who likes to dress in drag. His sister-in-law, Jean-Marc's mother, accepts Édouard the way he is. Mathieu is learning to accept Jean-Marc for the way he is, as the latter tries to open up, to reveal more of himself. All this happens contrapuntally rather than sequentially, with three children—Jean-Marc's father, a cousin, and Mathieu's son—blending into one. *La maison suspendue* premiered in Montreal, 1990. The same year the English version opened in Toronto with Guy Thauvette, Simon Fortin, and Claude Gai, directed by John Van Burek. § Tremblay, M. *La Maison Suspendue*. Trans. by J. Van Burek. Talonbooks, 1991. 101p.

206 *Once in a While the Odd Thing Happens* (1990) | **Paul Godfrey (1960–), English**

[Biographical study; 4M, 2W; flexible set.] Written in free verse and based on interviews that Godfrey conducted with Britten's sister and others who knew him, this *Play from the Life of Benjamin Britten* (1913–1976) offers impressionistic glimpses of the composer's years during which he collaborated with W. H. Auden (1907–1973) on *Paul Bunyan* and went on to write "the first grand opera in English," *Peter Grimes*. The latter is to star Britten's great love Peter Pears (1910–1986). Godfrey shows us the deep, if publicly restrained ties that existed between the two men, creating (in Clum's words, *Still Acting*, 194) "a gay artist-hero [...,] one contemporary gay men can unreservedly celebrate." A telling exchange occurs prior to a recital. Pears announces, "Passion overwhelms me"; Britten responds, "Is this the effect singing Michelangelo Sonnets / has upon you? Some say Michelangelo / wasn't you know and these love sonnets they / aren't either." Pears says, "So no one can complain when I sing of my love / for you in public?" The play also drops hints about Britten's abiding if chaste interest in young boys. The momentary appearance of a member of the opera's chorus gives us a glimpse of the homophobia that surrounds the two men. He pleads for a delay in the opera's premiere. After insisting that there is "nothing personal" in his request, the exchange accelerates to his labeling *Grimes* "Your precious opera with your 'friend' in the / starring role" and threatening, "you may regret this one day. / When we come to round up people like you." Britten declaims, "I am not ashamed! / [...] / Here / I am." The play opened in London, 1990, with Michael Maloney, Julian Wadham, and Stephen Boxer, directed by Godfrey. Alan Bennett later has his own take on Britten and Auden. § Godfrey, P. *Plays 1*. Methuen Drama, 1998. 145–232.

207 *Six Degrees of Separation* (1990) | John Guare (1938–), American

[Domestic comedy; 13M, 4W; unit set.] Based on the true story of a gay African American con artist, the play uses a narrative style, his victims describing their part in his scam as we see it unfolding. Paul targets the art dealers Flanders and Louisa Kittredge, appearing at their door covered in blood from an alleged mugging. He claims to know their two children at Harvard. Robbed, he throws himself on their mercy until he can meet up with his father, the actor Sidney Poitier. When Louisa goes to rouse him the next morning, she discovers him in bed with a hustler he has hired with the money they gave him. He says later, "I was so happy. I wanted to add sex to it." The Kittredges meet friends and discover they are not the first to be taken in. In the friends' case Paul was found "chasing this naked blonde thief down the corridor." The Kittredges find out that their children know nothing of Paul, but their schoolmate Trent Conway must have been his source of information. Indeed, this "Henry Higgins of our time" virtually created Paul while they were lovers for three months. Matters take a darker turn when Paul seizes upon a couple from Utah aspiring to become actors. He seduces the man and takes their cash reserve, which he then squanders on an evening on the town with him. Rick is ecstatic about their sex together: "I had never done anything like that [...] and it was fantastic. It was the greatest night I ever had." But when he has to face his girlfriend, he kills himself. Paul is arrested and disappears into the prison system. Louisa tries to find out what has happened to him, but no one knows his real name. The play opened in New York, 1990, with James McDaniel and John Cameron Mitchell, directed by Jerry Zaks. § Guare, J. *Six Degrees of Separation*. Dramatists, 1992. 63p.

208 *The Stanley Parkers* (1990) | Geraldine Aron (1951–), Irish

[AIDS romance; 2M; 1 set.] Speaking a loose verse directly to the audience, an Irish couple recount their life together. Stanley Parker worked for a design shop; Dimitri Papavasilopoulos designs lamp shades. They have bought a house together: "Graffiti appeared on the wall of our garden: / 'Two geriatric perverts live here' / Is that how folks see us? / I'm upset, I'll be honest. / Geriatric indeed. Bloody cheek!" Dimitri's mother approves of their relationship; Stanley's does not. They have flings with others—Stanley especially, to bolster his dwindling ego after he loses his position. As a result he contacts HIV, and his body begins to fail. Dimitri stays faithfully with him. The play concludes with his Zorba-like dance against the ravages of time. The play opened in Galway, 1990, with Des Keogh and Michael Roberts, directed by Garry Hynes. § Aron, G. *The Stanley Parkers: A Play*. French, 1995. 18p.

209 *Angels in America: A Gay Fantasia on National Themes* (1991–92) | Tony Kushner, American

[AIDS fantasy; 5M, 3W; flexible set.] The two-part play—*Millennium Approaches* and *Perestroika*—is undoubtedly still the most esteemed gay play on the American stage. Set in New York, it covers the period October 1985 through February 1986, with an epilogue set in February 1990. It mixes historical and fictional figures, living humans and ghosts, reality and visions, all in a highly theatrical manner. Kushner does not shy away from taking on politics and calling out traitors to the human spirit—in particular key figures in the Reagan administration, including the president himself: "Selfish and greedy and loveless and blind. Reagan's children." Roy Cohn (1927–1986) is a major character. He denies that he is homosexual, because homosexuals "have zero clout" and that does not describe him. By this logic, he cannot be suffering from AIDS because "AIDS is what homosexuals have." Therefore, he has "liver cancer." While lying in his hospital bed, he is haunted by the ghost of Ethel Rosenberg, whom Kushner accuses Cohn of having murdered. Questions are raised about the meaning of America. Belize, an African American nurse, ex–drag queen, admits he hates the country; he (inaccurately) claims, "The white cracker who wrote the national anthem knew what he was doing. He set the word 'free' to a note so high nobody can reach it." One of the main characters praises Mikhail Gorbachev after the fall of the Berlin Wall: "Whatever comes, what you have to admire in Gorbachev, in the Russians is that they're making a leap into the unknown." (The speaker clearly does not anticipate that the unknown will include Vladimir Putin.) Although Judaism plays an important role, Mormonism, an indigenous American religion, propels many of the key plot elements. It provides a comic moment when the two visionaries Prior Walter and Harper Pitt meet in a dream sequence. Harper says, "In my church we don't believe in homosexuals"; Prior responds, "In my church we don't believe in Mormons." Prior will become the new prophet: "This disease will be the end of many of us, but not nearly all, and the dead will be commemorated and will struggle on with the living, and we are not going away. We won't die secret deaths anymore. The world only spins forward. We will be citizens. The time has come."

The play has some thirty characters played by eight actors. The main plot involves the relationships among three gay men and a straight woman. Prior is suffering from the first onslaughts of AIDS. His lover of over four years, Louis Ironson, does not have the iron to face Prior's suffering and eventful death. He flees. Always talking, trying to philosophize, driven to cruising Central Park, he keeps crossing the path of Joe Pitt, "married probably bisexual Mormon Republican closet case." Louis brings Joe out, even as he continues to feel guilty about his shabby treatment of Prior. Joe allows the relationship to build, even as he feels guilty about having failed his wife Harper and his religion. Harper retreats to her visions. Prior is visited by an angel crashing through the ceiling of his bedroom at the end of Part One. More angels appear in Part Two. They are messengers, but "they have *no* imagination, they can *do* anything but can't invent, create, they're sort of fabulous and dull all at once." It is left to people to realize their "potential in the design for change, for random events, for movement forward." Roy dies. Belize learns forgiveness. Joe sheds his temple garment. Louis tries to return to Prior but gains no absolution. Harper ventures out into the real world. Prior accepts that "The Great Work Begins." The general consensus is that Part Two is not so powerful as Part One. It seems bloated in comparison to the muscular strength of the first part; Kushner admits that it did not gain the tight editing that Part One did. The English critic Sinfield (*Out*, 207) offers an interesting dissent to the general acclaim the play has received: "*Angels in America* slides into the cloudiness of irony, symbolism and produndity [*sic*] at moments where clear elucidation would be valuable." Part One, *Millennium Approaches*, premiered in San Francisco, 1991, with Michael Scott Ryan, Michael Ornstein, Stephen Spinella, John Bellucci, and Harry Waters, Jr., directed by David Esbjornson. Part Two, *Perestroika*, premiered in Los Angeles, 1992, with Jeffrey King, Joe Mantello, Stephen Spinella, Ron Leibman, and K. Todd Freeman, directed by Oskar Eustis and Tony Taccone. Kushner adapted the script for a 2003 television series. An opera version by Peter Eotvos opened in Paris, 2004. § Kushner, T. *Angels in America: A Gay Fantasia on National Themes.* Theatre Communications, 1995. 307p.

210 *The Best of Schools* (1991) | Jean-Marie Besset (1959–), French

[School drama; 4M, 2W; 1 set.] Besset was living in New York at the time he wrote *Grande École*. At core the play is a critique of the prevailing socioeconomic order in France. Paul Thabor and Louis-Arnault Real have been accepted to one of its *grandes écoles*, those prestigious schools of higher learning that graduate the country's elite; they share a student apartment. Louis-Arnault fits into the school easily by birth and by his interest in finance; Paul is the misfit, uninterested in economics but attracted by Louis-Arnault's aura. His girlfriend Agnes picks up on the attraction and challenges him to a contest: "Let's see which one of us can seduce Louis-Arnault first." Amid much talk of finance, literature, and philosophy, their lives play out. Louis-Arnault arrives back from a walk, seriously wounded by a street kid he called out for stealing a shopping cart. During his recuperation Agnes almost succeeds in seducing him, but is interrupted by Louis-Arnault's girlfriend. Paul spends the night with Mecir, a worker at the school, who turns out to be the one who stabbed Louis-Arnault. Paul stops him from assaulting the teenager, and Louis-Arnault quits the apartment. Paul and Agnes are left alone. Paul tells her he has won: "I had him. I had Louis-Arnault." He dates the encounter as the same evening he was with Mecir, leaving one to suspect he is lying. But Paul is clearly moving in a new, more egalitarian direction. The play was published, in English translation, in 1991. Its world premiere, in this translation, took place in New York in 1992 with Jonathan Friedman, Justin Walker, and Gil Bellows, directed by Evan Yionoulis. It did not appear in Paris until 1995. Besset prepared the screenplay for the 2005 film with its director Robert Salis, greatly fleshing out the story. § Besset, J.-M. *The Best of Schools.* Trans. by Mark O'Donnell. Ubu, 1991. 92p.

211 *Brave Hearts* (1991) | **Harry Rintoul (1956–2002), Canadian**

[AIDS romance; 2M; 1 set.] In this quiet play two men at a picnic table outside a home near Saskatoon talk. The older, Rafe, is a seismologist; G.W., some seven years younger, works on a horse ranch, having been kicked out of his home by his father because of his sexuality. He is largely at ease in his skin, though it comes out that he has invented a whopper to keep Rafe talking. Rafe is closeted, refusing to identify as fag or as gay. He claims, "I have a life. I don't have a lifestyle." He is also miserable, a recovering alcoholic who has no close friends. Through G.W.'s prodding, he realizes they have met once before when he was in an alcoholic haze. G.W. claims that Rafe saved his life: "I left the farm thinking I was nothing, that I was sick, that I didn't fit into the world and that the world had no place for me. I wasn't scared after I met you. I figured out for myself that I did fit." G.W. also reveals that he is HIV-positive, and for that reason he spurns a friendship. But Rafe responds, "I should decide that, not you." The play, Rintoul's most popular, ends with an ominous crack of thunder and G.W. in Rafe's arms. It opened in Toronto, 1991, with Murray Oliver and Ted Atherton, directed by Bryden MacDonald. § In Wallace, R., ed. *Making, Out.* 219–69.

212 *Bravely Fought the Queen* (1991) | **Mahesh Dattani (1958–), Indian**

[Family tragedy; 3M, 4W; 2 sets.] Dattani portrays a dysfunctional family suffering under the onus of a patriarchal society. The unseen Praful manipulated his two sisters into marrying his lover Niten and Niten's brutal, womanizing brother Jiten. Goaded by his mother, who discovers the sisters' mother was never legally married, Jiten savagely attacked his pregnant wife, causing her to deliver early and the daughter to be born deformed. His wife blocks out the world, living in her fantasies. Jiten's world falling apart around him, his last act is to deliberately kill a beggar woman who seeks refuge in their compound's courtyard. Niten refuses to give his wife children; she has become an alcoholic. He is promiscuous; not only does he regularly tryst with Praful, but he is also drawn to workers with muscular arms. His last act is to head to the back of the house, while his wife sleeps, to keep a rendezvous with a driver. This fierce attack on Indian hypocrisy opened in Mumbai in 1991 with Ashish Sen, directed by Dattani. § Dattani, M. *Collected Plays.* Penguin, 2000. 227–315.

213 *Flesh and Blood* (1991) | **Colin Thomas (1952–), Canadian**

[AIDS drama; 3M, 1W; flexible set.] Thomas wrote the play specifically for teenage audiences. Blood ties are tested when Jim, the older, gay brother, contracts AIDS. Allan, the younger, straight brother, fails to meet the challenge. Their growing up in a dysfunctional family, Jim has always tried to serve as a father-figure for Allan. When their mother overreacts to his having sex with his girlfriend, Jim takes him in. Reflecting the homophobic atmosphere in which they grew up, Jim is only mildly open about his relationship with Ralph, leading Allan to play semantic games: "Ralph's a fag. But Jim's not. I don't care what they do in bed, just so long's they don't go wavin' a flag about it." When Jim tests positive for the virus and becomes "afraid to have sex," even safe sex, he asks Ralph to leave. At first Allan reacts well to Jim's condition, but then he starts acting irresponsibly: getting drunk, forcing himself sexually on his girlfriend. When he finds that Jim may have picked up the virus by acting irresponsibly himself, he cuts out. Ralph remains faithful, reflecting again how families gays make are often stronger than the families we are given. He returns as Jim lies in a coma and confronts Allen: "You know what I think's really sad? Your brother's dying in there and you never even knew him." The play opened in Toronto, 1991, with Mark Saunders and Rob Osborne, directed by JoAnn McIntyre. § In Wallace, R., ed. *Making, Out*. 271–340.

214 *Furious* (1991) | Michael Gow (1955–), Australian

[Psychological drama; 3M, 3W; flexible set.] Earlier Gow presented *The Kid*, 1983, a satire about Australian culture. One character is gay, but the fact does not impact the plot. A more cunning work, constantly turning back upon itself in a self-referential way, *Furious* has as its central figure Roland Henning, a playwright who turns to his own past for his dramas. He is shocked to discover that his father was previously married and that he has a half-sister who disappeared after giving her son up for adoption. The first wife's niece delivers this unwelcome information; at the same time she asks Roland if he will coach her son Chris, 16, who is standing for a school exam on one of Roland's earlier works. With no warning, Roland asks the teenager, "You want to know the basic theme of the play? You want to know the basic theme of everything that's ever been written? *Roland goes straight to him, lifts him up and kisses him. Chris doesn't move. Roland releases Chris, but after the briefest moment, Chris pulls Roland back and kisses him.* You're so warm. Where's your room?" Roland recognizes that he has gone against social mores by having sex with a boy the same age as his unknown half-nephew. He tries to call the relationship off, but Chris resists. The mother finds out, but when she confronts Roland, he defies her. Having described graphically what the two do together, he sums up, "I've seen him do things you'll never see. I've seen him happier than you ever will. [...] I love your son." He begins a play based on his discoveries about his family and himself. Time and space blur so that it becomes difficult to know whether we are seeing the play or the play within the play as events repeat themselves in a distorted manner. Following a staged reading, *Furious* opened in Sydney, 1991, with Nicholas Eadie, directed by Gow. § In Parr, B., ed. *Australian Gay and Lesbian Plays*. 341–84.

215 *Mongrels* (1991) | Nick Enright (1950–2003), Australian

[Theater drama; 3M, 3W; flexible set.] The play fictionalizes the association of Peter Kenna and Jim McNeil. Katharine Brisbane in her introduction posits that Enright "chose to investigate this relationship between a pair of incongruous and yet confluent playwrights, and the artistic world they shared, as a way into an understanding of his own life and his own voice as a writer." Jealousy and mutual admiration define their troubled connection. Eddie Burke (McNeil) has the raw talent; Vincent O'Hara (Kenna) has the theatrical skill. Both are crippled: Burke by his personal demons which drive him to violence; O'Hara by a failing body which incapacitates his writing. O'Hara is openly gay; Burke has issues. Craig, an actor of ambiguous sexuality, admires O'Hara and dislikes the way he permits Burke to dominate him. By the end, Craig has become a successful playwright himself, having turned away from both their approaches and struck out on his own; he is also married. The play opened in Sydney, 1991, with Tony Sheldon, directed by Rhys McConnochie. § Enright, N. *Mongrels*. Currency, 1994. 77p.

216 *The Old Boy* (1991) | A. R. Gurney (1930–), American

[Social drama; 4M, 2W; unit set.] In a play so conventional that it seems to come from an earlier theatrical era, Gurney has one of his usual straight W.A.S.P. characters make an elegant plea for sexual understanding. Sam was "the old boy" assigned to mentor the new boy Perry Pell, another version of Tom Lee (*Tea and Sympathy*). Discovering Perry is gay, the womanizing Sam convinces him to "cure" himself by marriage to the girlfriend Sam is dropping as unsuitable for his career plans. Now back years later to deliver the commencement address at his old school, he meets up again with Perry's overbearing mother and the wife. For the first time, Sam learns that Perry's suicide resulted from his having AIDS. Against all advice from his assistant (Sam is planning to run for governor) he delivers his speech as a series of questions, asking "Why do we worry so much about unconventional forms of love? [...] If we so cherish religious tolerance, why not sexual tolerance as well? [...] What about the AIDS epidemic? Is this the result of sexual freedom, or sexual repression?" Overcome by emotion, Sam outs the dead Perry. Perry's mother is enraged. The play opened in New York, 1991, with Matt McGrath, directed by John Rubinstein. § Gurney, A. R. *The Old Boy*. Fireside, 1992. 108p.

217   *Raft of the Medusa* (1991) | Joe Pintauro, American

[AIDS drama; 8M, 3W; 1 set.] Dr. Jerry Rizzo presides over a largely dysfunctional AIDS support group. Its ten members include the ghost of a dead AIDS patient unseen by anyone save Jerry and Michael, the ghost's lover. Michael is a formerly married Vietnam veteran who alternately resents gays' promiscuity during the heady days of Gay Liberation and stands up against straights who blame gays for the epidemic and do nothing to find a cure. The other eight members are Alec, an actor who stands to lose his career if it is revealed he is gay and HIV-positive; two irrepressible clowns, an ex-model Tommy and a Hispanic construction worker Jimmy; two drug users, the provocative Alan, who contacted the virus either through a dirty needle or being gangbanged in prison, and Nairobi, a homeless black woman, a deaf mute; two straight women who were infected by their lovers, one who angrily blames gays for her plight, the other who is a lost Hispanic teenager; and Larry, a free-lance reporter against whom Michael reacts antagonistically, rightfully suspecting he is straight, HIV-negative, and a spy out to get a story. When Larry's recording device is exposed, Alan grabs him and Jimmy acts as if he is going to rape him. Jerry breaks up the scene, whereupon Nairobi rushes in and stabs Larry with a hypodermic needle. She lets him believe he has been infected before revealing that it is clean. Michael exclaims that they have witnessed "The miracle we've all been waiting for. [...] Of being delivered from it. He's got his whole life ahead of him." The play ends with a dance. Following an earlier lab production, the play opened in New York in 1991 with Steven Keats, Robert Alexander, and Reggie Montgomery, directed by Sal Trapani. The script was subsequently revised. This is not Pintauro's first AIDS play. *Rosen's Son*, 1987, is a moving account of a father berating his son's lover for not remaining faithful to his son's memory longer after his death from AIDS. § *Plays by Joe Pintauro: Full-Length Plays*. Broadway Play, 2005. 63–114.

218   *The Saints and Apostles* (1991) | Raymond Storey (1956–), Canadian

[AIDS drama; 3M, 2W; flexible set.] As indicated by the play's title, Storey attempts to bring a spiritual element to his story of doomed love, treating AIDS as if it were a Biblical plague. Daniel Vanderlee has a crush on stage director Michael Denton, fourteen years his senior. He initially frightens Michael by blurting out, "I'm HIV positive." Michael feels conflicted when he realizes he is about to "commit myself to something that I cannot understand. [...] I am so afraid of something that has everything—and nothing to do with illness. And has everything and nothing to do with you." Feeling as if he has had some sort of epiphany, however, he moves into "a world where caring and cautiousness are synonymous." Perhaps he becomes too needy in his feeling that Daniel needs him. Daniel decides, "Maybe it was a mistake [...] I'm supposed to fit into your life. But I don't want to fit into somebody else's life." He starts skipping his medication. His father, a physician, intervenes, and like that, Daniel disappears from Michael's world. All the characters, including Michael's housemate and his mother, are engaged in various questions of faith. Michael sums up his problem: "a belief in a conventional God entails the acceptance of a conventional morality but conventional morality denies my very existence and how can I embrace a morality that denies that I even exist?" The play opened in Toronto, 1991, with Storey and Steve Cumyn, directed by Edward Roy. § Storey, R. *The Saints and Apostles*. Playwrights Canada, 1993. 91p.

219   *Whale Riding Weather* (1991) | Bryden MacDonald (1960–), Canadian

[Absurdist drama; 3M; 1 set.] The online *Canadian Encyclopedia* describes the works of MacDonald as "a productively unstable tension between a raw and earthy physicality and a conspicuously self-conscious, urban (and urbane) sophistication."

The middle-aged Lyle and Auto, half his age, have become emotionally trapped in a small Toronto apartment with caged-up cats in the corner. Lyle fantasizes his past to such an extent that it is impossible to know what was real and what is imagined. Does he really have an ex-wife and a son? Apparently he did rescue Auto from a Montreal bar in which he found him, soaking wet, suffering from gonorrhea that he probably contacted while hustling. Then Auto encounters Jude, not named after the patron saint of lost causes—though he takes on that role, enticing Auto to quit the suffocating environment in which he finds himself. Apparently contemplating his death (suicide), Lyle releases the cats, tidies the apartment, and gives his blessing to Auto and Jude's leaving together to ride the symbolic whales. Written in loose verse, the play opened in Toronto, 1991, with Allan Gray, Randy Hughson, and Patrick Galligan, directed by Annie Kidder. § MacDonald, B. *Whale Riding Weather*. Talonbooks, 1994. 127p.

220 *The Baddest of Boys* (1992) | Doug Holsclaw (unknown), American

[AIDS farce; 3M; 2W; 1 set.] Too many deaths, too much despair, and AIDS becomes farce, humor another way to cope. As one of the characters says, "contrary to popular belief about the hearing, [...] it's the sense of humor that's the last to go." The setting is a café having trouble with staffing, so many of its hires keep dropping dead. Its specialty is chili. Its co-owner and keeper of the chili's secret ingredient is in the last stages of AIDS, his body attacked by the most outlandish diseases possible, combated by even more outlandish attempts at cures by his very pregnant lesbian doctor. The other co-owner is more concerned with his career as a performing artist. The Buddhist cook wants to know the secret ingredient (one hint dropped suggests that it is sperm), but realizes life with the doctor and her soon-to-be-born son is more important. Eric, a waiter, alternates between his various personalities but finally settles on being an activist. His lover Charles, the café's manager, seems to be the only one genuinely concerned with the dying man, whose last fungal infection reproduces the image of Jesus on his chest. The dark comedy opened in San Francisco, 1992, with Ken Steinmetz, Phil Vo, and B.G. Lacquemont, directed by Sabin Epstein. § In Jones, T., ed. *Sharing the Delirium*. 1–53.

221 *The Fastest Clock in the Universe* (1992) | Philip Ridley (1964–), English

[Shock drama; 3M, 2W; 1 set.] Like a creature in a demented version of *Peter Pan*, the narcissistic Cougar Glass is actually 30, but with the aid of his frustrated lover, the much older Captain Tock, he periodically celebrates his 19th birthday. On each occasion he throws a party whose sole aim is to seduce some available teenager. This time he has his sights on Foxtrot Darling, 15. Foxtrot throws Cougar's plans awry by showing up with his pregnant girlfriend, Sherbet Gravel. While her back is turned, Cougar precedes, nevertheless, to get into the complacent Foxtrot's pants. The sense of impending violence that has been growing since the young people's entrance accelerates when she turns and catches them in the act. Sherbet reveals that not only has she known Cougar's intentions all along but she also knows his real age, a disclosure that incites Cougar to go for her with the cake knife. But Sherbet has come prepared with a gun. The two are disarmed, whereupon Cougar punches Sherbet in the stomach so hard as to cause a miscarriage. Left alone, Cougar cryptically completes the fable that Tock has been developing by identifying the fastest clock in the universe as "Love." The play opened in London, 1992, with Con O'Neill, Jonathan Coy, and Jude Law, directed by Matthew Lloyd. Ridley is associated with the so-called In-Yer-Face theater. § Ridley, P. *Plays 1*. Bloomsbury, 2012. 97–193.

222 *Flaubert's Latest* (1992) | Peter Parnell, American

[Domestic fantasy; 5M, 3W; 1 set.] After a successful first novel Felix has taken as his next project to complete Gustave Flaubert's unfinished *Bouvard et Pécuchet*, but it is not going well. Thus he is beside himself when a psychic friend, with an explicit nod to Coward's *Blithe Spirit*, summons up no other than Flaubert himself, along with his friend Louise Colet. But the pleasure quickly dissipates as the French author demonstrates how unpleasant living with an artist can be—something Felix's lover Colin already knows. A dancer who is HIV-positive, Colin has accepted the fact that Felix is oblivious to everyone around him once he begins writing: "He never asks what I'm working on, or, worse, how it's going." Though Felix denies that Colin's viral status makes any difference, there is a palpable sense that it does. Collin turns to their gardener for physical comfort; the latter is unafraid: "We'll only be safe." Under stress, Colin is ready to leave Felix. Flaubert warns Felix, "Write *your own* book, and do not sacrifice your love." The psychic manages to teleport Flaubert and Colet back to their own time, and Colin and Felix seem to reconcile. The last we see of Felix he has immersed himself in another project. Perhaps he is finally heeding Colin's own advice to write "About today. About us. About what it's like to live with what we have to live with"? The play opened in New York, 1992, with Mark Nelson, Mitchell Anderson, and Gil Bellows, directed by David Saint. § Parnell, P. *Flaubert's Latest: A Comedy*. Dramatists, 1993. 77p.

223 *Heartbreak* (1992) | **Jack Heifner (1946–), American**

[AIDS drama; 3M, 2W; 1 set.] Jason's friends are shocked to discover that his posthumous novel, *Heartbreak*, is a *roman à clef* about them. They gather "for one last time. Just to go over all this and put everything away once and for all"—"Separate the truth from the lies"—in what becomes "a kinda crazy sort of memorial service." Mark was Jason's lover long enough for Jason to steal part of his novel from him and for Mark to become HIV-positive as a result of Jason's lying about being negative. Pamela is also HIV-positive, presumably from anonymous contacts she made trying to become pregnant. Karen is, in Jason's words, "an unmarried, overweight, fag hag," a writer of women romances. And Vincent is the token straight male friend. The spirit of Jason shows up on stage but engages with them only when they act out parts of the novel, before deconstructing it to reveal the reality behind the scene. They admit that Jason was not a very likable person, but for Vincent and the women he was the glue that kept them together as friends. And now, as Karen says, "The rotten, dear son of a bitch was gone." The play opened in Los Angeles, 1992, with Spencer Garrett and Joshua Fardon, directed by Milton Justice. § Heifner, J. *Heartbreak: A Play in Two Acts*. Dramatic, 1999. 86p.

224 *Jeffrey* (1992) | **Paul Rudnick (1957–), American**

[AIDS comedy; 7M, 1W; flexible set.] In the age of AIDS how can gay men love and have sex without fear or guilt? Jeffrey proclaims, "I *love* sex." Taking umbrage at stereotyping, he lashes out that "it's wrong to say that all gay men are obsessed with sex. [...] All *human beings* are obsessed with sex. All gay men are obsessed with opera. And it's not the same thing." He argues, "Sex wasn't meant to be safe, or negotiated, or fatal." But he has major difficulties coping with its dangers and cuts himself off from the possibilities of love. Steve is everything he ever wanted in a partner, save for the fact that he is HIV-positive. Jeffrey panics: "I hate sex! I hate love! I hate the world for giving me everything, and then taking it all back!" His friend Sterling, who is living with Darius, an HIV-positive dancer in *Cats*, tries to convince Jeffrey that he must let go of fear. Even the priest he turns to asks, "How dare you not lunge for any shred of happiness?" But Jeffrey is ready to return to the perceived safety of Wisconsin. Ironically, it takes the jolt of Darius's death to snap him out of his retreat from life. Meeting in the clinic where Darius has just died, Sterling tells Jeffrey, "You know, Darius said he thought you were the saddest person he ever knew. [...] he was sick. He had a fatal disease. And he was one million times happier than you." Jeffrey reconsiders: "I'm a gay man. And I live in the city. And I'm not an innocent bystander." Seeking another chance, Jeffrey meets Steve for a moonlit tryst. The play opened in New York, 1992, with John Michael Higgins, Tom Hewitt, Edward Hibbert, and Bryan Batt, directed by Christopher Ashley. Rudnick wrote the screenplay for the 1995 film. (He is responsible too for the over-admired film *In & Out*, 1997.) § *The Collected Plays of Paul Rudnick*. HarperCollins, 2010. 69–133.

225 *John, I'm Only Dancing* (w. 1992) | **Ken Duncum (1959–), New Zealander**

[School drama; 6M, 2W; unit set.] Duncum based his play on his experiences in high school in Rotorua 1973–77 and the impact David Bowie had on him as a teenager. John Jamieson, the prep school music teacher, decides to stage Bowie's *Ziggy Stardust* album (1972) as the school's annual musical production rather than turn out another Gilbert and Sullivan. In part his choice may be influenced by the fact that Head Prefect Alan Spencer is a big Bowie fan. John enlists his help along with that of two of his friends and two of their girlfriends and proceeds to fall in love with Alan. But also the choice may be in part his way to deliberately affront the headmaster Chote. John was formerly a student in the school; the other students called him Tinkerbell, and Chote made his life miserable. Having discovered subsequently that Chote cruises the public toilets whenever he is out of town, John questions: "So you thought you'd do me a favour by whipping it out of me? Or was it yourself you were beating?" As he has anticipated, the show draws Chote's ire and leads to John's being fired. John begs Alan to go with him, but Alan opts for heterosexuality and leaves with one of the girls—though not before telling John that he is "glad. Grateful" for the experience. The play is structured so that scenes from the eight-week rehearsal period alternate with excerpts from the final staged performance. Thereby, a happy ending is imposed upon reality. The play ends with Alan/Ziggy and John/Starman leaving this world together. Though Duncum finished the play in 1992, it was not published until 2011 and has yet to be produced because of problems obtaining music rights. § Duncum, K. *Plays 2: London Calling*. Victoria Univ. Press, 2011. 107–80.

226 *Lake Street Extension* (1992) | Lee Blessing (1949–), American

[Domestic tragedy; 3M; 1 set.] A child who was sexually abused by his father, and who in turn sexually abused his son, seeks atonement by taking in a refugee from the 1982 violence in El Salvador. When the son, Trace, shows up, old secrets spill out and new betrayals occur. Not only was Trace abused by Fuller, but also by Fuller's boss. At age 14 he ran away and became a street hustler. Now he returns to find Gregorio occupying his bedroom. The latter was politically abused by his country and by the CIA. Trace tracks down the boss, apparently searching for some renewed connection with him, and is badly beaten. When Immigration locates Gregorio, Fuller allows himself to become complicit in their actions. The two youths flee. Ten years later Fuller informs us that Gregorio was caught, deported, and eventually executed in the ironically named El Salvador; Trace simply disappeared without a trace. At one point Trace mentions that he knows about "the sex that gives you cancer in the legs, or whatever," letting the specter of AIDS hang over his disappearance. The play opened in Cincinnati, 1992, with Keith A. Brush and Gordon C. Greene, directed by Jeanne Blake, Blessing's first wife. § Blessing, L. *Patient A and Other Plays: Five Plays*. Heinemann, 1995. 165–210.

227 *The Law of Remains* (1992) | Reza Abdoh (IRN 1963–1995), American

[Theater of cruelty; 7M, 7W; flexible set.] The playwright has becomes something of a cult figure. It is impossible to summarize his kaleidoscopic pageant adequately, so much is going on at such a furious pace. One of the members of Andy Warhol's Factory recites the story at its core: "we are making a movie about a handsome, severely dyslexic young man who made stews out of human organs and it is an Indian movie." The young man is Jeffrey Dahmer (1960–1994), here generally called Jeffrey Snarling. Eleven of his seventeen victims are evoked by name, age, and ethnicity, revealing how many of them were persons marginalized by America racism, being African-, Asian-, Hispanic-, and Native-Americans. The last was a 14-year-old boy whom the police described as an "intoxicated Asian, naked male" and laughingly "returned to his boyfriend." Jarringly juxtaposed against this heart-wrenching moment are the totally tasteless jokes about Dahmer scattered throughout the play: for example, "What did the cops find when they looked in Jeffrey's shower? [...] Head and Shoulders." Jeffrey repeatedly claims, "I'm no fag." Schildcrout (*Murder*, 161) focuses on the idea that, "By putting the serial killer Jeffrey Snarling into a movie, Abdoh's Warhol is exploiting him as a commodity, creating him in a 'factory' and selling him like a can of soup." He goes on, "The play shows gay male characters as the perpetrators of violence, the victims of violence, and the exploiters of narratives about that violence. But it recognizes the larger social forces in which these characters exist, encouraging the audience to understand Dahmer's murders not as the expression of a pathological homosexuality but rather as the product of society's homophobia" (163). Around this core story swirl a maelstrom of noise and movement: repeated incantations, music, dances and choreographed movement, simulated sex, a multiplicity of languages. The final scene, in heaven, reveals that "God is a Puerto Rican drag queen with a frozen erection under a winter sun." The play premiered in an abandoned hotel in New York in 1992 with Peter Jacobs and Tom Pearl, directed by Abdoh. The audience was moved from room to room for each of the seven scenes. § *Plays for the End of the Century*; ed. by Bonnie Marranca. John Hopkins Univ. Press, 1996. 9–94. Also includes Maria Irene Fornes's AIDS play *Enter the Night*, 1993.

228 *My Night with Tennessee* (1992) | Sky Gilbert, Canadian

[Biographical study; 3M; 1 set.] Daniel MacIvor in his introduction to his play *His Greatness* remembers, "a few friends of mine told a few of us at a party a first hand account of his dark days in Vancouver and a meeting he had with Tennessee when Williams was there for the opening of his 'new' play *The Red Devil Battery Sign* [...]. Such a heartbreaking and darkly poetic tale it inspired my friend and fellow party goer, Sky Gilbert, to write his dark and poetic one-act play." Williams and his latest boyfriend Crummy Mullin are breakfasting in a café when Williams spots a 15-year-old boy, an angel who may assuage for a moment Williams's craving for beauty. He asks the boy to visit him in his hotel room, causing Williams and Crummy to quarrel and Crummy to leave. When the boy reveals that his last name is Angell, it seems a sign. He asks the boy to strip to his underwear and then read Rupert Brooke's sonnet "The Hill." For a moment satisfied, Williams bids the boy goodbye, calling him Frank—i.e., Frank Merlo. Crummy returns, and the two men reconcile. Williams confesses, "Frank is an idea. An idea of something that can never be gotten a hold of. [...] not even Frank was Frank." The play opened in Toronto, 1992, with David Ramsden and Peter Lynch, directed by Gilbert.

The play is an example of Gilbert's fascination with gay icons. He has written others about C. P. Cavafy (*Cavafy*, 1981), Pier Paolo Pasolini (*Pasolini/Pelosi*, 1983; *In Which Pier Paolo Pasolini Sees His Own Death in the Face of a Boy*, 1991), Truman Capote (*Capote: A Very Gay Little Musical*, 1990), Franz Schubert (*Schubert Lied: A Schubertirade*, 1998), William Inge (*Independence*, 1998), and Heliogabalus (*Heliogabalus: A Love Story*, 2002, unpublished). In *PlayMurder*, 1994, he toys with the idea that Libby Holman's husband Smith Reynolds may have been a closet case. § Gilbert, S. *This Unknown Flesh*. Coach House, 1995. 145–71.

229 *Party* (1992) | David Dillon (1957–), American

[Sexual comedy; 7M; 1 set.] In his introduction, Dillon recounts how tired he had become of "issue" plays that "bombarded [playgoers] with only the worst parts of our lives," how much he longed to see a gay play that was affirmative about gay life, including sex, and simply made him laugh in recognition. So he wrote a piece about six longtime friends who get together once a month, along with a new guy just entering the scene. In a backhanded homage to *The Boys in the Band*, they play an elaborate game based on "Truth or Dare." The results are a lot of stories, many of them quite humorous, a sense of comradery, a potential romance blossoming, and an evening that ends with everyone fully naked. Stereotypes are sent up: a leather guy suffers from the manic behavior of a musical comedy aficionado. Condoms are mentioned, but the plague for one evening is pushed aside. At the same time, the play avoids being frothy: the host has broken up with his partner of seven years. A lot of ribbing occurs, and some of the tensions that occur among old friends show up. The play ends with a dance. It opened in Chicago, 1992, with Jim Brown, Sal Iacopelli, Ted Bales, Kellum Lewis, Nic Arnzen, Robb Williams, and Sam Sakharia, directed by Dillon. § In Clum, J., ed. *Asking and Telling*. 5–96.

230 *Porcelain* (1992) | Chay Yew (SGP 1965–), American

[Ethnic tragedy; 5M; no set.] Though the playwright forbids the use of music during the play, dialogue charts the way *Madama Butterfly* morphs into the final scene of *Carmen*. It begins: "A man was found dead in a public lavatory in Bethnal Green in East London today [...]. The alleged murderer is said to be a nineteen-year-old Oriental male from nearby Whitechapel [...]. The victim, William Hope, a twenty-six-year-old male from South Hackney, was shot six times." When found, John Lee was cradling the dead body. Why? What led to the fatal moment? Police, reporters, and psychologist Jack Worthing (a name straight out of *The Importance of Being Earnest*, a "play about people pretending to be other people just to get laid") all seek answers: "So you're Oriental—a Chink. So you're gay, poof, queer. So what? Now's your chance to tell [us]." John recounts a story his father told him, about a crow who tried to fit in with sparrows, to discover that he belonged nowhere. William used John selfishly, ignoring his request to use a condom for example, then dropped him for fear of being seen with him. Claiming to be straight, William returned to cruising public toilets. Only John exists as a character in his own right. Four actors play all the other parts, including Hope. The poetic drama opened in London, 1992, with Daniel York, directed by Glen Goei and Stephen Knight. § In Clum, J., ed. *Staging Gay Lives*. 345-400.

231 *The School of Night* (1992) | Peter Whelan (1931-2014), English

[Historical tragedy; 8M, 2W, extras; flexible set.] The play was produced the year before the quatercentenary of Marlowe's death. The plague has hit London. Kit, along with Thomas Kyd, has taken refuge at Tom Walsingham's country house. Shakespeare shows up under the alias Tom Stone. Walter Raleigh also drops by. The last is out of favor with the queen because of his clandestine marriage. He fears that the papers associated with a group to which he and Kit belonged, the School of Night, may incriminate him further. Kit is also considered dangerous because of his work as a spy, not to mention his opinions and his sexuality. He tells Stone that the queen's "only concern is whether I should be killed for sodomy, atheism or treason." He leaves the impression that his atheism is a direct consequence of his sexuality: "My Creator?" he asks. "Surely He didn't create me? Creatures of my sort." Also in the house is an Italian actress trained in commedia dell'arte. She is smitten with Kit even though she knows, "He hasn't much use for a woman." She is attracted too to Stone. He has just completed *Henry VI*; Marlowe is working on *Dido, Queen of Carthage*. The two are also writing narrative poems. Kit recognizes that Stone's *Venus and Adonis* is greater than his *Hero and Leander*. It is arranged to have Kit stage a fake death and escape to Italy to meet the actress. But in the room at Deptford, Kit is killed. The play opened in Stratford-upon-Avon, 1992, with Richard McCabe, directed by Bill Alexander. § Whelan, P. *The School of Night*. Warner Chappell, 1992. 99p.

232 *Trafficking in Broken Hearts* (1992) | Edwin Sánchez (1954?-), Puerto Rican

[Urban tragicomedy; 3M; flexible set.] Sánchez has said he wanted to write plays that offered parts for Latinos other than those of gang members, pimps, and drug dealers. Nevertheless, the Latino here is a male prostitute. The play becomes a tangle of unlikely romantic fixations. Brian is a lawyer, "a twenty-six-year-old white male virgin" longing to make sexual contact with another man but petrified of contracting HIV: "Sometimes I feel like I'm going to die if I can't have sex; then other times I think I'll die if I do have it." Trying to get up nerve while cruising 42th Street, he encounters a Puerto Rican his age, a hustler moving beyond his prime. Papo will not admit to being "a faggot," but he is as beguiled by Brian as Brian is by him. The two stalk each other until finally Brian loses his virginity to him. Papo accepts that perhaps, after all, he is gay; he moves from "I don't kiss no faggots" to "The only trouble with being alone is there's no one there to kiss back." Although there is a quality of desperation in their relationship, the two men seem on the verge of creating some kind of life together. But Bobby complicates Papo's decisions. He is a 16-year-old runaway who latches onto Papo at the bus station and tries to recreate with him the life he had with his older brother, who regularly abused Bobby after forcing him to dress in their mother's clothes. When Papo quits Bobby to move in with Brian, Bobby jump out the window to his death, leaving Papo shaken. The play opened in Chicago, 1992, with Andrew Carrillo, Christopher Adam, and Woodrow James Bryant, directed by David Zak. § In Lane, E., and Shengold, N., eds. *Actor's Book*. 431-81.

233 *Two Weeks with the Queen* (1992) | Mary Morris (GBR 1944-), Australian

[Pre-adolescent comedy; 4M, 2W; flexible set.] A dramatization of the 1989 novel by Morris Gleitzman, this delightful and very funny play depicts the accelerated process of maturing that Colin Mudford, 12, experiences after he is shipped off to stay with his London aunt so he will not have to witness the suffering of his younger brother Luke from an incurable cancer. An idealist, Colin is convinced that if he can just get into Buckingham Palace, the Queen will send her best doctor to cure Luke. Thwarted at the palace gates, he persuades his overly protected cousin Alistair to help him scale the palace walls at night. Even when caught and chastised, he does not give up: he heads out to find the best cancer hospital to ask for the help of one of its specialists. There he encounters Ted Caldicot crying and is impressed that he is the first grownup he has met who can say the word *cancer*. Ted becomes the victim of a gay-bashing. Colin realizes now that the Griff he has been seeing is his mate, suffering from AIDS. With the simplicity of the innocent, Colin accepts their love as good and steals a wheelchair to get the injured Ted in to see Griff. He is there when Griff dies. Griff's family never accepted him and refused to visit the hospital. Colin realizes that the patients who seemed the happiest were those with family and friends. He knows that he needs to be with Luke and his parents. When his aunt refuses to sign the papers to allow him to fly alone, he gets Ted to do so. As a farewell present, Colin gives Ted a pink scarf. The strength Colin has drawn from his two weeks with a queen unexpectedly gives Alistair the courage to rebel against the coddling he endures. The play opened in Sydney, 1992, with Danny Nash, directed by Wayne Harrison. § Morris, M. *Two Weeks with the Queen* [...] *Based on the Novel by Morris Gleitzman*. Pearson, 2007. 89p.

234 *Beat the Sunset* (1993) | Michael Lewis MacLennan (1968–), Canadian

[AIDS drama; 2M, 2W; unit set.] In an unusual move MacLennan reminds his audience of ravages other diseases have taken on humans, most notably malaria and leprosy. His family, the Castorsons, have not dealt well with having a gay son. They have even more trouble when he becomes HIV-positive. Adam strikes back, but as his childhood "blood brother" says, "Your attitude's driving you down, not the disease." Sacha Pollock, however, is not doing that much better. His epileptic seizure, right after his first sexual experience with Adam when they were teenagers, effectively outed them. Sacha retreated into respectability and married. He is one of the few visitors Adam has, but he cannot admit that he loves him, "terrified," as he says to Adam, that "when you really will get sick again, when you'll need me. I think I'll fail you ... again." Yet the play convincingly builds to an affirmative ending. Confronted with virulent homophobia, Adam's mother speaks up for her son. Sacha repeats the blood oath he took when the two were young. And Adam begins working with ceramics again. The play opened in Victoria, B.C., 1993, with Phil Black and Kristian Martin, directed by MacLennan. § MacLennan, M. L. *Beat the Sunset*. Playwrights Canada, 1995. 96p.

235 *Beautiful Thing* (1993) | Jonathan Harvey (1968–), English

[Adolescent romance; 3M, 2W; 1 set.] Harvey is a laureate of welfare and working class London. It is a scrappy world in which politics are seldom mentioned and even the plague does not seem to be of great concern. *Beautiful Thing* is set in a housing project in the southeast part of the city. Sandra is a bartender who goes through boyfriends. She dotes on her son Jamie, 15, though they constantly bicker. Next door lives the overweight teenager Leah, who has a fixation on Mama Cass. Farther down is the flat belonging to Jamie's schoolmate Ste. His father is an abusive drunk; his brother Trevor is no better. The two boys together discover that they are gay. Sandra finds out they have been to a gay pub. She is taken aback, but when Jamie invites her to accompany him and Ste for an evening out, she accepts. The play ends magically with Jamie and Ste dancing together to Mama Cass's "Dream a Little Dream of Me," to be joined by Sandra and Leah as the stage turns into a nightclub. The premiere was in London, 1993, with Mark Letheren and Johnny Lee Miller, directed by Hettie Macdonald. Harvey also wrote the script for the much loved 1996 film. § In Wilcox, M., ed. *Gay Plays Five*. 147–211.

236 *Blue Dragons* (1993) | Gordon Armstrong (1960–1996), Canadian

[AIDS drama; 3M; unit set.] Armstrong was suffering from AIDS while writing this play; it is amazing how poetic the results are. Simon is trying to put to rest his sense of guilt that he failed Bram when the latter dies of AIDS. A sculptor whose work is more important to him than a relationship, Simon made Bram feel he was inhabiting a "corner in somebody's workspace." He moved in with Nick, who was the one who coped when Bram was diagnosed with the first of many illnesses. But it was Simon whom Bram asked to accumulate enough pills that he could choose his exit from life. Now Simon and Nick and their incarnated memory of Bram work to find meaning in what has happened. The language and the setting approach the level of poetry. Bram's descriptions of bodily failures are lyrical. Dominant symbols are clouds and dragons projected onto the scene and pomegranates, the literal eating of one closing the play. It premiered in Toronto, 1993, with Paul Boretski, Robert Persichini, and Alex Ferguson, directed by Bob Baker. (Another Armstrong play provides the title for the collection *Plague of the Gorgeous*.) § Armstrong, G. *Blue Dragons*. Scirocco Drama, 1993. 79p.

237 *Box 27* (1993) | **Michael Norman Mann (1966–), American**

[Military drama; 6M, 1W, extras; 1 set.] The "don't ask, don't tell" military policy instituted in 1993 resulted in the dismissal of over 13,500 service men and women, some of whom held vital wartime credentials such as the ability to speak fluent Arabic. The policy was repealed in 2010, leaving the play more a historical document than a political tract. But the argument Mann makes that gays should be allowed to serve their country with honor and dignity retains vitality. The play's dogmatism, however, does not wear well. Marine Captain Stephen Mills has reached the point where he does not "want to lie about being gay anymore." Having falsified the old enlistment form by not checking Box 27, identifying himself as a homosexual, he resurrects the form and includes it in his dossier seeking promotion. His father is a colonel in the Marines; his older lover, Major Howard Kurtis, is his father's friend. When the father learns the truth, he first recoils, then accepts that he loves his son even though he holds he has no place in the Marine Corps. Howard preserves his own career by continuing to lie. The play opened in Los Gatos, Calif., 1993. § Mann, M. N. *Box 27*. Actors Forum, 2008. 104p.

238 *Lonely Planet* (1993) | **Steven Dietz (1958–), American**

[AIDS drama; 2M; 1 set.] Diez was inspired by Eugene Ionesco's *Les chaises* to create a setting in which the chairs represent people who died of AIDS—although the acronym is never spoken in the course of the play. The scene is the map store Jody owns, dominated by a photograph of Earth from space: "a planet, small and alone, surrounded by enormous darkness." Jody describes the mapmaker as one who "takes a messy round world and puts it neat and flat," deciding "which distortions, which faulty perceptions he can live with," though sometimes "things on the periphery of lives that we distort" take on an importance so large that we cannot ignore them: "People I know are dying." His best friend is Carl. He claims to hold a variety of jobs, depending on his mood at the time. They have never been lovers, for which Carl is grateful, for "lovers are easy, *friends* are hard." It is he who brings the chairs to the store, creating an impromptu memorial so the dead will not be forgotten: "Like most of the people taken by this disease, we in the general public murdered them twice. First, by romanticizing them. Glamorizing their grief. And, then by ignoring them." Jody gets to the point that he cannot leave his store. Carl forces him to go to the clinic to be tested. He is HIV-negative. Presumably Carl is positive; he brings the chair that he has already identified himself with and begs Jody to keep it. The play opened in Evanston, Ill., 1993, with William Brown and Phil Ridarelli, directed by Dietz. § In Lane, E., and Shengold, N., eds. *Actor's Book*. 239–87.

239 *Pterodactyls* (1993) | **Nicky Silver (1960–), American**

[AIDS drama; 3M, 2W; 1 set.] Jimmy Fowler wrote in the *Dallas Observer* (August 8, 1996), "If Eugene Ionesco and filmmaker Peter Jackson were a couple, Nicky Silver is the baby they would adopt and raise into a disgruntled, ungrateful adult, taking revenge on his daddies with scatological two-acts using Ionesco's smug futility and Jackson's warped-aesthetic compulsion for finding beauty in the carnage of a car accident." The Duncans are the quintessential dysfunctional family. The alcoholic mother is interested only in appearances and revels in the opportunity to pull off a grand wedding for her mentally challenged daughter. She is disgruntled when her prodigal son returns with AIDS: "He had no right to get this disease. Who exactly does he think he is?" The father tries harder to understand, but he persists in calling his son Buzz, a good, masculine name that conceals his real name is Todd—*der Tod*, "'death' in German." Tommy, the daughter's suitor, is a film buff, only mildly interested in his engagement, more excited by his employment in the Duncan household as their maid since he gets to wear a maid's outfit. Till now he has had sex only with the priests at the orphanage where he was raised: "And they tied me up so all I had to do was shout the occasional 'Hail Mary.'" Todd infects Tommy, and he dies: "He went so fast. [...] It's good he choked, drowned. He got so ugly, all purple and swollen." His body remains in the Duncans' backyard, the ground too frozen for them to bury him. The daughter's ghost, after she kills herself when Tommy calls their wedding off, reports that his spirit "spends all his time with Montgomery Clift and George Cukor talking about movies." The title, like so many of Silver's, is misleading. Todd has discovered old bones in the backyard; throughout the play he assembles them to reveal the skeleton of a tyrannosaurus rex. He muses on their extinction: "they just ran their course, and their end was the order of things. And no tragedy. Or disease. Or God." The premiere was in New York, 1993, with T. Scott Cunningham and Kent Lanier, directed by David Warren. § Silver, N. *Etiquette and Vitriol: The Food Chain and Other Plays*. Theatre Communications, 1996. 69–150.

240 *The Rainy Season* (1993) | **Dwight Okita (1958–), American**

[Ethnic romance; 4M, 2W; flexible set.] Like Okita, the play's Harry is a third generation American of Japanese origins. And like "the many Latino boyfriends who [...] inspired this play," Antonio is Brazilian. They meet at a Chicago bus stop, and the attraction is immediate. The incurable romantic, Harry tries not to become carried away, but as he listens to Antonio's stories about life in Brazil, he opens himself up more and more. When Antonio proposes that he leave with him and go to Brazil, after initial resistance he buys his ticket, only to find that Antonio has made up most of the stories and has no attention of accompanying him. Harry concludes, "I have lousy taste in men." But he also realizes that he has to stop looking out windows, to "get out of the damn house. Go out into the rain. Get a little wet. And see for myself ... what's there." The play opened in Chicago, 1993, with Raymond J. Mark and Edward F. Torres, directed by Marlene Zuccaro. § *Asian American Drama: 9 Plays from the Multiethnic Landscape*; ed. Brian Nelson. Applause, 1997. 209–61.

241 *Stephen & Mr. Wilde* (1993) | **Jim Bartley (1952–), Canadian**

[Biographical study; 4M, 2W; 2 sets.] Bartley became intrigued by a relatively obscure interval in Wilde's life: his short visit to Canada as part of his 1882 North American lecture tour. He was accompanied by the African American Stephen Davenport. Bartley invents an entire biography for this unknown figure. An unscrupulous Toronto journalist uncovers that Stephen is really the ex-slave Henry Joyce, a fugitive wanted for the murder of a former brutal slave owner. Wilde's affection for his servant contributes to the writer's growing radicalism, and his defense of Stephen foreshadows the tactics he will pursue at his own trial. But at this point, Wilde is largely heterosexual. The rumor that at Oxford he pursued a "coy choir boy" has preceded him, but he patronizes a local brothel, forcing Stephen to accompany him. The brothel's owner tells Stephen, "He wants you, like his boys at Oxford," and the play ends with Wilde caressing Stephen's back, scarred by the many whippings he received as a slave. Anything sexual, however, remains latent. The play opened in Saskatoon, 1993, with Donald Carrier, directed by Bill Glassco. § Bartley, J. *Stephen & Mr. Wilde*. Blizzard, 1994. 79p.

242 *The Stillborn Lover* (1993) | **Timothy Findley (1930–2002), Canadian**

[Diplomatic mystery; 4M, 3W; unit set.] Inspired by two real-life diplomats (John Watkins, who died while being interrogated by the RCMP, and Herbert Norman, who committed suicide), Findley imagined a Canadian ambassador who in 1972 is called back from the U.S.S.R. after the murder of his 19-year-old Russian lover. The plot provides the opportunity to expose not only international intrigue but the domestic machinations such an event unleashes. Harry Raymond for years has been best friends with Michael Riordon, minister of external affairs who aspires to become the next prime minister. Thus Harry is a liability that he must deal with. Harry, however, has greater integrity: just as he refused to submit to Soviet blackmail, now he refuses to accept Mike's offer of a dishonest way out. The political becomes entangled in the personal in other ways. Harry's wife is suffering from the onset of Alzheimer's, so one cannot entirely trust her statements. Harry does not. But she claims to have set up his encounter with the youth in the baths at Yalta, just as she claims to have set up a much earlier meeting with an Arab youth in Cairo: "I was living with a man who was dying—of denial. [...] And I had to save his life." It is left unclear whether she knows that the Russian youth was in fact a Soviet pawn and that incriminating photographs exist. Harry's daughter must come to terms with the feeling that she not known her father; she accuses him of having lied to her by not disclosing his homosexuality. As to who killed the youth—that remains a mystery. The KGB? Harry's wife? Someone else? Findley also creates the suspicion that one of Harry's two RCMP interrogators is a closet case; certainly he is a tease. The play opened in Ottawa, 1993, with William Hutt, directed by Peter Moss. Jeremy Hole wrote the screenplay for the 1999 film, *External*

Affairs. § Findley, T. *The Stillborn Lover*. Blizzard, 1993. 92p.

243 *The Twilight of the Golds* (1993) | Jonathan Tolins (1964–), American

[Domestic drama; 3M, 2W; 2 sets.] Wagner's *Ring* cycle, particularly *The Twilight of the Gods* (*Götterdämmerung*), helps David Gold endure and transcend a desolating revelation of his family's hidden homophobia. His brother-in-law works with a firm on the cutting edge of unlocking the genetic secrets of DNA. When his wife becomes pregnant, he allows the fetus to be tested. They discover that the unborn son has a ninety percent chance of being gay and decide to terminate the pregnancy. David feels his sister is betraying him. Worse, he discovers that, even though his parents love him, they would have made the same decision. Rifts in the family are already apparent in their treatment of David's never seen lover Stephen. Ironically, the sister waits too long; when the doctor induces the abortion, complications occur that lead to his having to perform a hysterectomy. Not without pain, David bids his family farewell and turns to strengthening his own family that he is creating with Stephen. The premiere was in Pasadena, Calif., 1993, with Raphael Sbarge, directed by Arvin Brown. Tolins also wrote the script for the 1997 television film, in which the sister decides to keep the child, leading to a breakup with her husband. He wrote a number of episodes for *Queer as Folk*, 2001. § Tolins, J. *The Last Sunday in June and Other Plays*. Grove, 2004. 103–98.

244 *What's Wrong with Angry?* (1993) | Patrick Wilde (unknown), English

[School drama; 8M, 4W, extras; flexible set.] Though most viewers will be caught up emotionally by "the confusion and distress of a boy who can find gayness only in public toilets," the play, as Sinfield (*Out on Stage*, 350) informs us "was presented explicitly by its author as a contribution to the debate about the age of consent for gay men" going on in England. Steven Carter, 16, falls in love with the slightly older head boy at his Catholic school, John Westhead. The only person whom Steve feels safe to confide in is the overweight Linda Rodgers. John denies he is gay even as he has sex repeatedly with Steve. When John thinks he is found out by his schoolmates, he brutally attacks Steve to cover the truth. A closeted teacher at the school, Simon Hutton, tries to offer Steve reassurance that "it gets better. You have to keep fighting," but he inadvertently makes the situation worse. Steve's parents are alternately appalled and baffled, leading Steve to contemplate suicide. He decides, however, "to live … my life as I want to, no matter what it takes." At play's end he is alone. Its premiere was in London, 1993, with Tom Wisdom and Miles Petit, directed by Wilde. He also wrote the screenplay for the 1998 film *Get Real*, which departed from the play in ways large and small. § In Clum, J., ed. *Staging Gay Lives*. 63–118.

245 *As the Beaver* (1994) | Joel Drake Johnson (1950?–), American

[Domestic satire; 9M, 1W; unit set.] The play looks at adolescent sexuality by stripping the facade off the Cleaver (*Leave It to Beaver*), Ricardo (*I Love Lucy*), and Taylor (*The Andy Griffith Show*) television families to reveal the hypocrisy and homophobia behind their bourgeois respectability. When in 1966 June Cleaver catches her son Theodore (Beaver) kissing Little Ricky, she flies into a vindictive fury, riding roughshod over everyone else as she loudly proclaims that it is not her fault. Ricky Sr., reacts like a stereotypical Cuban father, beating up his son. June insists on calling in the minister, who so demoralizes Theodore that he tries to hang himself. The second part jumps twenty years ahead to 1986. Both Theodore and Opie Taylor, who are lovers, are HIV-positive. They stage a demonstration at a town parade (which June and Ward attend dressed as the Reagans) and are arrested. Mr. Ed, the talking horse, is so impressed with their courage that he finally has the courage to announce, "I am proud to say that today, yes, I am a gay horse!! God bless the Beaver!" Wally all along is the most supportive. At the end everyone wills a happy ending in which Theodore and Opie exchange marriage vows. The two declare: "Now I am a man and part of being a man […] Is becoming better and richer in soul. […] And so I will not be frightened […] And depressed and guilty any longer." After a 1992 staged reading, a revised version opened in Chicago, 1994, with Joel Sugerman and Scott Olson, directed by Timber Weiss. § Johnson, J. D. *As the Beaver*. Broadway Play, 2010. 58p.

246 *Babies* (1994) | Jonathan Harvey, English

[Urban comedy; 8M, 8W; flexible set.] Harvey here moves into the world of southeast working-class London. One of Joe Casey's students thinks he would make an excellent replacement for her dead father. In an effort to set him up with her mother, she invites him to her birthday party, not suspecting that Joe is gay and in a relationship, albeit a troubled one. Woody, his boyfriend, is hung up on drugs, so that the two men often go their separate ways. Joe attends the party, where the mother starts flirting with him. Her gay brother Kenny perceives the truth and also flirts with the now drunk Joe. When she questions Joe about his sexuality, he does not hide. He returns to Woody, and the two make peace. Meanwhile, young David, another of Joe's students, tries to make sense of his own sexual drive. He is uncomfortable when a drag queen shows up at the party to deliver a rousing chorus of "I Am What I Am." But there is a good chance he will realize he is gay; he and Joe bond as student-teacher. The play opened in London, 1994, with Ian Dunn and Karl Draper, directed by Polly Teale. § Harvey, J. *Plays 1*. Methuen Drama, 1999. 91–184.

247 *Bad Company* (1994) | Simon Bent (unknown), English

[Social drama; 6M, 2W; unit set.] Bonded by hormones, mutual antagonisms, and idleness, a group of youths while away their time in Scarborough. Ian Smith is the only one who has been to university. Labeled a "Ponce" upon his entrance, he claims that it "Doesn't bother [him] what people think." His sometimes sexual partner Paul Turner tells Ian, "It's easy for you, you've always known what you are, what you wanted, but I'm different." Paul claims that he likes girls, and perhaps he is bisexual. But when he has an opportunity to have sex with a young woman, he finds a pretext not to: "There's no protection. I haven't got any." Paul has just returned from London. He tells Ian how he became a rent boy there when he ran out of money. He and a certain Jim lived together; now that Paul is back in Scarborough, he keeps writing and telephoning Jim. When his friend Billy asks why he left Jim, Paul confesses, "I was beginning to like him." Billy's own sexuality is vague. He obviously looks up to Paul. In talking of Jim, he says, "It doesn't bother me you know." Paul spurns Ian's idea of their leaving together; instead, he heads back to London. Billy reports back on him: "Sounds alright." All the other characters are straight; they remain oblivious to Paul's troubled nature. The premiere was in London, 1994, with Stuart Laing and Kemal Sylvester, directed by Paul Miller. § Bent, S. *Bad Company: A Play*. French, 1994. 73p.

248 *The Beloved Disciple* (1994) | Tom Jacobson (1961?–), American

[Historical fantasy; 3M; flexible set.] The theater itself is a constant in Jacobson's plays. This one premiered the year after the quatercentenary of Marlowe's death. Kit, 29, has taken refuge with Henry ("Harry") Wriothesley, Earl of Southampton, 19. When an actor (who turns out to be Shakespeare) appears, Marlowe coaxes the two men into trying out his new play *The Beloved Disciple*, about the triangle consisting of Jesus (played by Kit), John (by Harry), and Judas (by Will). Kit's sensuality threatens to overpower Harry's basic reticence, and even Will almost succumbs at one point. He does eagerly pick up many of the lines in Kit's play (they will show up later in his own plays). Meanwhile, the court has become uneasy about Kit's atheism (as revealed by Thomas Kyd, played by the same actor who plays Shakespeare). The queen (also played by the same actor) dislikes that "'Tis noised about he hath succumbed to the sodomitical vice as well." After a passionate kiss between Harry and Kit, Harry recoils: "Thy John and Christ are sodomites!" Kit responds laconically, "Thou hast only now discovered this?" Playing the part of Judas, Will's line "Ecce homo!" should elicit a laugh. Warding off another kiss, Harry stabs Kit. But it is not mortal, and Kit prepares to depart for France, leaving the stage to Will. Much of the play is in blank verse. It opened in Los Angeles, 1994, with Cully Fredericksen, directed by Fred Sanders. § Jacobson, T. *The Beloved Disciple*. Broadway Play, 2014. 83p.

249 *Blade to the Heat* (1994) | Oliver Mayer (unknown), American

[Ethnic sports drama; 7M, 1W, extras; flexible set.] The world of contact sports ironically glorifies the idea of *machismo* even as its participants engage in blatantly homoerotic interactions. Without getting very deep into the psychological aspects, the play shows the confusion of violence, love, and sexual release in boxing: "Oh, you like to clinch! Almost like the real thing.... Except it ain't." Both the defeated champion Mantequilla Decima and the new star of the ring Pedro Quinn are accused of being faggots, revving up the tension between them. Pedro is a closet case, but when, under pressure, he breaks and admits his desire for his friend Garnet, their initial love-making turns violent. A variation of the scene repeats itself in the ring when Mantequilla and Pedro have their rematch. Other figures come across as sexually ambiguous. Set in 1959, there is also a sociological aspect to the play: the boxers represent various Hispanic cultures, while Garnet is trying to break into the African American music world. The premiere was in New York, 1994, with Kamar de los Reyes, directed by George C. Wolfe. The script was later revised. § Mayer, O. *Blade to the Heat*. Dramatists, 1996. 48p.

250 *The Food Chain* (1994–95) | **Nicky Silver, American**

[Sexual farce; 3M, 2W; 3 sets.] If Silver's play is an absurdist riff on Coward's *Design for Living*, their differences are signaled at once by their titles. In the first scene the needy Amanda Dolar, deserted by her husband after one week of marriage, calls a hotline, getting the aggressive Bea Woodnick. In scene two the needy Otto Woodnick pursues fashion model Serge Stubin. All come together in the last scene. Amanda's husband, Ford Dolar, has spent the two weeks having sex with Serge. He assures Amanda that she need not worry, however, because they practiced safe sex: "I consider myself extremely responsible." Otto follows Serge to the apartment, and Bea, who turns out to be his mother, also shows up. Amanda is Otto's old schoolmate. Sexual sparks fly between her and Serge. After Bea and Otto depart, they head for the bedroom, calling out for Ford to join them. Otto shows up one last time outside the door, begging: "Serge! If I sit, *quiet in the corner* … could ya love me!!?" The premiere was in Washington, D.C., 1994, with James Whalen, Christopher Lane, and Rob Leo Roy, directed by Silver. (In this version Otto kills himself.) It was revised before its New York debut. § Silver, N. *Etiquette and Vitriol: The Food Chain and Other Plays*. Theatre Communications, 1996. 1–67.

251 *Good Works* (1994) | **Nick Enright, Australian**

[Family tragedy; 3M, 3W; unit set.] This complex play moves freely in time, from 1928 to 1981, as well as in place, with actors playing multiple roles. It examines how religion, the pretense of good works, and class prejudices destroy people. At its center are two boys/men—Tim Donovan and Shane Grogan—half-brothers, a fact unknown to them (though in a childhood ritual they become "blood brothers"). Their father was pressured by his family into giving up Shane's mother and marrying Tim's. Tim grows up a fragile child, musically gifted but not enough to achieve the career he dreams of. Shane is physically abused by both the men who subsequently become part of his mother's life. There is a sexual attraction between the two boys as shown through a school play they are cast in, to Tim's family's disquiet. Shane rescues Tim from the physical abuse of a Catholic priest at the school, killing the priest with a knife, and is sentenced to prison. Now they meet up nineteen years later at a gay bar, at first uncertain who the other is. Shane calls himself John; Tim's gay friend insists he is Jack the Stripper who has been responsible for a number of robberies at knifepoint. Tim, feeling guilty about his part in the murder, wants atonement, but Shane refuses to grant it and leaves. Tim must live with his ghosts. The play opened in Penrith (Sydney), 1994, with Jamie Jackson, David Field, and Danny Adcock, directed by Adam Cook. (Four years later Enright would produce his international hit *The Boy from Oz*.) § Enright, N. *Good Works*. Currency, 1995. 57p.

252 *Joy* (1994) | **John Fisher (1964?–), American**

[Romance; 5M, 3W; flexible set.] The play depicts two couples—one gay, the other lesbian—through the stages of courtship, life together, and, for the gay couple, breakup. Paul is opinionated, overbearing, and often lovable. He himself says, "My politics are too demanding. My manner too honest." As his best lesbian friend says of a drag party Paul gives, "Well, it won't be the first party he's both thrown and ruined." When he first meets Gabriel, it is definitely not love at first sight. Then, as their paths keep crossing, they feel an attraction, which leads to sex and then to moving in together. But Paul constantly sabotages the relationship. After the disastrous drag party, he confesses, "It took Gabriel three days to get over it. It took me four to realize I had done something wrong." It is no surprise that Gabe moves on, falling in love with more of a fellow spirit in Darryl. Paul reminisces, "Joy is a state that transcend[s] happiness. [...] there was one year when I knew that transcendent joy." After being presented at UC-Berkeley, it opened in San Francisco in 1994 as *The Joy of Gay Sex* with Paul Tena, Gabriel Macen, Corey Scaeffer, Christian Milne, Darryl Stephens, directed by Fisher. It was subsequently revised. § Fisher, J. *Joy.* Broadway, 2007. 92p.

253 *A Language of Their Own* (1994) | Chay Yew, American

[Ethnic drama; 4M; minimal set.] The play examines Asian-Americans making their way in a white world. The title misleads. Oscar says, "The only thing that truly binds us together is being Chinese." Ming counters, "The only thing that truly pits us against each other is being Chinese." Oscar was born in China; Ming was born in the U.S. There are cultural differences, linguistic differences. Even such a simple statement as "I love you" takes on a different meaning depending on the speaker. In addition, Oscar is HIV-positive; Ming is negative. Robert sums up: "In the end we spoke different languages." After having been together for four years, Oscar decides the two of them should not see each other anymore: "It's not working out. We've become two very different people." Ming leaves and moves in with Robert, "a white guy." Oscar joins a group made up of people who have tested positive, learning "a new vocabulary, a new language." He begins dating again, attracted to Daniel, a Filipino: "a radical queer Asian who lives and breathes Sondheim." But Oscar and Ming realize that they still love each other. They also accept that they cannot return to their previous status; others are now involved. Ming, however, wants an open relationship, something that Robert cannot accept. They come to blows and split up. Daniel goes with other men without telling Oscar; he too tests positive. At Oscar's request he gets the pills to let Oscar slip away "alone in a sterile hospital room." Perhaps Ming and Robert will get back together. The audience must decide whether words fail them at the end or are simply unneeded. The premiere was in Los Angeles, 1994, with Dennis Dun, Chris Tashima, Anthony David, and Noel Alumit, directed by Tim Dang. § Yew, C. *Porcelain and A Language of Their Own: Two Plays.* Grove, 1997. 117–228.

254 *Love! Valour! Compassion!* (1994) | Terrence McNally, American

[Tragicomedy; 7M; flexible set.] McNally's play is for the 1990s what Mart Crowley's *Boys* was to the 1960s. Set in choreographer/dancer Gregory Mitchell's country home two hours from New York, it covers three weekends: Memorial Day, Fourth of July, and Labor Day. Its structure, however, is intricate; McNally uses narrative, simultaneous scenes, flashbacks, flashforwards, and other temporal and structural dislocations to portray eight men who, save for the fact that they are all connected in some way to the world of dance, lead rather ordinary lives. Gregory and Bobby (blind from birth) invite four friends to join them. Perry, a lawyer who has his demons, and Arthur, an accountant, have been rather staid partners for fourteen years. Lonely Buzz, HIV-positive, is a walking encyclopedia of musical comedy. John, a frustrated musician who acts as a rehearsal pianist, brings his latest sex object, the uninvited young dancer Ramon Fornos. John's twin brother, James (one actor plays both roles), also HIV-positive, shows up in Act 2. "James the Fair" is as loved as "John the Foul" is disliked, though Buzz had a brief affair with the latter. Ramon is a trickster figure, a deliberate mischief maker who unleashes all kinds of tensions. He effortlessly seduces Bobby, devastating Gregory when Bobby stupidly confesses and reminding Perry of Arthur's one-time infidelity and how badly he handled the situation. Ramon is also immensely talented. When Gregory realizes that his worn body is incapable of dancing his latest creation, the artist in him leads him to offer the role to Ramon.

Some degree of unity is achieved when all but Perry agree to perform the Pas des Cynges from *Swan Lake en travesti* as part of an AIDS fund raiser (and even Perry seems to grow during the summer). James, who has joined them, collapses. Buzz finds his role as caregiver even as he faces his own death. McNally takes a bold step, having each character now speak directly to the audience recounting how he will die. Gregory will outlive all of them, alone; Bobby will leave him for another man. James will commit suicide; Buzz will die even quicker than he expects. John will seek love, but is incapable of changing his unlovable nature. Despite the tensions that have occurred, the play ends on a relatively affirmative note. The final scene shows everyone save John skinny-dipping in the lake. The premiere was in New York, 1994, with Stephen Bogardus, Justin Kirk, John Benjamin Hickey, Stephen Spinella, John Glover, and Nathan Lane, directed by Joe Mantello. The well endowed Randy Becker's penis became the subject of a *New Yorker* Talk of the Town column. McNally also wrote the script for the 1997 film, with the same cast, save Lane. Buzz perhaps explains the British spelling of *Valour* when he kids the English-born James: "For people who insist on spelling 'valor' with a *u* [...] you're lucky we have a lenient immigration." § In Hodges, B., ed. *Forbidden Acts*. 653–741.

255 ***My Night with Reg* (1994) | Kevin Elyot, English**

[Sexual drama; 6M; 1 set.] Elyot's best known play is a wry comment on the dangers of promiscuity in the age of AIDS. It is set in London across several years in the 1980s. Reg is the never-seen but pivotal character. He is in a relationship with Daniel, but has an affair with John. He also has one-time sex with a couple, neither lover knowing about the other's infidelity. And he probably is the "Dwight" with whom the handyman Eric has a quick moment. At Reg's cremation (he dies from AIDS complications) even the vicar comments on how good he was sexually. Guy, the one man who has not had sex with him, is the one whom all the others confide in. Guy himself is hopelessly in love with John, but John is clueless about the fact until he begins sorting Guy's belongings after the latter's death from AIDS. (He was raped while on holiday by a Swindon mortician, who probably infected him.) Guy leaves John his flat; the first night John sleeps there, he beds young Eric, who seems in many ways the wisest of all the men. Sinfield (*Out on Stage*, 328) argues that the play "may well be a purposefully unAmerican, unheroic version of AIDS—wry and understated, furtive and thwarted, class-conscious, and virtually without uplift." On the last point, I would disagree. The premiere was in London, 1994, with David Bamber, John Sessions, and Anthony Calif, directed by Roger Michell. Elyot also wrote the screenplay for the 1997 film with the same cast. § Elyot, K. *Four Plays*. Nick Hern, 2004. 73–157.

256 ***What Are Tuesdays Like?* (1994) | Victor Bumbalo, American**

[AIDS drama; 5M, 1W; 1 set.] The play is another examination of coping mechanisms that came into existence as the plague continued. A mutual support group develops among three gay men and an African American woman who encounter each other each Tuesday in the waiting room of an AIDS clinic in New York over a period of six months. Scott is initially accompanied by Gene, who feels compelled to tell everyone, "I'm not sick. As a matter of fact, I'm not even HIV positive." A control freak, he acts as a nanny for Scott, until the latter rebels and takes control of his own treatment. They finally separate because, Scott says, "When that man looks at me, all he sees is a corpse. I'm not that." Jeff loses his lover. One of his friends makes the mistake of calling 911, with the result that Jeff is locked out of the apartment where the two have lived for nine years but which is not in his name. He tries returning to his mother in Miami, but feels smothered by her attention and returns to forage on his own in the city. He and Scott move in together to housesit for friends. Howard has already lost his lover. He prides himself on his self-control but finally breaks down and admits, "I'm so afraid." Denise, the one woman, must solve the problem of how to take care of her two children. The four discuss love, sex, and religion, but never politics. At the play's end a new patient shows up. Howard asks if he is going to become a Tuesday regular. The man asks, "Is it a good day?" Howard answers, "The best." The premiere was in Shepherdstown, W.V., 1994, with John Hollywood, Greg Stuhr, Court Whisman, and Anthony McKay, directed by Ed Herendeen. § In Lane, E., and Shengold, N., eds. *Actor's Book*. 1–48. In Jones, T., ed. *Sharing the Delirium*. 265–308.

257 ***You Should Be So Lucky* (1994) | Charles Busch (1954–), American**

[Farce; 3M, 3W; 1 set.] Written as a vehicle for the actor/playwright, it was one of the rare times when Busch appeared in a trousers role. Christopher Ladendorf's life changes when he plays the good Samaritan and invites Sy Rosenberg in after he passes out on the street outside Christopher's Greenwich Village apartment. Discovering Christopher is an electrologist, Sy decides to have unsightly hair removed. During their sessions Sy comes to look upon Christopher as a son and changes his will to leave half his estate to him. That happens sooner than anticipated when he has a heart attack (possibly brought on by a surge in electricity). At the same time, Christopher meets

Walter Zuckerman, an unlikely publicist who is every bit as neurotic as Christopher, and they begin dating. Sy's daughter decides to contest the will; Walter arranges for Christopher to go on a popular talk show to overcome the bad publicity she has generated. Unexpectedly, Sy's ghost shows up to help. Christopher does such a good job that the daughter renounces her lawsuit. He has a harder time voicing his emotions to Walter, to the point that Sy takes over Christopher's body to try to force the issue. But Christopher declares his love for Walter in his own voice and decides he must become his own person, banishing Sy back to the spirit world. The play opened in New York, 1994, with Busch and Matthew Arkin, directed by Kenneth Elliott. It now seems mostly a curiosity. § Busch, C. *You Should Be So Lucky: A New Comedy*. French, 1995. 109p.

Pre-Millennium, 1995–2000

AIDS cocktail introduced, 1995. U.S. Congress passes Defense of Marriage Act, 1996. South African constitution forbids discrimination based on sexual/gender orientation, 1996. Will and Grace debuts on television, 1998. Matthew Shepard murdered in Wyoming, 1998. Queer as Folk debuts on U.K. television, 1999. Scotland repeals Section 28, 2000. Vermont recognizes same-sex civil unions, 2000. Gay and lesbian soldiers permitted to serve in U.K., 2000. Queer as Folk debuts on U.S. television, 2000.

258 *Boom Bang-a-Bang* **(1995) | Jonathan Harvey, English**

[Dark comedy; 5M, 2W; 1 set.] Harvey continues to explore lives of ordinary Londoners. This play offers one rarely obtained glimpse of the time: Michael died of a brain tumor, but everyone is sure it is a cover-up that he had AIDS. Lee says, "Maybe it would have been easier if he had had AIDS. [...] We expect AIDS. We don't expect a brain tumour. I thought he'd gone off me coz it was always 'Not now Lee I've got a headache.'" As he had done when Michael was alive, Lee invites friends to watch the telecast of the Eurovision Song Contest. Things go awry. Lee's best friend Nick finds out that his girlfriend is in a relationship with Lee's sister. Nick moans, "Christ, Lee, why aren't I gay?" He accepts Lee's invitation to move in with him, leaving the playgoer to wonder how long he will remain straight. Steph, a bitter queen who passed up Michael's funeral, pulls several nasty tricks, further eroding his relationship with Lee. Lee is at ease in his skin, feeling that being gay is "Something special," but at play's end he is ready to take out his frustrations on his upstairs neighbor who has revealed a liking for bondage. Only bumbling Roy, who has outed the two women, remains pretty much the same, high on ecstasy and cocaine. The play opened in London, 1995, with Chris Hargreaves and Francis Lee, directed by Kathy Burke. § Harvey, J. *Plays 1*. Methuen Drama, 1999. 185–278.

259 *Clean* **(1995) | Edwin Sánchez, Puerto Rican**

[Ethnic drama; 5M, 1W; flexible set.] Sánchez takes on one of the strongest taboos in our culture: a romance between a pubescent boy and a priest—and does so with a fairly even hand. Gustavito is in love with his priest. The father begs him to back off: "I'm a thirty-year-old man, Gustavito, you're a ten-year-old boy. What you want is impossible. I'm not going to betray my life for you." Gustavito's father Kiko and his brother Junior threaten the boy and the priest. Norry, a drag artist for whom Gustavito's stepmother Mercy is making a wedding dress, further upsets the family's equilibrium, confusing the matter even more when he unexpectedly falls in love with Mercy and awakens conflicting feelings in Junior. In a rage Kiko takes the family back to Puerto Rico. They stay there for five years, returning to New York for Gustavito's mother's funeral. Gustavito heads straight for the priest to declare that his feelings are unchanged: "What I felt ... feel for you is not wrong, and what you feel for me is not wrong." The priest sadly tells him, "I know the world that we live in, there is no place for us there." But the play ends with their declaring their love before God. It opened in Hartford, Conn., 1995, with Joe Quintero, Neil Maffin, and A. Benard Cummings, directed by Graciela Daniele. (Sánchez's next play, *The Road*, 1999, about an estranged son dying of AIDS, feels like an older work he pulled from his trunk.) § Sánchez, E. *Clean.* Broadway Play, 1997. 77p.

260 *Comfort and Joy* (1995) | Jack Heifner, American

[Domestic comedy; 3M, 2W, 1X; 1 set.] The play builds on gay clichés. Scott is a closeted Hollywood studio publicist, the only child of a nouveau riche Texas family. His mother domineers him: she accepts that he is gay but not that he actually goes with other men. He feels guilty for having been in Houston with his family when his former lover died of AIDS. Tony, his partner for two years now, is an airline steward, one of three children born to an abandoned mother. Reared with Italian Catholic guilt but somehow managing to escape the burden, he sees life fairly steadily and whole. It is Christmas, and Scott has invited his mother. Tony's siblings unexpectedly show up also: Victor, who has been thrown out of his home by his ultra-conservative wife after confessing he cheated on her with a Disneyland apprentice and is now drinking himself into oblivion; and the "very pregnant" and unmarried Gina, who gorges on cheese and junk food. Heifner's innovation is to have a fairy—not a Tinkerbell or even an Ariel, but more an independent Puck—preside over the proceedings to bring all aright. The play opened in Portland, Ore., 1995, with Cameron Watson and Michael Mendelson, directed by Cliff Fannin Baker. § Heifner, J. *Comfort and Joy: A Play in Two Acts.* Dramatic, 1999. 102p.

261 *The Coronation Voyage* (1995) | Michel Marc Bouchard, Canadian

[Study of corruption; 8M, 6W; flexible set.] Three men of varying degrees of power are on a ship destined for the 1952 coronation of Queen Elizabeth. They are a minister accompanied by his outspoken wife and daughter, a mafioso chief fleeing Canada with his two sons; and a diplomat who has arranged, for a sizable fee, to furnish the chief and his family with new passports. When the diplomat sees Sandro, 13, he adds a proviso: they will get the passports "in exchange for one night with your youngest son." He coldly admits, "there's something titillating about committing an act that is illegal and immoral. It's always a delightful sensation." And he shows no remorse that afterwards "Their smiles are different, so are their eyes. Some of them become withdraw, others grow to like it."

He compares the sacrifice to that demanded of Abraham. The father agrees to the request. The diplomat hands over the boys' passports and promises to give Sandro the father's after their night together. But Étienne finds out what his father has done. He and Sandro show up the next morning to announce that the diplomat "fell overboard." Étienne casually adds, "We helped him," and Sandro mentions, "He said he had something for you in his vest pocket, but he didn't have time to give it to me." *Le voyage du couronnement* opened in Montreal, 1995. Its English premiere was in Calgary, 2000, with Todd Waite, directed by Roy Surette. § Bouchard, M. M. *The Coronation Voyage.* Trans. by Linda Gaboriau. Talonbooks, 1999. 128p.

262 *Dog Opera* (1995) | Constance Congdon (1944–), American

[Psychological drama; 6M, 1W; flexible set.] A series of vignettes reveal the sad lives of Peter and his best friend Madeline. They are perfect for each other, save for the matter of sex. As Tim, Peter's latest attempt at a gay relationship, tells him, "Do you know why you haven't gotten a lover before now? You never needed one. You just needed to get laid. You are in a celibate marriage with Madeline. The 'marriage of true minds' already happened when you were sixteen." Madeline's life goes nowhere. Peter loses Tim. It is mysterious how he contacts HIV since Tim is negative. Peter does have a fling with a Greek while he and his father are on vacation, and he has sex with a hustler, the even more lost Jackie, 16, whose poignant story weaves through the play. Increasingly brutalized, Jackie is finally murdered by someone he has picked up. The premiere was in New York, 1995, with Albert Macklin and Kevin Dewey, directed by Gerald Gutierrez. § In Lane, E., and Shengold, N., eds. *Actor's Book.* 87–166.

263 *Jim Dandy* (1995) | Sky Gilbert, Canadian

[Shock farce; 6M, 1W; 3 sets.] Ric Knoles (in E.-M. Kröller, *Canadian Literature,* 127) describes Gilbert as "a clever and provocative, if not always careful, playwright, dealing more in the audacious gesture than in the nuanced construction of action, language, or characterization. But at its transgressive best his dramaturgy functions effectively to implicate audiences in oppositional art, and to confront them with transgressive sexuality in a homophobic culture." This play is a perfect example. It is actually three one-acts held together by a "presenter" who, after portraying Wilde in a prologue, successively plays Andy Warhold, Radio Rooster, and himself. The first scene portrays a masochistic drag queen who shares an apartment with a male prostitute. He adamantly refuses to have sex with her, so she settles for provoking him to violence. (As part of the shock technique at one point he sits on the toilet in plain sight, uncertain whether he has gas or really needs to go.) The second scene occurs in a bathhouse. A lawyer meets a 19-year-old who bums cigarettes off him. For money he is ready to have sex. But when he drops that he has recently converted to Islam, the lawyer angers him by pointing out that he is not following Muslim principles of conduct. The lawyer ends up with the male prostitute. In the third scene, while talking on the telephone, a mother bets a friend that she can entice her teenage son to orally bring her to orgasm. Laying the receiver on the table, she begins her seduction act before bringing him in on the joke. They fake their big sex scene and claim the money. But after the blackout there is the possibility that the sex will become real. The play opened in Toronto, 1995, with Park Bench, Peter Lynch, Brendan Wall, Hugo Dann, and Balazs Koos, directed by Gilbert. § Gilbert, S. *Painted, Tainted, Sainted: Four Plays.* Playwrights Canada, 1996. 215–75.

264 *Minutes from the Blue Route* (1995) | **Tom Donaghy (1963?–), American**

[Domestic drama; 2M, 2W; 1 set.] Donaghy paints a dark portrait of a family one Labor Day weekend, showing them ineffectually trying to escape their confining existences. The father, 58, is losing his job due to his company's downsizing and wants to sell their house to move some place they can better afford, but their daughter, 21, cannot bring herself to leave its security after being irrationally traumatized by an airplane flight that had to be (safely) aborted. The son, 29, is HIV-positive. A magician, he is in an ill-defined relationship with the unseen Jonathan (only offstage characters have names). His parents have summoned him to talk the sister into staying in college, taking advantage of the full scholarship she has received. It becomes clear that he presents them a major worry: that they will be financially incapable of taking care of him if (they seem to mean *when*)

his health worsens. What is supposed to be an overnight visit stretches out to the full weekend, with the results that Jonathan fires him from his job even as Jonathan wants the two of them to move in together. Or so the son claims. In reporting to his sister how Saturday night he picked up her classmate Tommy (who had ran away from his own wedding), he comments, "No one's kissed me in such a long time." Several minor calamities paradoxically seem to liberate them. The father has saved an illustrated Bible the son made as a child; the last image in it represents Lazarus. This richly textured play opened in Poughkeepsie, N.Y., 1995, with Matt McGrath, directed by David Warren. In 1996 Donaghy's 1993 one-act play *The Dadshuttle*, about a gay son and his father on the way to a Philadelphia train station, was filmed. § Donaghy, T. *The Beginning of August and Other Plays.* Grove, 2000. 105–73. Includes *The Dadshuttle.* 1–22.

265 *Raised in Captivity* (1995) | **Nicky Silver, American**

[Domestic drama; 3M, 2W; flexible set.] *Whacky* and *bleak* are not adjectives that often go together—except in Silver's world. Twins Sebastian Bliss and Bernadette Dixon are the fulcrum on which the plot turns, but they, like the other characters, are alienated from others, having sealed off almost all their emotions. Bernadette longs to be an alcoholic. Her husband is a dentist who hates teeth; he quits his profession to become a painter, turning out white-on-white paintings that only a blind psychologist can see. Sebastian's very name is worth pondering: gay, wounded figuratively before the opening and literally during the course of action; anything but blissful. "I'm about to celebrate my eleventh anniversary of physical and emotional celibacy," he tells his failure of an analyst. He tries to fill the vacuum by corresponding with a prisoner serving a life sentence for murder. A graphic contrapuntal description of Sebastian's lover's death from AIDS and the convict's murder of his victim ends Act 1. In very different ways both men have been left numb, the one by what he witnessed, the other by the crime he committed. Act 2 ends on a guarded upbeat. The convict rejects Sebastian's dependence on him; Bernadette's husband leaves for Africa, taking the psychologist. The twins are left with her four-month-old child. Sebastian volunteers to act as the father. Yet his past clings, perhaps not in an altogether healthy way. He requests that the child be named after his lover, whom he judges to be another criminal: "Before he died, he slept with several people. I think. Willfully. [...] I think he killed them." The play opened in New York, 1995, with Peter Frechette, directed by David Warren. § Silver, N. *Raised in Captivity*. Dramatists, 1995. 82p.

266 *The Rise and Fall of Peter Gaveston* (1995) | Greg MacArthur (1970–), Canadian

[Biographical farce; 7M, 1W; flexible set.] The play wittily layers anachronistic contemporary views about sexual and political identity onto the medieval story of Edward II and Piers (Peter) Gaveston as recounted by Marlowe. Roles shift. Isabel says, "I'm a liberal woman. I'm no prude. I'm sure we can come up with some kind of arrangement." She too is bedded by Peter, and all three stand before the marriage altar so that when Edward makes his vows, it is unclear whether they are to Isabel or to Peter. Commenting on the drama are a brothel owner, two royal attendants, and two pensioners. One of the last remarks: "Even queers have a reputation to uphold. [...] You know, it's not so much their sex I object to. It's not their physical perversions. My father was a farmer. I understand primal urges. But you know, it's their culture. Their—Their tastes. Their feminine practices. Their extravagance. Their excessive behaviour. [...] That's the trouble with queers. Underneath all the make-up and pearls, they still have the hearts of men. And the arrogance of Kings." The brothel keeper says, "All I want is to suck a man's dick and make an honest living without the words imprisonment, sodomy, rape, pervert ringing in my ears." In one of the more farcical scenes, various pairings of lovers pop in and out of closed doors. When the country's economy is wracked by the king's excesses, Walter Langley moves to get rid of the "slut" and to seduce Isabel. The dead Peter ends "stuck" in a field of red poppies, a color he has always hated. The play opened in Toronto, 1995, with Clinton Walker and Michael McMurtry, directed by Sarah Stanley. § In Gilbert, S., ed. *Perfectly Abnormal*. 143–83.

267 *Roots and Wings* (1995) | Frank Vickery, Welsh

[Dark comedy; 3M, 3W; 3 sets.] Wisecracking Nigel lies in a hospital bed after his vehicular suicide-murder attempt fails; Kevin, his lover, is down the hall still in a coma. The two had a successful act as female impersonators. They were planning on raising Kevin's daughter after her stepfather rejected the child. Then suddenly, the same evening that Nigel embarrassed his father by calling him on stage during their drag act, Kevin announced that he was going to go back to his wife. The drama lies not between the two men, however, but among the four parents. Nigel's father cannot accept him; Kevin's father has. Nigel's mother is totally supportive; Kevin's mother less so, though she feels that Nigel is better than Kevin's ex-wife. Bit by bit they reveal that they all have messy secrets: physical and emotional infidelities that they have been concealing. Offstage, Kevin comes out of his coma and rejects Nigel's overtures, but the nurse challenges Nigel to fight for what he wants. The play opened in Cardiff, 1995, with Greg Ashton, directed by Phil Clark. § Vickery, F. *Selected Work*; ed. by Phil Clark. Parthian, 2007. 245–378. Includes also *Erogenous Zones*, 1992.

268 *Clocks and Whistles* (1996) | Samuel Adamson (AUS 1969–), English

[Urban romance; 3M, 2W; flexible set.] Henry seems incapable of handling the fact that he is maybe in love with a man he would normally deem unsuitable. Trevor is a self-educated poet whose output is of dubious value in Henry's eyes. Worse, he is blue-collar, complete with dropped aitches and lowbrow tastes, and bisexual to boot. Trevor beds Anne, Henry's best friend. Yet he radiates energy and more depth of knowledge and feeling than either Henry or Anne is willing to credit. A brief repartee about Isherwood's Sally Bowles, for example, suggests that Trevor is more astute than Henry about character. Trevor's soul is bared especially in one scene near the end in which he breaks down crying because he cannot donate blood. In contrast, Henry seems almost inarticulate about his feelings; he resorts to physical fury against the man he suspects of keeping Anne. Consequently, Henry may be redeeming himself when, in the end, he invites Trevor to move in with him, and Trevor accepts. I think Clum misreads Trevor, but he is on target when he writes that "few contemporary plays are as rich in presenting nuances of characters and relationships. Few plays present such a complex love story with such subtlety" (*Out on Stage*, 292–93). The play opened in London,

1996, with John Light and Neil Stuke, directed by Dominic Dromgoole. § In Clum, J., ed. *Asking and Telling*. 247-365.

269 *Deporting the Divas* (1996) | **Guillermo Reyes (CHL 1962-), American**

[Ethnic satire; 4M; flexible set.] Following the success of Reyes's monologue *Men on the Verge of a His-Panic Breakdown*, the play is something of a letdown. It is a postmodern attempt to meld noir parody, romance, and politics, particularly illegal immigration and AIDS issues, in a search for personal identity. Michael Gonzalez, a San Diego–based Latino border patrol agent who does not speak Spanish, becomes disturbed after a raid bursts in on a gay Mexican-American wedding. His wife leaves him, taking the children. He takes refuge in imagining himself "a character in a B-movie" and decides to take Spanish lessons. He is attracted to Sedicio, an undocumented Latino who is taking the class in hopes of finding a husband. The two click, but in the end Michael returns to his wife. All the characters are played by four male actors; the dialogue is self-conscious, with many asides to the audience and self-references to the playwright. Clum holds the play in high esteem, stressing its evocation of the borders that "exist between male-female, masculine-feminine, gay-straight, brown-white, Spanish-English, real-imaginary, real-theater" (*Out on Stage*, 315). The play opened in Los Angeles, 1996, with Julian Vicente (alternating with Robert Adanto), Christopher Liam Moore, Rene Moreno, and Rush Gomoz, directed by Jorge Huerta. It went through several rewrites for subsequent productions. § In Clum, J., ed. *Asking and Telling*. 111-87. In Clum, J., ed. *Gay Drama Now*. 319-412.

270 *Flipzoids* (1996) | **Ralph B. Peña (Philippines, 1962-), American**

[Ethnic drama; 1M, 2W; unit set.] The play's editor (419) asserts that it is "not only an important breakthrough in Filipino American theater, but a significant contribution to Philippine theater as well" for the way it "participates fully in the anticolonial and anti-imperialist discourses of Philippine nationalist texts." Three Filipino-Americans arrive at a beach in Southern California. An older woman, Aying, represents the unassimilated Filipina, still tied to her original home by rituals and memories. A younger woman is busily trying to fit in. Redford, in the words of the editor (425), is "a gay, confused young man, who struggles with his Filipino identity in the same way that he struggles with his relationships." Searching for a sense of identity, he spends much time in a toilet on the beach, saying, "I go in here, not to have sex, but to connect. [...] Sitting here, in one of the stalls, I can strip my soul naked to the occupant next door. I can let go." But the anonymous encounters do not fulfill him: "This is my prison. And my sanctuary." He turns to Aying for comfort, to ask, "can I find redemption in public places?" The play opened in New York, 1996, with Ken Leung, directed by Loy Arcenas. § *Savage Stage: Plays by Ma-Yi Theater Company*; ed. by Joi Barrios-Leblanc. Ma-Yi, 2006. 249-72.

271 *The Gay Detective* (1996) | **Gerard Stembridge (1958-), Irish**

[Crime drama; 6M, 1W; extras; unit set.] Set in the year 1993, when Ireland decriminalized homosexuality, it is the first Irish play in which identity politics is central. Pat is the Gay Detective, a label given him by his new lover Ginger. He accidentally solves the mystery of who was with Ginger the night he was mugged, though he does not learn the identity of the muggers. Through undercover work he also solves the mystery of who killed a closeted politician and a rent boy. But in this memory play he is ultimately more concerned with betrayal, his own and that of others. He betrays Ginger when he learns that the latter is HIV-positive and flees. His superintendent betrays him and his own profession when he refuses to arrest the powerful men responsible for the murders because Pat cannot provide the hard evidence to nail them for killing the politician, though he knows where the hustler's body is buried: "Do you seriously think we're going to arrest three distinguished citizens for the murder of a little shit, a little pansy rent boy," he says. Ginger accepts Pat back and points out that they may have many years together. So Pat may have the chance to solve the real mystery—"the big one"—of who he is. "At least I'm heading in the right direction now. Aren't I?" he says. Save for Pat and Ginger, all the roles are doubled. For some reason, the other characters have animal names. The play opened in Dublin, 1996, with Peter Hanly and Eddie Tighe, directed by Stembridge. § Stembridge, G. *The Gay Detective*. New Island, 1996. 80p.

272 *Shopping and Fucking* (1996) | **Mark Ravenhill (1966–), English**

[Sexual satire; 4M, 1W; flexible set.] Ravenhill certainly grabbed attention with his play's title. Its thesis is that almost every aspect of current existence is governed by consumerism: "Civilisation is money. Money is civilisation." Mark, Robbie, and Lulu form a *ménage à trois* that is far distant from the one in Coward's debonair *Design for Living*. Robbie and Lulu scramble to make money by selling the drug ecstasy (though Robbie gets high and gives their supply away) and providing phone sex. Mark is a drug and sex junkie. He hires a 14-year-old hustler for the sole pleasure of performing anilingus on him, to discover that Gary wants to be brutally assaulted anally the way his stepfather abused him. Robbie presumably speaks for Ravenhill when he says, "I think a long time ago there were big stories. Stories so big you could live your whole life in them. The Powerful Hands of the Gods and Fate. The Journey to Enlightenment. The March of Socialism. But they all died or the world grew up or grew senile or forgot them, so now we're all making up our own stories." The premiere was in London, 1996, with Andrew Clover and James Kennedy, directed by Max Stafford-Clark. § Ravenhill, M. *Plays 1*. Methuen Drama, 2001. 1–91.

273 *Some Sunny Day* (1996) | **Martin Sherman, American**

[SF farce; 4M, 2W; 1 set.] In the second part of *A Madhouse in Goa*, 1989, Sherman began drawing an apocalyptical vision of our present-day world. In this play he turns to science fiction, taking a matter as serious as the German threat to Cairo in 1942 and turning it into low comedy. Alec is "a bit of an upper-class twit," but Robin cannot help falling in love with him. What Alec does not suspect is that Robin is really "a creature from another world," who there has the form of "a two foot orange blob." On vacation to Earth, he has taken on the guise of a New Zealand journalist. The British officials have picked up on their relationship, but Alec isn't worried: "I don't think they really believe an officer might be queer, so *that* isn't an issue." They'll see it as "an undesirable friendship," convinced Robin is a spy. Though both men are important to the play, the plot is driven more by the complicated love life of a psychopathic propaganda official torn between a belly dancer and his wife, whom he kills. A fake duchess, a lesbian trying to escape to Palestine, also has a major role. The play opened in London, 1996, with Rupert Everett and David Bark-Jones, directed by Roger Michell. The same year the film *Alive and Kicking* about a dying dancer, based on Sherman's original screenplay, was released. § Sherman, M. *Some Sunny Day: A Play*. Amber Lane, 1996. 93p.

274 *Sordid Lives* (1996–2005) | **Del Shores (1957–), American**

[Blue collar comedy; 6M, 6W; 4 sets.] Shores always approaches his Texas background from a comic angle. Each of the four parts of *Sordid Lives* begins with Ty Williamson's session with his New York psychiatrist, detailing his fears of coming out to his family. His uncle Brother Boy has been committed to a mental institution for more than twenty years for "a severe case of homosexuality" and "transvestism." All comes to a head as a result of Ty's grandmother, Brother Boy's mother, leaving the motel bed she was sharing with a married Vietnam veteran, falling over his wooden legs, and slamming her head against the sink, killing her. Ty's mother wants to pretend none of her life is happening, but the other members of her family thwart her every attempt at respectability. She and Ty reconnect at the funeral; she confesses that she has known he is gay since he was five and long ago accepted the fact. How she will handle her brother may be another story. Wardell, the man who beat up Brother Bob, "my homo best friend[,] and sent him packing to the loony bin," faces up to his sense of guilt and springs him in time to attend the funeral. He appears in full, glorious drag and has the last word. The premiere was in Hollywood, Calif., 1996, with Kirk Geiger and Leslie Jordan (in a tailor-made role as Brother Boy), directed by Shores. It was revised for its 2005 publication to reflect additions made to the film version. Shores wrote the scripts for the 2000 film and the 2008 television series. He was also writing scripts for several episodes of *Queer as Folk*, 2003–05. § Shores, D. *Sordid Lives: A Comedy in Four Chapters*. French, 2005. 89p. + appendices.

275 *The Undertaking* (1996) | **Philip Osment, English**

[Psychological drama; 4M, 1W; flexible set.] The play is yet another exploration of the problems of familial communication. Following Irish-born

Henry's death from AIDS, his lover Howard, his former lover Michael (also Irish), his nurse Eamon, and Henry's friend Sheila undertake a pilgrimage from London to rural Ireland to scatter his ashes. The journey forces Michael to confront his demons. He came out while at Trinity (which is where he met Henry). As a result he felt alienated from his family and failed them when his sister needed help. His inaction set a pattern. When Henry needed him, he again failed, "terrified of being left on my own with him." Howard, HIV-positive, begrudges Henry's willing his property equally to Michael and him. He resents "Henry lying there dying and Michael getting off with his nurse." The van breaks down near Michael's brother's home. Under pressure from the others, he calls Patrick, with the unexpected results that the brothers begin the process of reconciliation. Michael and Howard talk, and Michael and Eamon move onto a new plane of their relationship. Michael admits to his much younger lover: "I might be older. Doesn't mean I'm more grown up." The play opened in Leicester, 1996, with Liam Halligan, Derek Howard, and John Lloyd-Stephenson, directed by James Neale-Kennerley. § Osment, P. *The Undertaking*. Oberon, 1997. 122p.

276   *Visiting Mr. Green* (1996) | Jeff Baron (1952–), American

[Psychological drama; 2M; 1 set.] Even though Baron updated the technology mentioned in the play for its most recent revision, and despite the fact that parents-children conflicts continue to disrupt lives, it feels like a period piece. After nearly hitting the elderly widower Mr. Green, Ross Gardiner is sentenced to pay him a visit once a week. Their relationship is an irritable one: Green resents Ross's intrusion in his life, Ross resents having to be there. Fed up with his parents' treatment of him, his feeling that he must hide his sexual orientation from his company (American Express!), and his self-imposed celibacy, Ross blurts out at the end of Act 1 that he is gay, a *faygele*. Green tries to convince him that he must be mistaken: "Jewish boys are not *faygeles*." While arguing whether one can equate the persecution of Jews with the persecution of homosexuals, including the Holocaust, and questioning whether being "a good Jew" means a son is "supposed to wreck a woman's life and wreck some kids' lives because [...] parents want grandchildren," Green lets slip that he has a daughter but sat *shiva* on her after she married a *goy*. It comes out that Green's wife, however, did not turn her back on her daughter. Green is reconciled with the family he has not known for thirty years, while Ross publicly stands up to his father's homophobia and walks out on him to claim his gay life. The play opened in Stockbridge, Mass., 1996, with Neal Huff, directed by John Rando. A 1999 German telecast *Besuch bei Mr. Green* and a 2003 Serbo-Croatian telecast *U poseti kod gospodina Grina* exist. § Baron, J. *Visiting Mr. Green*. Dramatists, 2005. 52p.

277   *As Bees in Honey Drown* (1997) | Douglas Carter Beane, American

[Satirical comedy; 3M, 3W; flexible set.] It is impossible to know whether Beane's bent for having his gay protagonists fall in love with a woman reflects his sense of the fluidity of sexuality or is a deliberate ploy to play mind games with both the gays and the straights in his audience. Or is it just his insurance for having a commercially successful drama? Con artist Alexa Vere de Vere chooses novelist Evan Wyler as her next victim. Even though he is gay, he falls in love with her and is first devastated and then revengeful when he learns how he has been duped out of $15,000. He seeks out her earlier patsies and meets painter Mike Stabinsky, who accidentally created Alexa. Evan learns from the experience. He writes his second novel, an exposé of Alexa, under his real name, Eric Wollenstein, and he and Mike become a couple. The relatively thin play is a tour de force for an actress. It opened in New York, 1997, with Josh Hamilton and T. Scott Cunningham, directed by Mark Brokaw. § Beane, D. C. *As Bees in Honey Drown*. Dramatists, 1998. 74p.

278   *Civil Sex* (1997–2000) | Brian Freeman (1955–), American

[Docudrama; 4M, 1W; flexible set.] Freeman was one of the founding actors of Pomo Afro Homos. This play is based on interviews he conducted with people who knew Bayard Rustin (1912–1987). It begins with Republican Senator Strom Thurmond denouncing Rustin as a sexual pervert in the senator's attempt to cast aspersions on the 1963 march on Washington. It has a double ending: the climax of that march on the steps of the Lincoln Memorial and Rustin's presence at the Gay Pride march in 1986. In between the play traces both his public life as part of the movement and his private life including a number of long-time relationships with white lovers. James Baldwin and Malcolm X have their moment in the drama. Rustin says, "Character is a matter of judgment within the context of a whole life. It is for my peers to judge me and my life." Freeman clearly judges him with deep affection, bringing "a shadowy figure" into the light. The play opened in Washington, D.C., 1997, with Duane Boutté, Michael Stebbins, and Freeman, directed by Freeman. It was subsequently revised for its New York opening, 1999, and its Berkeley, Calif., opening, 2000. § *The Fire This Time: African American Plays for the 21st Century*; ed. by Harry J. Elam, Jr., and Robert Alexander. Theatre Communications, 2004. 91–141.

279   *The Convergence of Luke* (1997) | Harry Rintoul, Canadian

[Sexual drama; 2M; flexible set.] The play follows the complex quasi-symbiotic relationship between two men over the course of fourteen years, 1984 to 1997. Both are trying to make their way in the world and largely failing. Luke is a hustler whom Grandon hires for an evening and ends up falling in love with. Luke feels no reciprocal feelings, much as he comes to depend on Grandon to bail him out of the various messes he ends up falling into: "Just because you have sex with someone, doesn't mean that person has to have an emotional attachment." As far as Luke is concerned, "All we had was sex. Pure an' simple." Luke is perhaps bisexual, perhaps gay for pay, perhaps unwilling to admit his own desires (out of the blue he offers Grandon a blow job). Dyslexic, supporting a woman and their children, he has trouble staying afloat financially. He ends up serving time because of a drug charge; he loses his family. While hustling he meets a university professor, Denholm, who teaches English and gay studies. Denholm teaches him to read; Luke falls in love with him. Meanwhile, Grandon is driven to prove himself but has one run of bad luck after another, perhaps because of his own character flaws. He goes steadily downward, until finally he is reduced to begging. Finding out that Denholm has died from a heart attack, Grandon pursues Luke, recognizing how the two of them have changed positions. Luke rejects him. The play opened in Winnipeg, 1997, with Arne MacPherson and Darcy Fehr, directed by Alan MacInnis. § In Gilbert, S., ed. *Perfectly Abnormal*. 1–78.

280   *Grace* (1997) | Michael Lewis MacLennan, Canadian

[Social drama; 3M, 3W; flexible set.] Six lost souls rattle around Vancouver, their lives intersecting in various, unexpected ways. Acting out of their own misery, they attack others; yet the six mysteriously offer the gift of grace to one another. Jared, having fled his small town Manitoba home, was picked up by Phil, but after Phil's suicide he is on his own, turning "Rent boy. To pay the rent." He is lured by a decoy into the woods and badly beaten by a gang of gay-bashers. Lonnie discovers him bleeding. She earlier lost her wallet, which he found and took the money from, to lose it during the beating. Instead of his looking for someone to save him, she tells him he should "save yourself." Lonnie knows something about abuse from her husband. She makes a temporary sexual connection with the poet Paula. Earlier Paula unreasonably attacks Hugh, who is fired from his high-paying job because of his alcoholism. A closet case, he tries, unsuccessfully, to pick up Jared. He runs into Paula again; this time she is forgiving. Finally, there is Ruth, who is still haunted by her dead husband whom she hates for having kicked their "deviant" son out of the house, causing her to lose him forever. At the end she seems on the verge of taking the mentally challenged Thomas in as her new son. The play opened in Victoria, 1997, with Todd Witham, directed by Gina Wilkinson. § MacLennan, M. L. *Grace*. Scirocco Drama, 1998. 87p.

281   *Gross Indecency: The Three Trials of Oscar Wilde* (1997) | Moisés Kaufman (VEN 1963–), American

[Docudrama; 9M; unit set.] Kaufman and his Tectonic Theater Project are leaders in documentary-style theater. Here the playwright has assembled texts recreating chief moments from the trials, intercut with both pre- and post-trial related material. Thus greater prominence is given to Frank Harris than usual, and even George Bernard Shaw has a role. Douglas has his hearing; Robert Ross and other close friends are conspicuous by their absence. The first trial is the result of Wilde's filing a slander charge against Douglas's father. Wilde loses, but so much comes out about his sexual activities that charges are brought against him. The second trial results in a hung jury. Because of the publicity, the charges are renewed. At the third trial he is found guilty and sentenced to the maximum penalty. Kaufman explains in his introduction that he "wanted to tell the *story—a story—* of these trials," but he also wanted simultaneously "to explore theatrical language and form." Clearly, other motives were to explore the relationship of art to its creator and to examine Wilde's importance to gay history. Both these concerns are articulated in an interview Kaufman had with Wilde scholar Marvin Taylor, which is recreated as a pivotal moment at the beginning of Act 2. Taylor holds that "Wilde was less interested in admitting that he had sex with men than he was interested in expressing his own intellectual ideas, his ideas about beauty and about art." But Taylor also emphasizes that, as a result of the trials, "people began identifying themselves as a specific type of person based on their attraction to people of the same sex." The play opened in New York, 1997, with Michael Emerson and Bill Dawes, directed by Kaufman. § Kaufman, M. *Gross Indecency: The Three Trials of Oscar Wilde.* Vintage, 1998. 134p.

282 *In Mortality* (1997) | **Leo Cabranes-Grant (1960–), Puerto Rican**

[Domestic drama; 3M; 2 sets.] So many plays in which a couple engage a third man in an attempt to spice up their sex life end disastrously for all concerned. Cabranes-Grant takes a different slant. Catholic James Gorman, a cancer research scientist, and Jewish Edgar Silverman, a lawyer, have been together for seven years. Rejecting monogamy—James had a brief affair with a woman living in their Boston South Side complex; Edgar has started exploring the baths—they take out an ad seeking a partner "to have safe fun with two white guys" as a way to celebrate Edgar's 40th birthday. Arturo Marquez responds. He is Puerto Rican, "one half [...] African-Caribbean black," an American history professor at the University of Massachusetts, and HIV-positive. This unlikely trio find their way through stereotypes and misconceptions, anxieties and uncertain feelings. The morning after, James reflects, "I made a few discoveries. I've never seen you [Edgar] doing certain things." Edgar ponders: "Maybe we were monogamous for so long because we were scared." Arturo envies the two of them having "a full life to think about. A future. That's what I miss the most. The sensation of having a lot of room, a lot of space ahead of me." The playgoer leaves with a sense that what began as simply a pornographic evening may be metamorphosing into something more meaningful for all three men. The play had a staged reading in Boston, 1997. § Cabranes-Grant, L. *Chat Room and Other Latino Plays.* Floricanto, 2007. 67–127.

283 *The Invention of Love* (1997) | **Tom Stoppard (TCH 1937–), English**

[Biographical study; 12M, 1W; flexible set.] Stoppard was earlier bemused by Wilde in *Travesties,* 1974. Wit and erudition here combine to depict the life of poet and classical scholar A. E. Housman (1959–1936) set against the Aesthetic Movement led by Wilde. Dead, Housman pauses on the shores of the Styx to look back at his younger self, hopelessly in love with his Oxford classmate Moses Jackson. Act 1 covers the Oxford years. We meet Walter Pater, John Ruskin, Benjamin Jowett, and other scholars. Housman matriculates the year Wilde finishes his studies (there is no record the two ever met). Housman fails to obtain his degree (Stoppard suggests he may have deliberately failed so as to stay close to Jackson) and takes a job in the Patent Office where Jackson works. A fictional gay friend reads Housman's unrequited passion only too well. Act 2 looks at significant moments in his life after Oxford: his finally declaring his love to Jackson, to the latter's discomfort; writing the poems that make up *A Shropshire Lad*; his reaction to Wilde's arrest and imprisonment. The two meet, and Wilde defends his martyrdom against Housman's timidity as the better choice. The play opened in London, 1997, with John Wood, Paul Rhys, Ben Porter, and Michael Fitzgerald, directed by Richard Eyre. § Stoppard, T. *The Invention of Love.* Grove, 1998. 102p.

284 *Martin Yesterday* (1997) | **Brad Fraser, Canadian**

[Psychological drama; 4M, 1W; flexible set.] "Y'a personne qui connaît personne," Yves says. Certainly Matt discovers how little he knows Martin Yesterday, the Toronto councilman with whom he falls in love. Matt writes a satiric comic book series with a gay superhero. He is on the verge of success, which brings its problems since his female partner is not included in an offer to move up. He would like to be part of a lasting gay relationship. The older Martin seems to promise stability. But his dark side emerges. He is keeping two younger men, Yves and Rex, at his house, but instead of offering them safe haven he is actually enabling their self-destruction. All three are HIV-positive, and Martin may well be the one who knowingly infected the two youths. After succumbing to a fit of madness himself, Matt realizes he needs to get out of the sick pattern Martin has created. Rex comes to the same conclusion, but Yves remains trapped. Beginning as a 1997 radio drama, it was adapted the same year to the stage with Steve Cumyn and Stewart Arnott, directed by Fraser. That script was radically reworked before it opened in Edmonton, 1998. During 2003–05 Fraser paused to write a number of scripts for *Queer as Folk*. § Fraser, B. *Martin Yesterday*. NeWest, 1998. 99p.

285 *A Question of Mercy* (1997) | David Rabe, American

[AIDS drama; 6M, 1W; unit set.] In 1991 Dr. Selzer published an article in the *New York Times* about his having been asked to assist a terminally ill patient's suicide. Rabe felt compelled to dramatize the story. In his version Thomas Ames calls Dr. Robert Chapman and asks him to assist his Columbian-born lover Anthony Calderon, suffering from the ravishes of AIDS, to meet his end as humanely as possible. Over the course of a month, the three, along with the lovers' friend Susanah, discuss the psychological, moral, professional, and legal ramifications of euthanasia. When it is too late, Anthony chooses life. The melodramatic arrival of two policemen to arrest Dr. Chapman comes across as a last-minute theatrical gimmick. The play opened in New York, 1997, with Stephen Spinella and Juan Carlos Hernandez, directed by Douglas Hughes. § Rabe, D. *A Question of Mercy, Based upon the Journal by Richard Selzer*. Dramatists, 1998. 75p.

286 *The Secret Fall of Constance Wilde* (1997) | Thomas Kilroy, Irish

[Biographical study; 2M, 1W, extras; unit set.] Though Wilde and Douglas again reenact their sexual argument, the voice of Oscar's wife is equally strong in this drama. It is left up to the playgoer, however, to decide what may be the connection between her being sexually abused by her father (Kilroy's invention) and her falling in love with a gay, or bisexual, man—a *Uranodiominge*, "an Urning who can also live with a woman." Oscar avers that the androgynous Bosie has healed the "great wound in Nature, the wound of gender" and fulfilled "the dream of Paradise [...] where there is no man, no woman, no duality, no contrary." As he moves toward his martyrdom, Bosie encourages him to hold fast against the "larger enemy," that "body of powerful interests in this country which hates love." Even Constance says, "There's something about sexuality that raises a primitive fear in people." What has made her literally fall then, injuring herself? What did she see at the top of the stairs? Her father? Oscar's affairs? Herself? The play opened in Dublin, 1997, with Robert O'Mahoney and Andrew Scott, directed by Patrick Mason. *My Scandalous Life*, 2004, depicting Douglas's reminiscences during the last year of his life, serves as a companion piece. § Kilroy, T. *The Secret Fall of Constance Wilde*. Gallery, 1997. 69p.

287 *The Soldier Dreams* (1997) | Daniel MacIvor (1962–), Canadian

[Psychological drama; 5M, 3W; unit set.] The playwright began as performance artist. He gradually moved to experimental two- or three-men pieces and finally to more conventional dramaturgy. He founded the theater company da da kamera in Toronto. He is a stage and film actor, having the starring role in Thom Fitzgerald's *Beefcake*, 1998. His screenplays include *Wilby Wonderful*, 2004. Generally his plays are small-scale, but here he is more expansive. Listening to the ramblings of a dying man, his family imagines he is referring to one event, but the audience is privy to the fact that he is remembering an entirely different occasion. They think David is recalling his sister's wedding (to which his lover Richard was not invited). In reality, he is remembering his encounter with a German student that occurred while he was in Ottawa for the wedding. Further underscoring the problem of communication, each person maintaining a vigil at David's bedside thinks he or she is the one who taught him sign language in order to converse privately. They agree only on one thing: that "if David had his way we'd probably all be dancing." Other motifs unite the play: for example, a suggestive joke about gays that David's brother-in-law tells and that Richard finds "homophobic [...] offensive" originated with David, who equally offended the student when he tried it out on him. The student holds that gays must remain vigilant at all times against homophobia: "Even when the soldier dreams the war goes on." At the end the ghost of the dead student awaits David: "No more living between 'was' and 'will be.'" The play opened in Toronto, 1997, with John McLachlin, Volker Bürger, and MacIvor, directed by MacIvor and Daniel Brooks. § MacIvor, D. *I Still Love You: Five Plays*. Playwrights Canada, 2006. 37–76.

288 *Corpus Christi* (1998) | **Terrence McNally, American**

[Spiritual drama; 13M; no set.] McNally grew up in Corpus Christi, Texas. One suspects there are many autobiographical elements in the text; certainly the tribute to his English teacher is one. In retelling the life of Christ in contemporary terms defined by thirteen gay men, the play's premise is summed up by Joshua (Jesus) as a paradox: "We're each special. We're each ordinary. We're each divine." The disciples come from all walks of life: doctor, lawyer, fisherman, masseur, hairdresser, hustler. Joshua emphasizes the play's basic message, "When we don't love one another, we don't love God." Taking on multiple roles the actors/disciples play out the events of Christ's life from nativity to crucifixion with the addition of contemporary events such as a senior prom, a gay wedding. The troubled premiere was in New York, 1998, with Anson Mount and Josh Lucas, directed by Joe Mantello. A documentary, *Corpus Christi: Playing with Redemption*, 2011, follows the preparations of a road company's production of the play, emphasizing its universality. § McNally, T. *Corpus Christi: A Play*. Grove, 1998. 81p.

289 *Dogeaters* (1998–2001) | **Jessica Hagedorn (PHL 1949–), American**

[Political tragedy; 9M, 7W; flexible set.] Using Brechtian techniques, Hagedorn adapted her 1990 novel to the stage. Incorporating a broad sweep of the 1982 Manila scene, the plot pivots on the assassination of Senator Domingo Avila (a fictional character). Having stolen Rainer Werner Fassbinder's camera bag, junkie/hustler Joey Sands, 16, flees and accidentally witnesses the murder. He turns to his pimp to protect him; instead the pimp sells him out. Suspecting something has gone wrong, Joey kills him and returns to the nightclub where he works as deejay. Its owner Perlita, a drag queen, arranges to have an insurgent group whisk him off into the mountains. At least for the time, the group gets him off drugs. There he meets the senator's daughter, who has been brutally raped by her uncle and his military men. The author's alter ego, prepares to leave the country, and the play ends abruptly, nothing resolved any more than it was in reality. The play opened in La Jolla, Calif., 1998, with Seth Gilliam, Alberto Isaac, Alec Mapa, and Christopher Donahue, directed by Michael Greif. It was subsequently revised before opening in New York, 2001. § Hagedorn, J. *Dogeaters: A Play about the Philippines*. Theater Communications, 2003. 109p.

290 *Down Dangerous Passes Road* (1998) | **Michel Marc Bouchard, Canadian**

[Psychological fantasy; 3M; 1 set.] Three brothers—three corpses: Victor, the suicidal driver of the wrecked truck; Ambrose, home for his youngest brother's wedding, minus his lover who is dying of AIDS in Montreal; Carl, the groom never to be—face the demons they have been battling for fifteen years, since they deliberately let their drunken embarrassment of a father, the town's laughing stock, die in the stream just below the road where their truck overturned, killing them. Carl thanks Ambrose for not bringing his boyfriend "to shock all the families." Victor regrets his not bringing him: his "kids would've liked to see it." Ambrose seems to be the most sensitive of the three; at least, he is the first to intuit that they are dead. But he judges himself harshly: "I'm pathetic. My boyfriend's dying of AIDS. I admit to my brother I used to be in love with him and I'm the one who criticizes other people for their clichés." The brothers are filled with memories; Victor seeks atonement; but they seem no closer to reconciliation, not even in their shared death. *Le chemin des passes-dangereuses* premiered in Montreal, 1998. It opened in Toronto, 2001, with David Jansen, directed by Sarah Stanley. § Bouchard, M. M. *Down Dangerous Passes Road*. Trans. by Linda Gaboriau. Talonbooks, 2000. 95p.

291 *The Dying Gaul* (1998) | **Craig Lucas (1951–), American**

[Revenge drama; 3M,1W; flexible set.] Lucas wrote the script for the much admired AIDS film *Longtime Companion*, 1989. This play is a far cry from that achievement. Robert has written an autobiographical screenplay *The Dying Gaul*, based on his and his late lover's experiences. It describes Malcolm's sufferings from the ravages of AIDS; it does not reveal that Robert eased him into death. A bisexual producer, Jeffrey, buys the script with the proviso that Robert turn it into a heterosexual tragedy. Soon the two men are having an affair. Jeffrey's wife becomes suspicious. Discovering that Robert has become addicted to online chat rooms after Malcolm's death, she disguises herself as a gay man and searches him out on his favorite site. There she pretends to be Malcolm speaking from the dead. When Robert discovers the ruse, he first considers suicide, but then he cuts up the monkshood he has thought to ingest and mixes it into a salad she has prepared. Shortly afterwards she crashes her car into a concrete divider, killing herself and her two children. The play opened in Glasgow, 1998, with Stephen Scott and Henry Ian Cusick, directed by Jon Pope. Revised, the American production opened the same year in New York with Tim Hopper and Cotter Smith, directed by Mark Brokaw. Lucas wrote and directed the 2005 film. Schildcrout treats play and film with great respect in *Murder Most Queer*; I find both repugnant. § Lucas, C. *What I Meant Was: New Plays and Selected One-Acts.* Theatre Communications, 1999. 1–78.

292 *Family Values* (1998) | Charles Deemer (1939–), American

[Domestic drama; 3M, 3W; unit set.] Setting his play on July 4, 1976, Deemer weaves together two very different themes: parenting and the right to die. Thomas Wellington, who takes too much after his father, is not having an easy time accepting the changes coming to his family even though he has earlier been brave enough to come out to them. His father accepts that his son is gay, but will not permit him and his partner Victor to share a room when they are summoned for an extended visit. Thomas also faces his father's disapproval when he tells him that his ex-wife is voluntarily giving their son over to the men. His sister Emily is also there, once again warring with her father over her liberal beliefs. Thomas is not ready to hear that his father plans to kill himself to escape the ravages of a virulent cancer and the onset of Alzheimer's. Vincent, though kept on the margin of the family, provides a point of stabilization for them all. He opens and closes the play with his rewrite of Thomas Jefferson's Declaration of Independence to apply to a need to redefine family. The play opened in Salem, Ore., 1998, under the title *Famililly*, with Tripp Robbins and David Egan, directed by Laney Roberts. § Deemer, C. *3 Plays about Family.* Round Bend, 2016. 7–117.

293 *Four* (1998) | Christopher Shinn (1975–), American

[Psychological drama; 3M, 1W; flexible set.] Finding no interest in his plays in New York, Shinn began his career with the Royal Court Theatre in London. Yet his work is very American. In *Four* two couples try to connect linguistically and physically on the Fourth of July. Despite much talk and finally sexual intercourse, both couples fail; when the fireworks go off, each is alone. It is telling that most of their time together, they are aimlessly driving. Joe, 40, an African American English professor, meets the improbably named June, 16, white, via computer hookup. Often a pompous ass, Joe lectures June about his tastes, takes pleasure in the fact that he is being adulterous (without ever mentioning that he is on the down low), but never seems to examine his motivations. June wants the encounter, but he sneers at a classmate for acting too much "Like a faggot" (though the words are actually Joe's). Simultaneously, Joe's daughter, 16, is enacting a similar pattern of invitation followed by withdrawal with a boy of Puerto Rican descent, 19. The play opened in London, 1998, with Joseph Mydell and Connor Ratliff, directed by Richard Wilson. It opened in New York, 2001, with Isiah Whitlock, Jr., and Keith Nobbs, directed by Jeff Cohen. Joshua Sanchez wrote the screenplay for the 2012 film. § Shinn, C. *Where Do We Live and Other Plays.* Theatre Communications, 2005. 1–50.

294 *Handbag: The Importance of Being Someone* (1998) | Mark Ravenhill, English

[Farce; 3M, 3W; flexible set.] A revamped *Importance of Being Earnest* gets mixed up with a contemporary London set of relationships. Mauretta and Suzanne, a lesbian couple, want a baby. Tom, one half of a gay couple, provides the sperm for Mauretta. These parents turn out to be the most stable characters in both the play and the play within the play. Their partners stray. Suzanne is attracted by Lorraine, one of the women she is using in an advertising gimmick. David picks up the hustler Phil, who becomes dependent upon him. David and Tom separate. But then Phil and Lorraine become a couple. Lorraine, like Prism in *Earnest*, is hired as the nanny for Mauretta's son Jack. She and Phil steal the child, but he dies while Phil is looking after him. Meanwhile, Cardew (also from *Earnest*) is accused of molesting the boys in his charge. One boy has already run away from his school. As the two worlds collide, Cardew momentarily mistakes Phil for the lost boy. The play ends with Prism arranging to mix up her charge and her novel so Cardew can take the baby as his own. It opened in London, 1998, with Paul Rattray, directed by Nick Philippou. § Ravenhill, M. *Plays 1*. Methuen Drama, 2001. 141–226.

295 *The Judas Kiss* (1998) | **David Hare** (1947–), **English**

[Biographical study; 6M, 1W; 1 sets.] Hare chose to depict Wilde's state just before his arrest and soon after his release from prison. The drama grows entirely out of the relations between Wilde, Douglas, and Robert Ross. Douglas emerges as a totally self-centered individual, "full of cunning," ready to use Wilde when it is convenient and to betray him when his usefulness is over. Towards the end of the play he announces his heterosexuality and gives a glimpse of his future religious conversion. The play is probably the least sympathetic to Wilde of all the ones written about him, though there is a certain noble, even tragic finality in his inaction: "I am cast in a role. My story has already been written. How I choose to play it is a mere matter of taste. The performance of the actor will not determine the action." Hare eschewed any real attempt to reproduce Wilde's witticisms. The tensions between the English and the Irish are referenced. Robbie and the offstage Constance draw our sympathy. We can take pleasure in the wrongness of Douglas's assessment of Wilde's future reputation. The play opened in London, 1998, with Liam Neeson, Tom Hollander, and Peter Capaldi, directed by Richard Eyre. § Hare, D. *The Judas Kiss*. Grove, 1998. 115p.

296 *The Most Fabulous Story Ever Told* (1998) | **Paul Rudnick, American**

[Religious satire; 4M, 5W; flexible set.] Act 1, somewhat in the style of Thornton Wilder's *The Skin of Our Teeth*, retells Bible stories from the creation to the nativity. God begins his divine plan by placing Adam and Steve and then Jane and Mabel in the Garden of Eden. The four leave the Garden, endure the flood, make it out of Egypt, and end up in Bethlehem. Adam is perpetually filled with wonder; Steve is ever the logical atheist. These traits continue with them in Act 2, set in a Greenwich Village loft on Christmas Eve. Often politically incorrect, characters take potshots at all kinds of gay stereotypes (including oblique references to Kushner's *Angels in America*). Adam voices how happy he is. He becomes a father when Jane delivers her baby girl (perhaps to be called Satan). And he finally decides to take full control of his life when Steve forces him to face up to the fact that he, Steve, will die from AIDS. The comedy wears well. It opened in Williamstown, Mass., 1998, with Alan Tudyk and Bobby Cannavale, directed by Christopher Ashley. § *The Collected Plays of Paul Rudnick*. Itbooks, 2010. 135–246.

297 *On a Muggy Night in Mambai* (1998) | **Mahesh Dattani, Indian**

[Sexual drama; 7M, 1W; unit set.] In his introduction, John McRae asserts that this is "the first play in Indian theatre to handle openly gay themes of love, partnership, trust, and betrayal." Kamlesh is ready to defy the Indian social code: "Let them talk! If two men want to love one another, what's the harm?" But he and Sharad break up, even though Sharad loves him deeply and is everything Kamlesh has ever wanted, because Kamlesh cannot let go of his former lover Prakash. Kamlesh continues to pine for him even after Prakash proposes to Kamlesh's sister Kiran in an attempt "to be a real man" and seems paralyzed to take any action. Kamlesh's friends are horrified that he has not warned Kiran. But he convinces himself that Prakash is telling the truth when he says "he is heterosexual now." It takes Sharad's performing a parody of "real" men "thrusting themselves on to the world [with] all that penis power" for Kamlesh to realize how stupid he has been to give Sharad up: "he has the courage to live with me, we both do— to live openly as two men in love." For the first time Kamlesh says, "I love you," and means it. Prakash's hypocrisy and cynicism thus hits Kamlesh all the harder when Prakash privately upbraids him: "You fool. Can't you see? [...] Once we are married, I could see you more often without causing any ... suspicion." Finally recognizing that his friends are correct, he tells Kiran the truth, allowing her to see a photograph that makes his and Prakash's previous relationship unmistakable.

Kamlesh's other friends represent varying attitudes about homosexuality. A lesbian is happily in a committed relationship; she feels a sisterly obligation to Kiram and is instrumental in pushing Kamlesh to do the right thing. Ranjit fled India for England ("I can't seem to be both Indian and gay"); he has been living there for twelve years with his lover and is briefly back only in his professional role of "Working with HIV counsellors." Bunny is doubly closeted. A television personality who got his job because he matches the "common perceptions of what a family man ought to look like," he conceals that he is Sikh and gay. After Kamlesh comes clean with his sister, Bunny, rather implausibly, reveals that the evening has convinced him to tell his wife the truth. He even contemplates coming out "in the nine hundredth episode" of his television series. Prakash plays out a dramatic suicide attempt, thwarted by the others. His last gesture is to turn to a guard (who earlier has a sexual rendezvous with Kamlesh) and beg him, "*almost childlike*," "Will you help me?" Sharad exits singing, leaving unresolved whether he will accept Kamlesh back or not. All the while the faint sounds of a traditional wedding going on in the courtyard provide an ironical counterpoint. The play opened in Mumbai, 1998, with Rituraj, Amar Talwar, Joy Sengupta, Denizil Smith, Sanjit Bedi, and Pawan Chopra, directed by Lillette Dubey. Dattani also wrote and directed the very flat 2002 film, *Mango Soufflé*. The screenplay has also been published. § Dattani, M. *Collected Plays*. Penguin, 2000. 43–111.

298   *The Backroom* (1999) | **Adrian Pagan** (BEL 1968?–2007), **English**

[Sexual drama; 7M; 1 set.] Set in an Earls Court male brothel on five consecutive Saturdays, the play depicts the tensions among six rent boys and their self-centered male madam. Charlie and Sandy quickly feel more than just a sexual attraction. But any future is beclouded by Charlie's problems with truthfulness. He invents a whole background and then constantly changes it to the point that one cannot be sure what is authentic and what is made up. Craig, an Australian, is a nurturer who is attracted to Sandy. Dallas is a back-biting troublemaker from Manchester. Madonna is the youngest, a Spaniard who likes to camp. Paul is a troubled army vet. Gary lords it over them all while playing a number of dirty tricks, such as sending Paul to perform anilingus on a client with anal warts. The boys get back at him by identifying the professional footballer with whom Gary is having an affair and threatening to out them, with the result that the footballer drops Gary out of fear. After a series of betrayals on Charlie's part, he and Sandy seem heading for a breakup, especially as Charlie is indirectly instrumental in the police closing down the house. But a romantic epilogue establishes that the two are now running their own sex business together. The play opened in London, 1999, with Ben Price, Justin Salinger, Paul Thomas Hickey, Patrick Baladi, James Lance, Darren Tighe, and Luke Healy, directed by Jonathan Lloyd. § Pagan, A. *The Backroom*. Bush Theatre, 1999. 93p.

299   *Chat Room* (1999) | **Leo Cabranes-Grant, Puerto Rican**

[Psychological drama; 2M, 1W; 1 set.] A play about playing games, the drama has so many twists and turns that at the end the audience cannot be sure what has been real and what has been planned lies or fake spur-of-the-moment improvisations. It begins as an ordinary internet hookup. Drew arrives at Raul's Brookline, Mass., apartment for sex. Both admit that some of the stuff they put on the web was lies: age, size, previous experience. Then, just as it seems that they are ready to move into sex, Drew knocks Raul out with a karate chop. Between scenes Leslie arrives. She may be Drew's incestuous sister, half-sister, accomplice, or betrayer. She undoes Raul's handcuffs and eggs him to treat Drew the way he has been treated, then to call the police. But that will mean publicity and the ultimate outing of the Puerto Rican who has already confessed that his family has refused to acknowledge his sexuality and that he is closeted in his profession. The play may have received a staged reading in Boston in 1999. § Cabranes-Grant, L. *Chat Room and Other Latino Plays*. Floricanto, 2007. 1–65.

300   *Coffeehouse* (1999) | **Michael D. Jackson (1968–), American**

[Romance; 5M, 5W; 1 set.] The play is the first written of a set of twelve in which Jackson examines gay and lesbian history from the 1880s through 2000. They are his bid to write the kind of theater he was not seeing. He notes, "there seemed to be few […] examples of gay life" outside of plays about AIDS or those with "a gaggle of gay men in a New York apartment making gay wise-cracks and bitching or taking off their clothes or both." He wanted to create something that offered "a wider scope to the gay experience" including lesbians.' The setting is a coffeehouse run by Margie, a lesbian who has lost her partner to breast cancer but is finally ready to take a chance on love again. Her waiter Jeremy, 19, has been out since high school, even taking a boy to his senior prom. He is now at the awkward age, too young for the bars, searching for dates via personal ads and the internet. The timid Scott, 21, responds and then freaks when he meets Jeremy the evening the coffeehouse inaugurates a karaoke night with a drag queen in charge and lesbians everywhere. His reaction angers and saddens Jeremy, although he reveals he too has a hang-up about drag. Harry, an older gay who witnessed the Stonewall Inn rebellion, offers advice, praising the role of drag queens at that historic event. Jeremy and Scott's youthful ignorance of their heritage allows him and Margie to offer a hit-and-miss primer of gay history. At evening's end couples pair off: Margie with a fired schoolteacher, Jeremy and Scott, Harry and the drag queen. The play opened in Sacramento, Calif., 1999, with Thomas Richards, Paul Farmer, Talbott Smith, and Bradley Moates, directed by Colleen Griffiths. § Jackson, M. D. *Making Progress: America's Queer History in 12 Plays.* AuthorHouse, 2004. 619–96.

301 *Compleat Female Stage Beauty* (1999) | Jeffrey Hatcher (1957–), American

[Historical study; 9M, 5W; flexible set.] Edward (Ned) Kynaston (1640?–1712), one of the last "boy players" on the English stage, loses his métier when Charles II allows women actors. In a series of cascading events, he also loses his appeal for George Villiars [sic], Second Duke of Buckingham: the latter says, "When I did 'spend time' with you.... I saw you as a woman. [...] I don't know who you are now." Ned discovers that his dresser Maria has long loved him. He protests, "I have never slept with a woman. Except myself." Ned apologizes to Maria for his failure: "I had been trying to act a man, but hadn't found the role." Charles commands him, "Act a man, Kynaston. How hard could it be?" He moves to male parts. In instructing an inept actress how to play Desdemona, particularly how to die, he finally comes alive as a male. Villiars seems to have second thoughts, but they go their separate ways. The play premiered in Shepherdstown, W.V., 1999, with Dallas Roberts and Lee Sellars, directed by Ed Herendeen. It went through numerous revisions over the next several years. Hatcher wrote the screenplay for the 2004 film, *Stage Beauty*. A chamber opera, *Prince of Players*, with music by Carlisle Floyd, was performed in 2016. § Hatcher, J. *Compleat Female Stage Beauty.* Dramatists, 2012. 74p.

302 *Die Mommie Die!* (1999) | Charles Busch, American

[Comic mystery; 3M, 3W; 1 set.] In a parody of the myth of Agamemnon, Edith goads her gay brother Lance to revenge the murder of their father by the woman they think is their mother. However, Angela is actually their Aunt Barbara, their mother's identical twin, as talentless as their mother was gifted. Jealous, Barbara murdered her sister and took her place. The well-endowed and bisexual Tony Parker is a federal agent in disguise as a tennis pro. He cozies up to Angela/Barbara, hoping to prove his father's suspicions were right when the older Parker investigated "Barbara's" suspicious death. Both Edith and Lance vie for Tony's attention. The siblings break the case by interrogating Angela/Barbara while she is under the influence of LSD. The play ends with the improbable resurrection of the father and a murdered maid, and Barbara accepts her fate, glad finally to be herself. The play opened in Los Angeles, 1999, under the title *Die! Mommy! Die! The Fall of the House of Sussman*, with Carl Andress and Mark Capri, directed by Kenneth Elliott. It opened in New York, 2007, with the present title. Busch wrote the script for the naughtier 2003 film. § Busch, C. *Die Mommie Die! A Comic Thriller.* French, 2008. 80p.

303 *Dolly West's Kitchen* (1999) | Frank McGuinness, Irish

[Domestic romance; 5M, 4W; 2 sets.] World War II Ireland is neutral, but the West household is fighting its own wars. They live in Buncrana, near the border with Northern Ireland, and all kinds of borders are crossed in this richly layered play. There are three siblings. Esther has married a man she does not love; Dolly was not able to declare her love for the bisexual Englishman Alex; and Justin is hiding his homosexuality. Alex, now a soldier stationed in Derry, returns to Dolly's life, and her mother invites Jamie and Marco, two American soldiers stationed there, home with her.

Jamie stirs up emotions in both Esther and the servant girl; his openly gay cousin Marco instantly recognizes his affinity with Justin. By the end of the war Esther is reconciled with her husband and has given him a child (whom he may not be the father of). Dolly has let slip that she loves Alex. She asks him, "Tell me what you need. Woman or man?" He answers, "Both," and she responds, "You can have both in me." And Justin and Marco have come to terms with their troubled pasts. Marco's parents threw up to him that he was a "Twisted, mean cissy queen." Their disapproval led him to adopt his often campy behavior; it also explains why he enrolled in the army. Though suffering from PDST, he is proud that he "fought better than any straight man." Justin remembers the priest who thought he was coming onto him when he tried to talk about his sexual desires. He admits that before he met Marco he was a "Twisted, miserable git." He no longer hides his love for the American, and the two prepare to set up life together. The play opened in Dublin, 1999, with Michael Colgan, Perry Ojeda, and Anthony Calf, directed by Patrick Mason. § McGuinness, F. *Plays Two*. Faber & Faber, 2002. 171–263.

304 *Hushabye Mountain* (1999) | Jonathan Harvey, English

[Domestic fantasy; 4M, 2W; flexible set.] The play marks a departure for Harvey: an excursion into the world of fantasy. Danny, having died from AIDS, is stuck at the Pearly Gates. While waiting to learn whether he can pass over, scenes from his and his friends' lives play out, but not in chronological order. Thrown out of his Liverpool home when his parents discover he is gay, Danny goes to London to school. There he becomes good friends with Lana and pushes her to take Lee's attention seriously; at the same time he falls in love with Lee's brother Connor. Danny's mother, both literally and figuratively, haunts him, appearing in various guises. He conceals from Connor that she wrote both of them seeking to atone for her guilt as she grew to despise her husband. Connor's last act will be to write her. Connor has become a kind of off-and-on guardian of HIV-positive Ben, who has been living with the virus for years and has found, grace of the new combination drugs, that he may live yet longer. Ironically, Ben has more trouble dealing with this new hope than he did facing death. The 1999 national tour began in Crewe, England, with Andrew Lincoln, Stuart Laing, and Nick Bagnall, directed by Paul Miller. § Harvey, J. *Plays 2*. Methuen Drama, 2002. 115–218.

305 *Kilt* (1999) | Jonathan Wilson (unknown), Canadian

[Domestic / military drama; 3M, 2W; flexible set.] Wilson had his first success with his one-man show *My Own Private Oshawa*, 1996 (filmed 2002). *Kilt* is more ambitious. Tom's mother, a dance instructor, fled Glasgow, seeking to leave behind her humble origins, her knowledge that her father loved another man during World War II and even after his marriage, and her own lustful memories of her ruffian husband killed in a football riot. But she did take her father's kilt and gave it to Tom. The two became estranged when he gave up Scottish dancing in competition and came out to her sexually. Now, upon her father's death, she tracks him down to the Toronto bar where he performs as a stripper wearing the kilt. She wants it back for her father to be buried in. Tom reluctantly agrees to accompany her to Scotland, wearing the kilt. In Glasgow he meets his grandfather's lover. Tom and his grandfather resemble each other so closely that Tom is like the ghost of his ancestor. (The actor who portrays Tom also portrays the grandfather.) The play constantly shifts between the present and 1942 North Africa. As they scatter the dead man's ashes, Tom's mother seems to move towards some acceptance of the realities; she asks her sister to read Robert Burns's poem "A Man's a Man for A' That." The lovers in wartime Africa have the final scene in the play. It opened in Toronto, 1999, with Paul Braunstein and Brendan Wall, directed by Andy McKim. § Wilson, J. *Kilt*. Playwrights Canada, 1999. 96p.

306 *Night Queen* (1999) | Mahesh Dattani, Indian

[Sexual comedy; 2M; 1 set.] Raghu picks up Ash while cruising in the park. Raghu recognizes that Ash is negotiating a marriage with his sister; Ash is unaware of the connection at first. When he realizes the truth, he lashes out, and the two fight. But Raghu forces him to confront hard truths. Ash became fixated on his brother when he saw him masturbating and tried to instigate sex between them. The brother beat him badly and drug him to the park to show him how "unhappy and miserable" gays are, "worst than lepers." Raghu turns the argument around: "Why didn't you beat him up when you saw him with his girlfriend? Why didn't you tell him that unless he slept with a man, he is as ugly as a leper? Why didn't he go down on his knees and plead with you to help him?" Unexpectedly, the two men kiss, and the play ends in laughter. It was published in 1999. The title refers to a flowering shrub, but it obviously has a double meaning. Dattani has gone on to create other plays, radio pieces, and films that address gay and transgender themes. § *Yaraana: Gay Writing from South Asia*; ed. by Hoshang Merchant. Penguin, 2010. 60–76. Includes R. Raj Rao's story/screenplay *Six Inches*. 138–52.

307 *Rescue and Recovery* **(1999) | Steve Murray (unknown), American**

[Domestic comedy; 4M, 1W; no set.] For Clum (*Still Acting*, 300) the play is about "the possibility of negotiating relationships in a culture that has no moral code to support them. Terms like love, fidelity, and loyalty have no stable referents, but still stand as ideals for the central characters." Cameron, an Atlanta physician and former addict, and Janie, a lawyer, narrate the story of their life after divorce, brought on when Cameron confessed to having an affair with a male internist. The two have a son who is often mentioned but who seems to play no part in their emotional life. Rather the play focuses on their relationships with three men. Timothy is an actor, suffering from AIDS. Jay is his longtime partner, whom he sets up with Mark. The last is a rather naive bank teller, "a walking contradiction." Cameron falls in love with him, but Mark moves in with Jay soon after Timothy dies. Jay also has sex with Cameron and Janie. Both Cameron and Janie move on, even as they remain emotionally co-dependent. Cameron sums up: "I admit I am powerless over my own [...] heart. And its power to hurt me. And the people I love. Or thought I loved. And still love, God help me cause I can't help it." The play opened in Atlanta, 1999, with Brad Sherrill, Jeff McKerley, Rob Beams, and Jeff Feldman, directed by Chris Coleman. § In Clum, J., ed. *Asking and Telling*. 366–455.

308 *Somewhere in the Pacific* **(1999) | Neal Bell, American**

[Military drama; 7M; flexible set.] An almost hallucinatory drama set aboard a Liberty ship and then a life-raft in 1945, the scenes present snapshots of men in war riddled by fear of the unknown. Clum (*Still Acting*, 309) writes, "What unites the men on this ship is the anguished familiarity with death their war experience has already given them. [...] Though the interactions of the marines and sailors on the nameless ship demonstrate a variety of forms of male-male love—the love of father for son, husband for wife, comrade for comrade—what separates the men is their response to the possibility of male-male desire, the wild card of homosexuality." Billy DuPre is gay; Hobie is a closet case; McGuiness is a study of institutional homosexuality. Billy and Hobie have a sensual, almost romantic encounter that Hobie has trouble dealing with. McGuiness is quite willing to accept a blowjob from Billy—and to cry foul when the two are caught *flagrante delicto*. Their captain meanwhile, suffering from guilt that his son committed suicide (probably because the man he was in love with was killed), sets the ship up as a target. It is taken out by two torpedoes. Only Billy, McGuiness, and a by-the-rules aide to the captain survive. The play premiered in Durham, N.C., 1999, with Eamonn Farrell, Adam Smith, and Adam Saunders, directed by Jody McAuliffe. § In Clum, J., ed. *Asking and Telling*. 188–244.

309 *Wonderland* **(1999) | Chay Yew, American**

[Ethnic tragedy; 3M, 1W; flexible set.] The play poetically portrays a minority family's failure to achieve the American Dream. The father aspires to be a major architect but ends up designing shopping malls. Tragically, he makes structural changes in the design of the Santa Monica Wonderland Mall to compensate for the expensive materials he imports for its facade, and the roof collapses, killing shoppers. He loses his license, and the family is denied his insurance when he kills himself. His Singapore-born wife discovers that America is not an Elizabeth Taylor movie even as she and her son inappropriately reenact scenes from her films. This son tries to talk to his father about his sexuality, only to have "Leviticus twenty thirteen" thrown in his face. He runs away from home, intending to become an actor, and ends up in the Los Angeles sex industry. The premiere was in La Jolla, Calif., 1999, with Alec Mapa, directed by Lisa Peterson. § Yew, C. *The Hyphenated American: Four Plays*. Grove, 2002. 277–454.

310 *The Beginning of August* (2000) | Tom Donaghy, American

[Domestic drama; 3M, 2W; 1 set.] Jackie's wife deserts him after the birth of their daughter. His widowed stepmother, having offered to look after the child, is surprised to discover that Jackie is a total control freak. The house painter whom he has dismissed refuses, however, to leave. As he and the stepmother get drunk together, he reveals that he is in love with the missing wife. Ted, who lives two doors down and takes care of the yard, shows up and casually lets drop that he and Jackie had a sexual encounter after the wife's disappearance, information the stepmother uses to get her way when Jackie returns from work. Jackie pulls the old "I was drunk" routine, but Ted refuses to let him off. The two embrace. Pam reappears. At play's end the five seem prepared to create a new configuration of family, a *ménage à quatre* with the stepmother as a sort of guardian figure. After its premiere in Costa Mesa, Calif., 2000, it opened in New York with Garret Dillahunt and Ray Anthony Thomas, directed by Neil Pepe. § Donaghy, T. *The Beginning of August and Other Plays*. Grove, 2000. 175–247.

311 *The Crumple Zone* (2000) | Buddy Thomas (unknown), American

[Dark comedy; 5M; 1 set.] The setting is a Staten Island apartment at Christmastime. Two lines provide the arc of the drama: "You can't help who you fall in love with" and "Move on [...] you got a choice," spoken respectively by Buck and Terry. Alex and Matt have been in a relationship for four years, but while Matt is on tour with a musical comedy, Alex falls in love with Buck. Terry too is in love with Buck but desperate to be with anyone who will have him. That includes Roger, a married man ready for quick sex with men on the side. As Terry's life comes undone, in an unstoppable series of quips he lets slip the truth to Matt when he unexpectedly shows up to celebrate Christmas with Alex. The television special *How the Grinch Stole Christmas* irritates Terry because of its happy ending, but he is the one who advises Matt to get out of the crumple zone. The play opened in New York, 2000, with Mario Cantone, Gerald Downey, Josh Biton, Steve Mateo, and Paul Pecorino, directed by Jason Moore. § Thomas, B. *The Crumple Zone: A Comedy*. French, 2001. 70p.

312 *Elizabeth Rex* (2000) | Timothy Findley, Canadian

[Historical drama; 10M, 4W, 1X, extras; 1 set.] In thinking about how boys played women's role in Elizabethan theater, Findley pondered whether men would not have been needed to play the more mature women. He invented the character Ned Lowenscroft. Then, as he explains in his introduction, the play's title popped into his mind and he saw "the possibility of a glorious, theatrical confrontation—between the woman who throughout her reign had played the role of a man, and the man who in his theatrical career had played the role of a woman." He decided to set the piece on the night of Shrove Tuesday/Ash Wednesday 1601 when the Earl of Essex was awaiting execution. Also imprisoned with him, but escaping beheading, was Shakespeare's patron and perhaps lover, the Earl of Southampton (whom the queen alleges is also Essex's lover). In Findley's conceit, the queen has summoned Shakespeare's company to perform *Much Ado about Nothing*. She chooses to pass the night with the players in a palace barn to distract her from Essex's imminent death. Adding complexity, Ned, who has just played Beatrice, is dying of syphilis contracted from one of Essex's soldiers, the great sores on his head clearly corresponding to AIDS sarcomas. The queen learns that Shakespeare is working on *Antony and Cleopatra*, providing another role for Ned should he live, but one which echoes too close her relationship with Essex. Verbal challenge after challenge occurs till news comes of Essex's death and the queen takes her departure, saying "Master Lowenscroft—I would rather I had known you than anyone, but one, I ever met." There are also brief mentions of same-sex encounters other players have had; sodomy does not seem of particular concern, though Shakespeare certainly wants his sex life to remain hidden. Findley credits Paul Thompson's help in the development of the play. It opened in Stratford, Ont., 2000, with Brent Carver, directed by Martha Henry. Kate Miles Melville wrote the screenplay for the 2004 film. § Findley, T. *Elizabeth Rex*. Harper Perennial, 2003. 141p.

313 *Hijra* (2000) | Ash Kotak (1966?–), English

[Ethnic romance; 4M, 4W; flexible set.] Kotak was born in London of Indian parents. As his publisher says, "Bombay and Wembley collide in this comedy drama which explores community, sexuality and identity." A *hijra* is a "third gender" person, neither male nor female, who traditionally has the power to grant wishes and to cast spells and who thus must be courted. Raj has been adopted, as is the custom, by a *guru hijra*. While cruising on a Mumbai beach, he meets up with Nils, an Indian living in Wembley, whose mother has inveigled a return to India to search out an appropriate wife. Reluctant to tell his mother the truth, Nils finds himself torn. There is also a practical problem: Raj cannot secure an ordinary passport to allow him to emigrate to the U.K. The *guru hijra* steps in with a scheme to disguise Raj as a woman so Nils can take him back to London as his "wife." The scheme quickly unravels when they discover Raj may have to keep the disguise for years for fear of deportation. Also, Raj demands equality in their relationship as two men together. Under stress, Nils blurts out to a woman that he is gay; the news spreads quickly. But Nils has underestimated his mother's love. She has already discerned the truth, and she now sets out to find a way to bring Raj legally into the country. The play opened in London, 2000, with Emil Marwa and Raj Ghatak, directed by Ian Brown. § Kotak, A. *Hijra*. Oberon, 2000. 87p.

314 *In Extremis: A Love Letter* (2000) | Neil Bartlett (1958–), English

[Biographical study; 1M, 1W; no set.] Bartlett is very much a man of the theater, but he has written few conventional plays. Tantalized by Wilde (he has written a book-length tribute to him, *Who Was That Man?*), this playlet was written as a companion piece to actor Corin Redgrave's interpretation of Wilde's *De Profundis*. It imagines what might have happened during Wilde's real-life visit to a palm reader shortly before his third trial. Both Wilde and Mrs. Robinson are speaking from their graves. What emerges is a cameo portrait of the playwright and a possible explanation for his choosing martyrdom. When Wilde asks her, "What will happen if I stay," she fabricates, "I see a triumph. A very great triumph." Buoyed up by her statement, Wilde delivers a paean to Douglas. The dead Mrs. Robinson, clearly thinking of Wilde's continuing high reputation, has the final word: "Well, was I lying?" The play, directed by Trevor Nunn, was given in 2000 in commemoration of the hundredth anniversary of Wilde's death. In *Stella*, 2016, Bartlett returned to the Wilde era, but his biographical study of Ernest Boulton, aka Stella Clinton, is a story of gender fluidity rather than one about gay identity. § Bartlett, N. *In Extremis: A Love Letter*. Oberon, 2000. 13–52.

315 *Kit Marlowe* (2000) | David Grimm (1965–), American

[Biographical study; 13M; flexible set.] Grimm is a theater virtuoso. Each new play stakes out a different period of drama to examine, generally through a gay perspective. For his story of Marlowe and Elizabethan theater, he combines an affectionate pastiche of Marlowe's lines with his own blank verse. Kit, despite his genius, becomes a pawn in the political rivalries of the day, in part because of Thomas Walsingham's love for him, in greater part because of his unrequited worship of Sir Walter Raleigh. The play opens with Kit's dramatic appearance on stage, completely naked, dripping with water from a swim, to throw himself on Thomas. Thomas's uncle, Sir Francis Walsingham, brings pressure upon Kit to become involved in England's network of spies. The rivalry between Raleigh and the Earl of Essex dooms him. Kit despairs even of his literary reputation lasting, his having attended a play with "Language such as I've never heard before, dropping like gems from off the pen of a small man from Stratford." Heeding his hero Tamburlaine's advice to look to his soul and know himself, he questions, "How does one learn oneself? I want no longer the divine—only to know who is he calls himself Kit Marlowe." And so he faces his death heroically. Thomas grieves, but even he believes that Kit's memory will one day fade. The tragedy opened in New York, 2000, with Christian Camargo and Sam Trammell, directed by Brian Kulick. § Grimm, D. *Kit Marlowe*. Dramatists, 2001. 74p.

316 *The Laramie Project* (2000) | Moisés Kaufman, American

[Docudrama; 4M, 4W; minimum set.] The month after Matthew Shepard (1976–1998) died, Kaufman and six members of his company traveled to Laramie, Wyo., to interview townsfolk. Upon their return they organized the different voices to form a three-act play. Act 1 ends with the finding of Shepard's body; Act 2 with his death on October 12, 1998; and Act 3 covers memories of his funeral and the sentencing of the two murderers. The script is gripping: hearing the varying emotions recalled by very ordinary people thrust into extraordinary positions. Some of the images it evokes—a growing parade, angels shutting out hate speech—engrave themselves on the playgoer's mind. Glimpsing the personal emotions of the theater troupe as they gathered this information (for they too become voices in their own right) adds a sense of integrity. The play opened in Denver, 2000, with John McAdams, Stephen Belber, Andy Paris, and Greg Pierotti, directed by Kaufman. The same group prepared the screenplay for the 2002 film.

They returned to Laramie ten years later, interviewing many of the same people and adding new respondents, including political figures, the two murderers, and Shepard's mother. They found a great many people wishing to put the murder behind them, some of them now convinced by a *20/20* segment that it was not a hate crime but a drug deal gone wrong. Their accounts are interesting, but the new play seems flabby in comparison with the original work. Rather surprisingly (especially in view of reactions voiced against *20/20*), it does not record anyone's take on *The Laramie Project* itself, play or movie. How did the community members feel seeing themselves on stage? We are not told. § Kaufman, M., et al. *The Laramie Project [...] and The Laramie Project: Ten Years Later*. Vintage, 2014. 198p.

317 *Mambo Italiano* (2000) | Steve Galluccio (1960–), Canadian

[Ethnic comedy; 3M, 4W; flexible set.] Galluccio finds humor in the Italian-Canadian family structure. Angelo is an award-winning television script writer living in Montreal, but he still feels he must conceal from his parents that he and his former schoolmate are lovers sharing an apartment. As he says, "there is no fate worse than being gay and Italian." When his sister goads him into coming out, the histrionics begin. Angelo stands up to his parents, but his lover Nino capitulates and allows his widowed mother to push him into marriage with a balls-breaking Italian-Canadian woman. When Nino's mother next meets up with Angelo's parents, they indulge in a bout of one-upmanship, crowned with Angelo's father's triumphant cry, "No one's gayer than my son!" Angelo proudly marches in the next Gay Pride parade, while poor Nino ends up having male/male sex on the sly. The play's premiere was in Montreal, 2000, in a French translation. The first English production was in Montreal, 2001, with Andreas Apergis and Joseph Gallaccio, directed by Gordan McCall. Galluccio co-wrote the screenplay for the 2003 film with director Émile Gaudreault. § Galluccio, S. *Mambo Italiano*. Talonbooks, 2004. 126p.

318 *Other People* (2000) | Christopher Shinn, American

[Psychological drama; 5M, 1W; flexible set.] The characters talk and talk and talk, punctuated now and then by long silences, but no one communicates. Petra says, "Life is other people." The man with her responds, "So is hell, or so someone said." Petra ripostes, "Well then so is heaven." But even when Petra makes a series of astute observations about the untruthfulness of the rock musical *Rent*, she shrugs off her commentary, "I'm not used to having to think too hard when I'm here." *Here* is a bar where she works as a stripper even as she aspires to be a writer. Her gay roommate Stephen is the master of the unfocused monologue. One sympathizes with his ex-lover Mark when he screams out, "Can you SHUT UP for a second?" But Mark is the ultimate liar. Having become a druggie while making a documentary film, he disappeared from Stephen's life to find God. Now he is back, seeking refuge from the world. So what does he do? Pick up a hustler who specializes in masturbating in public places. Stephen focuses briefly: "It's not fair. [Mark] can't be honest with me? I love him. I love him and I've done nothing except try to help him." The new year 1998 arrives: Mark is set to join his hustler in jacking off at a hotel window where "people could see us"; Petra announces that she is leaving New York. Stephen is alone. The play has many comic moments; they serve to make the play that much darker. It opened in London, 2000, with Daniel Evans, James Frain, and Neil Newbon, directed by Dominic Cooke. The American production occurred the same year with Neal Huff, Pete Starrett, and Ausin Lysy, directed by Tim Farrell. § Shinn, C. *Where Do We Live and Other Plays*. Theatre Communications, 2005. 51–120.

319 *The Queen & Peacock* (2000) | Loughlin Deegan (unknown), Irish

[Ethnic drama; 4M; 1 set.] Deegan wrote an earlier, unpublished gay play, *The Stomping Ground*, 1997. This one, set in a London pub, looks at Irish immigrants to the city, revealing a generational difference. Ciarán, Fergal, Paul, and Willie are the focus. Ciarán never appears, indeed dies offstage of AIDS during the course of the play. In Ireland Fergal was put down for being a sissy-boy; in London he erases all traces of his origins and became Mark—aka Gertrude, a drag queen and prostitute. Paul fled his small-town environment, lacking courage to come out to his parents. Young Willie, whom Mark has picked up, cannot understand either Paul or Mark, his having been open with his mother, who "knew I was a bleeedin' Nellie years before I did." Goaded by the barman, Paul finally telephones his parents and contemplates returning to Ireland, at least to Dublin. Mark rejects any such idea: "This is [...] home now." Other secrets emerge, but the play seems overly long, even tedious. Its premiere was in Waterford, Ireland, 2000, with Tony Flynn, Charlie Bonner, and Alan Leech, directed by Jim Nolan. § In Walsh, F., ed. *Queer Notions*. 17–70.

320 *Singapore* (2000) | **John Palmer, Canadian**

[Domestic farce; 5M, 2W; 7 sets.] Sam Stone's father is moving into full-blown Alzheimer's. What ensues as a result provokes farce, not pathos. His ex-wife is upset that a gold digger half his age is after his money. She tries to enlist Sam's help to obtain power of attorney. Sam genuinely loves his father and seems indifferent to the money. At the moment he is gaining extra cash by catering to the S/M needs of Roberto Tasii, a man even older than his father, but is trying to break up with him. For Sam—"a middle-aged, neurotic, unsuccessful fairy"—has problems with relationships: "If it's a pick-up I can do it with him. If it's a stranger. But if we get to know each other, I can't do it. I'm paralysed." Bucky Wilson—sometimes waiter, sometimes tennis coach, always gigolo—is carrying on with the wife-to-be. Sam suggests that guys would also go for him. Bucky rejects the idea until he finds out how much Roberto is willing to pay. Roberto manages to get even the rabbi who comes to perform the wedding. Sam remains unmoved through it all; he is last seen having a Thanksgiving meal with his now institutionalized father. The comedy opened in Toronto, 2000, with Alon Nashman, Louis Negin, Shaun Benson, and James Harkness, directed by Palmer. § Palmer, J. *Singapore*. Fredericton, 2001. 86p.

321 *Southern Baptist Sissies* (2000) | **Del Shores, American**

[Spiritual drama, 6M, 2W; unit set.] Four members of the Texas Calvary Baptist Church are gay. When "extreme adolescence kicked in," along with "desires of the flesh, pains of the heart, mixed with fundamentalist doctrine," their major problem becomes how to love themselves. As Mark, the play's narrator, says, the church preaches love, but ironically it "is where we learned to hate ourselves." Seeking some kind of stability, each of the four chooses a different route. T.J. suppresses his sexual urges, goes to Baylor University, and marries a woman. Benny becomes a drag queen "Iona," losing himself in her persona. Andrew hangs himself when his mother, on the preacher's advice, confronts him. In his commentary, laced with sarcasm and comic asides, Mark lashes out—"righteous in [his] unrighteousness," T.J. tells him. An older gay man (a part tailor-made for Leslie Jordan) spends his time drinking at the club where Benny performs; his wry comments provide much of the play's comedy, but he is essentially a sad queen who would like to save the boys but is incapable, ineffectual. The premiere was in Hollywood, 2000, with Robert Lewis Stephenson, Ted Detwiler, Michael Taylor Gray, Sam A. McConkey, and Jordan, directed by Shores. A production of the play was filmed in 2013. § Shore, D. *Southern Baptist Sissies: A Play in Two Acts*. French, 2005. 90p.

322 *Thief River* (2000) | **Lee Blessing, American**

[Domestic drama; 6M; 1 set.] Three decisive meetings chronicle the doomed relationship between the openly gay Gil and the closeted Ray. The evening of Gil's prom, 1948, he is beaten up and urinated on by a homophobic classmate. Returning with a gun, he shoots off his oppressor's fingers (for which he is sentenced to serve time). Ray cleans him up. But a drifter comes across them and threatens to kill them both. Ray's grandfather arrives in the nick of time and kills the man; he and Ray bury the body in a field. When Gil finishes serving his time, he leaves for New York. For twenty-five years Ray writes him every week. Gil pops back into his life in 1973, unfortunately bringing his jealous lover the day of Ray's son's wedding rehearsal. The lover disgraces himself and then tries to out Ray. Gil breaks off the relationship, and the lover becomes an early AIDS victim. When the last meeting occurs in 2001, Ray's wife is dead, and he has suffered a stroke and can no longer write. The play ends nostalgically, the relationship still unresolved. The play had a staged reading in Waterford, Conn., 2000, directed by Michael Engler. Gil and Ray are portrayed by three different actors for each stage of the relationship; the six also take on the other roles. § Blessing, L. *Thief River*. Dramatists, 2002. 57p.

323 *Vincent River* (2000) | **Philip Ridley, English**

[Psychological drama; 1M, 1W; 1 set.] Anita River becomes aware that a teenage boy is stalking her; she assumes his presence has something to do with the murder of her closeted son. Finally exasperated, she invites him into her new apartment, and the play begins. Davey blurts out, "I found the body." But it turns out that he was the one whom Vincent had sex with in the abandoned railroad station toilet just before he was killed by five queer-bashers. According to Davey, had the 33-year-old not panicked, he would probably not have been discovered: ironically, his fear of exposure led to his being outed in death. It occurred at the same time Davey's mother died, allowing him to get out of a sham engagement. Now Davey seeks to expiate his guilt by confessing all to Vincent's mother. In a symbolic gesture she lets go of the past, and Davey leaves. The premiere was in London, 2000, with William Mannering, directed by Matthew Lloyd. Ridley also wrote the script for the television film, 2006. § Ridley, P. *Plays 2*. Bloomsbury, 2009. 1–70.

Early Contemporary, 2001–2007

Destruction of World Trade Towers, 2001. Quebec enacts civil union bill, 2002. U.S. Supreme Court decriminalizes homosexual acts, 2003. Section 28 repealed in rest of U.K., final decriminalization of homosexual acts, 2003. Canada enacts same-sex marriage laws, 2005. U.K., enacts civil union laws, 2005. South Africa enacts marriage laws, 2006.

324 *Flamingos* (2001) | Jonathan Hall (unknown), English

[Sexual drama; 5M; flexible set.] Though the play does not delve into the reasons behind the paradox, Cliff sums up the dilemma of gay men: "We want it all ways—committed relationships and free love." He is the proprietor of a Blackpool bed and breakfast, who has recently lost his partner of twenty-seven years to a heart attack. Cliff holds that "the thing that really made us go the distance—was the fact that we didn't really love each other." This weekend he has four guests. Gavin is a gay Lothario who comes down on the side of free sex. His two friends Phil and Mark are a couple, but both become emotionally entangled with the fourth guest, Richard; he deliberately cuts loose from his own partner this weekend to make up for his having never gone through the "slapper stage." Richard has sex first with Mark, then with Phil. The two face that "*a turning point has come*" in their relationship. Phil admits to Richard that he does not love Mark, but that "it's okay. I'd rather be with someone than not. We're good friends. We're all right." Richard skips out on the luncheon date that he and Phil have in order to return to his partner. But before he leaves, he accepts Gavin's telephone number. The play opened in London, 2001, with Fred Pearson, Mike Grady, Ian Reddington, Francis Lee, and Ian Curtis, directed by Mike Bradwell. § Hall, J. *Three Plays*. Oberon, 2004. 7–74.

325 *Mouth to Mouth* (2001) | Kevin Elyot, English

[Psychological drama; 5M, 2W; 3 sets.] Often comical, the play, nonetheless, is a mordant portrait of a self-centered, predatory homosexual. Frank feels guilt, but its precise nature is never identified even though the body of the play is a flashback. Does it stem from the fact he seduced his best friend's teenage son, a third his age? Or from the fact that the son, essentially straight, was killed in a motorcycle accident just after Frank tried to seduce him again? Nor do we know whether this guilt leads to his decision to stop his medications warding off the full onset of AIDS. All the straight adults are just as self-centered, never listening to each other, never listening to themselves even. They also have their secrets, most notably that the boy is actually his uncle's son. The play opened in London, 2001, with Michael Maloney, directed by Ian Rickson. Elyot's last original play was *Forty Winks*, 2004, with a gay couple in a minor role. He went on to write the screenplays for *Clapham Junction*, 2007, and Isherwood's *Christopher and His Kind*, 2011. § Elyot, K. *Four Plays*. Nick Hern, 2004. 249–305.

326 *Out in the Open* (2001) | Jonathan Harvey, English

[Urban romance; 3M, 3W; 1 set.] Frankie McAdam was struck dead by lightning while cruising Hampstead Heath. For seven years he was Tony's partner but during their last year he was also having an affair with Brett on trips to Manchester. Tony's best friends—the alcoholic Kevin, who is secretly in love with him; Monica, a frustrated singer—both know about Brett but conceal their knowledge from Tony. Thus they are shocked when Tony brings home Iggy, no other than Brett using his second name (Ignatius). Tony is HIV-positive, but he does not let that unduly affect his life. Only towards the end of the play does it come out that Iggy has known from the beginning who Tony is and that Tony had popped in on Frankie in Manchester and discovered him in Iggy's company. By then Tony questions whether Kevin and Monica are truly friends and seems prepared to accept Iggy's invitation to join him in Manchester. Frankie's mother figures prominently in the drama; she also proves capable of growing, changing. The comedy opened in London, 2001, with Mark Bonnar, James McAvoy, and Sean Gallagher, directed by Kathy Burke. § Harvey, J. *Plays 2*. Methuen Drama, 2002. 219–324.

327 *Prok* (2001) | Brian Drader (1960–), Canadian

[Biographical study; 2M, 1W; flexible set.] A much earlier, unpublished play by Drader, *The Fruit Machine*, 1993, dramatized RCMP's 1960s attempt to root out homosexuals by measuring eyes' dilation when presented with sexual scenes. So it was a natural progression to bring Alfred Kinsey (1894–1956) to center stage. Influenced by James Jones's biography, the play does not shy away from Kinsey's attraction to young males, particularly Victor (i.e., Ralph Voris). One of his informants recalls his first meeting with Kinsey at "a particularly 'gay' evening" hosted by Monroe Wheeler. Another character accuses Kinsey of falling in love with a "young German prostitute" whom he engaged to help him with his research. But these are only incidents in the complex portrait presented. Still, Kinsey's wife closes the play by recalling: "A short time after his death, a young couple arrived on my doorstep. It was two men, but I knew instantly that they were a couple. They were comfortable with each other, at ease. They were themselves. [...] they'd come to pay homage. They believed that they would not have been able to accept themselves, and each other, as normal, if Alfred hadn't started that dialogue. [...] they loved each other, and they wanted to thank him for that. [...] I would have liked very much for him to have met that couple. I think it would have made him very happy." The play opened in Winnipeg, 2001, with Richard Hurst and Arne McPherson, directed by Margo Charlton. § Drader, B. *Prok*. Scirocco Drama, 2003. 80p.

328 *Say You Love Satan* (2001) | Roberto Aguirre-Sacasa (1973–, Nicaraguan), American

[Sexual fantasy; 4M, 1W; flexible set.] Aguirre-Sacasa's vision has been formed in great part by his love of comic books and *outré* fiction. Andrew, a graduate student studying Russian, is swept off his feet by Abaddon, aka Jack, whom he meets in a laundromat. Spending his nights with him, Andrew neglects his friends: Jerrod, a medical student, the epitome of good, and Bernadette, his oldest friend, a stereotypical "fag hag," as well as Chad, his ex-lover who cheated on him on his birthday and dumped him on Valentine's Day. When Andrew realizes that a birthmark is getting larger since he has been with Jack, he freaks. Then Jack's ex-lover, the angel Rafael, shows up. When Jack demands that Andrew kidnap one of the abandoned babies at the shelter Jerrod volunteers for, he realizes that he must get out of the relationship or risk losing his soul. Bernadette calls her ex-boyfriend, "Druidic Cult" Martin. Martin advises the two of them how to trick Jack. The crisis over, Andrew and Jerrod make peace, and Andrew recalls his favorite passage from Dostoevsky's *The Brothers Karamazov*, in which Ivan affirms life. The dark comedy opened in Atlanta, 2001, with Dan Triandiflou, Tim Cordier, and John Fischer, directed by Sean Daniels. § Aguirre-Sacasa, R. *Say You Love Satan*. Dramatists, 2005. 43p.

329 *The Shooting Stage* (2001) | Michael Lewis MacLennan, Canadian

[Sexual tragedy; 5M; flexible set.] In this ambitious play MacLennan explores the difference between photographic art and pornography, the legacy of abuse, teens' fear of sexuality and bullying, and the effects of emotional denial. Malcolm and Len were child actors in a short-lived series, both abused by the person they call the Old Man. Grown, Len has retreated behind the safety of the camera lens. An innocent picture he took at age 14 of Malcolm, 16, in their television mother's dress, clearly sporting an erection—and unwisely included in an exhibit—has landed him in court. Malcolm, now a lawyer, reappears to prepare him for cross-examining. Malcolm's secrets spill out. He confesses that he liked the attention he received from the Old Man. He himself is exploiting Derrick, 17, paying him for pornographic selfies. Under the shock, Len reevaluates his relationship to his subjects and renounces photography even as a jury vindicates his work. Meanwhile, Derrick turns out to be an abusive schoolmate of Malcolm's son. Elliot, 16, is gay. He also likes to dress up in his dead mother's clothing and participates in drag shows run by managers not too strict about age. He is attracted to a third teenager, Ivan, likewise bullied by Derrick. The brooding tension among the boys breaks out at a bird sanctuary (the trumpeter swan becomes an important symbol). Elliot reveals Ivan's homosexuality. Ivan goes wild: he peels away Derrick's bravado and shoots Elliot in the leg. In a final attempt to reassert himself, Derrick presents Malcolm with photos he took of the evening, seeming to suggest Elliot is dead. Malcolm commits vehicular suicide. At the funeral Len tries to comfort Elliot, who announces he has decided to become a photographer. The play opened in Vancouver, 2001, with Clarence Sponagle, Kevin MacDonald, Paul Anthony, and Gerry Mackay, directed by Stephane Kirkland. MacLennan was also working on *Queer as Folk* at the time. § MacLennan, M. L. *The Shooting Stage*. Playwrights Canada, 2002. 92p.

330 *The York Realist* (2001) | Peter Gill, Welsh

[Psychological drama; 4M, 3W; 1 set.] In the early 1960s, George, a Yorkshire farmer, becomes involved with a group putting on the York mystery cycle. As an actor in the crucifixion play, he meets John, the assistant director, and the two begin a discreet affair. Unlike his brother-in-law, with whom he had his first sexual experience, George has no trouble accepting his sexuality. But he is equally realistic about his and John's chances of a life together: John's career lies in London; George feels obligations to his aged mother. After her death, he tells John that it is too late for him to uproot: "You got to be seventeen, eighteen, true. And, you know, I've got no…. That's it. I'm not ambitious. […] I've none. I live here." Meanwhile, a neighboring woman sets out to grab him in marriage. The play is structured as a flashback, beginning and ending with John's entreaty to George to leave Yorkshire and join him in London. The play opened in London, 2001, with Lloyd Owen and Richard Coyle, directed by Gill. § Gill, P. *Plays Two*. Faber & Faber, 2008. 217–94.

331 *The Coffee Lover's Guide to America* (2002) | Jonathan Hall, English

[Romance; 2M; flexible set.] Joe, an Englishman who has just finished a town planning job, is in Key West checking out the gay scene. Gregg, an American looking for sexual adventures, cruises him in a Starbucks. Learning that Joe's very closeted partner has reneged on flying over to join him for a trip across the States, Gregg proposes to take his place. The two set off on an unorthodox tour (with some strange geographical routes). Joe goads Gregg into returning to his hometown in Virginia, where it turns out he was the center of a schoolboy scandal involving his married neighbor. Having fallen in love with Joe, Gregg proposes he stay in America. Joe counters with the reverse offer. The last scene occurs in another Starbucks—this time in Joe's home country. Gregg is about to fly back to the U.S., but Joe promises he will follow as soon as he gets Gregg's call. The play opened in London, 2002, with Daniel Rabin and Trevor White, directed by Nigel Townsend. § Hall, J. *Three Plays*. Oberton, 2004. 75–150.

332 *Gates of Gold* (2002) | Frank McGuinness, Irish

[Historical romance; 3M, 2W; 1 set.] In 1928 lovers Hilton Edwards (1903–1982) and Micheál Mac Liammóir (1899–1978) founded the Gate Theatre in Dublin. Mac Liammóir died in 1978; Edwards followed in 1982. Their story inspired McGuinness. In his play the two men become Conrad and Gabriel, who is dying. They bicker, as old lovers do, as they look back on their life together: "We were dangerous. We were men who loved each other and lived together openly as lovers when it was a […] crime to do so." Alma is hired as nurse; Gabriel's sister and nephew arrive. They all have stories to tell—stories which may, or may not, be authentic in the details but are true in spirit. Conrad tries to hold onto Gabriel, but Gabriel moves fearlessly toward death: "Open the door. Open the gate. The gates of gold." Their final union is a kiss. The play opened appropriately at the Gate Theatre, 2002, with Alan Howard and Richard Johnson, directed by Kent Paul. § McGuinness, F. *Gates of Gold*. French, 2002. 58p.

333 *Lovesong of the Electric Bear* (2002) | Snoo Wilson, English

[Biographical fantasy; 5M, 2W; flexible set.] Wilson's play is more inventive than Huge Whitemore's. Here Porgy, Alan Turing's teddy bear, recounts the salient facts of Turing's life: his youthful crush on a classmate, his part in saving Britain during World War II, his research into artificial intelligence, his reticence around women, his fateful encounter with Arnold Murray that leads to his being "prosecuted for an act of gross indecency," and his suicide by eating a poisoned apple—the symbolic fruit that has been teasing his imagination ever since he saw Walt Disney's *Snow White and the Seven Dwarfs*. The relationship between his intellectual pursuits and his sexual needs remains vague, the nearest the play comes to offering an explanation being the admonition offered by an American working for Bell Telephones: "The bottom line is, you just don't realise how important it is to interact with people." Dramatic unity is provided by the bear's unconditional love for Alan. His final gesture after Alan's death is to tear out his own heart from his straw-filled chest. The play opened in Edinburgh, 2002, with Alexander Gilmour. § Wilson, S. *Lovesong of the Electric Bear*. Bloomsbury, 2015. 80p.

334 *The Men from the Boys* (2002) | Mart Crowley, American

[Dark comedy; 9M; 1 set.] After *The Boys in the Band*, Crowley wrote four plays, none of which was as successful. He returned to *Boys* for a sequel set thirty years later. Six of the original group gather at Michael's for a "celebration of life" in honor of Larry. He has died of cancer. Despite their problems seen in *Boys*, he and Hank held together for all that time. Michael and Bernard are both on the wagon; Bernard has married a woman. Donald is now alcoholic. Emory remains relatively unchanged, though notably more subdued. And Harold is still Harold. After all the others leave, he confides to Michael that he has been diagnosed HIV-positive and has had his first bout with an AIDS-related illness. Three much younger men show up also. Scott is using Michael; Rick and Jason both had a crush on Larry. Jason represents the politically motivated generation; Michael finally blasts him: "if it weren't for boys like us, there wouldn't be men like you." Emory, in fact, was one of those caught up in the Stonewall Inn riots. *Men* is a lesser play, but it reminds us just how revolutionary *Boys* was. *Men* premiered in San Francisco, 2002, with Russ Duffy, Will Huddleston, Terry Lamb, Peter Carlstrom, Michael Patrick Gaffney, and Lewis Sims, directed by Ed Decker. § *The Collected Plays of Mart Crowley*. Alyson, 2009. 385–458.

335 *Original Sin* (2002) | Peter Gill, Welsh

[Sexual tragedy; 15M; flexible set.] Inspired by Wedekind's *Lulu* plays, Gill reimagines the story from a gay perspective. An *homme fatal*, Angel is picked out of the gutter by a wealthy newspaper publisher. When Angel becomes a teenager, the publisher foists him off on a doctor who lusts after him. The doctor commissions his portrait, to lose Angel to the painter. But Angel is still seeing the publisher. The doctor dead, the painter a suicide, the publisher becomes the next victim, shot by Angel. The publisher's son gives testimony that shortens Angel's prison sentence. Another suitor devises a scheme to spring him from captivity and escape to Paris. The money dwindles away. In the last scene Angel, his father (who has been lurking on the fringes of the action throughout the play), and the publisher's son are reduced to returning to London and a miserable life in a garret. Angel returns to the street: his third client is Jack the Ripper. The play opened in Sheffield, 2002, with Andrew Scott, directed by Gill. § Gill, P. *Plays 2*. Faber & Faber, 2008. 295–410.

336 *Take Me Out* (2002) | Richard Greenberg, American

[Sports drama; 11M; flexible set.] In this baseball story, Darren Lemming's teammate Kippy Sunderstrom narrates much of what happens after Darren comes out of the closet, but he is not privy to several pivotal incidents that occur this summer. Darren's best friend Davey Battle, who plays for another team literally and figuratively, provides the catalyst for Darren's decision. When they meet on the crucial day that changes everything, Darren remembers their conversation thus: "You told me to reveal my true nature. You said I could only do this through love." He is taken aback when Davey lashes out, "That before I knew you were a pervert." Darren retorts, "Drop dead." Shane Mungitt, on his way to the showers, overhears the last words. Shane has earlier been suspended for blurting out during an interview about his teammates, "I don't mind the colored people—the gooks an' the spics an' the coons an' like that. But *every night* t'have'ta take a shower with a *faggot*?" Darren happens also to be half white, half black, so Shane's insults are doubled. When Shane later insists to Darren, "You wunt who I's talkin' about. You wunt the faggot," Darren accuses him of "lashin' out at what you fear," turns the accusation, "You're colored, aren't ya, Shane," and then changes course again and kisses him as they both stand naked. Whether Shane is or is not gay is left unanswered. But called in to be the relief pitcher, just as Davey steps up to the plate, he fires off his specialty ball straight into Davey's skull, killing him. He is banished forever from baseball. After the funeral, Kippy tries to rekindle his and Darren's platonic friendship, but Darren turns to his financial investor Mason Marzac, who may or may not be gay. Mason calls the season "tragic"; Kippy describes it as "a 'mess.'" The play opened in London, 2002, with Daniel Sunjata, directed by Joe Mantello; it transferred intact to New York. § Greenberg, R. *Take Me Out.* Dramatists, 2004. 67p.

337   *Where Do We Live* (2002) | Christopher Shinn, American

[Social drama; 7M, 2W; flexible set.] Beginning with this play, Sinn became increasingly political. The place is New York; the time is August 9 to October 9, 2001. Stephen lives in an apartment with a window onto the World Trade Towers. An idealist, he feels intellectually for the poorer families that live in his building; whether he feels empathy or love for them, even he does not know. His best girlfriend tells him that he needs to "make room for just—who people are" instead of "always looking for something that isn't there—something better—as opposed to reality. Who someone might be." At a party Stephen blows up at one of his boyfriend's Republican pals so explosively that the boyfriend walks out of his life. Stephen spends a night with an Asian-American who is even more articulate about society's shortcomings than he, but they do not connect even sexually. The deeply pessimistic play opened in London, 2002, with Daniel Evans, Adam Garcia, and Ray Panthaki, directed by Richard Wilson. It opened in New York, 2004, with Luke Macfarlane, Jacob Pitts, and Aaron Yoo, directed by Shinn. § Shinn, C. *Where Do We Live and Other Plays.* Theatre Communications, 2005. 231–308.

338   *Big Bill* (2003) | A. R. Gurney, American

[Sports drama; 4M, 1W; flexible set.] This relatively superficial play is a disappointment. A biographical study of the life of tennis star William Tilden (1893–1953), the drama focuses heavily on his keen sense of fair play, blemished by his inability to resist the sexual attraction of older teenagers. Even standing before a judge, he remains convinced that telling the truth is all he need do; he is shocked when he is sentenced to prison. Gurney delves little into Tilden's psychology. The best he offers is Tilden's statement to the judge, "I know my own nature. In the end, I'm back to little Junie Tilden, the sissy, fooling around behind the barn." The premiere was in Williamstown, Mass., 2003, with John Michael Higgins, directed by Mark Lamos. § Gurney, A. R. *Big Bill.* Broadway Play, 2004. 76p.

339   *Cherish* (2003) | Ken Duncum, New Zealander

[Domestic tragedy; 2M, 2W; flexible set.] Tom has fathered both of Jess's and Maeve's girls, with the understanding that the third child will be his and William's. But Jess, early in her pregnancy, decides she cannot give up the son she is carrying. Tom, who may be lovable, is also hopelessly immature (he misses his baby's first scan because he is cheating on William). When William, a lawyer, tells him he has no legal recourse to obtaining the child, he in essence blackmails Jess and Maeve by serving notice he is taking them to court for fifty-fifty custody of the girls. Maeve retaliates by dragging up William's past: at age 17 he was arrested for having sex with a 15-year-old. The case was dropped, but Maeve's lawyer is clever enough to know he can destroy William's reputation with the information. Tom kidnaps the girls, then faces the fact, "I've blown it, haven't I?" William answers truthfully, "You'd blown it before you started." Adding to the tension, Maeve's daughter is autistic, a real danger to Jess's daughter. Jess, who matches Tom in immaturity, opts for a heterosexual family and marries her lawyer, his assuming the role of father for her two children. Tom tells Maeve, "You were right. I had to grow up. I couldn't do that with William," then impulsively proposes to her. The play ends with William's dancing manically to the Rolling Stones' "You Can't Always Get What You Want." It opened in Wellington, 2003, with Edwin Wright and Bruce Phillips, directed by Katherine McRae. § Duncum, K. *Cherish*. Victoria Univ. Press, 2004. 79p.

340 *The End of the Tour* (2003) | **Joel Drake Johnson, American**
[Dark comedy; 4M, 3W; flexible set.] The play is a portrait of an estranged family. Andrew receives a call from his sister Jan that their mother is in a nursing home. David, his lover, thinks he should visit her. Arriving there, Andrew's emotional insecurities spill out, symbolized by his refusal to hold David's hand when David takes Andrew's. He remembers how his stepfather tormented him by calling him a sissy until his mother sent him to live with another family. David insists that both of them need "to get away from this damaged soul stuff." Jan's ex-husband Chuck suffers from his wife's rejection of him, clinging to his dying cat, still dependent on Jan for advice. His best friend Tommy tries to comfort him. (Tommy is enduring an unhappy marriage as the result of his wife's becoming super-religious.) The shadow of Ronald Reagan, in whose boyhood hometown the play is set, looms over the entire piece. It ends with all of them continuing on, trying to cope. Andrew says, "I'm going to try, you know, David." The play opened in Chicago, 2003, with Timothy Hendrickson and Andrew Rothenberg, directed by Sandy Shinner. § Johnson, J. D. *The End of the Tour*. Broadway Play, 2007. 69p.

341 *Hardcore* (2003) | **Jonathan Hall, English**
[Psychological drama; 4M; no set.] Using a cinemagraphic style, the play presents quick cuts showing four men preparing to shoot and then celebrating the completion of a porn film. Craig, who already has two porn flicks behind him, seems to be the most self-assured as he prepares the others for the mechanics of sex on film, but he turns out to be the most vulnerable. After an evening spent with him, Martin is ready to fall in love. But when he is spurned, he goes on to become the star of the film with the possibility of an American career ahead of him. Robert is in an ambivalent relationship with a much older man who approves of his making the film. Kevin claims to be straight, doing it to prove his versatility in order to kickstart his acting career, but the others are dubious about his claims. The play provides the men's backgrounds by the equivalent of voice-overs, but the drama is thin. The premiere was in Edinburgh, 2003, with Alex Hassel, Phil Matthews, Simon Thomas, and Christopher Redmond, directed by Russell Labey. § Hall, J. *Hardcore*. Oberon, 2004. 95p.

342 *Last Romantics* (2003) | **Michael Lewis MacLennan, Canadian**
[Biographical study; 5M, 3W; flexible set.] The artists-couple Charles Ricketts (1866–1931) and Charles Shannon (1863–1937) seem to be almost forgotten, yet they were intimates of Wilde and never deserted him even in prison. They were also friends of the lesbian couple collectively known as Michael Field. And Ricketts was rival in book-illustrations with Aubrey Beardsley. All of them show up, as does MacKenzie King, Canada's prime minister for whom Ricketts served as advisor for the national art gallery. Their own collection was notable for bringing to light overlooked art works. Some of the tension in the play is sexual: Ricketts is exclusively homosexual; Shannon is bisexual, capable of falling in love with a female model. The script moves toward the tragic when Shannon falls off a ladder and permanently damages the front part of his brain. Their collection is sacrificed a bit at a time to pay for his care. But a great deal of the play ponders the plight of connoisseurs who have exquisite taste for past art and no sympathy for, or insight into, the present and the potential future. The two men champion Purvis de Chavannes but make fun of Cézanne and Picasso. MacLennan credits J. G. P. Delaney's biography of Ricketts as his major source; the resulting script is his most assured play. It opened in Toronto, 2003, with Julian Richings and Oliver Dennis, directed by Richard Rose. § MacLennan, M. L. *Last Romantics*. Playwrights Canada, 2003. 115p.

343 *The Last Sunday in June* (2003) | **Jonathan Tolins, American**
[Dark comedy; 7M, 1W; 1 set.] Gay friends assemble in a Christopher Street apartment overlooking the Gay Pride march. Representing a

variety of professions, they have in common that they are all up on the latest thing in the arts and quite aware of their gay heritage. It does not take long for one to notice how much they resemble the script for a play in the tradition of *The Boys in the Band* (mentioned by name) or *Love! Valour! Compassion!*: "a bunch of gay guys in an apartment or a country house bitching and cracking jokes about what it means to be gay [...] who] play a truth game and reveal ugly secrets about each other! [...] And then [...] do a dance. Curtain. [...] It's so postmodern." So they proceed to act out "another gay play." A couple for seven years, Michael and Tom are their unplanned hosts for the event. Two announcements by guests set into motion complementary plots examining the nature of commitment. James, who was formerly Tom's lover, tells them that he is dropping out of the gay scene and marrying a woman. Brad, one of James's former boyfriends, HIV-positive (though only Tom and Michael are aware of the fact), blurts out, not entirely inadvertently, that Tom has been having hookups with other men when he is out of town on business trips.

Tom deliberately invites James's fiancée to drop by in order to sabotage his plans, but she proves that the two have thought through the implications of their marriage quite thoroughly. It is Tom and Michael who have not examined their commitment. Joe, another guest, reveals that he and Michael have had cyber sex. Then Scott, an object of Tom's street flirtations, walks in to use their bathroom ("The unexpected arrival of the shirtless hunk. You can't have a gay play without one"). He seems to recognize Michael and knows exactly where the bathroom is located. The parade ends. Joe suggests it is time to go dancing even though the truth game has not been played. Tom and Michael are "the last two left onstage [...]. The ending's up to [them]. Gay plays end happily now." But Michael follows through on Scott's admonishment that "the old rules didn't make much sense, and the new ones aren't any better. No one knows how we're supposed to be anymore. I think people just have to make it up as they go along. As long as they tell each other the truth." Michael confesses that not only has he had sex with Scott, but also with others.

Rifts in the two men's relationship have already emerged. Now the audience discovers they have become "glorified roommates," not having had sex with each other in five months. Michael rues that they have "been playing these stupid roles for everyone to see. Maybe if we had talked about it." In retrospect, they do not seem that dissimilar from James. They, after all, have been planning to leave the gay scene and move to Nyack; they have been hobnobbing with straight couples; they are onlookers rather than participants in the parade. Young Joe, the irrepressible refugee from homophobic America, stands in strong contrast. Just before his exit, he proudly proclaims, "Let's show everybody! 'We're here, we're queer, we're average and insecure [...] and horny, and confused, get used to it!'" Tolins developed the script under the title *Another Gay Play*. The New York premiere, 2003, had Johnathan McClain, Peter Smith, David Turner, Arnie Burton, Donald Corren, Mark Setlock, and Matthew Wilkas, directed by Trip Cullman. § Tolins, J. *The Last Sunday in June and Other Plays*. Grove, 2004. 1–102.

344 *Mr Elliott* (2003) | Jonathan Hall, English

[Social drama; 3M, 2W; flexible set.] In an England in transition, sexual liberation intertwines with the social problems of new immigrants. Rob Elliott, 45, has taught in the same school using virtually the same methods for twenty years. The internet, however, sweeps him into the world of gay sex, and he learns the cruising places in his town. One evening he has sex with a youth, only to realize that he is Ash Al-kalid, 19, one of his former students. Realistic fears surface on Elliott's part, even though Ash reassures him that he himself must be discreet because of his homophobic Pakistani family. But he scares Elliott even more by blurting out, "I think I'm falling in love with you." A flamboyantly open gay man associated with the Urban Challenge movement roils matters by putting on a play that crudely reflects the realities of the poverty-ridden town and its uneasy mix of ethnicities. After witnessing the performance Elliott blows up and says things to Ash, one of the actors in the play, that he does not deserve to hear. His safety off, Elliott heads home to announce to his wife that he is gay. Ash plans to escape to Manchester, but his family traps him into marriage. At play's end, Elliott is rearranging his classroom. Whether he will manage to rearrange his life is left unanswered. The premiere was in London, 2003, with Gary Cady, Elyes Gabel, and Marcus Rogers, directed by Nigel Townsend. § Hall, J. *Three Plays.* Oberon, 2004. 151–221.

345 *My Big Gay Italian Wedding* (2003) | Anthony J. Wilkinson (unknown), American

[Ethnic comedy; 8M, 5W; flexible set.] Wilkinson clearly mines his own biography. Anthony Pinnunziato becomes engaged to Andrew Polinski and gets his family to agree to a traditional wedding. His mother sets two conditions: their Catholic priest must perform the ceremony, and Andrew's homophobic mother must give her son away. The priest's absence is explained by an attack of kidney stones; a friend dresses in drag as the mother. Both lies are, of course, exposed. Then both Andrew's and Anthony's best men independently decide to inform Anthony that Andrew was unfaithful Memorial Day weekend at Fire Island. The play charges along with no pretense at subtlety to the requisite happy ending (Andrew proves his love by singing for the first time in public). It opened in New York, 2003 (in repertory with *Naked Boys Singing*), with Wilkinson and Bill Fischer as the grooms, directed by Peter Rapanaro. A sequel, *My Big Gay Italian Funeral*, 2013, offers more of the same. It contains the information that Andrew indeed proves to be fickle. *My Big Gay Italian Mid-Life Crisis*, 2015, has yet to be published. § Wilkinson, A. J. *My Big Gay Italian Wedding.* French, 2011. 77p.

346 *2 Lives* (2003) | Arthur Laurents, American

[Domestic fantasy; 4M, 4W; 1 set.] In part an autobiographical play, it opens with the last day in the life of Howard Thompson, 65, as his lover Matt Singer, 80, tries for a comeback in the theater. Matt is writing a new play; he is trying to cajole a Hollywood producer to back another play in New York. The two men's relationship is low-key. Howard is completely supportive of Matt. An actress friend points out to Matt that "the true center [of his life] is and always has been [his] work." Still, when Howard dies of an aneurysm at the end of Act 1, Matt cannot let him go. Howard's spirit remains in the garden that he created. Howard's dotty mother provides black humor to the scenes in which she appears. The premiere was in New York, 2003, with Tom Aldredge and James Suto-rius, directed by Nicholas Martin. § Laurents, A. *Selected Plays.* Back Stage, 2004. 365–427.

347 *Your Loving Simon* (2003) | Robert Colman (1959–), South African

[Biographical homage; 2M; minimal set.] Simon Nkoli (1957–1998) was a black anti-apartheid activist who was accused of treason and arrested in 1984 as part of the Delmas 22. While in prison, he came out as gay; he also discovered he was HIV-positive. Released in 1988, he became both a gay activist who fought, successfully, for the decriminalization of same-sex acts under the new constitution and an AIDS spokesperson. Colman traces Nikoli's evolution through a series of conversations with his straight cellmate in prison, interspersed with excerpts from the letters he actually wrote to his lover. According to the play the cellmate had trouble accepting Simon's sexuality, but after Simon's suicide attempt (triggered by his discovery he was positive) he begins to understand Simon's earlier point: "Why can't I be honest, true to myself? I've got nothing to hide. I don't have a problem. If it is a problem for you, then that is your problem not mine." The play opened in Johannesburg, 2003, with Fourie Nyamande, directed by Coolman. § In Malan, R., ed. *S.A. Gay Plays 2.* 7–50.

348 *Youth* (2003) | Olivier Py (1965–), French

[Absurdist drama; 6M, 4W; flexible set.] In a radical revision of his 2001 play *Au monde comme n'y étant pas*, Py introduces a gay theme. In a meaningless world all the characters are searching for direction—atheists looking for a heavenly father in "this theatre of joyful filth" in which their earthly fathers have failed them. The play opens with Aurélien jacking off over a note he intends to send his parent: "Father, now I don't owe you anything." He discovers that Thomas, 17, the waiter in the café he frequents, received the scar on his face from his abusive father. Thomas initiates Aurélien into homosexuality, perhaps love, but Thomas also provokes Aurélien to renounce his love for his brother Paul. Paul is in a sexless marriage; he sublimates his desires through physical activity at the gym with two friends who work at the same place he does. Paul faces yet another treachery. His boss calls him in and declares his love for Paul, then announces that one of the two friends must be fired and Paul must make the decision. Hard on this betrayal, Paul casts himself out a window. He lives but falls into a coma; his wife announces, "Only Aurélien can bring Paul back from the kingdom of the dead." Aurélien's last act is to paint a white cross on the wall. Published in 2003, *Jeunesse* was first performed in 2006 in Paris. § Py, O. *Four Plays*. Trans. David Edney. Univ. Press of America, 2005. 141–205.

349   *Beautiful Child* (2004) | Nicky Silver, American

[Domestic tragedy; 2M, 3W; 1 set.] Silver's play takes the unthinkable and makes the playgoer think about it. What should parents do if they discover their 30ish-year-old schoolteacher son is molesting an 8-year-old student? Isaac confronts his parents with this problem. They have accepted that he is gay; they are appalled to discover that he is a pederast with no feelings of remorse, convinced the child loves him in return. His cry, "I LOVED SOMEONE," is all the more ironic given that his father is having a loveless affair with his secretary and that his mother admits she has never loved her husband. She especially feels they must do something since she knows of an earlier case of abuse that she has tried to put out of her mind: that of Isaac's troubled student Victor, who while at Columbia jumped from a window. The parents agree to protect Isaac on the condition that he "never see another child." Literally. They blind him. Now Isaac may once again be their "beautiful child." The premiere was in New York, 2004, with Steven Pasquale, directed by Terry Kinney. § Silver, N. *Beautiful Child*. Dramatists, 2004. 51p.

350   *Beauty of the Father* (2004) | Nilo Cruz (CUB 1960–), American

[Domestic fantasy; 3M, 2W; 1 set.] Cruz is fascinated with García Lorca, one of his literary sires. His drama *Lorca in a Green Dress*, 2003, has five actors representing different aspects of Lorca; the eponymous actor symbolizes Lorca's ardent desires. In *Beauty* Lorca acts as a ghostly advisor to the middle-aged artist Emiliano. Emiliano's daughter arrives at his home after the death of her mother. She knows her father is gay, but she is not prepared for the muddle she discovers. His Moroccan lover Karim is in an arranged marriage in order to get his papers. He is not gay, only using Emiliano. To the father's distress Karim now woos the daughter. Lorca tries to advise the father how to behave. When a confrontation becomes inevitable, Lorca takes the bullets Karim meant for Emiliano and attempts to bring peace to the troubled house. The play opened in Coral Gables, Fla., 2004, with Carlos Orizondo and Roberto Escobar, directed by Rafael de Acha. § Cruz, N. *Beauty of the Father*. Theatre Communications, 2008. 65p.

351   *Dog Sees God: Confessions of a Teenage Blockhead* (2004) | Bert V. Royal (1977–), American

[Dark adolescent comedy; 4M, 4W; flexible set.] Royal had a surprise hit with his "unauthorized parody" of the comic strip *Peanuts*. It covers issues facing high school students, not only sexuality and drug use but also the meaning of life and the possibility of an afterlife. CB's (i.e., Charlie Brown's) dog contacts rabies and has to be euthanized. Distraught, he writes his old pen pal even though he has never responded to his letters and searches for some meaning with his school friends. Displaying numerous contradictions, after having previously tormented Beethoven (Schroeder) for being a "faggot," he impulsively kisses him, first in the privacy of the piano rehearsal room and then before everyone at a party that Marcy (Marcie) gives. CB's friend Matt (Pig-Pen) goes berserk, causing Tricia (Peppermint Patty) to realize, "Matt's in love with CB. That's what this is all about. […] Repressed homosexual anger isn't all that uncommon." Totally out of control, Matt destroys Beethoven's hand, so he will never play again. Beethoven kills himself. CB reverts to his previous callous self. His sister (Sally) counsels him: "Find. An. Identity." He finally receives a response from his pen pal. It is now revealed that his initials are CS (Charles Schultz). He assures CB, "You are a good man." The play opened in New York, 2004, with Michael Gladis, Benjamin Schrader, and Jay Sullivan, directed by Susan W. Lovell. § Royal, B. V. *Dog Sees God: Confessions of a Teenage Blackhead*. Dramatists, 2006. 49p.

352   *Happy Endings Are Extra* (2004) | Ashraf Johaardien (1974–), South African

[Sexual melodrama; 2M, 1W; unit set.] At the beginning of 2003 nine persons were murdered and one severely injured in a gay massage parlor in Cape Town. Two men were arrested, but no motive ever came through for the mass murder. Johaardien says that the play "started out as a tribute to the victims," and indeed the massacre is mentioned a few times, but the focus shifted to the troubled life of a bisexual man Gabriel Ruddick. He is engaged to Chantelle, who is somehow drawn to bisexuals, perhaps receiving affirmation when they return to her. But Gabriel's growing desire for teenage rent boy Chris tests their relationship, and she has sex with an anonymous man. The play ends melodramatically. By accident Gabriel discovers that Chris is his son and that the boy set out deliberately to seduce his father. Gabriel goes into a tailspin and shoots himself. Chris finds absolution of some kind to get on with his life. The premiere was in Grahamstown, 2004, with Paul Harris and Rory Acton-Burnell, directed by Nevil Engelbrecht. § In Malan, R., ed. *S.A. Plays 1*. 7–59.

353 *The History Boys* (2004) | Alan Bennett, English

[School drama; 11M, 1W, extras; flexible set.] Eight boys at an English public school would be more logical candidates for a redbrick university, but their hopes (and the headmaster's) are set on gaining entrance to either Oxford or Cambridge. Three teachers—two in history, one in English—prepare them for the examinations they will have to set. Each teacher represents a different approach to education, creating a play of ideas that is the heart of the drama. It happens that Hector, the English teacher, likes to caress his charges, groping their genitals as they ride behind him on his motorbike. None of them minds; it's part of the game. Irwin, the new history teacher, turns out to be closeted. Dakin, though straight, sees through his facade and offers himself for a blow job out of gratitude for his teaching. Dakin is also the one who blackmails the headmaster into granting Hector a reprieve after he is sacked. And he does not mind that he is the object of young Posner's affection. In a flash forward the audience is informed that all the boys make it into the school of their choice. But matters go awry for the two teachers and Posner, Hector's spiritual heir. Hector offers Irwin a ride on his motorbike. They crash, killing Hector and paralyzing Irwin's legs. Posner becomes a recluse who "has long since stopped asking himself where it went wrong." The premiere was in London, 2004, with Richard Griffiths, Stephen Campbell Moore, and Samuel Barnett, directed by Nicholas Hytner. It came to New York with the same cast, who also appeared in the 2006 film scripted by Bennett. § Bennett, A. *The History Boys*. Faber & Faber, 2004. 109p.

354 *Liar* (2004) | Brian Drader, Canadian

[Psychological drama; 3M, 1W; unit set.] Jeremy picks up Mark, a consummate con artist, in a gay bar. They end up on a rooftop tripping on ecstasy. When Jeremy tries to initiate sex, Mark declares that he is straight. And then Jeremy falls (or is pushed?) to his death from the ledge. Mark ingratiates himself with Jeremy's sister at the funeral, leaving the impression that he and Jeremy were longtime lovers. Her husband picks up that there is something suspicious, but even he is won over during a drunken evening on the town, just the two of them, and Mark accepts his offer to make their home his "temporary" headquarters. It comes out that Jeremy has told Mark about his indirect responsibility for the disappearance of his nephew, snatched while waiting for his father after school when Jeremy got stoned and called to say he could not pick the boy up. Though the sister wants another child, the husband refuses. There is a suggestion that Mark impregnates her. But by the time this is discovered, he has disappeared, having absconded with their savings and maxed out their credit cards. Jeremy remains almost as much an enigma as does his death. The play opened in Winnipeg, 2004, with Carson Nattrass, directed by Stephane Kirkland. § Drader, B. *Liar*. Scirocco Drama, 2004. 72p.

355 *Match* (2004) | Stephen Belber (1967–), American

[Domestic drama; 2M, 1W; 1 set.] Belber was part of *The Laramie Project*, both play and film. Here he uses a traditional structure. Seattle policeman Mike Rinaldi and his wife show up at former dancer/choreographer Tobias Powell's Manhattan apartment. Lisa has arranged the visit on the pretext of interviewing him about the dance world in the 1950s. But Mike's probing reveals the true reason for their visit: Mike wants to prove that Tobi is his father, the result of indiscriminate sex forty-three years earlier. He resents that his mother had to quit dancing to support them "because the *faggot* who knocked her up wouldn't take responsibility for what he did." When Tobi denies paternity, Mike forcefully scrapes his mouth to obtain tissue sampling for DNA testing. While he is gone, Tobi confesses that he is the father and even helped pay for Mike's college costs. But he understands that it is too late to change wrongly-made choices, that all of them need to move on with their lives. Upon his return, Mike seems to accept the point. The play opened in New York, 2004, with Frank Langella, directed by Nicholas Martin. Belber wrote and directed the 2014 film version. § Belber, S. *Match*. Dramatists, 2004. 57p.

356 *The Paris Letter* (2004) | **Jon Robin Baitz (1961–), American**

[Psychological drama; 4M, 1W; flexible set.] Baitz eschews chronological order in Anton Kilgallen's narration of his fifty-year relationship with the tormented Sandy Sonnenberg. They spend four intense months together November 1962 to February 1963, but Sandy seeks the help of a psychiatrist specializing in conversion therapy. Both Anton and Sandy's mother, in her oblique fashion, try to convince him he is re-enacting his father's emotional frigidity. Anton sums up, "Your problem is not at all sex, Sandy. It is pleasure—it's joy." Sandy follows his father into banking. Though it takes him a long time to do so, he marries a friend of Anton's and fathers a child. Then late in life he becomes smitten with a financial advisor, young Burt Sarris, who takes economic risks that ultimately bankrupt his prominent clients. Sandy advises Burt to kill himself and turns to trying to recover the losses, abandoning wife and son in the process. His last letter, from Paris, reaches his wife just as she, unknown to him, is dying from cancer. She begs Anton to bring Sandy back, but she dies before he can depart. In November 2002 Anton finds Sandy, informs him that he is aware of Sandy's culpability in Burt's death, and cold-bloodily serves him a drug-laced glass of bourbon. The ponderous script opened in Los Angeles, 2004, with Lawrence Pressman, Neil Patrick Harris, and Josh Radnor, directed by Michael Morris. § Baitz, J. R. *The Paris Letter*. Dramatists, 2006. 53p.

357 *Spatter Pattern, or How I Got Away with It* (2004) | **Neal Bell, American**

[Crime drama; 3M, 1W; flexible set.] The lies one tells oneself and the lies one presents to the world can both lead to self-destruction. Straight teacher Marcus Tate is called out by one of his students for the myth he has fabricated about himself as a Navy SEAL. Shortly thereafter her throat is slashed. Is he the killer? Gay scriptwriter Edward Dunn is forever reediting what he has said into what he wishes he had said. He feels that he emotionally betrayed his partner of twenty-three years, dead of a heart attack, by ceasing to love him and not trying to stop him from drinking and smoking. He tries to redeem his shortcomings by providing Tate with a fake alibi. When Tate asks why, Dunn answers simply, "I wanted someone to escape." The play ends with Dunn scattering his lover's ashes on the beach and Tate disappearing into the water, perhaps to follow the current down shore to a new life. The play opened in New York, 2004, with Peter Frechette, directed by Michael Greif. § In Clum, J., ed. *Gay Drama Now*. 413–89.

358 *Valhalla* (2004) | **Paul Rudnick, American**

[Historical study; 4M, 2W; flexible set.] Valhalla, the Norse hall of the slain, represents beauty, aspiration, fulfillment. Both Ludwig II of Bavaria (1845–1886) and the fictional James Avery of Texas, who lives during the middle of the 20th century, are in quest of a beautiful life. The playgoer witnesses significant snippets from their lives from the time both are ten until after their deaths. Ludwig's is somewhat embroidered upon, but the main outline remains true. James is bisexual, hungry for experience, yearning for more than the humdrum life his small-town environment offers. He steals beautiful objects, and is consequently abused by his father. He falls in love with Henry Lee Stafford. He impregnates Henry Lee's fiancée and then takes her place at the wedding. The two men leave together to fight in World War II. They are parachuted into Bavaria to report on enemy lines, and there James becomes enraptured of Ludwig's castles. After James's death his daughter looks into the reliquary he has stolen; designed to hold Ludwig's heart, it now holds the crystal swan James stole when he was ten. Wagner's music permeates the entire drama in what is Rudnick's most mature play to date. It opened in New York, 2004, with Peter Frechette, Sean Dugan, and Scott Barrow, directed by Christopher Ashley. § *The Collected Plays of Paul Rudnick*. Itbooks, 2010. 321–406.

359 *Blowing Whistles* (2005) | **Matthew Todd (unknown), English**

[Domestic drama; 3M; 1 set.] The play offers

a caustic variant on the results of a couple having a threesome. Nigel, 37, and Jamie, 32, have lived together for ten years. At Nigel's instigation they celebrate their anniversary by inviting Mark, a 17-year-old he has found on the internet, for an evening of sex. The couple represent almost stereotypical gays as portrayed by the media. Mark is a rougher, more complex character whose games are entirely different. The next day is London's Gay Pride. Jamie becomes fed up and returns home. Mark turns up and makes overtures to Jamie, trying to persuade him to leave Nigel. Upon Nigel's tardy return, he and Jamie have it out. Nigel swears that nothing happened at Pride after Jamie left and that he will give up other men to preserve their relationship, even cut off his membership in the online meeting site. Jamie is ready to forgive when a message arrives from Mark revealing that he and Nigel met at Pride and had sex. Jamie leaves. The play opened in London, 2005, with Neil Henry, Joe Fredericks, and Peter McNicholl, directed by Phil Willmott. § Todd, M. *Blowing Whistles*. Dramatists, 2006. 61p.

360 *The Boy Who Fell from the Roof* (2005) | Juliet Jenkin (unknown), South African

[Elegy; 2M, 2W, narrator; unit set.] Jenkin creates a moving tribute to a life cut short. Simon Lyndsay, 18, falls from a roof trying to reach a ball for his best friend Georgina Marais. Just a moment before he has shouted, "I am a gay man." At his funeral, narrated by a chorus figure, Georgina, Simon's mother, his boyfriend Leonard Jackson, 25, and Simon's ghost recall key moments in his brief existence. He never came out to his mother, though she gave him the opportunity when he wore a green carnation to a dance. He rejected the idea that "sexuality equals character" but lamented that "no straight kids have to agonise over this sort of thing." He scorned the plot of too many gay works: "Be gay. Meet gay person. Fall in love, experience carnal delights, grow up a little more, fall out of love, remain firm friends, meet more gay people, fall in love with them or don't and have sex with them or don't, mature, learn valuable life lessons about love respect sexually transmitted disease, write a book about it and die." Leonard, 25, rejects such an easy summary. He is a math student, a "coloured man," whom Simon met at a Seven Eleven. But Simon died before they had a chance to alter the script. The play opened in Cape Town, 2005, with Francesco Nassimbeni and David Johnson, directed by Roy Sargeant. § In Malan, R., ed. *S.A. Plays 1*. 61–113.

361 *Bunbury: A Serious Play for Trivial People* (2005) | Tom Jacobson, American

[Literary fantasy; 5M, 3W; flexible set.] In another inventive riff on *The Importance of Being Earnest* (*A Trivial Comedy for Serious People*), Edgar Bunbury, having no idea that he is a never-seen character in the play encounters a kindred spirit, the never-seen Rosaline of *Romeo and Juliet*. He thinks she is a joke sprung on him by his lover Algernon Moncrieff and goes in angry pursuit of Algy (his having decamped to London), encountering Jack Worthing on the way. As a result Bunbury discovers the double game that Algy and Jack have been playing. He is further disillusioned when he learns that Algy intends to marry Cecily Cardew. Picking up a lily that Jack has dropped, he leaves with Rosaline. They save Romeo and Juliet and, as a result, change the course of literary history. Poe now writes a poem to a peacock that says "Anytime"; the three sisters take off for Moscow; Allan Grey does not kill himself but discovers the pleasures of Bunburying, so Blanche does not have a fatal encounter with Stanley; and George and Martha's son (*Who's Afraid of Virginia Woolf?*) shows up. Appalled by the way they have changed literature, the two return to Juliet's tomb, and Rosaline stages the lovers' deaths. It is too late: history remains changed. Vladimir and Estragon hail Bunbury as their long awaited Godot. He meets up finally with the aged Algy, to find that the latter has never heard of Wilde. Bunbury himself has not aged since he knows he is only "a plot device, a mere joke." At the end they watch the moon landing together: the never assassinated Robert Kennedy says, "Thank you, Jack, for leading us to this day," seeming to merge JFK and Worthing. The comedy opened in Los Angeles, 2005, with Sean Wing and Zach Dulli, directed by Mark Bringelson. The year before Jacobson produced another speculative drama, *Ouroboros*, whose five scenes can be played in either direction. § Jacobson, T. *Bunbury: A Serious Play for Trivial People*. Broadway Play, 2008. 69p.

362 *Curtsy* (2005) | Brian Drader, Canadian

[Domestic tragedy; 3M; flexible set.] The figure at the center of Drader's play offers all sorts of dramatic possibilities. Dillan is an intersex person who self-identifies as gay. A writer, he has for eight years been the partner of Randolph, a sociology professor. But Drader chose the easy course of serving up clichés rather than take the viewer on a journey of discovery. Dillan is a drug addict. Randolph cheats on him with Bart, a burnt-out hustler. Bart shows up at their home and provides Dillan more drugs. Randolph throws them out. Dillan overdoses in a sleazy bathhouse. Bart retreats into romantic fantasy. Dillan sought inspiration for his next novel from Conrad's *Heart of Darkness*. His anti-hero Barblow was going to go in search of Curtsy, a drag queen lost in "the *urban* jungle." But Dillan confesses he never finished Conrad's story: "It was so wretchedly depressing. All those dark jungles and testosterone-fueled philosophical waxing." It is a good description of the play. It opened in Ottawa, 2005, with Greg MacArthur, Julian Doucet, and Hubert Proulx, directed by Emma Tibaldo. § *Three on the Boards: New Plays for Three Actors*; ed. by Kit Brennan. Signature, 2007. 9–76.

363   *Questa* (2005) | Victor Bumbalo, American

[Psychological drama; 5M, 2W; flexible set.] The play probes the nature of guilt, love, and redemption. Paul goes into an alley behind a Greenwich Village bar looking for sex. Instead, he is attacked by a homophobic straight man who has dashed into the darkness to urinate. Paul strikes back and accidentally kills him. Unbeknownst to Paul, the altercation is witnessed by an African American street person Daniel. He comes forward to the police and describes the killer as someone who resembles Paul not in the least. The gay community assumes the killing is another gay-bashing and rallies behind the mother. Ironically, though she works in a hair-dressing salon popular with gays, she is equally homophobic and often made fun of her boss to her son. Paul begins stalking her, even as Daniel starts stalking him, realizing that he's falling in love. Paul's lover, his brother-in-law's best friend, has died of AIDS. Daniel has lost his brother to drugs. The hairdresser Richard likewise has lost his partner. (Paul says, "Gay boys have so much in common. Our love for divas and dead boyfriends.") Now they are trying to reconnect with others, Paul understandably having the most trouble. As for the heterosexuals, Paul's sister and her husband are having serious communication problems, chiefly because she clings to Paul, and the dead man's mother is having an affair with her Catholic priest. There are no epiphanies at the end, but at least there is quiet. The premiere was in Los Angeles, 2005, with Michael Hagerty, Dorian Harewood, and Bruce Nozick, directed by Joe Cacaci. The title comes from Paul's childhood memory of a visit to the Edenic New Mexican village, a symbol of innocence to which he can never return. § Bumbalo, V. *Questa*. Broadway Play, 2006. 70p.

364   *Rope Enough* (2005) | Sky Gilbert, Canadian

[Crime drama; 4M, 1W; flexible set.] Playing with language and its relationship to perception, Gilbert may be satirically sending the audience up or engaging in a serious postmodern discussion of the nature of knowledge. The detective in the case is aptly named John Trick. The supposed perpetrators constantly deconstruct the stories they tell. Ichabod Malframe and Dylan Short may or may not have bludgeoned Ichabod's parents and sister to death. Ichabod may be a genius, a charlatan, a mentally disturbed person—or perhaps all three. Although there is no evidence to connect him to the murders, he confesses to Trick during a sexual encounter to excite him. (One of the minor mysteries is where the very naked Trick was concealing a wire.) Sex is a driving force for the stories told. For the last year, the youths' association with the grisly deaths have both turned on and frightened off potential partners. A female journalist takes up their case and finds herself wandering through the worlds of Leopold and Loeb, *Will and Grace*, Einstein, Foucault, and Oprah. A key philosophical question—posed by Bobbi LaCreme, head of Canada's Rainbow TV Channel, to Trick—becomes "How do you feel about unsafe sex?" Upon their encounter with Trick, Dylan (sounding very much like Ichabod) admits they bareback: "But we don't go around *talking* about barebacking all the time, like some icky people. Have you ever met a serious bugchaser? What crashing bores they are, and some of them call themselves AIDS radicals." The last sounds heard in the drama come from an old television interview by Phil Donahue with "men who deliberately infect others with AIDS." The play, with its teasing title, opened in Toronto, 2005, with Gavin Crawford, David Tomlinson,

Ryan McVittie, and Patrick Conner, directed by Gilbert. § Gilbert, S. *Rope Enough*. Playwrights Canada, 2005. 51p.

365 *Romance* (2005) | **David Mamet (1947–), American**

[Satire; 7M; 3 sets.] Tom in Tolins's *Last Sunday in June* asks, "What's a 'straight play'?" to which Michael answers, "Mamet." One can understand Michael's riposte even given the homoeroticism that drives so many of Mamet's plays, including outright homosexuality in such earlier plays as *Edmond*, 1982 (the basis for the 2005 film), and *The Shawl*, 1985. *Romance* comes across as the playwright's deliberate attempt to prove Michael wrong. Five of the seven characters in this pointless farce are gay. However, all seven are caricatures, and the plot is deliberately politically incorrect. The setting is a courtroom in a city where a major peace conference attended by the Israeli and the Palestinians is in session. The gay Bernard, aka Bunny, is the pivotal character. He is the prosecutor's lover, but he went on a vacation to Hawaii with the defendant while pretending to be in Atlantic City with the prosecutor's mother. The defendant, a chiropractor, is charged with some unspecified crime. He devises a plan to bring peace to the Mideast by manipulating all the leaders' necks. The judge pops so many pills that he is befuddled throughout the trial. He and the bailiff are also lovers on the side. The play opened in New York, 2005, with Keith Nobbs, Bob Balaban, and Larry Bryggman, under Neil Pepe's direction. Mamet went on to write yet another gay play, *Keep Your Pantheon*, 2007, about two gay actors in Roman times. § Mamet, D. *Romance: A Play*. Vintage, 2005. 118p.

366 *Sir Richard Wadd, Pornographer* (2005) | **Shawn Postoff (1974–), Canadian**

[Sexual drama; 5M; unit set.] The play wittily focuses on the attraction of gay porn: "Cum *ergo sum*." It also addresses the question of adolescent sexuality and the laws governing it. Sir Richard Wadd has an internet site for which he directs sexual acts between young males, describing what they are to do in heroic couplets, to wit: "All scenes depicted, expressed or implied, / Are meant to contain graphic narrations / Of explicit sexual relations / Among safe, sane and consenting adults. / Given, therefore, their intended results, / Entrance to minors is prohibited." Kevin, 14, disregards this interdiction. Enamored of Wadd's poetry and the performances he obtains from college-age men, Kevin shows up on his doorstep with a sample of his own poetry. Wadd turns him away because of the danger he poses: "I'd be arrested. I'd become the latest in a long and distinguished line of sex monsters to grace the pages of the hysterical *Times*." Kevin is taken in by the amoral John, who offers him drugs and promises that "my friends are gonna like you." The premiere was in Toronto, 2005, with John Healy, Jefferson Guzman, and Jason Fraser, directed by Postoff. He followed it with two yet unpublished sequels: *Sir Richard Wadd, Topographer*, and *Sir Richard Wadd, Paleographer*. Postoff was also a writer for *Queer as Folk*, 2003–05. § In Gilbert, S., ed. *Absolutely Abnormal*. 101–41.

367 *A Strange and Separate People* (2005) | **Jon Marans (unknown), American**

[Ethnic drama; 2M, 1W; unit set.] This play of ideas encourages audiences to think about Orthodox Judaism's stance on homosexuality. Phyllis Berman, a former caterer, is coping the best she can with an autistic child. She strikes up an unexpected friendship with Stuart Weinstein, a gastroenterologist seeking her catering services. He is quite frank that he intends to strive to be "the first of a new breed of gay orthodox men. Discreet but open." He is not frank that he is her husband's lover. Jay Berman is a therapist who ironically used "reparative therapy" on men suffering from "Same Sex Attraction Disorder" before he met Stuart (although Stuart is not the first man he has been with since marriage). When Phyllis realizes the truth, she orders Jay to leave. He and Stuart set up house, adapting orthodox dogma as needed. Jay outs himself to the President of the synagogue, who suggests he would be happier elsewhere. But Stuart cannot match him in honesty: "How do I tell G-d that some of his laws I'm going to completely ignore." Phyllis, almost against her will, feels compassion for Jay and begs Stuart to join her in standing up to the President, but he walks away. At that point Jay tells Phyllis that he thinks their son "should be bar mitzvah'd here," and the two face the world both alone and somehow together. The premiere was in Stony Point, N.Y., 2005, with Sam Guncler and Arnie Burton, directed by Joe Brancato. § Marans, J. *A Strange and Separate People: A New Play*. Chelsea Station, 2012. 21–109.

368 *Strangers in Between* (2005) | Tommy Murphy (1979–), Australian

[Adolescent comedy; 3M; flexible set.] King's Cross, Sydney, became part of the gay literary landscape with the 1961 publication of Jon Rose's semifictional autobiography *At the Cross*. It inspired Alex Harding's 1988 musical comedy *Only Heaven Knows*. Murphy returns to the scene to offer a very different view. Shane, a runaway, is a mass of contradictions. He is more naive than the most naïf, yet sexually rather pushy. He doesn't know how to do his laundry and is cold-cocked when he gets a case of anal warts, yet he know how to get his way by admitting at calculated moments that he is not 19 but 16. He has fled an abusive brother, but is haunted by his spirit. Clearly his attraction to Will grows out of his resemblance to this brother (the two characters are played by the same actor). The much older Peter becomes a surrogate father, the first person to whom he says "I'm gay." He is terrified he will be mugged in the city, but he has been attacked only in his small hometown. Shane can shift course within the same sentence, adding to the comedy and the bewilderment of the two men who end up caring for him whether they want to or not. The play opened in Sydney, 2005, with Sam Dunn, Brett Stiller, and Anthony Phelan, directed by David Berthold. § Murphy, T. *Strangers in Between*. Nick Hern, 2016. 76p.

369 *Telstar: The Joe Meek Story* (2005) | Nick Moran (1969–), English

[Biographical study; 9M, 1W; 1 set.] Moran became fascinated with the life and suicide of record producer Joe Meek (1929–1967), whose *Telstar* became the first British single to top American charts despite the fact that Meek himself was not a musician. Moran enlisted the aid of James Hicks to sort myth from fact (not always successfully according to some). Act 1 is largely taken up with technical matters and personnel. As it builds, we see Meek's attraction to straight singer Heinz Burt, who is willing to play gay to forward his career. Two calamities strike: a French composer sues for plagiarism, and Joe is arrested for "Importuning in a public convenience." Act 2 shows his mental breakdown, acerbated by threats after newspaper publish articles about his arrest. As Joe becomes increasingly paranoid, he loses his studio; his landlady is posed to evict him. Always spooked by February 3 as an unlucky day, he grabs a hunting rifle and kills her before turning the weapon upon himself. His last faithful friend, Patrick Pink, is left to handle the mess. The play opened in Cambridge, 2005, with Con O'Neill, directed by Paul Jepson. The pair also wrote the screenplay for the 2008 film. § Moran, N., with J. Hicks. *Telstar: The Joe Meek Story*. Oberon, 2005. 106p.

370 *The Agony & The Agony* (2006) | Nicky Silver, American

[Farce; 4M, 2W; 2 sets.] In a note to the play, Silver reveals that he was so depressed by the negative reviews of *Beautiful Child* that he contemplated giving up writing. He decided to have one last fling, to write a light-hearted play just for the fun of it. So he wrote about a depressed gay playwright, Richard, a total hypochondriac, in an open marriage to an independently wealthy but failed actress. She invites over gay producer Anton Knight, the man who rejected Richard's last play, hoping to land the part of Blanche in a new production of *Streetcar*. One of her sexual partners, the versatile Chet, shows up to borrow money to bail out his pregnant girlfriend's father from jail. He decides to stay around when he hears Anton is expected; his dream is to play Nugget in *Equus*, Anton's next scheduled production after *Streetcar*, and he is willing to go gay to get the part. Nathan Leopold, of Leopold and Loeb, also shows up: he is unhappy at finding himself a character in Richard's latest play. He becomes even more unhappy when he discovers what a lousy script it is. The only solution Nathan decides is to write his own play. It is not totally clear whether the final results are his or Richard's, but the play read aloud to the producer is the one the audience has just seen. It opened in New York, 2006, with Harry van Gorkum, Michael Esper, and Silver (as Richard), directed by Terry Kinney. § Silver, N. *The Agony & The Agony*. Dramatists, 2008. 62p.

371 *Based on a Totally True Story* (2006) | Roberto Aguirre-Sacasa, American

[Hollywood satire; 4M, 1W; flexible set.] The play opens with an old-fashioned prologue giving away the plot: "This is a story about a guy, a writer [Ethan], and another guy, also a writer [Michael], and a dad (the first guy's dad), and a play the first guy wrote [its title never given, but clearly Aguirre-Sacasa's *The Muckleman*, 2001], and the people in Hollywood who want to turn that play into a movie, and what happens with the people in Hollywood, the first guy, the second guy, the first guy's dad, and what they learn about themselves and the world." Ethan becomes so immersed in Hollywood's pipe dreams that he ignores Michael. For more complicated reasons he fails his father when the latter confesses to having an affair with a married woman. The Hollywood agent keeps demanding rewrites until the script little resembles the play it is based on. On a trip to meet potential producers, Ethan has a one-night stand with a Hollywood wannabe and then, despite counsel to keep silent, confesses to Michael. Just as Ethan's mother leaves his father after he confesses to the affair, Michael leaves Ethan. The one constant in his life remains his work for a comic book series. He is invited to rewrite an old horror movie (an eerie foreshadowing of Aguirre-Sacasa's rewriting *Carrie*); the play ends with the cast watching the finished film. The audience is told at the beginning that the semi-autobiographical play is "a *slightly* familiar story." One could add *self-indulgent*. Its premiere was in New York, 2006, with Carson Elrod and Pedro Pascal, directed by Michael Bush. § Aguirre-Sacasa, R. *Based on a Totally True Story*. Dramatists, 2008. 64p.

372 *Circuitry* **(2006) | Andrew Barrett (unknown), American**

[AIDS fantasy; 4M; unit set,] Following three friends and a dead lover's ghost, Barrett takes audiences on a nostalgic if judgmental look at the world of drug-fueled circuit parties. The time is 1994–96, when the new AIDS cocktail was introduced. Brian, a Village rare-book dealer, has lost his partner to AIDS. In an effort to jump-start his life again, his two friends David and Lenny become his guides to four circuit parties. HIV-positive David seduces Brian while Lenny is high on everything from ketamine to meth. Though Brian is the only one able to see him, his dead partner Paul shows up to urge Brian to move on with his life. After a major confrontation, all four reevaluate their existence. Lenny sums up, "What a mess of our lives we've all made. But we can clean it up." Happy that at least he lived that life for a few months, Brian puts it behind him and finally comes out to his Jewish mother. The premiere in New York, 2006, was titled *Rainy Days & Mondays*; the cast included Michael Carbonaro, Ander del Rio, Benjamin Gabriel, and Jamyl Dobson, directed by Niegel Smith. § Barrett, A. *Circuitry*. French, 2007. 94p.

373 *Citizenship* **(2006) | Mark Ravenhill, English**

[Adolescent drama; 6M, 7W; flexible set.] In his introduction, Ravenhill discusses his motive for writing about teenage sexuality: "The sexualised teenager is a recurrent icon in the global marketplace. Fears about children and sex are everywhere, and yet unsensational, clear-eyed writing is still pretty rare." Tom and Amy, both 15, are the leads, but Tom gains the greater attention in his search to decide whether he is gay or straight. He is pretty sure his social science teacher is gay, but De Clerk deflects all his questions. Though the school celebrates diversity, the biggest slur the students can hurl at anyone is the accusation that the person is gay. Tom has sex with Amy, impregnating her in their one time together. Through a chatroom he meets Martin, 21, who is interested only in "Money. Sex. Fun." Tom wants love: "I want everything and I want…. I want…. I want to find out everything." He is ready to grow up and strike out on his own. The premiere was in London, 2006, with Sid Mitchell, Javone Prince, and Richard Dempsey, directed by Anna Mackmin. In addition to other gay-themed plays, Ravenhill most recently created the television series *Vicious*. § Ravenhill, M. *Plays 2*. Methuen Drama, 2008. 233–92.

374 *Danny and Chantelle (Still Here)* **(2006) | Phillip McMahon (1979–), Irish**

[Psychological drama; 1M, 1W; flexible set.] The title characters spend an evening in Dublin high on Ecstasy. They have been best friends for years, "Joined at the hip" (like French conjoined twins, who are mentioned several times). Their E-supplier is Swiss-Tony, openly gay. The first time they met, he warned Danny against a "chicken hawk" cruising him; they ended up "on the couch of some hairdresser, with Swiss-Tony in between us, educating us on chickens, and chicken hawks, poppers and rimming, cock rings and anal beads." Danny accuses his best friend Stephen (Steo) of being overly touchy about Tony: "homo-haters are actually homos themselves." And in fact he catches Steo openly kissing Chris, a guy whom Tony was cruising. Confronted, Steo accuses Danny of also being "a bender," reminding him how they used to kiss when younger—something Danny emphatically denies. By now the audience is on Steo's side. Two actors play all the parts. The play opened in Dublin, 2006, with McMahon, directed by Deirdre Molloy. § In Walsh, F., ed. *Queer Notions*. 184–208.

375 *The Drowning Room* (2006) | Verity-Alicia Mavenawitz (1957–), Irish

[Psychological drama; 6M, 1W; 1 set.] Seán's family and friends gather in the early hours of the morning in a secluded site to spread his ashes, having vowed to keep them till the gay-bashers who killed him were sentenced. Waiting for the sun to rise, they drink and reminisce. Seán was obviously a good human, but, to the dismay of his brother Cillian and his former lover Bob, the irreverent Leo brings out that he was no saint. Maura, the mother of Seán's child, accepts the revelations with equilibrium. She is also the one willing to listen when the father of one of Seán's muggers unexpectedly shows up. Kevin, Seán's closest friend since childhood, straight, sums up, "Seán was a man of honour and he had great dignity, so tonight [...] should be about dignity and respect, and if not forgiveness, then ... acceptance." Cillian and Bob resist, but after the father reads aloud his son's private confession, they experience a muted catharsis. The play ends with an improvised ritual: Seán always wore lip gloss; Kevin recalls how as early as the third grade, when the teacher accused him of wearing lipstick, he had replied, "No, sir! Just because I'm gay doesn't mean I wear lipstick." Now, as they get ready to spread the ashes, Kevin brings out a lipstick, and one by one they each in turn put it on another's lips, including the father's. The premiere was in Dublin, 2006, with Simon Fogarty, directed by Nuala Kelly. § In Walsh, F., ed. *Queer Notions*. 136–83.

376 *Dying City* (2006) | Christopher Shinn, American

[Psychological drama; 1M, 1W; 1 set.] The play moves back and forth between two scenes, one in July 2005 and one in January 2004. Identical twin brothers (played by the same actor), Peter is an actor, gay, promiscuous, his brother's hero worshipper; Craig is a military officer deployed to Iraq, unhappily married to a therapist, a student of Faulkner, a suicide. Kelly the wife, despite her training and occupation, has her own issues with both brothers. Peter has just walked out of a production of *Long Day's Journey into Night* (the actor playing the father told him, "You're never going to be a good actor till you stop sucking cock") to show up unannounced at Kelly's door. The raw wounds of their troubled childhoods (the twins' father was a Vietnam veteran suffering from PDST; hers offered money in place of love) and the messy failures of their adult interactions are exposed anew, but the small epiphanies that occur offer no more promise for resolution and healing than does the mother's muted memories at the end of O'Neill's play. Much about the trio's emotional bonds remains unexplored: the exact nature of the twins' relationship; the desire for a baby not to be fulfilled; the meaning of their reactions to one of Kelly's clients; Peter's unfaithfulness with his boyfriend Tim; the significance of Craig's reading of Tim. The title city is Bagdad, but it is also New York after 9/11. It premiered in London, 2006, with Andrew Scott; it opened in New York, 2007, with Pablo Schreiber; both productions were directed by James Macdonald. § Shinn, C. *Dying City*. Dramatists, 2007. 40p.

377 *The Golden Thug* (2006) | Ed Roy (unknown), Canadian

[Biographical study; 4M, 1W; 1 set.] The play recreates Jean Genet's final days in 1986 in a seedy hotel in Paris, peppering his script "with truths, half-truths and bald-faced lies." While supposedly working on the final draft of *The Prisoner of Love*, Genet becomes intrigued by the proprietress's nephew/son, the young Pierre in whom he sees a reflection of his younger self. Enamored of his friend Luc, Pierre allows him to propel the two of them into a life of petty crime. Luc talks him into stealing from the hotel patrons, including taking what they think is the sole manuscript of *Prisoner*, intending to demand ransom for its return. Genet outmaneuvers the two youths and then reveals that the publisher has had a copy all along. Their antics cause Genet to flash back to key moments in his own life. The young Genet was used by men for sexual pleasure with no commensurate investment of emotional involvement. Now Genet uses people. Pierre becomes raw material for his notebooks. Genet coldly says, "Who are you to me? You played your hand and I played mine. We made our choices, good or bad, and now we have to live with them." Genet dies cogent of Pierre's foreboding (if mistaken) prophesy that his works will be forgotten.

The premiere was in Toronto, 2006, with William Webster and Andrew Hachey, directed by Roy. § Roy, E. *The Golden Thug*. Playwrights Canada, 2008. 105p.

378 *Holding the Man* (2006) | **Tommy Murphy, Australian**

[Coming out/AIDS drama; 4M, 2W; flexible set.] Murphy dramatizes Tim Conigrave's posthumous memoir and tribute to his lover John Caleo. Both men died of AIDS, John in 1992 and Tim in 1994. The play opens when Tim, 9, first realizes he is "a poofter" and concludes with an epilogue revealing his death, not quite 35. Between those events the audience witnesses adolescent love, the differing reactions of the two families, Tim's restlessness, which leads to a trial separation as they pursue different goals (Tim in theater; John in health care), activism, and then the ravages of AIDS. Tim must accept that he is probably the one who infected John: "I've killed the man I love." The two men turn to raising people's awareness. Tim's play *Soft Targets*, performed in 1986, was probably Australia's first AIDS play. (Passing mention is also made of Alex Harding's later play.) But the emphasis in Murphy's own play is almost exclusively on the personal. Its premiere was in Sydney, 2006, with Guy Edmonds and Matt Zeremes, directed by David Berthold. Murphy also wrote the screenplay for the 2015 film. § Murphy, T. *Holding the Man, Adapted from the Book by Timothy Conigrave*. Nick Hern, 2010. 110p.

379 *In Gabriel's Kitchen* (2006) | **Salvatore Antonio (1976–), Canadian**

[Ethnic tragedy; 4M, 1W; unit set.] The play provides a graphic example of the way families destroy gay children. It alternates between present time and the crucial period three years earlier when Gabriel Montesano and Matthew Finnerty, both 18, explore their sexuality together. Matt advises Gabriel that his family often moves because of his father's profession, but when he begs Gabriel to set up a home with him, Gabriel feels constrained by his family heritage. This does not prevent him from telling them the truth, whereupon his parents react like stereotypical Sicilians. Gabriel feels that he has no recourse but to kill himself. His last act of defiance before hanging himself is to wear his rosary like a necklace as a statement, "How can it be a sin if it comes from God?" Matt provides an attempt at a moral, to the effect that we all must learn to live appropriately in the cosmos. The premiere was in Toronto, 2006, with Marc Bendavid and Kristopher Turner, directed by David Oiye. § Antonio, S. *In Gabriel's Kitchen*. Playwrights Canada, 2007. 106p.

380 *The Little Dog Laughed* (2006) | **Douglas Carter Beane, American**

[Hollywood satire; 2M, 2W; flexible set.] Mitchell Green is posed to make it big in Hollywood, but his agent is worried. Mitchell "suffers from a slight ... recurring case of homosexuality." At the moment, in New York, he is getting a bit too serious about an escort he has hired, Alex Eatenbrook. Alex claims he is safe; he has a girlfriend after all. But then he realizes, "I have feelings for this guy." The relationship could complicate "straight" Mitchell's life as he is preparing to play a gay man on the screen. As his agent says, "If a perceived straight actor portrays a gay role in a feature film, it's noble. It's a stretch. [...] If an actor with a 'friend' plays a gay role, it's not acting, it's bragging." So which is it to be: happiness with Alex or fame as a star? Of course, Mitchell chooses the latter, but with a twist. Alex's girlfriend is pregnant. He will marry her and take on the role of father for Alex's child. Alex takes a deep breath, so to speak, and moves on: "My life is beginning." The agent sums up: "The little dog laughed to see such sport and the dish ran away with the spoon." The premiere was in New York, 2006. with Neal Huff and Johnny Galecki, directed by Scott Ellis. § Beane, D. C. *The Little Dog Laughed*. Dramatists, 2007. 52p.

381 *Measure for Pleasure: A Restoration Romp* (2006) | **David Grimm, American**

[Sexual comedy; 4M, 3W, extras; 8 sets.] In this pastiche, the playwright captures the spirit of Restoration comedy with a gay twist. Two of the three intertwined plots follow heterosexual hijinks, complete with "masks and mad disguises." The young rake Captain Dick Dashwood and the randy old goat Sir Peter Lustforth, though the latter is married, both pursue young Hermione Goode, who herself means to reform Dashwood. But the third plot centers on valet Will Blunt's love for young Molly Tawdry, a male prostitute in drag. Completely aware of Molly's gender, Blunt manages to get him a place in the household as a lady's maid and then is pained to see Molly also fall amorous of Dashwood. However, after many a twist and turn, the couples are paired off correctly. In a final flourish, with an implicit nod to *The Importance of Being Earnest*, Molly resumes masculine clothes and reveals that he is Valentine Lustforth, the son given up by the mother in a pique against her unloving husband. Vowing his continuing love for the youth, Blunt observes, "In classical terms, this is what's called a Homo ex Machina." Molly/Valentine recognizes Blunt's true value and proposes, "Marry me, Will." He has the final lines in the play: "For life is short and love is sweet. Give pleasure without measure." The premiere was in New York, 2006, with Michael Stuhlbarg and Euan Morton, directed by Peter DuBois. § Grimm, D. *Measure for Pleasure: A Restoration Romp*. Dramatists, 2006. 65p.

382   *Regrets Only* (2006) | **Paul Rudnick, American**

[Political satire; 2M, 4W; 1 set.] Fashion designer Hank Hadley is recovering from the death of his lover of thirty-eight years. He calls upon old Manhattan friends, the McCulloughs, to discover that Jack and his daughter Spencer, both lawyers, are headed to Washington at the invitation of the president to help draft an airtight amendment to the Constitution defining marriage as between only a man and a woman. Hank feels betrayed. He and his gay friends ponder, "What would this city, what would this world, be like, without gay people? [...] what if we all just decided to, oh say, take the day off?" The answer, of course, is that the city would be virtually paralyzed. Hank also realizes that "the president and his posse, they're all following fashion. Which is easy. And scary." Hank further observes that, to date, all twenty-seven amendments save the ones dealing with Prohibition are "big-hearted." He notes that the opening to the Declaration of Independence is "so gay. [...] It's like a party invitation." These trenchant political observations are surrounded by swathes of banter and wit. The comedy opened in New York, 2006, with George Grizzard, directed by Christopher Ashley. Rudnick next turned his attention to a series of short plays. § *The Collected Plays of Paul Rudnick*. Itbooks, 2010. 407–72.

383   *Some Men* (2006–07) | **Terrence McNally, American**

[Historical sketches; 9M; flexible set.] Opening and closing with a gay wedding, the play offers a dozen vignettes of gay American life from 1922 through 2007. Since they are not presented in chronological order, it takes some time to realize that the interconnected backstories of the wedding party and their guests are being presented: how they met, how they interacted with each other, who their relatives were, and how they link to various important stages in the history of gay New York. One thread follows Bernie, married with children: he gets up the courage to have sex with a hustler, later meets Carl at a bathhouse and falls in love, and the two embrace Bernie's gay son when he comes out and accept his lover Perry. Perry is the grandson of a chauffeur, a rich man's lover whom we meet in the earliest vignette set on the Hamptons in 1922. At the bathhouse Bernie briefly meets Aaron, who is there with his partner Scoop. Aaron is a physician, thus in the midst of the AIDS crisis when it breaks. They are latter interviewed by Fritz and Pat, who meet in a chatroom. Scoop dies before the wedding, but there is a possibility that Aaron will go out with Marty, who keeps pushing himself to write the story of his uncle, one of the drag queens in the Stonewall riots. (The hustler is also present.) Fritz meets Paul, who lost his lover in war in the Mideast. In short, there are far fewer than six degrees of separation in this frieze of gay history. The 2006 premiere was in Philadelphia with John Glover, Don Amendolia, Stephen Bogardus, Brandon Bales, Malcolm Getz, Gregory Wooddell, and Duane Boutte, directed by Philip Himberg. A much revised script that eliminated women's roles debuted the next year in New York. § McNally, T. *Some Men*. Dramatists, 2008. 67p.

384   *Southwark Fair* (2006) | **Samuel Adamson, English**

[Social comedy; 5M, 2W; 4 sets.] Playing with the differences that short shifts in time and perspective can make, the play tells the same story twice. Simon is excited that the man who took his virginity when he was 14 wants to meet up with him eighteen years later. Patrick Mulligan was the drama coach; the moment occurred "during the interval of a summer school production of *A Midsummer Night's Dream*." When they meet at a restaurant, however, Simon discovers that Patrick has mixed him up with the teenager who played

Lysander and that it is the latter he expected to see. Intersecting their story is that of the Hungarian waiter Aurek, who is excited about his upcoming civil union with a London deputy mayor, only to be left waiting at city hall when the latter gets cold feet. Aurek is appalled to discover that Patrick once had sex with the underaged Simon and won't believe that Simon feels no residual emotional problems. All the while Patrick's wife has been tailing first him and then Simon. An Australian sidewalk bird whistle seller also crosses everyone's paths. Act 1 sets forth the bare outlines of the stories; Act 2 fills them in and extends the bizarre—and quite humorous—set of circumstances. Patrick wanders off and disappears. His wife and the bird whistler pair up, and Aurek turns his attention to Simon. A doddering old dear who is convinced some new film director will recognize her potential based on her cameos in the long ago *Carry On* series adds her own brand on inanity to the proceedings. The play opened in London, 2006, with Rory Kinnear, Con O'Neill, Michael Legge, and Rhashan Stone, directed by Nicholas Hytner. § Adamson, S. *Southwark Fair*. Faber & Faber, 2006. 111p.

385 *All That I Will Ever Be* (2007) | Alan Ball (1957–), American

[Social drama; 5M, 1W; flexible set.] Ball turned out a number of short plays with gay themes before his resounding success with the film *American Beauty* and the television series *Six Feet Under*. In this full-length play he pursues the meaning of identity. Omar is a hustler, a con artist ready to don whatever persona is needed by his client. Is his name then Omar, Joseph, or something else? Is he Lebanese, Armenian, or Persian? If he feels as deeply for Dwight as it appears he does, why does he antagonize him so? What part does the hatred unleashed after 9/11 against Muslims play in explaining his mercurial personality? When he pushes Eddie White so hard in the last scene in the play, is he enjoying his power or has he mysteriously turned his own pain into a source for healing others? Consider this curious exchange: "Eddie. So … are you just gay for pay? / Omar. I started out that way. Then I started to like it. / Eddie. Really…? You're not just lying about that? / Omar. I don't lie. / Eddie. What do you like about it? / Omar. I like everything about it. I like losing myself in another man … making his body mine, and mine his … discovering that secret place in him that's just like that secret place in me … until he finally drops all his inhibitions … any last fear of letting me see who he really is." Do we see the real Omar as he cradles the frightened Eddie? He has not disclosed his name, even when stripped of the hustling name (Carlito) he has adopted. It is the type of play that generates conversation afterwards. It opened in New York, 2007, with Peter Macdissi, Austin Lysy, and David Margulies, directed by Jo Bonney. Ball's next resounding success was the television series *True Blood*. § Ball, A. *All That I Will Ever Be*. Dramatists, 2008. 60p.

386 *Dalliances* (2007) | Pieter Jacobs (1980–), South African

[Urban tragedy; 3M, 1W; flexible set.] The play is about four losers. Perhaps we are meant to see them as social victims (one is badly beaten by his brother when he is found with another boy), but they seem to have pretty much victimized themselves. Janet is hooked on drugs and obsessed with death. She is in an ill-defined relationship with the promiscuous Leo. The abusive Ken and the younger, suicidal Andy have been living together for three years. Though Ken is HIV-positive, he has unprotected sex with all three. Andy impulsively kills him and then hacks his body up into three parts. Putting it in garbage bags, he delivers them to Leo and Janet. The play ends with a whimper. It opened in Cape Town, 2007, with Stephen Jubber, Clayton Boyd, and Keenan Arrison, directed by Neville Engelbrecht. § In Malan, R., ed. *S.A. Plays 1*. 115–71.

387 *The Giant* (2007) | Antony Sher (ZAF 1949–), English

[Historical drama; 12M; 1 set.] In a note Sher records how he was early drawn to Michelangelo (1475–1564) for his portraits of nude males but became equally enamored of Leonardo (1452–1519) as he developed this play. He writes, "Nowadays it's generally accepted that both were gay […] yet they seemed to have remained celibate. Why? I became more and more drawn to exploring something which fascinates me: the link between creativity and sexuality. And their link to power—for Machiavelli was in Florence too." Both artists were candidates to carve David. The play, covering the years 1501–04, imagines what may have passed between them. Both men sublimate their sexual desire in art. Leonardo, who was arrested for sodomy, is accompanied by his minion Salai, but he has taken "a vow of purity" as a result of the arrest. Michelangelo falls in love with the model for David, but is able to voice his feelings only over the youth's sleeping body. That model, Vito, is tempted to stray, not by Michelangelo but by Leonardo, but he returns to his wife and daughter, content that his youthful beauty has been forever preserved in the statue of the "uncircumcised Hebrew." The play opened in London, 2007, with John Light, Roger Allam, and Simon Trinder, directed by Gregory Doran. § Sher, A. *The Giant*. Nick Hern, 2007. 105p.

388 *His Greatness* (2007) | **Daniel MacIvor, Canadian**

[Biographical study; 3M; 1 set.] MacIvor explains how both he and Sky Gilbert (see *My Night with Tennessee*) were influenced by the same story about Williams. He avers, "*His Greatness* is not a play about Tennessee Williams. [... It] is a play about three lost men who have forgotten their dream of a life, and as a result of the events of two days come to remember, if not their dream, at least that they once had a dream." But the setting is Vancouver, and the occasion is mounting a new production of a revised play. So the Playwright (the only name he has in the script) is inescapably Williams. He is with his Assistant—his business manager, protector, and sometimes sexual partner. The Playwright picks up an ill-educated hustler and fills him with dreams. The Young Man and the Assistant engage in a tug of war, the one trying to maintain the status quo, the other wanting the dream of success the Playwright has invoked. When the playwright's new production is panned, the hustler urges him to fight back. Finally having had enough, the Assistant walks out. The Young Man too succumbs to reality. Alone on stage, the Playwright starts composing aloud his new play. It may well be the play the audience has just watched. It opened in Vancouver, 2007, with Allan Gray, David Marr, and Charles Gallant, directed by Linda Moore. § MacIvor, D. *His Greatness*. Playwrights Canada, 2008. 80p.

389 *Shadow of Himself* (2007) | **Neal Bell, American**

[Mythological/military drama; 4M, 1W, chorus; unit set.] The play moves back and forth between the time of Gilgamesh and the present. Using modern diction, Bell condenses the main action of the epic: the taming of the wild man Enkidu; their joint battle against Humbaba, guardian of Cedar Mountain; Enkidu's death; Gilgamesh's journey to the land of the dead to try to save his friend; and his failure to stay awake the required seven days. Here the hero is called Gil, and his friend is NK. Throughout, their comradery is stressed; little is made of their physical desire for each other. At one point Gil does say, "You're a part of me. / [...] You know you are: / blood, bone, sweat, smile, / muscle, cock, shining eye." A chorus comments, "As they fight, they cannot help but feel the other's sweat-slick body. / And they have thoughts, without words: / the words come later—thousands of years." Two modern soldiers who have been grafted onto the story do not hesitate to call them "Homos." These two soldiers are having greater trouble admitting their love for each other. When an observer points out, "you fell, and he was on top of you. [...] And he was inside you," the soldier growls, "Shut *up!*" When the more open of the two declares he cannot leave his friend behind, it is NK who asks, "Because you love him?" The play was first tried out in Durham, N.C., 2007. § *The Civilians: An Anthology of Six Plays*; ed. by Steven Cosson. Playscripts, 2009. 217–75.

390 *Special Forces* (2007) | **John Fisher, American**

[Military melodrama; 5M, 1W; minimal set.] The year: 2003; the setting: Kuwait and Iraq. Bush's war: SNAFU. A four-person Marines unit is sent out to target an opposition leader. The assignment is placed under the command of a female psychopath instead of the more logical command of Tom Hazlitt. The latter is suspected of pushing Don't Ask Don't Tell: in fact, the bisexual lieutenant is currently enamored of a drag artist, "Dinah Blue," performing at a nightclub in Kuwait City. Everything goes wrong with the mission, including the discovery that they have been sent to take out the wrong individual (the names resemble each other enough to confuse intelligence). If they succeed in their original objective, all four will be killed themselves. The colonel, who meets Blue when he goes to close down her act, lets this information slip in her hearing. Like some heroine out of an old movie, Blue dons a burka and sets off across the desert to find them. The play ends with Hazlitt and Blue leaving the front on the same airplane. It opened in San Francisco, 2007, with Matthew Martin and Elias Escobebo, directed by Fisher. § Fisher, J. *Special Forces*. Broadway Play, 2012. 63p.

391   *Speech & Debate* (2007) | **Stephen Karam (1980?–), American**

[School drama; 2M, 2W; unit set.] The play examines teenage angst: three Salem, Ore., teenagers struggle to find their identities and their place in the world. New student Howie came out when he was ten, but he is freaked when he goes on chatline and ends up being propositioned by his English teacher (who thinks Howie is in Portland). Solomon attacks the hypocrisy of political leaders and teachers even as he conceals that he is a closet case and that he has already seduced the same teacher. (His well-to-do, socially prominent parents have sent him to a conversion therapy camp.) Diwata yearns to be an actress, but she is consistently passed over because she does not fit the type. (The script leaves unclear whether her acting skills also leave something to be desired.) The three come together via a series of accidents (Diwata sees Solomon with the teacher in the boys' restroom; Howie sends what he thinks is a private email to Diwata, but one that is public, giving his telephone number, which Solomon discovers.) Wanting to gain attention from the drama coach, Diwata blackmails the two boys into joining her Speech & Debate group. Howie talks her and Solomon into supporting his Gay/Straight Alliance. Solomon resigns himself to another session at Camp Exodus but begins a new chapter in his life by joining a gay chatline group. Diwata may get her revenge against the drama coach; she lands the position of understudy to all the girls in *Fiddler on the Roof*. Howie plugs along. The play opened in New York, 2007, with Gideon Glick and Jason Fuchs, directed by Jason Moore. Karam wrote the screenplay for the 2016 film. § Karam, S. *Speech & Debate*. Dramatists, 2008. 70p.

Recent Contemporary, 2008–2014

U.S. lifts ban on gays in military, 2011. President Obama cites Stonewall in second inaugural address, 2013. Russia begins a crackdown on gay rights, 2013. India recriminalizes homosexuality, 2013. U.S. Supreme Court legalizes same-sex marriage in all states, 2015. Ireland approves same-sex marriage by popular vote, 2015. Pulse nightclub massacre, Orlando, 2016. President Obama designates Stonewall Inn area a national monument, 2016.

392 *Fucking Men* (2008) | **Joe DiPietro (1961–), American**

[Sexual drama; 10M; flexible set.] DiPietro serves up another gay adaptation of Schnitzler's *Reigen*. Ten men engage in a circular series of sexual encounters: hustler, soldier, graduate student, undergraduate, a married couple, porn star, playwright, movie star, television journalist, and back to hustler. The adaptation is inventive in having each sexual blackout bridged by a speech from the next man to enter the circle. The pairings discuss promiscuity, fidelity, monogamy, love, honesty, emotional and physical connections. The playwright says, "I think that's what sex is all about—connecting on the most wonderful human level." If the married couple is having problems—one confesses that he is promiscuous only because his husband is—the hustler and the soldier discover love and are unexpectedly rewarded by a gift from the movie star to ease their life together. It is also the playwright who says, "Let's just be kind. Kindness is so valuable"—though he willfully outs the movie star when the latter reneges on a verbal agreement. Also discussed are the significance of disclosing one's HIV status, the power of the closet, the particular problems a celebrity has. The first word of the title functions as both participle and catch-all expletive. The premiere was in London, 2008, with Shai Metuki, Nick Keith, Chris Polick, James Kristian, Timothy Lone, Morgan James, Adam Unze, Scott Capurro, Guy Fearon, and Patrick Poletti, directed by Phil Willmott. The American debut was in Los Angeles, 2009, directed by Calvin Remsberg. § DiPietro, J. *Fucking Men* [...] Adapted from La Ronde by Arthur Schnitzler. Dramatists, 2014. 48p.

393 *Now or Later* (2008) | **Christopher Shinn, American**

[Philosophical drama; 4M, 2W; 1 set.] Shinn explores the contradictory political stances that Western culture has fallen into. When cartoons depicting Muhammad are posted on a college campus, "the Muslim Student Association tried to use that to change the university's freedom of speech policy." So John pens "an editorial defending [...] freedom of expression." One woman takes up the Muslim cause, but then throws a "naked party." On a whim, John goes dressed as Muhammad (and gets his friend Matt to pose as a fundamentalist Christian preacher) to point out "the contradiction between her throwing this libertine party and her support for a group that was trying to stifle freedom of expression, including expression critical of Islam's regressive views on female sexuality." Pictures are taken and posted on the internet. The problem: his father is soon to be named U.S. president-elect. The father's staff wants John to issue a public apology. Acting the spoiled kid, John refuses until his father informs him that people have been killed in riots in Pakistan. John's sexuality plays little part in the drama, though he does make some comments about religious homophobia. The play opened in London, 2008, with Eddie Redmayne, directed by Dominic Cooke. The star possibly saved the show; John is not very likeable. § Shinn, C. *Now or Later.* Dramatists, 2014. 35p.

394 *Octopus* (2008) | Steve Yockey (1976–), American

[AIDS fantasy; 5M; flexible set.] Through the trope that gives the play its title, Yockey pulls off an affirmative ending to an AIDS drama. Blake is reluctant to engage in a four-way sex session with another, older couple, Max and Andy, but his lover Kevin feels that their relationship would somehow be strengthened. In the encounter, however, Blake ends in the middle of the tangle of naked bodies, while Kevin becomes the outsider, enthralled by the pornographic action he is witnessing to the point that he does not interfere when Andy enters Blake without a condom. This fact does not emerge until after the arrival of a mysterious telegram delivered by a wet telegraph boy. Kevin finds out that Andy tested positively for HIV at his next regular checkup, and that Max relegated him to the bottom of the ocean where a deep-sea monster devours him. Kevin betrays Blake a second time when he admits, "I don't know if I can stay with you if you have it." Blake too disappears into the depths: "The people that go, the ones like Blake, they choose to go, because they get thrown away." The telegraph boy charges Kevin with engaging in meaningless words, but Kevin has an epiphany, the nearly drowned Blake returns from the sea, and the tragic ending is snatched away—though the telegraph boy counters Kevin's optimism with a cynical, "We'll see." The play opened in Atlanta, 2008, with Joe Sykes and Brian Crawford, directed by Kate Warner. § Yockey, S. *Octopus.* French, 2008. 61p.

395 *Plague Over England* (2008) | Nicholas de Jongh (1944–), English

[Historical polemic; 9M, 1W; unit set.] The play sets the 1953 arrest of actor Sir John Gielgud (1904–2000) on the trumped up charges of "persistently importuning male persons for immoral purposes" into the larger social context of the time.

In the eyes of many, there seemed to be a concerted campaign on the part of authorities to, in the words of Home Secretary Sir David Fyfe, "eliminate homosexuality," which he views as "an infectious plague over England." An American character has fled the U.S. because of the witch-hunts conducted against gay federal employees, the so-called Lavender Scare. The arrest of Lord Montagu is alluded to. And we see the various ways gays around Gielgud react to his public disgrace. In de Jongh's telling, one of the ironies is that the arresting officer, Constable Terry Fordham, is a closet case who falls in love with Greg Lightbourne, the son of a homophobic justice, and then breaks off the affair when Greg cannot free himself of class and family. The last part of Act 2 jumps to 1975 and a Gay Pride march. Gielgud refuses to be a spokesperson, but Greg acknowledges: "First time since Oscar Wilde—you brought gayness out in the open. [...] If it wasn't for you it would have taken years longer to change the law." The play opened in London, 2008, with Jasper Britton, Robin Whiting, Leon Ockenden, and Timothy Watson, directed by Tamara Harvey. De Jongh co-wrote the screenplay for the 2016 film. § De Jongh, N. *Plague over England: A Play.* French, 2009. 96p.

396 *The Pride* (2008) | Alexi Kaye Campbell (GRC 1966–), English

[Sexual drama; 3M, 1W; flexible set.] Reviews of London and New York productions of *The Pride* indicate that the play in performance is less confusing than the play on paper. Here is the gimmick: The scenes alternate between 1958 and 2008. In both time periods we have a triangle: two men and a woman, named Philip, Sylvia, and Oliver. They are not the same people, and their respective stories only link thematically. John Lahr in his review for the *New Yorker* (March 1, 2010) cites one possibility: that the 1958 story "demonstrates the punishing consequences of repression," the 2008 story "the punishing consequences of liberation." The 1958 Philip is dissatisfied with selling real estate, a profession he inherited from his father, and dreams of emigrating to Africa. His wife illustrates children's books. She invites Oliver, the current author with whom she is working, to join them for a meal so the two men can meet. Something clicks between Philip and Oliver, and they have sex. Oliver says, "All my life I've been waiting for some sort of confirmation that I'm not alone." He goes on to avow that "it was the first time, when we were together, when we were embracing that I felt that I had a pride. A pride for the person I was." Philip is conflicted about his feelings, including his relationship with Sylvia. He brutally rapes Oliver and then checks himself into a clinic that promises to cure him through aversion therapy. The 2008 Philip finally has enough of his Oliver's nonstop promiscuity and leaves him. Thinking Oliver is out of the apartment, he returns to pick up a last package and catches him in an S/M scene with a hustler dressed as a Nazi. Oliver insists that such scenes are meaningless, that it is Philip he loves. Oliver is a journalist; he is hired by a magazine to write a piece on the freedom of contemporary gay sexuality: "Kind of like gay sex for the straight man." Consequently, he can pass off his promiscuity as research. Sylvia, his best friend, plans to join him at the Pride march. When he unexpectedly balks, she tells him it is important he go. She arranges for him and Philip to meet. Oliver says he wants to change. The premiere was in London, 2008, with JJ Feild and Bertie Carvel, directed by Jamie Lloyd. § Campbell, A. K. *The Pride*. Dramatists, 2010. 77p.

397   *Secrets of the Trade* (2008) | Jonathan Tolins, American

[Coming out drama; 4M, 1W; flexible set.] Famous director Marty Kerner muses that it is through contacts between older and younger gays that "the culture is passed down." But as Andy Lipman discovers: it is and it isn't. The play covers ten years, from the time Andy, 16, writes a fan letter to Marty, the man he idolizes, to the time he finds himself, now 26, cast unwillingly into the same role with a younger male. By then Andy has given up his dream of being the next great writer for Broadway and settled for writing for a Los Angeles-based television series. Between the two dates he discovers that he cannot rely on Marty to find the footing he wants. He comes out to his parents and alternates between appreciating his mother's sincere interest in him and being threatened by her over-possessiveness: "I'm tired of you interviewing me like I'm a Foreign Exchange Student and you're pretending to find my culture fascinating," he says. Bradley, Marty's unchanging assistant, may be the wisest in settling for what he can get. Or perhaps he is to be pitied. At one point Marty speaks of Andy's fascination with the scrim as a stage device: "What is a scrim. It's something we use to hide what's really there. To mask. Conceal. It only makes its effect when we throw some light behind it, when we show what's really going on." The short speech seems apropos of Tolins's drama. No one is better at depicting gay culture, yet he never seems to illuminate it fiercely enough to lift his portrayals to greatness. The play opened in Los Angeles, 2008, with Edward Tournier, John Glover, and Bill Brochtrup, directed by Matt Shakman. § Tolins, J. *Secrets of the Trade*. French, 2011. 100p.

398   *Sissy* (2008) | Ricardo A. Bracho (MEX 1966?–), American

[Adolescent pageant; 5M, 3W; flexible set.] Ernest Hardy's online blog sums up the script beautifully: "By the time 12-year-old Latino homo Sissy holds a dance-off with his sneering older sister [...] Bracho's play has settled into a raucously charming groove of digestible Marxist theory, redemptive Negro pop culture and odes to the uncharted complexities of Latino identities. The story—a day-in-the-life tale set in Culver City, 1978, on Sissy's 12th birthday—whisks us through scenes of sibling rivalry, parent-child conflict, cholo bullies, tranny whores dropping wisdom and show-stopping musical sequences set to the gamut of '70s black music [... as the boy] struggles to hone not just his queer sexuality but also his Latino identity, when the absence of large-scale Latino representation made black culture the default setting for nonwhite identification." The play opened in Los Angeles, 2008, with Xavier Moreno, directed by Armando Molina. § In Clum, J., and Metzger, S., eds. *Awkward Stages*. 167–225.

399   *Slipping* (2008) | Daniel Talbott (1976–), American

[Adolescent drama; 3M, 1W; flexible set.] Another play about teenage angst, it begins and ends with the main character in the hospital. Eli comes from a dysfunctional San Francisco family. His mother, an English professor, has a series of lovers. His father dies in an automobile accident, perhaps a suicide. His boyfriend Chris's family wants their son to stop seeing Eli. He begins cutting himself. Three months later Eli and his mother relocate to a college town in Iowa. The mother continues to be promiscuous. Eli is attracted to Jake. Everyone at their school assumes Eli is gay, to Jake's discomfort. They have sex, but Jake tries to remain in the closet. Eli begins cutting himself again. Perhaps his experience with Jake seems too similar to that with Chris, and he outs him in class. But the play ends with Jake calling on Eli in the hospital with a bouquet of flowers, and the lights come down on them laughing at Eli's adolescent jokes. The play opened in Chicago, 2008, with Nate Santana, Daniel Caffrey, and Adrian Gonzalez, directed by Adam Webster. § In Clum, J., and Metzger, S., eds. *Awkward Stages.* 227–355.

400 *Steve & Idi* (2008) | **David Grimm, American**

[Fantasy; 5M; 1 set.] Just prior to this play, Grimm penned a very different work from the theatrical pastiches by which he gained his reputation: *Chick* is a distillation of the life and influence of the bisexual director of the Wadsworth Atheneum in Hartford, Conn., told in three monologues. *Steve & Idi* is yet another departure, inventive in a different way. Steve is a New York playwright suffering from writer's block. His actor boyfriend, absent on a Chicago engagement, dumps him via email. His agent likewise drops him. His writing friends Ralph and Max are concerned about Steve's frame of mind but are put off by his obnoxiousness. Steve admits, "I test. Everyone. Always." Totally despondent, he tries to kill himself, but is saved when the ghost of the Ugandan dictator Idi Amin bursts through his window like some demented angel (à la *Angels in America*) and demands that Steve write the story of his life. When Steve questions why he has been chosen for the task, Idi suggests, "Perhaps because I am your mirror image." The resulting play seems to be the one the audience is watching. It is a cruel work filled with allusions to cruel politicians on the American scene (Bill O'Reilly and Ann Coulter particularly draw ire). Feathers, presumably of angels, appear at the end of the play, but they provide only a fake resolution. The New York premiere, 2008, starred Grimm, Greg Keller, and Michael Busillo, directed by Eleanor Holdridge. § Grimm, D. *Steve & Idi.* Dramatists, 2009. 45p.

401 *Wig Out!* (2008) | **Tarell Alvin McCraney (1980–), American**

[Ethnic drama; 8M, 3W; flexible set.] In all his works McCraney celebrates his roots as a man of color. In this campy drama Eric encounters Nina in her masculine aspect as Wilson. Eric plays the passive partner and is uncertain how to react when he discovers Wilson belongs to a group of drag queens "Where a daughter that once was a son ... / Can find family." For Nina, "Her / Body read man, gave you butch, but secretly she / Believed she was a woman." Life becomes more complicated for Eric when he realizes he has "kicked it" with the group's male protector Lucian. Lucian makes fun of him for allowing "trannie girls on [his] back." Nina/Wilson has already said to Eric that the scene "wigs you out." At the end, as Wilson, he asks Eric to leave. At the same time another transwoman, Venus, is redefining her relationship with the DJ, Diety/Adrian. Act 3 is given entirely to a drag ball, in which the group's roles get shuffled. As is usual with the playwright, many of the stage directions are spoken aloud as part of the drama. Written in free verse, the play premiered in London, 2008, with Alex Lanipekun, Danny Sapani, and Leon Lopez, directed by Dominic Cooke. It came to New York later that same year. § McCraney, T. A. *Wig Out!* Faber & Faber, 2008. 121p.

402 *Cock* (2009) | **Mike Bartlett (1980–), English**

[Domestic debate; 3M, 1W; no set.] Bartlett obviously could not resist an eye-catching title. It may refer to the penis. More likely it should convey the idea of an arrogant man. The plot dynamics are analogous to a cockfight; in fact, the playwright would prefer it be performed in the round with the audience on benches. A gay couple has begun to drift apart. John, the only character with a name, has an affair with W (woman). He turns to his lover M (man) for consolation. In Part 2 John and W have a long discussion, while Part 3 takes place at a dinner for the three of them. M, however, invites his father (F), who acts as a sort of referee. He tell John, "You're being selfish. I think you need to work out what you are. Fast." John throws out the possibility that he suffers from "some psychosis caused by a homophobic society or something." But basically he rejects all labels: "Gay straight, words from the sixties, sound so *old*, only invented to get rights." He gets more support from M, but sex with W is better. The play ends inconclusively. One might also remember that *cock* is British slang for nonsense. The play is a *tour de force* for the actors; reviews suggest productions of it so far have been a literal pain in the butt (because of the seating). Another problem also exists: it is difficult to care one way or the other about John. The premiere in London, 2009, was with Ben Whishaw and Andrew Scott, directed by James Macdonald. Bartlett permitted the 2012 New York production to be advertised in the media as *The Cockpit Play*. § Bartlett, M. *Cock*. Dramatists, 2013. 108p.

403   *The Habit of Art* (2009) | **Alan Bennett, English**

[Biographical study; 11M, 2W; no set.] Though both Godfrey's *Once in a While* and Bennett's play cover much the same ground, Godrey's is documentary-style while Bennett's is wildly inventive. The audience here is witnessing a rehearsal of a play, *Caliban's Day*. It records a fictional meeting between poet W. H. Auden and composer Benjamin Britten at the time Britten is struggling with his opera *Death in Venice*. Auden notes a curious coincidence: he is Thomas Mann's son-in-law, having married Erika to help her escape the Nazis ("What [else] are buggers for?") Also prominent in *Caliban's Day* are Humphrey Carpenter, who wrote biographies of both men, and a rent boy Stuart, who symbolically stands for Caliban. There is much about sex, including Auden's habit of using rent boys and Britten's attraction to adolescent boys—a facet of his emotions that now scares him as he plunges deeper into his opera. Their lovers, Chester Kallman and Peter Pears, are mentioned. But there is as much talk about the habit of art, how Auden cannot escape words, just as Britten cannot escape music. In a fantasy sequence Words and Music even engage in a dialogue. Auden, however, argues that for both writer and composer "Will is paramount [...] grim application." There is also discussion of the role of biography. Auden sees it as mere "idle curiosity," morally questionable, and notes, "A biographer is invariably second-rank even when he or she is first-rate." Stuart criticizes biography on the grounds that his kind is unfairly omitted from it: "Because if nothing else, we at least contributed. We were in attendance, we boys of art." The actors constantly break character to discuss the play they are rehearsing, in the process revealing something of themselves. The comedy was first performed in London, 2009, with Richard Griffiths, Alex Jennings, and Stephen Wight, directed by Nicholas Hytner. § Bennett, S. *The Habit of Art*. Faber & Faber, 2009. 88p.

404   *I Have AIDS* (2009) | **Sky Gilbert, Canadian**

[AIDS comedy; 3M; 1 set.] From *Theatrelife* on Gilbert has taken an idiosyncratic approach to the plague. Prodon tells his lover Vidor about his HIV status quite casually: "Oh yeah. I almost forgot. I have AIDS." Reflecting upon his low-keyed response, he ponders how gays could have "become so blasé about such an extraordinary thing." He then sets up the play's scheme: "first there's denial, then partying, then loss of control, then religious conversion, then acceptance. Then death," although he dislikes the idea of ending with the last: "All AIDS plays end in death and it's just so boring, so dramaturgically predictable." It quickly becomes clear that by denial he is speaking of personal responsibility for transmission. He blames heterosexuals for their lack of understanding to the point that Vidor accuses him of turning into "Canada's Larry Kramer." Shifting to the next stage, Prodon looks at partying as an opportunity "to be a gift giver." The actual party scene turns out to be an exercise in grossness morphing into loss of control. Vidor comes to the rescue. Recovered, Prodon now slavishly follows his doctors' every suggestion. He meets Ron Friend, who delivers a long monologue about how "You have to learn to embrace adversity" in order to become a better person. Prodon converts to acceptance. But in another political barb (of the many scattered throughout the play), he observes, "I think people are glad that AIDS is not about fags anymore. It was always hard to lend support to effeminate, sexual, partying gay men who got AIDS because deep down most people just find us so disgusting—but hey, they've got no problem giving support and help to African children." The play may end in his death. It may not: Prodon's last word is "Yes?" The premiere was in Toronto, 2009, with Gavin Crawford, Ryan Kelly, and David Yee, directed by Gilbert. He subsequently revised the play. § Gilbert, S. *I Have AIDS!* Playwrights Canada, 2010. 66p.

405   *The Intelligent Homosexual's Guide to Capitalism and Socialism with a Key to the Scriptures* (2009–11) | **Tony Kushner, American**

[Domestic drama; 6M, 5W; 1 set.] For seven years the play's forthcoming publication has been announced; the latest projection calls for mid 2017. From online reviews one can gather the basic plot: the family patriarch Gus Marcantonio, a former longshoreman, labor leader, and Communist party member, has summoned his three children to his Brooklyn brownstone to prepare them for his imminent suicide before he succumbs to Alzheimer's. Maria Teresa (aka Empty), a labor lawyer, is in a lesbian relationship but enjoys sex with her ex-husband. Pier Luigi (aka Pill), a gay high school history teacher, is in a relationship with a theological professor but given to outside sexual adventures, at the moment infatuated with a hustler. Vito (aka V), a contractor, is straight and married. Gus's sister Clio, an ex-nun who is now a Maoist, is also present. What follows is a lot of talk both about the children's mundane needs and the larger issues addressed in the title. Jayne Blanchard, in one of the fullest summaries, ends: "But you still may wonder—what does it all mean? Could be a lot of delectably perfumed hot air, for all we know. That doesn't necessarily detract from your enjoyment of Kushner's sprawling, ambitious work that forces us to think once again about class struggles and the power of the people." The play first opened in Minneapolis, 2009, with Stephen Spinella, Michael Potts, and Michael Esper, directed by Michael Grief. A revised script came to New York in 2011. It has subsequently been performed in various cities. § Unpublished so far.

406 *Marcus, or The Secret of Sweet* (2009) | **Tarell Alvin McCraney, American**

[Adolescent drama; 5M, 5W; unit set.] The play is the third of the trilogy *The Brother/Sister Plays*. Marcus Eshu, 16, begins to understand his sexuality. Save for one youth, his Louisiana community has no problem with his being "sweet," an alternate label for gay. As he talks to friends and family, the nature of the hold that his dead father Elegba had over one of the Size brothers (in the second play in the trilogy, *The Brothers Size*) becomes clearer. Marcus has his first sexual experience with Shua, or Joshua, a young black on the down low from the Bronx visiting the parish where Marcus lives. The fact that Joshua is having an affair with Marcus's best friend (female) makes his own relationship seem somehow a betrayal, but otherwise the experience is positive. A hurricane bears down on the parish, but the storm is entirely external. The play, written in free verse, was inspired by Yoruba myths. Characters are simultaneously ancient African gods and modern-day African Americans. Further heightening a sense of theatricality, they speak not only their lines but also their stage directions. Blanks in the script allow the director a great deal of leeway to fill them with action. The play opened in Princeton, 2009, before moving to New York with Alano Miller and Samuel Ray Gates, directed by Robert O'Hara. § McCraney, T. A. *The Brother/Sister Plays*. Theatre Communications, 2010. 241–361.

407 *Me, as a Penguin* (2009) | **Tom Wells (1986?–), English**

[Dark comedy; 3M, 1W; 1 set.] Wells's plays provide a welcomed remove from the usual gay London scene. His are set in his native Yorkshire. In *Me*, Stitch, 22, who worked in a crafts shop in his hometown Withernsea, has fled the decaying seaside resort for Hull to test "The whole gay thing." He is staying with his "heavily pregnant" sister Liz and her boyfriend Mark. At the end of a turbulent twenty-four hours he has to face up to the fact that his excursion has failed, and he prepares to return to Withernsea. In that time he has impulsively stolen a sad-looking penguin that he identifies with from the local aquarium where he has taken his nephew. The visit was an attempt to get closer to Dave, a zoo worker who has inspired him by his story about two gay penguins in the New York zoo. But the story seems to have been more a ploy on Dave's part to get Stitch excited enough to give him a blow job. Mark calls Dave to come rescue the stolen bird; he shows up in the penguin suit he wears when working with children at the aquarium. They discover the penguin has died. Liz and Mark rush to the hospital to deliver Stitch's new niece. Stitch tries to kill himself, but mistakenly takes his kelp supplement instead. His vomit irreparably stains the sofa that Liz has been trying to persuade Mark to get rid of. The play ends with Mark asking Stitch to help him take it out to the garbage pickup. The play opened in Leeds, 2009, then in London, 2010, with Ian Bonar, directed by Chris Hill. § Wells, T. *Me, as a Penguin*. Nick Hern, 2010. 55p.

408 *The Miracle at Naples* (2009) | **David Grimm, American**

[Romantic comedy; 4M, 3W; 1 set.] In his stroll through theater history, Grimm here arrives at 16th-century Italian commedia. A traveling troupe appears in Naples on the day the blood of San

Gennaro traditionally liquefies. One of the local girls, Flaminia, wants to be with a man, but her nurse counsels her to maintain her vaginal virginity. When two members of the troupe, Matteo and Tristano, offer her a love potion, she gladly drinks it with them and offers herself anally. As Matteo watches, he realizes that it is Tristano he wants. They kiss, blaming it on the potion. When the seller reveals that it was merely aqua vitae and they were drunk, the two reconsider. Though they are undoubtedly "degenerates," Tristano argues they do not have to act on their feelings, while Matteo argues the reverse. Meanwhile, Flaminia is pursuing Giancarlo, another actor, a vain Casanova who becomes furious when he discovers Matteo and Tristano have had sex with her. He tries to kill Tristano, but Matteo steps in and takes the wound. Thinking he has lost Matteo, Tristano admits that he loves him, whereupon Matteo revives. They can happily be degenerates together. This may be the greater miracle than the liquidization of the saint's blood. The heterosexual plots are as complicated, but not nearly so romantic. The play opened in Boston, 2009, with Gregory Wooddell and Pedro Pascal, directed by Peter DuBois. § Grimm, D. *The Miracle at Naples*. Dramatists, 2010. 65p.

409   *Muscle* (2009) | **Tom Wainwright (unknown), English**

[Dark comedy; 3M; 1 set.] The characters' identities, stories, and relationships all shift and repeat themselves in so many different ways that one is left uncertain what is real, what is fabricated, what is actually said, and what is voiced thought. They try out various scenarios, even to the point of taking on the personas of other, offstage characters. On the simplest level, Steve has lost his looks to such a point he turns his wife off sexually. He becomes aware she is seeing another man, Dan. He gets his gay friend Terry to invite him to his gym to begin workouts. In walks Dan, and there may (or may not) be a confrontation. Violence lurks just below the surface, sexual in nature, but Steve ends up hitting Terry instead, while Dan masturbates in the changing room. Terry keeps admitting and then denying that he is gay. Both Steve and Dan intermittently come across as closet cases, Steve attempting to kiss Terry. In a bit of bravura acting Dan plays Steve's wife, heightening a sense of homoerotic dynamics between him and Steve. The repeats of dialog are farcical and weirdly resonant. The play opened in Bristol, 2009, with Paul Mundell, Sion Pritchard, and Stewart Wright, directed by Lee Lyford. § Wainwright, T. *Muscle: A One-Act Comedy*. Oberon, 2011. 75p.

410   *The Muscles in Our Toes* (2009) | **Stephen Belber, American**

[Political comedy; 5M, 1W; 1 set.] Gayness is and isn't one of the play's focal points. Four former friends converge at their twenty-fifth class reunion. Phil is the one gay (though he keeps pushing the notion that Les is a closet case). The others alternate between kidding him and wishing he would shut up about his sexuality. Their big concern is their friend Jim, who has been kidnapped by a terrorist group in Chad, where he has a shoe factory. They blame the FBI for inciting the kidnapping by "illegally detaining that Chadian dude in California" so that the "dude's buddies over in Chad [...] kidnapped Jim in revenge." They decide to force "the FBI to give in to the Chadian terrorist demands and just let the California guy go free." Phil argues that he couldn't be a terrorist anyway, because he is gay. (The evidence? Phil knows "a guy who gave him a blowjob.") So they plot how to get their message out without hurting anyone and finally compromise on blowing up a file cabinet in a local FBI office. A momentary setback occurs when Jim shows up to announce he wasn't kidnapped; he just disappeared to have a romantic interlude with a local worker. They decide to go on with the plot, however, making a video to convey their message, but the evening ends as a rite of exorcism instead. Les keeps the video for their fortieth reunion. The play opened in Los Angeles, 2009, with Bill Tangradi, directed by Jennifer Chambers. § Belber, S. *The Muscles in Our Toes*. Dramatists, 2015. 49p.

411   *Myth of Andrew & Jo* (2009) | **Gideon van Eeden (unknown), South African**

[Sexual comedy; 2M, 2W; unit set.] The characters freely mix Afrikaan with English; the published script provides translations, but they are not really necessary. A drug-fueled encounter between a gay man and a lesbian results in a pregnancy. It is the last thing either Andrew, a set designer for operas, or Jo, a nature photographer, wants. Both are in long-term relationships: Andrew with Lawrence, a copywriter, a man of color; Jo with Saartjie, a game warden and huge rugby fan. Jo's news threatens to destroy both relationships, but these are good-hearted people of strong will. A heavenly voice assures them, "You didn't choose this child. This child has chosen you. You have created it, now create with it." And so they do, working out the rough patches, sometimes in hilarious ways, as they create an unconventional but stable environment for the child. Lawrence muses, "Do you realise how lucky we are? A bunch of queers having a baby together and being able to share their lives with this kid and not having to worry any more about maintaining the pink lifestyle or constantly being reminded of *moffie*-this, gaypride-that, drugs, party and all that shit." The upbeat, life-affirming play opened in Cape Town, 2009, with Dean Roberts and David Johnson, directed by Roy Sargeant. It deserves to be more widely known. § In Malan, R., ed. *S.A. Plays 1*. 225–92.

412   *Next Fall* (2009) | Geoffrey Nauffts (1961–), American

[Religious drama; 4M, 2W; flexible set.] The play got good reviews and was nominated for a number of awards. Reading the script leaves one wondering why, the relationships depicted seem so unbelievable. Luke is a Christian fundamentalist and closeted gay. Adam is an atheist and out. He cannot stop needling Luke about his beliefs, and Luke defends them to the max. He does not try to reconcile his sexuality with his beliefs (he prays after sex), and he lies about his true nature to his family (surely another sin). On Adam's part, he is a hypochondriac who at times has thought whatever imaginary illness he may have may be a punishment from his nonexistent god. Unlikely as it seems, the two stay together five years until Luke is struck by a New York taxicab. The play opens in the waiting room outside an ICU unit at a Jewish hospital (undoubtedly some irony here, since Jews will not be saved at the rapture). It then alternates between scenes in the hospital and scenes from the past portraying the two men's religious and medical discussions with some glimpses of their lives outside the apartment. Luke dies. His mother has guessed the truth by then; the father probably has too but will not acknowledge it. And Adam has his final moment of self-delusion: "And, you know, all the doubts, everything I've been questioning for the past five years, none of it meant anything, all of a sudden. It was just us.... Me and Luke....

That's all that mattered [...]. And it was like ... *finally*.... I believed." The play opened in New York, 2009, with Patrick Breen and Patrick Heusinger, directed by Sheryl Kaller. Nauffts has written the screenplay for a proposed film. § Nauffts, G. *Next Fall*. Dramatists, 2010. 71p.

413   *Prick Up Your Ears* (2009) | Simon Bent, English

[Biographical study; 2M, 1W; 1 set.] The fourth play about Orton and Halliwell, it portrays key moments in their lives from their arrest for defacing library books to Ken's murder of Joe. The setting is the claustrophobic bedsitter in which they lived, whose walls Ken decorates with collages, and which he never leaves. As a result the emphasis is more on him than on Joe. A third character, their upstairs neighbor Mrs. Corden, provides comic relief. (When Ken describes finding his father dead with his head in the kitchen oven, she instantly pops out, "Killed by the Gas Board," and goes on to declare, "The Gas Board should only issue ovens to people of sound mental health." Clearly, the pair's wit is contagious.) The play largely skirts Orton's promiscuity, mostly relying on Ken's vitriol to provide glimpses of Joe's cottaging, and it does not address what might have been in the missing final pages of the diary that so set Halliwell off. By ignoring Joe's point of view it also leaves what kept the two men together so long in such a small space another mystery. The dark comedy opened in London, 2009, with Matt Lucas and Chris New, directed by Daniel Kramer. § Bent, S. *Prick Up Your Ears: Inspired by John Lahr's Biography and the Diaries of Joe Orton*. Oberon, 2009. 99p.

414   *The Temperamentals* (2009) | Jon Marans, American

[Historical romance; 5M; flexible set.] Marans turns history into riveting theater in retelling the story of the first years of the Mattachine Society. Harry Hay (1912–2002) and his lover Rudi Gernreich (1922–1985), a fashion designer, launch the organization in Los Angeles in 1950. The playwright captures the paranoia (and reality) of the times. He also depicts how early gay liberation was an outgrowth of an interest in Communism (Bob Hull asks, "Do you *actually* think a radical organization is born from moderate people?") and an identification with the oppression of the Jewish minority. The group's big moment comes when Dale Jennings is entrapped by a rogue vice squad officer. Instead of pleading guilty and paying the fine, the group finds him a lawyer and sets out to fight the trumped up charges. Hay also sees the occasion as a perfect opportunity to argue that homosexuals (or "temperamentals") make up another "oppressed minority." A hung jury frees Dale. Matters move quickly. Hay and Gernreich's romance is strained by the latter's wishing to make it in the fashion world. Hay is called to testify before HUAC. The other members of the society realize he is becoming a liability to the organization's growth. The original group is disbanded (to be reorganized in San Francisco). Each character tells the audience about his subsequent life and final days. The play opened in New York, 2009, with Thomas Jay Ryan, Michael Urie, Tom Beckett, Matthew Schneck, and Sam Breslin Wright, directed by Jonathan Silverstein. § In Clum, J., ed. *Gay Drama Now*. 217–318.

415 *True Love Lies* (2009) | Brad Fraser, Canadian

[Domestic drama; 3M, 2W; flexible set.] David McMillan reappears (see *Love and Human Remains*), but here the focus is on his former lover Kane Sawatsky and his family. After a series of failed ventures, David returns to his hometown to open a restaurant; Kane's daughter Madison applies for a job as waiter. When David finds out who she is, he refuses to hire her. Madison confronts her parents, who believe in being honest with their children. The former relationship comes out, and the family's life changes forever—perhaps for the better after some rough patches on the way with David acting as the catalyst. Taking a blasé highroad, Madison rushes through life saying whatever she feels like divulging. She sees David as a sexual challenge. He finally convinces her: "A secret's not the same as a lie." Her asexual brother Royce, suffering from bipolar disorder, affects a worldly attitude until he breaks completely. He threatens David life, but it is David who saves him by forcing the family to get him the help he needs. Carolyn, the wife, finally lets out all the repressed hatred she has felt for her husband and David's relationship. She walks out of her family, perhaps her wisest move. At the end the possibility is held out that Kane and David will again become friends. The dialog sometimes comes across as theatrically artificial, but in many ways this is Fraser's most mature play. Its premiere was in Manchester, Eng., 2009, with Jonny Phillips and John Kirk, directed by Braham Murray. It opened in Toronto the same year under Fraser's direction. § Fraser, B. *True Love Lies*. Playwrights Canada, 2009. 135p.

416 *With Bated Breath* (2009) | Bryden MacDonald, Canadian

[Psychological drama; 3M, 3W; flexible set.] Willy, a homeless gay teenager from Cap Breton, makes an impression on everyone he meets, but he himself is lost. After he disappears in Montreal, those who were closest to him explore their memories of their time with him. Bernie, who is more than twice his age, in particular loses all sense of direction when Willy disappears. A farmer, he is married but closeted; his wife is openly bisexual. Even the women whose lives he touched feel adrift without Willy's presence. Only Float, a Québécois, who is a stripper at the same bar where Willy finds work, is relatively unmoved. Despite the amount of information the playgoer is presented about the boy, much remains unexplained, leaving one to ponder meaning itself. Written in a loose verse form, the play debuted in Montreal, 2009, with Michael Sutherland-Young, Neil Napier, and Éloi Archambaudoin, directed by MacDonald and Roy Surette. § MacDonald, B. *With Bated Breath*. Talonbooks, 2010. 127p.

417 *Canary* (2010) | Jonathan Harvey, English

[Social satire; 6M, 2W; flexible set.] After taking time out to write screenplays for television (*Gimme Gimme Gimme*; *Beautiful People*), Harvey returned to the stage with this ambitious look at British gay life from 1962 through 2010. Skipping back and forth in time and space, even engaging in fantasy, it opens with Mary Whitehouse's launching her Festival of Light and ends with two boys (Mickey and Russell) dressed in drag spinning merrily around in a garden. In between, it covers earlier gay arrests (with passing mention of Alan Turing), the use of aversion therapy, gays' support of striking miners, the impact of AIDS and Margaret Thatcher's indifference, gay-bashing, and irresponsible barebacking. The central character is Tom Harris, a police captain. After being caught having sex with Billy Lynch, he is coerced by his father, also a policeman, into perjuring himself. He claims that he was sexually attacked. The judge sentences Billy to psychiatric treatment, but he emerges seemingly whole and becomes an activist for gay and lesbian rights. At one point he quotes activist Peter Tatchell: "Women and gay people are the litmus test of whether a society respects human rights. We're the canaries in the mine." Years later, however, he meets the psychiatrist in a gay nightclub, picks him up, and murders him. All the time Tom remains in the closet. Only when his gay son Mickey is dying from AIDS can he bring himself to tell Mickey, "How proud I was of you. Able to be yourself and stuff the consequences." But he still goes along with his wife when she puts out that Mickey died in a moped accident. Mickey's childhood friend Russell Dowler snaps: he outs Tom and the real cause of Mickey's death. With the press on his doorstep Tom prepares a statement: "I do not regret who I am, but I do regret my deceptive behaviour over the years." It opened in Liverpool, 2010, with Philip Voss, Kevin Trainor, Ben Allen, and Sean Gallagher, directed by Hettie Macdonald. § Harvey, J. *Canary*. Methuen Drama, 2010. 101p.

418 *Courageous* (2010) | **Michael Healey (1951–), Canadian**

[Social satire; 4M, 2W; 3+ sets.] The inadequate title unites two discursive plays, loosely connected by the overlapping of three characters and an examination of some common themes: personal and civil rights, religion, government, refugees, love, commitment, marriage, identity. In the first play Tom, a civil servant, marries a heterosexual couple despite their obvious relationship problems. But when Brian, a lawyer, arrives to exchange vows with Martin, he refuses, even though he himself is gay: "the tenets of my faith don't allow me to marry homosexuals." Brian files a complaint with the Ontario Human Right Commission. When the two men meet in the antechamber, they discuss the situation. Tom admits, "I've had to question every aspect of my faith in order to reconcile the gay me with the Catholic me." At base, he questions the entire institution on the grounds that "it's done more to oppress people, women mostly, than anything else I can think of." Tom refuses to marry Arthur, his lover, a refugee from war-torn Somalia. Brian himself is more interested in marriage as a public rather than a private statement: "Every time [gays] walk down the steps at city hall, it's like, I dunno, Mandela walking out of prison." Martin senses this. Brian wins his case; Tom is dismissed from his post; but Martin and Arthur end up together. The second play follows the ups and downs of the heterosexual couple's union. They too end up going their separate ways. The play opened in Toronto, 2010, with Tom Barnett, Patrick Galligan, Tom Rooney, and Maurice Dean Wint, directed by Richard Rose. § Healey, M. *Courageous*. Playwrights Canada, 2010. 103p.

419 *Mary* (2010) | **Thomas Bradshaw (1980–), American**

[Social satire; 5M, 2W; flexible set.] Bradshaw has courted controversy throughout his career. *Mary* combines an exposé of black economic slavery with an examination of black prejudice against homosexuality. Mary's ancestors were slaves for the same Baltimore family where she and her husband now work for an "allowance," clothing, and a cabin to live in. David has always disliked the way his parents treat them, but when he brings his lover Jonathan home to meet his parents, seeing the situation from Jonathan's perspective galvanizes him to act. He forces his mother to allow Mary to take adult literacy classes and to treat her less like a slave. David's parents have only one problem with his and Jonathan's sexuality: that "the dang homo hides his homosexuality from us." Mary, however, feels strongly that it is an abomination: she quotes at length from memory the story of Sodom and declares, "God wants us to help little Davie to overcome these unnatural desires." Blaming Jonathan, she urges her husband to shoot him in the crotch with his BB gun. Mission fulfilled, she feels bad, especially after Jonathan is so nice to them, and decides that instead of quoting the Old Testament, she should pay attention only to Christ's sayings. Time passes. Learning to read, Mary starts formal schooling and becomes the oldest student ever to graduate from her college. In her valedictory speech, she reveals that her pursuit of a degree in theology has caused her to revert to her previous mindset. Calling David on stage with her, she denounces gays' "perverse and abnormal lifestyle" and announces, "I have made the primary mission of my ministry to end the practice of homosexuality on this planet." Published in 2010, the play opened in Chicago, 2011, with Alex Weisman and Eddie Bennett, directed by May Adrales. § Bradshaw, T. *The Bereaved and Mary*. PAJ, 2010. 57–103.

420 *Banana Boys* (2011) | **Evan Placey (can 1984?–), English**

[Adolescent drama; 8M, 11W; flexible set.] Placey describes his approach to playwriting thus: "I ignore the adults: the parents and the teachers. I'm not writing for the gatekeepers, but for the young people in the audience, and the young people performing in the play." He sets as one of his goals to address matters that actually concern them, without censorship. Here he tackles the question: what do you do if you're the 16-year-old captain of your football team and know you are gay? Such is Cameron's plight. He is surrounded by boys whose usual putdowns include "That's so gay." He conceals his feelings from Calum, his best friend; he tries to act like the other boys around girls. Ben, the one openly gay student, challenges his cover. Cal catches Cam and Ben together. He has to decide whether he is angry because his best friend is a fag or because Cam has lied to him. Various girls are finding their way through the hazards teenage heterosexuality poses. A fantasy trio, the Banana Girls, wind their way through the plot in something of the manner of the trio in *Little Shop of Horrors*. The play opened in London, 2011, with Myles Howard and Tom McDermott, directed by Debra Glazer. § Placey, E. *Girls like That and Other Plays for Teenagers*. Nick Hern, 2016. 1–106.

421 *Bootycandy* (2011) | **Robert O'Hara (1970?–), American**

[Adolescent drama; 3M, 2W; flexible set.] O'Hara is interested in finding links between racial and sexual repression, now and in the past, but the relationship is not always clear in such overwhelming theatrical works as *Insurrection: Holding History*, 1995, or *Antebellum*, 2009. More satisfying is this lower-keyed, semi-autobiographical collection of comical skits. The African American playwright Sutter is O'Hara's alter-ego; the skits the playgoer watches are written by him and three other characters (who are introduced at the end of Act 1). One theme that runs through the evening is Sutter's discovering the use of his penis, his bootycandy. He reaches out to his mother and stepfather when a man starts following him when he leaves the library, but they assume that Sutter is responsible, with the results that the scene becomes a fandango of cross-communications. (We later learn that the man took Sutter's anal virginity when he was 16.) In a darker sketch, he and a friend pick up a white man who is straight but longs to be mistreated; Sutter is accused of raping him with a black dildo, followed by the man's jumping off the roof of his hotel. In the last skit Sutter sums up his philosophy: "I think that if Boys was just allowed to lick other Boys' BootyCandies, there would be peace in the world cuz then they wouldn't be mad at each other and start tryin' to kill each other cuz they BootyCandies would be happy." The premiere was in Washington, D.C., 2011, with Phillip James Brannon, directed by O'Hara. § O'Hara, R. *Bootycandy*. French, 2014. 94p.

422 *Edith Can Shoot Things and Hit Them* (2011) | **A. Rey Pamatmat (unknown), American**

[Adolescent drama; 2M, 1W; flexible set.] In several plays Pamatmat explores issues of ethnicity, sexuality, and adolescence. *Thunder Above, Deeps Below*, 2009, portrays the friendship of three homeless people: a gay-for-pay hustler, a transwoman, and a woman thrown out of her home for having a child with an African American. *Edith* has a different triad of relationships but some similarities. Kenny, 16, and Edith, 12, have been virtually abandoned by their widowed father, a physician. Benji, 16, is thrown out of his house when his mother discovers he is gay and in love with Kenny. Edith copes by creating a fantasy world where she vows to protect them all. Kenny turns himself into a robot to avoid deep emotions. The perpetually horny Benji justifies himself by recourse to scientific language. He urges Kenny to confront his father. Kenny pleads that he doesn't know how. Benji argues, "You'll figure it out. You take it up the butt, remember? You can do anything." He continues, "I don't want us to hide. I don't want you to hide. Tell him the truth. They threw us out, or threw us away. They have no right anymore to tell us what to do." And so the three bravely face the future despite their youth. The playwright imagined the siblings as Filipino-Americans, but save for some references to foods there is nothing that marks the story as ethnically based. The premiere was in Louisville, Ky., 2011, with Jon Norman Schneider and Cory Michael Smith, directed by May Adrales. § In Clum J., and Metzger, S., eds. *Awkward Stages*. 13–165.

423 *Falling in Time* (2011) | **C. E. Gatchalian (1974–), Canadian**

[Ethnic tragedy; 3M, 1W; flexible set.] The lines Gatchalian gives one of his characters is the task he imposes on the audience: "What there are are random happenings on which we as humans impose meaning and narrative. In and of itself, nothing has meaning." The play moves back and forth between Vancouver in 1994 and Korea in the early 1950s. The major characters are five, none Canadian: Chang Hyun, 22, a Korean student, was raped while serving in the military. Jamie, 30, his Kansas-born ESL teacher and lover, feels he lost his father in the Korean war to PTSD. Steve Wendland, 65, an American and Chang's sexual partner, is a Korean war veteran dying of cancer. Ju Cheol, aka "Tyrone O'Brien" (played by the same actor who plays Chang), was Steve's wartime buddy, a South Korean soldier killed by a Chinese soldier. Eun Ha, 65, Chang's grandmother, was Ju Cheol's fiancée, later raped by Steve. Chang abandons Steve and Jamie to return to his dying grandmother without any of them knowing about their intertwined histories. Steve kills himself. Jamie finds some degree of tranquility. Chang returns to the unknown. As their stories unfold, a giant doraji (Korean bellflower) blossoms on stage. The expressionistic play opened in Vancouver, 2011, with Nelson Wong, Allan Morgan, and Kevin Kraussler, directed by Seán Cummings. § Gatchalian, C. E. *Falling in Time*. Scirocco Drama, 2012. 106p.

424   *Go Back to Where You Are* (2011) | David Greenspan (1956–), American

[Fantasy; 5M, 2W; minimal set.] Greenspan is interested in theatricality. Here actors speak aloud their dialogue, thoughts, and stage directions with great gaps in chronology unaccounted for. He plays with the conceit that Passalus, a failed actor from Classical Greece, is actually writing the play that contemporary playwright Bernard is presenting as we watch. Passalus has been given a mission by God to free the never-seen Caroline from the clutches of her actress mother Claire, with the proviso that he must not interfere with anyone else's life. If he succeeds, Passalus will gain the bliss of total annihilation. He plays gender games by taking on the persona of Constance Simmons and promptly becomes entangled in the lives of five gay men. He falls in love with Caroline's uncle Bernard, who lost his lover to AIDS sixteen years ago. Wally, Claire and (unbeknownst to everyone) Tom's son, has just lost his lover to prostate cancer. Tom is a director; he was enamored of Claire's dead husband and, so Claire says, "got to Robert through me." Tom's present partner is the set designer Malcolm. They are going through a rough patch because of Tom's infidelities with chorus boys. As a result of Passalus's entering their lives, God announces their pact is null. Passalus and Bernard begin a relationship. The play opened in New York, 2011, with Brian Hutchison, Stephen Bogardus, Michael Izquierdo, Tim Hopper, and Greenspan (as Passalus), directed by Leigh Silverman. § Greenspan, D. *Go Back to Where You Are*. French, 2013. 44p.

425   *House of the Rising Son* (2011) | Tom Jacobson, American

[Philosophical drama; 4M; flexible set.] When the aptly named Felix first encounters Professor Trent Varro giving a lecture about parasites in Los Angeles, it is love at first sight. Among Felix's many attributes, Trent is impressed by his sexual freedom and his lack of interest in Trent's family wealth. He wants Felix to return with him to New Orleans to meet his family. He lures the lover of ghost stories with the promise of how haunted the city is. There Felix meets Trent's father Garret, a restoration architect, and his grandfather Bowen, a scatological poet. In the final moments of Act 1, he is shocked to discover Trent and his father in a passionate kiss. It comes out that none of the members of the Varro family is biologically kin. Each has legally adopted the younger member to preserve the line: they have "figured out how to cheat the world, how to sidestep hetero hegemony." Trent wants to adopt Felix. Trent's lectures on the purpose of parasites in the world muddle the situation. He seems to connect gays to parasites, but then turns his argument around and makes the case that gays "are not an accident, a fluke—we help the species survive." Trent, however, is indirectly responsible for disrupting the order of succession in his family. Though he knows Felix is searching for "something [...] *reliable*," Trent picks up a dancer at a gay bar. When he realizes that Tod (German for "death") is dangerous, he gets away from him. Tod shows up at their house while Bowen is alone. The audience has been led to expect Bowen's death from prostrate cancer; now when Tod threatens him with a broken goblet stem, we assume he is killed. Instead, it is Garret, who has returned home unexpectedly. Trent accepts his responsibility. He is prepared to leave New Orleans and join Felix in Los Angeles. Their final embrace is joined by Garret's ghost. The play opened in Los Angeles, 2011, with Steve Coombs, Paul Witten, Patrick John Hurley, and Rod Menzies, directed by Michael Michetti. § Jacobson, T. *House of the Rising Son.* Broadway Play, 2012. 81p.

426 *The Kitchen Sink* (2011) | **Tom Wells, English**

[Dark domestic comedy; 3M, 2W; 1 set.] It is striking that Billy's sexuality is of so little concern for his Withernsea family and his sister's would-be boyfriend (Pete) that it is scarcely mentioned. Other, important matters focus the attention of his blue-collar family: the fact that the life they know is falling apart and that they must struggle to change. Or perhaps, in Billy's case, it would be more accurate to say, must fight to remain true to himself. He gains entry to art school with his loving tribute to Dolly Parton, but his professors see his painting as deliberate kitsch. The day they deride his performance piece as karaoke he realizes that he must leave if he is going to maintain his love of art. He feels validated when he quits their office to discover someone has liked his paintings enough to steal them. Meanwhile, his parents adjust to the challenges of the father's failed business, his sister promises that she will try again after failing to obtain her black belt, and Pete decides to take a vacation from it all in Australia. The play opened in London, 2011, with Ryan Sampson, directed by Tamara Harvey. § Wells, T. *The Kitchen Sink.* Nick Hern, 2011. 81p.

427 *The Lyons* (2011) | **Nicky Silver, American**

[Domestic comedy; 3M, 3W; 2 sets.] Dying, Ben Lyons uses the occasion to berate everyone in his family. His wife, who has never loved him, makes a point of letting him know she intends to redecorate the house as soon as he is gone. Their daughter Lisa falls off the wagon again when her brother reveals that her ex-husband abused her. In retaliation she discloses that, though Curtis may be gay, all his lovers have been imaginary. Perhaps the truth goads him into pretending to buy a Manhattan apartment from his real estate neighbor whom he has built his latest fantasy around. The two connect, but not in the way Curtis envisioned. The man brutally beats him, destroying his spleen, so that he ends up in the same hospital his father died in, acting much the way his father did. Lisa decides not to return to her husband but to comfort a dying man down the hall. Their mother announces she is eloping with Lisa's AA sponsor. Now it is Curtis's turn. The nurse reminds him of the choices he has: "Some people are happy. And some people are just lonely, mean and sad." The premiere in New York, 2011, was with Michael Esper, directed by Mark Brokaw. § Silver, N. *The Lyons.* Theatre Communications, 2012. 72p.

428 *Rattigan's Nijinsky* (2011) | **Nicholas Wright (ZAF 1940–), English**

[Biographical study; 7M, 4W, extras; flexible set.] Wright has described the play's origin: "Philip Franks rang me [...] to ask if I'd be interested in adapting a [never produced] Rattigan screenplay about Nijinsky." Having independently become intrigued by the closeted playwright whose career gradually faded away, he leapt at the chance. The results is a play "written by Rattigan and Wright in roughly equal parts." The Wright part, set in 1974 in Claridge's, sees the story as the tragedy of a playwright who could never bring himself to be open about his sexuality even as he longed to. Just as Diaghilev destroys Nijinsky (1890–1950) and thus himself, Rattigan loses his last chance to be honest by giving in to Nijinsky's widow's threat, in an attempt to block the project, to out him in court if he permits the screenplay to be filmed. Time and space, through Rattigan's imagination, become fluid so that Rattigan and Diaghilev are sometimes together, sometimes apart with Rattigan looking on. The familiar story of the Ballets Russes is recounted, building to Diaghilev's lie: "there's a limit to how long one man can sustain erotic interest in another." His ghost begs Rattigan: "You have two years left to live, you say. Live them honestly!" Rattigan tries to justify his reticence: "my queerness is there all the time, only it's under the surface. If I became ... *officially* a queer, if I had a big sign saying 'queer' hanging over my head, then there'd be *nothing* under the surface. It would all be obvious. All banality. I'd be a preacher. That's not acceptable." His sex drive gone, due to medication, he takes comfort from lying next to one of the hotel employees (played by the same actor who plays Nijinsky). The play opened in Chichester, 2011, with Malcolm Sinclair, Jonathan Hyde, and Joseph Drake, directed by Philip Franks. §

Wright, N. *Rattigan's Nijinsky* [...] *Based on the Screenplay by Terence Rattigan*. Nick Hern, 2011. 93p.

429 *Sons of the Prophet* (2011) | Stephen Karam, American

[Ethnic drama; 5M, 3W; flexible set.] A Lebanese-American family living in Nazareth, Penn., very distantly related to the poet Kahlil Gibran, has more than its share of woes. Joseph suffers from a series of mysterious ailments. Brother Charles was born without one ear. Their father wrecks his car swearing to avoid a deer decoy a high school student placed in the road as a prank; two weeks later he dies of a heart attack. The judge decides to postpone the student's punishment until football season has finished (he is a star) but leaves it up to the school board to do whatever they want. The two sons are left responsible for their wheelchair-bound uncle. Joseph's boss, a book agent on hard times, comes up with the idea of writing a family history emphasizing the Gibran connection—the title of the play being the title of her proposed book. Joseph has a short-lived relationship with a reporter covering the school board's decision and Charles seems attracted to the African American football player, but sex plays little part in the plot. The ending is sudden and a bit too deft. The premiere was in Boston, 2011, with Kelsey Kurz and Dan McCabe, directed by Peter Dubois. § In Clum, J., ed. *Gay Drama Now*. 491–586.

430 *Tom at the Farm* (2011) | Michel Marc Bouchard, Canadian

[Psychological drama; 2M, 2W; flexible set.] After William's death in a motorcycle accident, Tom drives to his lover's boyhood home to attend the funeral. He discovers that neither the mother nor the brother Francis has ever heard of him, though Francis says, "I knew you'd show up someday." Tom also discovers that William was a habitual liar, that he really knows nothing about the man he lived with. He feels he should leave, but is mysteriously compelled to remain on the farm even as he suffers increasing physical abuse and threats against his life from the homophobic Francis. Struck by how much the brothers resemble each other, Tom seduces Francis. He warns Tom that he literally tore apart the face of William's friend when they were teenagers because the boy wanted to talk to him about the relationship. Becoming aware how much is wrong, how little she knew her son, the mother reads the journals he left behind and finds the key to William's lies in this horrendous act: "*He tore Paul's beautiful face apart. I saw the whole thing. I didn't lift a finger.* [...] *I didn't defend him. I didn't do a thing. I think we should never tell the truth. Never.*" Events inexorably propel Tom, wearing William's clothes, to murder Francis and to dispose of his body at a site where it will never be discovered save by coyotes. *Tom à la ferme* premiered in Montreal, 2011. The English version opened in Toronto, 2015, with Jeff Lillico and Jeff Irving, directed by Eda Holmes. Bouchard wrote the screenplay for the 2014 Xavier Dolan film. § Bouchard, M. M. *Tom at the Farm*. Trans. by Linda Gaboriau. Talonbooks, 2013. 80p.

431 *Trade* (2011) | Mark O'Halloran (unknown), Irish

[Psychological drama; 2M; 1 set.] O'Halloran focuses on the moments before a sexual encounter between a rent boy, 18, and an older man, late 40s. Neither self-identifies as gay. The older man is married, with a son the same age as the rent boy. The hustler lives with the mother of his baby daughter. Yet the older man confesses that he told his son, after the two had a fight, that "I loved you more then [sic] I loved him." Hurt and outraged, the son bloodied his father's nose, whereupon the latter called the hustler for another sexual encounter. The man is emotionally drained. He has lost his job as the result of his shipping company being taken over and its staff being downsized. He wants to talk to the younger man, explain his life. He wants to admire his near-naked body. And he wants to again be the passive partner in sex. But before that, he begs the teenager to just let him hold him for a moment. After a public reading the year before, the play opened in Dublin, 2011, with Phillip Judge and Ciarán McCabe, directed by Tom Creed. § In Conway, T., ed. *Contemporary Irish Plays*. 47–81.

432 *The Twentieth-Century Way* (2011) | Tom Jacobson, American

[Historical drama; 2M; 1 set.] Sharon Ullman in her book *Sex Seen* described a 1914 case of police entrapment in Long Beach, Calif.; Lillian Faderman and Stuart Timmons retold the story in their *Gay L.A.* (Basic Books, 2006), where Jacobson encountered it. Two professional gay-baiters, W.

H. Warren and B. C. Brown, were hired as vice specialists by the police chief. Jacobson imagines the two men as actors competing to be hired for a position. Warren challenges Brown to a bout of improvisations: "The better actor wins the right to stay." They play out various scenarios, all recounting the sequence of events that unwound in Long Beach as they take on the roles of the real-life victims, the police chief, a journalist, a lawyer, and their own assumed guises as gay bait. As a result, "The line between the actor and role blurs and turns hazardous," and Brown queries, "Have we become our parts? Gotten emotionally involved." After initially resisting the suggestion, Warren gives in to his attraction to Brown, and the play ends with a kiss: *"passionate and unfeigned, raw."* The premiere was in Pasadena, Calif., 2011, with Will Bradley and Robert Mammana, directed by Michael Michetti. § Jacobson, T. *The Twentieth-Century Way*. Broadway Play, 2012. 77p.

433   *Band Fags! / BFs!* (2012) | **Frank Anthony Polito (1970–), American**

[Adolescent comedy; 2M; 1 set.] The play follows two boys, age 14 to 18, living in a Detroit suburb during the years 1984–88. Both are members of the high school band, though very little is made of the fact. The focus is almost entirely upon their relationship. Brad Dayton, the only son of a blue-collar family, has known since he was a child that he is gay, and he accepts the fact. He suspects his best friend Jack Paterno, who comes from a more affluent family, is also, as does Jack himself. But Jack is not willing to admit it, and Brad hesitates to push the idea. The problem with the nearly two-hour play is that nothing much happens. There is no real sense of angst, few bumpy moments in their friendship, and no great change even when Jack finally comes out. The play began as a shorter work, *John R.*, 2001. *Band Fags!*, had a staged reading in 2006. In 2008 the story became a novel. The script was then revised to follow the novel; its premiere was in Omaha, Neb., 2012, with Predrag (PJ) Sudar and Joey Galda, directed by Thomas Lowe. The play was subsequently reissued as *BFs!*, 2015. § Polito, F. A. *Band Fags! A Play*. Woodward Avenue, 2012. 118p. *BFs! A Play*. Woodward Avenue, 2015. 126p.

434   *The Best Brothers* (2012) | **Daniel MacIvor, Canadian**

[Domestic comedy; 2M; flexible set.] Kyle and Hamilton's mother is killed in a freak accident when a drag queen falls off a Pride float and lands on her. Now the brothers have the responsibility of preparing her funeral service and taking care of her estate, including her dog. Tensions arise. Hamilton feels that Kyle was more loved than he and blames her death on him: "Mother never would have even been at a Gay Days Parade if not on the hunt for a husband for you." His own marriage dissolves, the dog serving as the catalyst for his wife to walk out on him. Kyle is in a relationship with a grammatically challenged sex worker (i.e., hustler). Hamilton is rigid, logical; Kyle is scatterbrained, emotional. The former is an architect; the latter is a real estate agent. The brothers' very different world views provide the humor of the piece. At intervals each takes on the role of the dead mother, revealing their view of her. In the end they accept their differences and reconcile. The play opened in Stratford, Ont., 2012, with John Beale, directed by Dean Gabourie. § MacIvor, D. *The Best Brothers*. Playwrights Canada, 2013. 84p.

435   *From White Plains* (2012) | **Michael Perlman (unknown), American**

[Social drama; 4M; flexible set.] Perlman pens a riff on Rudnick's opening for the film *In & Out*. In this case a gay Oscar winner, Dennis Sullivan, outs the straight bully who he feels caused his best friend to take his life fifteen years ago. In the age of Facebook his speech, of course, is just an opening salvo. The bully, Ethan Rice, feels he must respond. Dennis responds, and the debate escalates without any real clarity from either side. Dennis's lover Gregory begs him to let it go instead of letting it consume his life. Ethan's friend John does the same. There are complications for both: Gregory is still in the closet as far as his parents are concerned; John has not disclosed to Ethan that his brother is gay. Nothing seems resolved at the end—probably by design, to force the audience to think through the issues raised. The play opened in New York, 2012, with Karl Gregory and Jimmy King, directed by Perlman. He credits the two, along with the other two actors, Aaron Rossini and Craig Wesley Divino, as collaborators. § In Clum, J., and Metzger, S., eds. *Awkward Stages*. 401–568.

436   *Harbor* (2012) | **Chad Beguelin (1969–), American**

[Domestic comedy; 2M, 2W; flexible set.] The

play begins with a portrait of Kevin and Ted's seemingly picture-perfect marriage. Deep rifts become visible, however, when Kevin's sister and niece descend on their Sag Harbor home. Ted likes having Kevin depend upon him, but he is not willing to consider introducing even a pet, let alone a child, into their life. Now, without Ted's knowledge, Donna talks Kevin into agreeing to adopt her unborn child. Donna's basic immaturity and irresponsible behavior are apparent as soon as she opens her mouth. Kevin's own immaturity takes longer to manifest itself, though the fact that he has worked for ten years on a novel and still does not know its plot hints at his inadequacies. The teenage niece Lottie is the one grownup. When Kevin announces that he is leaving Ted to join the homeless Donna in her van, Lottie begs Ted to let her stay with him. The last we see, she is finishing up the brochure that Kevin was supposed to be writing and could not finish, while her uncle and her mother are driving away recreating their childhood games together. The play opened in Westport, Conn., 2012, with Bobby Steggart and Paul Anthony Stewart, directed by Mark Lamos. § Beguelin, C. *Harbor*. French, 2014. 75p.

437 *Special Thanks to Guests from Afar* (2012) | **Nicholas Spagnoletti (unknown), South African**

[Sexual comedy; 2M, 1W; 2 sets.] Spagnoletti introduces a seldom-seen character: a completely asexual man. Neither Luke, a gay Cape Town professor of economics, nor Thabisa, a straight black South African emigrant to Zurich, have a chance sexually with him. He is the groom's brother at a German wedding; old friends, Luke and Thabisa have taken the opportunity of the wedding to get back together after being apart for so long. Luke is still floundering three years after his lover left him. (The catalyst strangely was a car accident that injured them both). Thabisa feels in a kind of limbo, unable to face returning to her still racially troubled country, but keenly aware of European slights that her skin color provokes. Nothing really happens, but all three grow a bit as a result of their meeting. Most important, the playgoer comes to care about these people. The play opened in Cape Town, 2012, with Nicholas Dallas, directed by Matthew Wild. § In Malan, R., ed. *S.A. Gay Plays 2*. 191–243.

438 *Vanya and Sonia and Masha and Spike* (2012) | **Christopher Durang, American**

[Domestic comedy; 2M, 4W; 1 set.] A collage of memorable moments from Chekhov's major plays, the play emerges, nevertheless, as an original work. Still, such a line as Sonia's repeated "I am a wild turkey" is that much funnier for its echo of Nina's "I am a seagull." Their parents being college professors, Vanya and Masha and adopted sister Sonia are named after his characters and share more than a few similarities with them and others in his plays. Masha is a self-absorbed actress facing a declining number of roles. She supports her siblings. Sonia and Vanya both have settled into largely meaningless existences following the slow demises of their parents. Neither has apparently even glimpsed the man of her/his dreams. It takes Masha's arrival with her latest boy toy and an invitation to a party (the setting is Bucks County, Penn.) to shake them out of their lethargy. Sonia secures a date after she upstages Marsha with her Maggie Smith impersonation. Vanya at least admires eye candy (the new boyfriend spends as much time in his underwear as he does dressed). Spike, Masha's young and very temporary lover, and the maid Cassandra have wandered in from a non–Chekhovian world; they indirectly provide the impetus that resets the siblings' values, bringing them together in some kind of unity. The play began in Princeton, N.J., 2012, and went on to New York with David Hyde Pierce, directed by Nicholas Martin. § Durang, C. *Vanya and Sonia and Masha and Spike*. Grove, 2013. 90p.

439 *The View* (2012) | **Philip Rademeyer (1986–), South African**

[Dystopian drama; 1M, 1X; unit set.] Rademeyer records how his play was a reaction to the homophobic comments of the fundamentalist American preacher Charles Worley, who proposes penning up all "lesbians and queers" and letting them die out. But Rademeyer stresses, "Beyond its politics, it is simply a very human story of a young man brutally separated from his loved ones, purely because of who he is." The cast consists of a Boy, a young male, and an Actor, either male or female, who plays twelve different roles, including the Angel Africanii from Kushner's *Angels in America*. Boy exists in some "hermetically sealed pod," a limbo that only voices or perhaps memories can pierce. He looks out on the ruins of a post-apocalypse world. He has lost his lover, will never have the child he wanted (he comments on "how easy Neil Patrick Harris and his picture-perfect family makes it look"). He lost the family he was born into because of his father's disapproval of his sexuality; his mother mourns his loss to her and to the world. The text consists of twenty-five monologues; the last momentarily becomes dialogue with Boy having the final words: "Here I am," repeated sixty-two times. The play opened in Cape Town, 2012, with Gideon Lombard, directed by Rademeyer. A second play by him, *Ashes*, 2014, about three gay murders, has also been published. § Rademeyer, P. *The View*. Junkets, 2013. 59p.

440 *The Whale* (2012) | **Samuel D. Hunter (1981–), American**
   [Dark comedy; 2M, 3W; 1 set.] The play depicts the last five days in the life of Charlie. He became compulsively, morbidly obese after his lover Alan wasted away from not eating and is now trapped in his room like some beached whale. Alan's sister tries to look after him the best she can. Charlie is visited by Joseph Paulson, aka Elder Thomas, 19, who wants "to see Mormonism help *one person*." Charlie's daughter Ellie, 17, also shows up. Her mother says she's "evil." Her father claims she's very honest in spite of the fact that Ellie almost kills him. The mystery Charlie wants most to solve is what happened to Alan when Alan's father forced him to attend a Mormon service; he begs Elder Thomas to find out. It turns out the sermon was about Jonah. Elder Thomas interprets the message to be that Alan "tried to escape God's will, he chose his lifestyle with you over God. And when he heard this story, when he heard *God's word*, he knew." Charlie rejects this reading. In his mind this story becomes intertwined with an essay Ellie wrote in the eighth grade about the sadness in *Moby-Dick*. The play opened in Denver, 2012, with Tom Alan Robbins, directed by Hal Brooks. § Hunter, S. D. *The Whale / A Bright New Boise*. Theatre Communications, 2014. 1–100.

441 *Wolves: A Predatory Fairy Tale* (2012) | **Steve Yockey, American**
   [Crime drama; 3M, 1W; unit set.] In this deconstructed version of the Little Red Riding Hood story as an urban legend, Jack (wearing a red hoodie, naturally) picks up Wolf at a local bar and brings him back for sex. When Wolf responds to Jack's egging him into rough sex, Ben—Jack's former lover, still his apartment mate—goes berserk and kills Wolf with an ax that just happens to be handy. The Narrator tells us that Jack is "a little too willing to see the world through Ben's eyes and a little too weak to stop when he should have." Jack aids Ben in cutting up Wolf's body and depositing the pieces in garbage bags. Even though the dead Wolf and the Narrator discuss what has happened, the playgoer obtains no real understanding of the victim's viewpoint. Nor do Ben and Jack receive our sympathy. The playgoer may leave the play feeling that it has functioned as some kind of warning, but the Narrator informs us early on not to look for "a regular, lesson-learned kind of story," rather it is one which a person would be "hard pressed to reconcile a moral with." The play opened in Atlanta, 2012, with Joe Sykes and Brian Crawford, directed by Melissa Foulger. § Yockey, S. *Wolves: A Predatory Fairy Tale*. French, 2014. 59p.

442 *Arigato, Tokyo* (2013) | **Daniel MacIvor, Canadian**
   [Psychological drama; 3M, 1W; flexible set.] Two different cultures meet, think they are communicating, but fail. Carl Dewer, a Canadian writer, comes to Tokyo on a book tour. As he says, "If you've read my books you know my recipe for being 'evolved' is sex, drugs, and sex'n'drugs." The drug of preference is cocaine. As for sex: "Many women. More men. Several in between." His interpreter, Nushi Toshi, is in love with him. If anyone attracts Carl, it is her brother Yori, a Noh actor. The one time he is with Nushi, apparently nothing happens between them. ("Perhaps less sake next time," she says.) It is quite different with Yori, but his sister claims, "This betrayal will stop him from being a great actor." Etta Waki, his guide from a previous tour, also makes a play for Carl, but he returns to Vancouver alone. He is perhaps marginally wiser, but not by much: "still I thank you for this burden." Of the two Japanese words that approximate *thank you*, he chooses *arigto*, translated by Nushi as "this kindness you show me makes it difficult for me to find a way to repay you," delivered to someone you know, not to a stranger. Heavily influenced by Noh, the play opened in Toronto, 2013, with David Storch, Michael Dufays, and Tyson James, directed by Brendan Healy. § MacIvor, D. *Arigato, Tokyo*. Playwrights Canada, 2013. 71p.

443 *Choir Boy* (2013) | **Tarell Alvin McCraney, American**

[School play; 7M; 5 sets.] After the critical failure of *American Trade: A Contemporary Restoration Comedy*, 2011, with its bisexual entrepreneur hero, McCraney returned to his roots with this play. Written in a loose verse form and interspersed with spirituals, it follows a year in the life of Pharus Jonathan Young at an all African American prep school. He is a contradictory mixture: sometimes irritatingly brash, sometimes overly vulnerable. His every mannerism gives him away as gay. Not surprisingly, he has to deal with slurs, especially from the headmaster's nephew, who becomes his nemesis. He is slugged when he comes onto one of his classmates in the showers. On the other hand, his roommate is quite supportive; one of the most touching moments is his giving Pharus a haircut. Much of the play is taken up with a discussion of the meaning of spirituals. The idea that they acted as coded guides to ways to escape slavery is set against their promise of a heavenly afterlife. How either reading affects Pharus's life is not made explicit. The play opened in New York, 2013, with Jeremy Pope, directed by Trip Cullman. § McCraney, T. A. *Choir Boy*. Dramatists, 2014. 59p.

444 *Chomi* (2013) | **Pfarelo Nemakonde (1988–), South African**

[Ethnic drama; 9M; unit set.] Nemakonde has taken as his mission to fill the void of scripts about gay black middle-class men in South Africa. His first play, in his words, "follows the lives of four twentysomething black men and their friendships with each other, their relationships with others, and—most importantly—their perceptions of themselves." In a rigid allocation of sexual roles, the four are the girls, bottoms, who identify themselves by their relationships with the guys, tops. Percy has been "married" to Mandla for over three years; now that they can legally marry, they plan a wedding at which the other three girls will be bridesmaids. Before that can occur, Mandla is killed in a car accident, and Percy sinks into alcoholism. Rudzani has a perfect relationship with Akim, but he is so self-centered that he cannot see what they have together and ends the relationship. Too late he understands what he has lost, but Akim has moved on. Sicelo is a therapist, blind to his partner's infidelities. When he discovers that his friends have all known about Mike's philandering, he says some hurtful things to them. Thabang, the fourth, has refused ever to commit, liking sex too much. But his white partner Kevin has different ideas which Thabang seems increasingly to consider. On the day that was supposed to be Percy's wedding day, Rudzani, surprisingly, is the one who makes overtures to bring the girls back together and reaffirm that they are friends, *chomi*. The play was published in 2013. It was staged in Cape Town, 2014, with Thabang Sidloyi, Anele Situlweni, Robert Haxton, Yanga Mkonto, Sipho Mahlatshana, and Mandisi Sindo, directed by Motlatji Ditodi. § In Malan, R., ed. *S.A. Gay Plays 2*. 245–322.

445 *Jumpers for Goalposts* (2013) | **Tom Wells, English**

[Sports romance; 4M, 1W; 1 set.] The Barely Athletic football (soccer) team is pretty bad. Lesbian Rovers, Man City, and Tranny United all outperform them. But over a period of six matches we learn to admire and care about the five of them. Fiery lesbian pub owner Viv is the sponsor and one of the players. She has recruited her straight brother-in-law Joe, recently widowed and badly out of shape. He has taken in Beardy Geoff after he was gay-bashed. Geoff has other problems: he scores for the other team; he cannot resist going after one of the players for Man City. He is also preparing to try out to be one of the Pride singers. Danny, working to get his coaching certificate, is using the team for his placement. While studying in the library, he became smitten with young, innocent Luke and recruited him for the team. Fearful, Danny waits too late to tell Luke that he is HIV-positive. Luke initially freaks, but then he rereads his diary (the team has given him the nickname "Bridget") and remembers how he felt the day Danny brought the recruitment poster to the library. As a result, Luke summons the courage to say, "Honestly, Danny, there's no one in this world I'd rather put a condom on than you. *Luke fishes in his pocket*. Got ribbed, extra-safe. Pineapple." Geoff, who has been instrumental in bringing the two back together, cannot resist a final schmaltzy moment and chooses *You'll Never Walk Alone* as his Pride entry, dedicated to "anyone who needs to hear it." It does not matter that they have come in last in football; they have all been "good losers" and can hold their heads high. The play opened in Watford, 2013, with Jamie Samuel, Philip Duguid-McQuillan, and Andy Rush, directed by James

Grieve. § Wells, T. *Jumpers for Goalposts*. Nick Hern, 2013. 79p.

446 *Late Company* (2013) | **Jordan Tannahill (1988–), Canadian**

[Domestic drama; 3M, 2W; 1 set.] Joel Shaun-Hastings, 16, committed suicide, presumably because of homophobic bullying. His classmate Curtis Dermott was identified as one of the principal perpetrators. Joel's parents invite Curtis's over for a meal ostensibly to work toward some kind of closure. Instead, accusations fly, and secrets come out. An empty plate is set for Joel; he is the focus of the dialogue; but he remains elusive. We learn that he suffered from depression, a family trait; it may (or may not) have contributed to his suicide, but his parents deny its importance. Though they pride themselves on their support of their son, they actually knew little about him. His father, a politician, spent little time with him, and his mother, an artist, was not as close to him as she thought. They have no idea, for instance, that Joel posted a series of videos online of him in drag lip-syncing to songs. Curtis claims that his sexuality, however, played no part in the bullying: the fact that he was deliberately weird was "what was annoying, that he tried to be a freak and did it in everyone's face." Curtis's parents seem to be as clueless about much of their son's life. We might wonder about his sexuality. Certainly we must wonder why he returns to the Shaun-Hastings home after his parents' acrimonious departure. The play's basic premise, that these two sets of people would agree to a dinner engagement, seems contrived, but that is not to deny the impact the evening can have on playgoers. It premiered in Toronto, 2013, under Peter Pasyk's direction. § Tannahill, J. *Late Company*. Playwrights Canada, 2015. 104p.

447 *Mothers and Sons* (2013) | **Terrence McNally, American**

[Domestic drama; 3M, 1W; 1 set.] In 1988 McNally presented a short play *Andre's Mother* as part of an evening with nineteen other playwrights. Cal, his father, his sister, and his lover's mother gather to memorialize Andre's death from AIDS. The mother never speaks, but it comes out that she never really knew her son. Two years later an expanded version giving her a voice was broadcast on PBS. Now twenty years after the memorial service (redated to 1994) she unexpectedly shows up at Cal and his husband's Central Park West apartment to return her son's diary. She remains a sad portrait of what parents lose when they cannot accept their children as they are. Cal has moved on with life. He has married a man fifteen years younger than he, and they have a son, 6. Cal tells her that people can change, but they "have to want to change." Their son, just by being the boy that he is, offers her that chance. The premiere was in New Hope, Penn., 2013, with Manoel Felciano and Bobby Steggert, directed by Sheryl Kaller. § In Osborn, M. E., ed. *The Way We Live Now*. 189–93. McNally, T. *Selected Works*. Grove, 2015. 607–58.

448 *The Nance* (2013) | **Douglas Carter Beane, American**

[Historical comedy; 4M, 4W; 4 sets, drop.] Beane records his indebtedness to George Chauncey's *Gay New York*. Presumably his naming his lead character Chauncey Miles is his homage to the social historian. Beane's Chauncey is a nance, generally a straight man who played the part of a pansy in burlesque shows during the period between the world wars. Chauncey is unusual in being a gay man. Just as strange, he is "a pansy who's for the Republicans [...] like a Negro Klan member or the League of Jewish Nazi Voters." When the mayor launches a campaign against vice (meaning against homosexuals), he deludes himself that it is merely a political stunt to gain reelection. Yet when the crackdown begins, after years of being very careful, he suddenly becomes a crusader for freedom of expression on the stage, taunting the license commissioner when he shows up in the audience and delivering a burlesque routine before the judge. Also strange for such a self-avowed conservative, he turns out to be driven to promiscuity, ignoring his newly found lover who adores him. This is Ned, a country boy who moves into Chauncey's apartment and joins Chauncey's vaudeville company. In the remarkable space of three months Ned grows enough to be offered a position in the chorus of Cole Porter's *Red, Hot, and Blue*. Their farewell occurs in the same automat where they met. Chauncey impulsively kisses him goodbye and is arrested by a passing cop. The curtain falls with Chauncey still having faith that the current situation is a momentary blip, that one can yet count on Republicans. A vehicle for its star, this is Beane's most dishonest drama. It opened in New York, 2013, with Nathan Lane and Jonny Orsini, directed by Jack

O'Brien. § Beane, D. C. *The Nance*. Dramatists, 2016. 65p.

449 *Teddy Ferrara* (2013) | **Christopher Shinn, American**

[School drama; 8M, 3W, extras; flexible set.] Shinn once again captures the contradictory nature of confrontational politics and hidden motives. Gabe is trying to raise the university's consciousness about issues queer students face, but after the apparently motiveless suicide of the title character, Gabe's past encounters with the multi-sided Teddy bring him to realize how complicated events are. Activists want to use the death as a rallying point, but Gabe rejects both "the way people make themselves out to be such victims" and the "herd mentality—the vigils, the shrines, the status updates"—which prevents "having an honest discussion." Gabe's own life is a mess: he allows himself to be dominated by Drew, the ruthlessly ambitious editor of the school newspaper, who drops him, then picks him up again, only to casually mention how he has made out with Gabe's supposedly straight best friend Tim. Gabe goes into a tailspin and reaches out, too late, to Jay, whom he had rejected because Jay is wheelchair-bound. He self-destructively heads to the ninth floor of the library, from which Teddy had jumped. Gabe, however, goes into the men's room looking for quick sex, to be busted by the campus police. The story goes up on the campus newspaper's website (the clear implication being that Drew is behind it), so now, as Tim says, "For the rest of his life it'll be on the internet—so when [Gabe] applies for a job or—" The play opened in Chicago, 2013, with Liam Benzvi, Adam Poss, Ryan Heindl, Rashaad Hall, and Christopher Imbrosciano, directed by Evan Cabnet. § Shinn, C. *Teddy Ferrara*. Dramatists, 2013. 85p.

450 *Another Day on Willow St* (2014) | **Frank Anthony Polito, American**

[Domestic drama; 3M, 1W; flexible set.] Stacy the mother-to-be and Paul the lawyer at two different points provide the play's moral: "It happens all the time. People put things off and put things off and put things off…. Till one morning they wake up and find their life is over." The play covers the two weeks before the morning of September 11, 2001. Paul Green and Mark Gray have a long-distance relationship. Paul's firm is based in Boston; Mark is seeking an acting career in New York. He lives on Willow Street in Brooklyn, with its view on lower Manhattan, just across from Stacy Gold, a Random House editor, and Ian Brown, an investment banker. Since they are shortly expecting their first child, Stacy resigns from her job, losing, she feels, an essential part of her identity. Ian is so involved in building up a nest egg for his unborn daughter than he misses important moments with his wife. Paul wants to live openly as a couple, but Mark fears coming out to his parents. All four come to realize they need more give and take in their relationships. But it is too late. That fateful Tuesday morning Paul boards AA flight 11 out of Boston, and Ian ascends a World Trade Tower set of elevators to the 105th floor. The play was workshopped 2006–07. It premiered in Annapolis, Md., 2014, with Anthony Bosco and Jonathan Taylor, directed by Lucinda Merry-Browne. Polito's husband is Craig Bentley, with whom he performed the gay couple in one of the earlier versions. § Polito, F. A. *Another Day on Willow St: A Play*. Woodward Avenue, 2015. 131p.

451 *Concord Floral* (2014) | **Jordan Tannahill, Canadian**

[Adolescent drama; 3M, 7W; no set.] In this slight but inventive drama, several teenagers, in particular two girls, must come to terms with the way they humiliated a third girl just because she wore the same sweater to school that one of them had bragged online about buying at a bargain with the intention to show it off the next school day. One of the boys—Just Joey, in whose basement the teens hang out—uses Craigslist to try to hook up with men. One of his schoolmates' dad responds, and they have a sexual rendezvous in an abandoned greenhouse, witnessed only by a fox. When Joey sees the dad a week later, he remembers: "He looked right at me but didn't recognize me / Or if he did, he didn't let on." Written in a loose verse form, the play opened in Toronto, 2014, with Liam Sullivan, directed by Erin Brubacher, Cara Spooner, and Tannahill. § Tannahill, J. *Concord Floral: A Play*. Playwrights Canada, 2016. 135p.

452 *A Hard Rain* (2014) | **Jon Bradfield (1979?–) and Martin Hooper (unknown), English**

[Liberation drama; 5M, 1W; 6 sets.] The authors take us to the Baker's Inn, an imaginary Mafia-run gay bar opened in 1969 in the Village just over from the Stonewall Inn. Frank Ravelli, its overweight manager, "has a weakness for pretty boys." So when Miss Jimmy, 16, shows up again (he has been earlier with Frank), he is willing to use the boy to run his errands and occupy the bed above the bar. Angie, an unwed mother, serves as bartender. She meets Danny Kirkpatrick, a crooked cop with a heart of gold, when he comes in to pick up the bar's payoff to police, and they begin an uneasy relationship. Ruby, a drag queen with a dishonorable discharge from the Army, is a regular; his boyfriend, Josh, a Wall Street broker, follows him. Ruby has violence-management problems that prevent him from fitting into the Mattachine Society. His erratic behavior presents problems for the ambitious Josh, and he accepts a post to London after the two are caught in a raid on the bar. Danny becomes indirectly responsible for Jimmy's murder; knowing he cannot get the evidence on Frank, he blackmails him into disappearing. Fed up with the whole crooked system, he literally throws his policeman hat away. In the final scene Josh brings news of an uprising against the police occurring at the Stonewall Inn. Ruby is ready to do his part: "This is it, kids. This is the night when we show we ain't taking no more. The storm's been brewing a long time. [...] the world starts tonight." The play opened in London, 2014, with Michael Edwards, Oliver Lynes, James El-Sharawy, and Nigel Barber, directed by Tricia Thorns. § Bradfield, J., and Hooper, M. *A Hard Rain*. Nick Hern, 2014. 98p.

453 *Pronoun* (2014) | Evan Placey, English

[Adolescent comedy; 4M, 3W, extras; flexible set.] Are sex and gender as complicated as society makes them, or infinitely simpler? Josh, 16, returns from holiday to discover that his girlfriend Isabella has come out as Dean (a name he has taken in homage to James Dean). Dean is adamant about one point: "Love me. And if that's too much to ask. Then hate me. But don't tolerate me." The young are more resilient than the old. While Dean's parents have problems losing their baby girl, Dean and Josh's friends are supportive. Josh finds he still loves Dean, but he has to cope with labels. He tells Dean, "I'm not gay." Dean is. He goes to a bar and picks up another boy, causing Josh to feel jealous: "You dumped me for a guy in a farmer's dungarees!" Josh affirms, "There are days when I'm like I can do this. It's all normal. It's just a pronoun." Dean warns him, "It'll be worse for you, Josh. Worse for you than me. They'll give you a harder time than me." But attending their best friends' wedding, Josh recalls their roles in a school production of *Twelfth Night*: "I always thought Olivia should've married Viola, and Sebastian should've married Orsino." He insists, "Some stories have a happy ending, Dean. You're allowed to make yourself a happy ending." The proof of his acceptance of Dean is most unexpected to both: under goading from Dean, he gives him a black eye, just like he would to any other boy. The play was given in 2014 in youth theaters across the U.K. as part of Connections. § Placey, E. *Girls like That and Other Plays for Teenagers*. Nick Hern, 2016. 237–302.

454 *Riding in Cars with (Mostly Straight) Boys* (2014) | Sam Brooks (1991?–), New Zealander

[Sexual comedy; 2M; a car.] The play makes sport of gay guys who fall in love with straight men. Kyle has never learned to drive. He depends on "Hot, straight, male friends" to take him places. On the ride he invariably makes adolescent passes at them. Mike throws him out of the car. Shane, after a year, admits that he is gay, whereupon Kyle loses interest: "I'm in love with straight, gorgeous, everly unattainable Shane. [...] Not gross, gay, present, there, Shane." So, of course, openly gay Trent is not appealing at all. Kyle's best friend Jay, even after Kyle declares his love, puts up with him. He makes Kyle face up to the fact: "It's easier to want something you can't have [...] than it is to want something you can have and get hurt." He forces Kyle to get his learner's permit and prepares to give him his first driving lesson. Kyle is played by one actor; the other four characters are played by one other. The play premiered in 2014 in a miked car parked on the Wellington waterfront, with Dan Veint and Calum Gittins, directed by Brooks. § *Here/Now: 8 Plays by Award-Winning NZ Playwrights*; ed. by David O'Donnell. Playmarket, 2015. 339–409.

455 *Sextet* (2014) | Morris Panych (1952–), Canadian

[Sexual farce; 4M, 2W; unit set.] Panych takes a chamber orchestra, strands them in a provincial motel in the winter, and lets them reveal the desires and tensions that have build up among the group during their several years performing together. Harry, a cellist, is a neurotic closet case whom everyone has long figured out. The motel has only limited space, so Dirk, a violist, suggests he and Harry share a room, not knowing (or admitting that he knows) that Harry has a crush on him. Dirk avows he is in love with Sylvia, the other cellist and Harry's best friend, whom they all suspect of being lesbian, but he flirts with Harry. Then there is the married Gerard, the violinist and head of the troupe: he has an extra X chromosome which affects his sexuality, so he makes up for it by going for an open marriage and being bisexual. That creates its own problems since his wife Mavis, who has her own fertility problems, wants a child. Sylvia will donate an egg if Mavis will promise to use Harry's sperm. Despite all the crosscurrents and miscommunications, when the sextet plays, their music is beautiful. Harry has the curtain line: "The universe plays us; all we can do is play back." The play opened in Toronto, 2014, with Damien Atkins, directed by Panych. § Panych, M. *Sextet: A Play*. Talonbooks, 2016. 137p.

456   Versailles (2014) | Peter Gill, Welsh

[Historical polemic; 7M, 6W; 2 sets.] Set in 1919, the play in quasi–Shavian fashion exposes how so many of the problems which have plagued the western world ever since grew out of decisions made at the Versailles Peace Conference, as witnessed here by Leonard Rawlinson. He is part of the British delegation, in particular responsible for the clauses relating to the Saar Basin. Of course, it is easy to have characters predict the future when one is writing from that future, but Gill puts Leonard's forebodings into terms that seem plausible for the period. To add authenticity Gill has even resurrected the feel of early 20th-century drama: it is a three-act play, two acts set in a drawing room. Leonard is discreet. We never learn, for example, what, if anything, happens between him and the German he dines with in Paris. His lover Gerald is outspoken. He affirms, "I took it that, since he made me, God was on my side," followed immediately by a comment to Leonard: "you continue to have the most beautiful arse." He objects to Wilde's penchant to view "The working class as sexual objects for the privileged" but himself refers to the maid's boyfriend's "enormous penis, waving about when we went swimming in the river." Gerald faults Leonard for not being willing to take risks, to put up with uncertainty, for wanting to "behave as [the straights] do." Gerald though is a ghost. He was killed during the war. The play ends with a flashback to 1914 as the two men prepare to depart for the front. The play opened in London, 2014, with Gwilym Lee and Tom Hughes, directed by Gill. § Gill, P. *Versailles*. Faber & Faber, 2014. 136p.

Appendix A: Performance Pieces

John Clum in a note in his anthology *Staging Gay Lives* (401) remarks that "the one-person show is the ideal form for the age of identity politics." These performance pieces are often autobiographical in nature, designed to be performed by the author, but sometimes they depict a fictional character, and sometimes the actor channels a number of voices, resulting in a work that approaches a conventional play. David Román in his introduction to the anthology *O Solo Homo* (6) writes that "in the pre–Stonewall era and to a lesser extent in the immediate years following it, there were very few queer performers creating solo work and even fewer doing autobiographical work." He notes that such works first appeared in bars, nightclubs, and drag revues. No one seems to have studied the role that standup comedians have played, though DVDs have captured actual performances. The following list is far from complete. An entire guide could be written on gay one-man and one-woman shows.

Holly Hughes and Román compiled their anthology *O Solo Homo: The New Queer Performance* (Grove, 1998), using only American examples: Luis Alfaro's *Downtown*; Craig Hickman's *Skin & Ornaments*; Gary Indiana's *Roy Cohn*, performed by Roy Vawter; Michael Kearns's *Attachments*; Alec Mapa's *I Remember Mapa*; and Tim Miller's *Naked Breath*. In 1990 Miller involuntarily became one of the so-called NEA Four—four performance artists whose NEA grants were rescinded under pressure from Republican Senator Jesse Helms and other self-appointed moral guardians. Miller has selected examples of his work for *Body Blows: Six Performances* (Univ. of Wisconsin Press, 2002). Alfaro has published performance pieces in a wide variety of anthologies. Kearns has published *Intimacies / More Intimacies* (in Helbing, T., ed. *Gay and Lesbian Plays*), *T Cells & Sympathy* (Heinemann Drama, 1995), and *Life Expectancies* (Heinemann Drama, 2005). He has also written guides: *Getting Your Solo Act Together*, 1997, and *The Solo Performer's Journey*, 2005. Other American collections include those by Robert C. Reinhart, *Telling Moments: Fifteen Gay Monologues* (Applause, 1994); Will Scheffer, *Falling Man and Other Monologues* (Dramatists, 1998); and Dan Bernitt, *Dose: Plays and Monologues* (Sawyer House, 2008).

Bernitt channeled four characters in his play about homophobia in a fraternity house, *Phi Alpha Gamma* (Sawyer House, 2008). Other plays with multiple characters that could be presented by more than one actor include Godfrey Hamilton's *Road Movie*, performed by his husband, actor Mark Pinkosh (Nick Hern, 1996), which follows the journey of a man across the U.S. hoping to reunite with the man he fell in love with, only to discover that he has died of AIDS; and Jonathan Tolins's *Buyer & Cellar*, performed by Michael Urie (Dramatists, 2014), about an employee of Barbra Streisand, who ponders her stardom. Then there are plays that include self-contained monologues, such as the two plays by Pomo Afro Homos (Djola Bernard Branner, Brian Freeman, Eric Gupton, Marvin K. White)—*Fierce Love* (Plume, 1986) and *Dark Fruit* (in Clum, J., ed. *Staging Gay Lives*)—and the second part of Christopher Durang's *Laughing Wild* (in Osborn, E., ed. *Way We Live Now*).

Other individual pieces include George Birimisa's *The Back Row of the Strand* and *Looking for Mr. America* (in *Birimisa*; ed. by L. Baugniet and P. Sagan, Sweetheart, 2009); Lanford Wilson's *A Poster of the Cosmos* (in Osborn, E., ed. *Way We Live Now*); Charles Busch and Kenneth Elliott's *Après Moi, Le Déluge* (in Barnes, N., and Deutsch,

N., eds. *Tough Acts*); Dan Butler's *The Only Thing Worse You Could Have Told Me*, performed by Scott Allyn (Dramatists, 1997); Colman Domingo's *A Boy and His Soul* (Oberon, 2007); David Drake's *The Night Larry Kramer Kissed Me* (Anchor, 1994), which was filmed; Steven Fales's *Confessions of a Mormon Boy* (Alyson, 2004); Martin Moran's *The Tricky Part* (Dramatists, 2005) and *All the Rage* (Dramatists, 2013); Robert Patrick's *One Person* (in Berman, E., ed. *Homosexual Acts*) and *Poof Positive*, an AIDS comedy performed by Terry Talley (in *Untold Decades*. St. Martin's, 1988); and Guillermo Reyes's *Men on the Verge of a His-panic Breakdown*, performed by Felix A. Pire (in Clum, J., ed. *Staging Gay Lives*). Joe Mantello adapted David Sedaris's *The Santaland Diaries and Season's Greetings*, performed by Timothy Olyphant (Dramatists, 1998).

Canada has two anthologies. Sky Gilbert assembled *Gay Monologues and Scenes: An Anthology* (Playwrights Canada, 2007), but only a few performance pieces are actually included: Peter Lynch's *Dig the Leaves Outta Your Hair and Then Variety Store*, performed by Carl Bart Davies; and David Roche's *David Roche Talks to You about Love* and *Why I Am Not a Transvestite*. Jean O'Hara highlights the art of First Nation monologists in her anthology *Two-Spirit Acts: Queer Indigenous Performances* (Playwrights Canada, 2013): Kent Monkman's *Taxonomy of the European Male, Séance*, and *Justice of the Piece*; and Waawaate Fobister tragedy *Agokwe*, about two boys whose families have forgotten the importance of its two-spirited members. The last would easily work with multiple actors. Daniel MacIvor has performed one-man shows throughout his career. Published scripts include *House Humans* (Coach House, 1993), *Wild Abandon* (Playwrights Canada, 1997), *Monster* (Scirocco Drama, 1998), *Cul de Sac* (Talonbooks, 2005), *One Voice* (Playwrights Canada, 2009). and *This Is What Happens Next* (Playwrights Canada, 2014). Other important works include Maxim Mazumdar's *Oscar Remembered* (Personal Library, 1977), a portrait of Wilde through the eyes of Lord Douglas; Michael Achtman's *Nazi/Jew/Queer* (in Gilbert, S., ed. *Perfectly Abnormal*); Walter Borden's *Tightrope Time* (Playwrights Canada, 2005); Ken Garnhum's *Beuys Buoys Boys* (in Wallace, R., ed. *Making, Out*); and the first part of Colin Thomas's *Sex Is My Religion* (in Armstrong, G., et al. *Plague*). Jonathan Wilson's *My Own Private Oshawa* (PUC, 1999) has been filmed. Two of the three plays in Jordan Tannahill's *Age of Minority* (Playwrights Canada, 2014) concern gay youth: *rihannaboi95*, about a lip-synching youth on YouTube, and *Peter Fechter: 59 Minutes*, about a German youth killed scaling the Berlin Wall.

Neil Bartlett is England's most published solo performer. His two collections are *Solo Voices: Monologues 1987–2004* (Oberon, 2006), which includes the original version of his tribute to the painter Simon Solomon, *A Vision of Love Revealed in Sleep*, famously performed by Bartlett in the nude, and *Queer Voices* (Oberon, 2012). Tom Wells appended two monologues to the script of *Me, as a Penguin* (Nick Hern, 2010): *About a Goth*, performed by Owen Whitelaw, and *Notes for First Time Astronauts*, performed by Ben Webb. The second part of Webb's *The Well and Badly Loved* (Oberon, 2012) is a gay rewrite of The Song of Songs, performed by Sean Hart. Chris Goode performed his complex *Men in the Cities* (Oberon, 2015). Neil Watkins, Irish, has published *A Cure for Homosexuality* (in Walsh, F., ed.,*Queer Notions*) and *The Year of Magical Wanking* (in Conway, T., ed. *Contemporary Irish Plays*).

The first gay Australian play to achieve renown was Steve J. Spears's *The Elocution of Benjamin Franklin* (in Chan, Kevin, and Israel, Ken, eds. *Drag Show*. Currency, 1977)—in great part because of the virtuoso acting of its star Gordon Chaer, who incarnated a 56-year-old Melbourne voice/acting teacher and drag queen seduced by his 12-year-old pupil Ben Franklin. The Indian playwright R. Raj Rao wrote *The Wisest Fool on Earth* (Brown Critique, 1996), a scatological soliloquy by a male prostitute, played by Rajit Kapur, looking out the window of the toilet where his lover has hidden him when the latter's father unexpectedly appears.

Appendix B: Musical Theater

After the second world war, if not before, the musical comedy buff—the trivia expert who knows the songs of even the most obscure shows—became a gay stereotype. Buzz in McNally's *Love! Valour! Compassion!* is a sterling example; Ethan Mordden is his real-life counterpart. John Clum has written an entire study: *Something for the Boys: Musical Theater and Gay Culture* (St. Martin's, 2001). See also Claude J. Summers, ed., *The Queer Encyclopedia of Music, Dance & Musical Theater* (Cleis, 2004). Even before the war it was assumed that male theater gypsies were gay, as well as some leading men. Many hit shows, even if not gay themselves, owed their existence to gays: *West Side Story*—the collaborative effort of four gay men: Leonard Bernstein, Arthur Laurents, Jerome Robbins, and Stephen Sondheim—is a prime example. Lyrics by Noël Coward, Lorenzo Hart, Cole Porter, and Sondheim take on added meaning when read from a gay perspective, while Jerry Herman has penned openly gay songs.

W. S. Gilbert and Arthur Sullivan's *Patience*, 1881, parodies Wilde, but as an aesthete, not a "sodomite." Book musicals with gay characters, both in secondary and principal roles, perhaps began with *Lady in the Dark* with Danny Kaye playing an obviously gay fashion photographer. They flourished, particularly in the U.S., from 1969 on. J. D. Doyle, *Queer Music Heritage: Gay Musicals* (online: queermusicheritage.com/gaymus), has provided a useful guide. Because they demand a different kind of talent, I early decided to eliminate musicals from consideration even if they are very much part of the gay repertoire. Virtually all have a cast recording, but relatively few have been published for the general reader. The creators' names are listed here in order of book, lyrics, and music.

Lady in the Dark (New York, 1941) | B: Moss Hart; L: Ira Gershwin; M: Kurt Weill. § Random House, 1941. 182p.

Joyce Dynel: An American Zarzuela (New York, 1969) | B: Robert Patrick. § *Robert Patrick's Cheep Theatricks*; ed. by Michael Feingold. French, 1972. 173–230.

Applause (New York, 1970) | B: Betty Comden, Adolph Green; L: Lee Adams; M: Charles Strouse. § Random House, 1971. 147p.

Coco (New York, 1969) | B/L: Alan Jay Lerner; M: André Previn.

The Faggot (New York, 1973) | B/L/M: Al Carmines.

Mercy Drop, or Marvin Loves Johnny (New York, 1973) | B/L: Robert Patrick; M: Richard Weinstock. § *Mercy Drop and Other Plays*; by R. Patrick. Calamus, 1979. 1–85.

The Rocky Horror Show (London, 1973) | B/L/M: Richard O'Brien. § French, 1983. 54p.

Let My People Come (New York, 1974) | L: Earl Wilson, Jr., Phil Oesterman; M: Earl Wilson, Jr.

Lovers (New York, 1974) | B/L: Peter del Valle; M: Steve Sterner.

Boy Meets Boy (New York, 1975) | B: Donald Ward; B/L/M: Bill Solly. § In Hoffman, W., ed. *Gay Plays*. 47–125.

A Chorus Line (New York, 1975) | B: James Kirkwood, Nicholas Dante; L: Edward Kleban; M: Marvin Hamlisch. § Applause, 1995. 145p.

Fascination (New York, 1975) | B: Michael Bottari; L/M: Michael Greene, Quitman Fludd III.

Gulp! (New York, 1977) | B/L: J. B. Hamilton; B: Stephen Greco; L: Robin Jones; M: Scott Kingman.

In Trousers (New York, 1979) | L/M: William Finn. § *The Marvin Songs*. Fireside, 1991. 1–87.

March of the Falsettos (New York, 1981) | L/M: William Finn. § *The Marvin Songs*. Fireside, 1991. 89–175.

Spin Cycle (Chicago, 1981) | B/L/M: Rick Karlin, Frank DePaul.

Sparkles (Los Angeles, 1981) | B/L: Michael Lewis; M: James Murdock.

La Cage aux Folles (New York, 1983) | B: Harvey Fierstein; L/M: Jerry Herman. § French, 1987. 111p.

Dance a Little Closer (New York, 1983) | B/L: Alan Jay Lerner; M: Charles Strouse.

In Gay Company (New York, 1984) | L/M: Fred Silver.

Xposed (Philadelphia, 1984) | L/M: Dan Martin, Michael Biello.

Sit on It and Swivel (New York, 1985) | B: G. Simpson, Betty LaMorte; L/M: Scott McLarty.

Ten Percent Revue (Boston, 1985) | L/M: Tom Wilson Weinberg.

Only Heaven Knows (Melbourne, 1989) | B/L/M: Alex Harding. § Currency, 1988. 69p.

Capote at Yaddo (Toronto, 1990) | B/L: Sky Gilbert; M: John Alcorn. § In Wallace, R., ed. *Making, Out.* 95–188.

Dirty Dreams of a Clean-Cut Kid (San Francisco, 1990) | B/L: Henry Mach; M: Paul Katz.

Falsettoland (New York, 1990) | B; James Lapine; L/M: William Finn. § *The Marvin Songs.* Fireside, 1991. 177–248.

Kiss of the Spider Woman (New York, 1990) | B: Terrence McNally; L: Fred Ebb; M: John Kander. § French, 1997. 90p.

2-2-Tango: A-Two-Man-One-Man-Show (Toronto, 1990) | B/L/M: Daniel MacIvor. § In Wallace, R., ed. *Making, Out.* 189–217.

AIDS! The Musical! (Los Angeles, 1991) | B/L: Wendell Jones, David Stanley; M: Robert Berg. § In Jones, T., ed. *Sharing the Delirium.* 207–63.

Pageant (New York, 1991) | B/L: Frank Kelly; M: Bill Russell.

The Harvey Milk Show (Atlanta, 1991) | B/L: Dan Pruitt; M: Patrick Hutchison. § In Clum, J., ed. *Staging Gay Lives.* 5–62.

Prom Night of the Living Dead (Edmonton, 1991) | B/L: Brad Fraser; M: Darren Hagen. § *The Wolf Plays*; by B. Fraser. NeWest, 1993. 113–250.

An Unfinished Song (New York, 1991) | B/L/M: James J. Mellon.

Queen of Angels (Los Angeles, 1992) | B/L: James Carroll Pickett; M: Jon Cohen. § In Jones, T., ed. *Sharing the Delirium.* 87–140.

All That He Was (Los Angles, 1993) | B/L: Larry Johnson; M: Cindy O'Connor.

Elegies for Angels, Punks, and Raging Queens (London, 1993) | B/L: Bill Russell; M; Janet Hood.

Get Used to It (New York, 1993) | L/M: Tom Wilson Weinberg.

Hello Again (New York, 1993) | B/L/M: Michael John LaChiusa. § *Hello Again.* Dramatists, 1995. 76p.

Howard Crabtree's Whoop-Dee-Doo! (New York, 1993) | L: Charles Catanese; M: Dick Gallagher et al. § French, 1995. 84p.

Night after Night (London, 1993) | B/L: Neil Bartlett; M: Nicolas Bloomfield. § Methuen Drama, 1993. 57p.

One Foot Out the Door (New York, 1993) | L/M: Stephen Dolginoff.

The Ballad of Mikey: The Birth of an Activist (New York, 1994) | B/L/M: Mark Savage.

Cruisin' (Toronto, 1995) | B/L/M: various artists.

Fairy Tales (Chicago, 1995) | L/M: Eric Lane Barnes.

In the Blood (St. Louis, 1995) | B/L/M: Scott Miller.

Most Men Are (New York, 1995) | L/M: Stephen Dolginoff (New York, 1995).

Victor/Victoria (New York, 1995) | B: Blake Edwards; L: Leslie Bricusse; M: Henry Mancini, Frank Wildhorn.

Howard Crabtree's When Pigs Fly (New York, 1996) | B/L: Mark Waldrop; M: Dick Gallagher. § French, 1999. 112p.

Rent (New York, 1996) | L/M: Jonathan Larson. § Weisbach, 1997. 141p.

The Gay 90s Musical (Los Angeles, 1997) | L/M: various artists.

The Last Session (New York, 1997) | B/L/M: Steven Schalchlin.

Under Wraps: A Spoke Opera (St. John's, N.L., 1997) | B: Robert Chafe; M: Petrina Bromley. § Playwrights Canada, 2014. 110p.

The Boy from Oz (Sydney, 1998) | B: Nick Enright; L/M: Peter Allen.

Cabaret (New York, 1998) | B: Joe Masteroff; L: Fred Ebb; M: John Kander. § *Cabaret: The Illustrated Book and Lyrics*, ed. by Linda Sunshine. Newmarket, 1999. 17–99.

Hedwig and the Angry Inch (New York, 1998) | B: John Cameron Mitchell; L/M: Stephen Trask. § Dramatists, 2003. 63p.

Kooky Tunes (New York, 1998) | L/M: Keith Thompson.

Naked Boys Singing! (Los Angeles, 1998) | L: Robert Schrock; M: Stephen Bates.

A New Brain (New York, 1998) | B: James Lapine; B/L/M: William Finn.

The Rainbow Room (New York, 1998) | L/M: Rick Knight.

A Perfectly Normal Boy (New York, 1999) | L/M: Paul Bruce.

Ship in a Bottle (St. Louis, 1999) | B/L/M: Jerrold Rabuska.

Tom Bogdan's L'Amour Bleu (New York, 1999) | L/M: various artists.
Bare (Los Angeles, 2000) | B/L: Jon Hartmere, Jr.; B/M: Damon Intrabartolo.
Bed, Boys, and Beyond (New York, 2000) | B/L: Jeff Dobbins; M: Alfredo Alvarez.
Cowboys! (New York, 2000) | B/L: Clint Jefferies; M: Paul L. Johnson.
The Full Monty (New York, 2000) | B: Terrence McNally; L/M: David Yazbek. § Applause, 2002. 148p.
Mother Clap's Molly House (London, 2000) | B/L: Mark Ravenhill; M: Matthew Scott. § *Plays Two*; by M. Ravenhill. Methuen Drama, 2008. 1–152.
Out on Broadway (St. Louis, 2000) | L/M: various artists.
Outrageous! (Toronto, 2000) | B/L: Brad Fraser; M: Joey Miller.
Prodigal Son (Perth, 2000) | B/L: Dean Bryant; M: Matthew Frank.
The Wild Party (New York, 2000) | B/L/M: Andrew Lippa.
The Wild Party (New York, 2000) | B: George C. Wolfe; B/L/M: John LeChiusa.
Bourbon Street (New Orleans, 2001) | B/L: Hiram Edwin Taylor; M: Irvin Decker.
Closer to Heaven (London, 2001) | B: Jonathan Harvey; L/M: Pet Shop Boys.
Dirty Little Showtunes (New York, 2001) | L/M: Tom Orr.
Portraits (New York, 2001) | L/M: Mark Alan DeWaters.
The Producers (New York, 2001) | B/L/M: Mel Brooks. § *The Producers.* Miramax, 2001. 192p.
Avenue Q (New York, 2002) | B: Jeff Whitty; L/M: Robert Lopez, Jeff Marx. § Applause, 2010. 151p.
Convenience (Rochester, N.Y., 2002) | B/L/M: Greg Coffin. § Dramatists, 2004. 72p.
Flower Drum Song (New York, 2002) | B: David Henry Hwang; L: Oscar Hammerstein; M: Richard Rodgers. § Theatre Communications, 2003. 120p.
A Man of No Importance (New York, 2002) | B: Terrence McNally; L: Lynn Ahrens; M: Stephen Flaherty. § Stage & Screen, 2003. 108p.
The Pink Files (Adelaide, 2002) | B: Ian Purcell; L/M: Sean Peters.
Taboo (London, 2002) | B: Mark Davies Markham; L/M: Boy George.
The Boy from Oz (New York, 2003) | B: Martin Sherman; L/M: Peter Allen.
Joe Starts Again (Melbourne, 2003) | B: Mark Fletcher; B/L: Martin Croft; M: Dean Lotherington.
Not Me (New York, 2003) | L/M: Hector Coris, Paul L. Johnson.

Radiant Baby (New York, 2003) | L: Ira Gasman, Stewart Ross; L/M: Debra Basher, Stewart Ross.
Rudolph the Red-Hosed Reindeer (Chicago, 2003) | B/L/M: David Cerda.
Thrill Me: The Leopold & Loeb Story (New York, 2003) | B/L/M: Stephen Dolginoff. § Dramatists, 2006. 72p.
Zanna, Don't (New York, 2003) | B/L: Alexander Dinelaris; B/L/M: Tim Acito.
The Big Voice: God or Merman (New York, 2004) | B/L/M: Steve Schalchlin, Jim Brochu. § French, 2008. 60p.
108 Waverly (New York, 2004) | B/L: Dan Clancy; M: Lynn Portas.
Pyrates (New York, 2004) | B/L: Barbara Kahn; M: Jay Kerr.
Breathe (Chicago, 2005) | L: Michael Biello; M: Dan Martin.
Fleet Week (New York, 2005) | B/L/M: Mac Rogers.
Oh My Godmother! (Alameda, Calif., 2005) | B/L/M: Ron Lytle.
Songs from an Unmade Bed (New York, 2005) | L/M: Mark Campbell.
Trolls (New York, 2005) | B/L: Bill Dyer; M: Dick DeBenedictis.
Yank! (New York, 2005) | B/L: David Zellnik; M: Joseph Zellnik. § In Clum, J., ed. *Gay Drama Now.*
Ain't We Got Fun (Cleveland, 2006) | B: Michael McFaden; L/M: various artists.
Bathhouse (Orlando, 2006) | L/M: Tim Evanicki, Esther Daack.
Muscle-Man vs. Skeletonman (New York, 2006) | L/M: Richard J. Hinds, Gina Trello.
Play It Cool (Los Angeles, 2006) | L: Mark Winkler; M: Phil Swann.
Priscilla, Queen of the Desert (Sydney, 2006) | B: Stephen Elliott, Allan Scott; L/M: various artists.
Spring Awakening (New York, 2006) | B/L: Steven Sater; M: Duncan Sheik. § Theatre Communications, 2007. 112p.
[title of show] (New York, 2006) | B: Hunter Bell; L/M: Jeff Bowen.
What's Your Problem? (New York, 2006) | L: Mark Coris; M: Paul Johnson et al.
I Was A Teenage Homo (Los Angeles, 2007) | B/L: Bill Fagan; B/L/M: Jeff Scott.
Over the Rainbow (New York, 2007) | B/L/M: Michael Penny.
Bash'd: A Gay Rap Opera (New York, 2008) | B/L: Chris Craddock, Nathan Cuckow; M: Aaron Macri. § Talonbooks, 2011. 96p.
A Catered Affair (New York, 2008) | B: Harvey Fierstein; L/M: John Bucchino.

The Fancy Boy Follies (New York, 2008) | B/L/M: David Pevsner et al.
Glory Days (New York, 2008) | B: James Gardiner; L/M: Nick Blaemire.
Road Show [Wise Guys / Bounce] (New York, 2008) | B: John Weidman; L/M: Stephen Sondheim. § *Look, I Made a Hat*; by S. Sondheim. Knopf, 2011. 178–291.
My Big Phat Gay Musical (New York, 2009) | L/M: John Paul Sharp.
Our Country (New York, 2009) | B: Dan Collins; L/M: Tony Asaro.
Boys Will Be Boys (New York, 2010) | L: Joe Mioscla; M: Kenneth Kacmar.
The Kid (New York, 2010) | B: Michael Zam; L: Jack Lechner; M: Andy Monroe.
Nowhere Town (Chicago, 2010) | B/L/M: Hal Duncan.
Cleveland Street (London, 2011) | B/L: Glenn Chandler; M: Matt Devereaux.
Little Miss Sunshine (La Jolla, Calif., 2011) | B: James Lapine; L/M: William Finn.
Soho Cinders (London, 2011) | B; Elliot Davis; B/L: Anthony Drewe; M: George Stiles.
Kinky Boots (New York, 2012) | B: Harvey Fierstein; L/M: Cyndi Lauper.
Out! (Palo Alto, Calif., 2012) | B: Molly Hersage; B/L/M: Nancy Gilsenan Hersage. § Dramatic, 2013. 82p.
Chance (San Francisco, 2013) | B/L/M: Richard Isen.
Sodom (unproduced, 2013) | B/L/M: Hal Duncan.
Fun Home (New York, 2013) | B/L: Lisa Kron; M: Jeanine Tesori. § French, 2015. 77p.
Upstairs (New Orleans, 2013) | B/L/M: Wayne Self.
Rent Boy (London, 2015) | B/L: David Leddick; M: Andrew Sargent.
The Jamb (New York, 2016) | B/L/M: J. Stephen Brantley.
Poster Boy (Williamstown, Mass., 2016) | B: Joe Tracz; L/M: Craig Carnelia.
The Sins of Jack Saul (London, 2016) | B/L: Glenn Chandler; M: Charles Miller.

Another gay cliché is the opera queen, each with his favorite female diva. He has been portrayed most notably as an arch-stereotype in McNally's *The Lisbon Traviatta*. Wayne Koestenbaum has written a study, *The Queen's Throat: Opera, Homosexuality, and the Mystery of Desire* (Poseidon, 1993). What may be surprising is the number of gay operas set to an English text that exist. Creators' names are listed by first the librettist, then the composer.

The Knot Garden (London, 1970) | L/M: Michael Tippett. § Philips, 1974. 15p.
Death in Venice (Aldeburgh, 1973) | L: Myfanwy Piper; M: Benjamin Britten. § London, 1974. 54p.
A Quiet Place (Milan, 1984) | L: Stephen Wadsworth; M: Leonard Bernstein. § Deutsche Grammophon, 1987. 379p.
Harvey Milk (Houston, 1995) | L: Michael Koric; M: Stewart Wallace. § Teldec, 1998. 105p.
Edward II (unproduced, 2001) | L/M: Scott Eric Smith.
Angels in America (Paris, 2004) | L: Mari Mezci; M: Peter Eotvos.
Three Decembers (Houston, 2008) | B: Terrence McNally; L: Gene Scheer; M: Jake Heggie. § Albany, 2008.
Stonewall (Greeley, Colo., 2012) | L: John Stirling Walker; M: David Conte.
Oscar (Santa Fe, 2013) | L: John Cox; M: Theodore Morrison.
Two Boys (London, 2013) | L: Craig Lucas; M: Nico Muhly.
Under the Rainbow (Orlando, 2013) | L/M: Alan Gerber.
Brokeback Mountain (Madrid, 2014) | L: Annie Proulx; M: Charles Wuorinen. § Bel Aire, 2015. 18p.
Sentences (London, 2015) | L: Adam Gopnik; M: Nico Muhly.
Fellow Travellers (Cincinnati, 2016) | L: Greg Pierce; M: Gregory Spears.
Pleasure (London, 2016) | L: Melanie Challenger; M: Mark Simpson.
Prince of Players (Houston, 2016) | L/M: Carlisle Floyd.

General Bibliography

Anthologies

Armstrong, Gordon, et al. *Plague of the Gorgeous & Other Tales.* Scirocco Drama, 1996.

Barnes, Noreen C., and Nicholas Deutsch, eds. *Tough Acts to Follow: One-Act Plays on the Gay/Lesbian Experience.* Alamo Square, 1992.

Berman, Ed, ed. *Homosexual Acts: Five Short Plays from the Gay Season at the Almost Free Theatre.* Inter-Action, 1975.

Clum, John M., ed. *Asking and Telling: A Collection of Gay Drama for the 21st Century: Six Scripts.* Stage & Screen, 2000.

_____, ed. *Gay Drama Now: An Anthology.* Cambria, 2013.

_____, ed. *Staging Gay Lives: An Anthology of Contemporary Gay Theater.* Westview, 1996.

_____, and Sean A. Metzger, eds. *Awkward Stages: Plays about Growing Up Gay.* Cambria, 2015.

Conway, Thomas, ed. *The Oberon Book of Contemporary Irish Plays.* Oberon, 2012.

Gilbert, Sky, ed. *Perfectly Abnormal: Seven Gay Plays.* Playwrights Canada, 2006.

Helbing, Terry, ed. *Gay and Lesbian Plays Today.* Heinemann, 1993.

Hodges, Ben, ed. *Forbidden Acts: Pioneering Gay & Lesbian Plays of the Twentieth Century.* Applause, 2003.

_____, ed. *Out Plays: Landmark Gay and Lesbian Plays of the Twentieth Century.* Alyson, 2008.

Hoffman, William M., ed. *Gay Plays: The First Collection.* Avon/Bard, 1979.

Jones, Therese, ed. *Sharing the Delirium: Second Generation AIDS Plays and Performances.* Heineman, 1994.

Kourilsky, Françoise, and Catherine Temerson, eds. *Gay Plays: An International Anthology.* Ubu, 1989.

Lane, Eric, and Nina Shengold, eds. *The Actor's Book of Gay and Lesbian Plays.* Penguin, 1995.

Loisel, Clary, ed. *Mexican Queer Theater.* Floricanto, 2015.

_____, ed. *Out of the Closet onto the Stage: An Anthology of Contemporary Mexican Gay and Lesbian Theater.* Floricanto, 2012.

Malan, Robin, ed. *S.A. Gay Plays 1: The Artscape Dublin Festival Plays.* Junkets, 2011.

_____, ed. *S.A. Gay Plays 2: An Anthology of Plays 1994–2013.* Junkets, 2013.

Parr, Bruce, ed. *Australian Gay and Lesbian Plays.* Currency, 1996.

Osborn, M. Elizabeth, ed. *The Way We Live Now: American Plays and the AIDS Crisis.* Theatre Communications, 1990.

Osment, Philip, ed. *Gay Sweatshop: Four Plays and a Company.* Methuen, 1989.

Senelick, Laurence, ed. *Lovesick: Modernist Plays of Same-Sex Love, 1894–1925.* Routledge, 1999.

Shnipper, Brian, et al. *Standing on Ceremony: The Gay Marriage Plays.* Dramatists, 2013.

Shewey, Don, ed. *Out Front: Contemporary Gay and Lesbian Plays.* Grove, 1988.

Susoyev, Steve, and George Birimisa, eds. *Return to the Caffe Cino: A Collection of Plays and Memoirs.* Moving Finger, 2007.

Wallace, Robert, ed. *Making, Out: Plays by Gay Men.* Coach House, 1992.

Walsh, Fintan, ed. *Queer Notions: New Plays and Performances from Ireland.* Cork Univ. Press, 2010.

Wilcox, Michael, ed. *Gay Plays.* 5v. Methuen, 1984–1994.

References

Aldrich, Robert, ed. *Gay Life and Culture: A World History.* Universe, 2006.

Australianplays. Online: http://australianplays.org/category/gay-lesbian-themes.

Banham, Martin, ed. *The Cambridge Guide to Theatre.* Cambridge Univ. Press, 1995.

Charlebois, Gaeton, et al. "Gay and Lesbian Theatre." *Canadian Theatre Encyclopedia.* Online: http://www.canadiantheatre.com/dict.pl?term=Gay%20and%20Lesbian%20Theatre.

Chauncey, George. *Gay New York: Gender, Urban Culture, and the Making of the Gay Male World, 1890–1940.* Basic Books, 1994.

Clum, John M. *Still Acting Gay: Male Homosexuality in Modern Drama.* St. Martin's, 2000.

Crompton, Louis. *Homosexuality & Civilization.* Belknap/Harvard Univ. Press, 2003.

Curtin, Kaier: *"We Can Always Call Them Bulgarians": The Emergence of Lesbians and Gay Men on the American Stage.* Alyson, 1987.

de Jongh, Nicholas. *Not in Front of the Audience: Homosexuality on Stage.* Routledge, 1992.

Dynes, Wayne R., ed. *Encyclopedia of Homosexuality.* 2 vols. Garland, 1990.

Franceschina, John. *Homosexualities in the English Theatre from Lyly to Wilde.* Greenwood, 1997.

Gerstner, David A., ed. *Routledge International Encyclopedia of Queer Culture.* Routledge, 2006.

Grassi, Samuele. *Looking through Gender: Post-1980 British and Irish Drama.* Cambridge Scholars, 2011.

Haggerty, George E., ed. *Gay Histories and Cultures: An Encyclopedia.* Garland, 2000.

Harbin, Billy J., Kim Marra, and Robert A. Schanke, eds. *The Gay & Lesbian Theatrical Legacy: A Biographical Dictionary of Major Figures in American Stage History in the Pre-Stonewall Era.* Univ. of Michigan Press, 2007.

Hawley, John C., ed. *LGBTQ America Today: An Encyclopedia.* 3v. Greenwood, 2009.

Hurley, Michael. *A Guide to Gay and Lesbian Writing in Australia.* Allen & Unwin, 1996.

Kerr, Rosalind, ed. *Queer Theatre in Canada.* Playwrights Canada, 2007.

Kröller, Eva-Marie, ed. *The Cambridge Companion to Canadian Literature.* Cambridge Univ. Press, 2004.

Lacey, Brian. *Terrible Queer Creatures: Homosexuality in Irish History.* Woodwell, 2008.

Malinowski, Sharon, ed. *Gay & Lesbian Literature,* [v1]. St. James, 1994.

Miller, Carl. *Stages of Desire: Gay Theatre's Hidden History.* Cassell, 1996.

Nelson, Emmanuel S., ed. *Contemporary Gay American Poets and Playwrights: An A-to-Z Guide.* Greenwood, 2003.

_____, ed. *Encyclopedia of Contemporary LGBTQ Literature of the United States.* 2v. Greenwood, 2009.

New Zealand Playwrights: Playmarket. Online: http://www.playmarket.org.nz.

Norton, Rictor. *Mother Clap's Molly House: The Gay Subculture in England 1700–1830.* GMP, 1992.

Oddy, Julian. *The Playwrights Database of Modern Plays.* Online: www.doollee.com.

Pendergast, Tom, and Sara Pendergast, eds. *Gay & Lesbian Literature,* v2. St. James, 1998.

Playwrights Guild of Canada. Online: https://www.playwrightsguild.ca/playwrights.

Rayter, Scott, et al., eds. *Queer CanLit: Canadian Lesbian, Gay, Bisexual, and Transgender (LGBT) Literature in English.* Coach House, 2008.

Sarotte, Georges-Michel. *Like a Brother, like a Lover: Male Homosexuality in the American Novel and Theater from Herman Melville to James Baldwin.* Trans. by Richard Miller. Anchor/Doubleday, 1978.

Schildcrout, Jordan. *Murder Most Queer: The Homicidal Homosexual in the American Theater.* Univ. of Michigan Press, 2014.

Sinfield, Alan. *Out on Stage: Lesbian and Gay Theatre in the Twentieth Century.* Yale Univ. Press, 1999.

Spencer, Colin. *Homosexuality in History.* Harcourt Brace, 1995.

Summers, Claude J., ed. *The Gay and Lesbian Literary Heritage: A Reader's Companion to the Writers and Their Works, from Antiquity to the Present.* Holt, 1995.

Vining, Donald. *A Gay Diary.* 5v. Pepys, 1979–1993.

Woods, Gregory. *A History of Gay Literature: The Male Tradition.* Yale Univ. Press, 1998.

Index of Authors and Titles

References are to entry numbers

Abdoh, Reza 227
Absolute Hell (Ackland) 185
Achtman, Michael Appendix A
Ackerley, J. R. 23
Ackland, Rodney 185
Adam and the Experts (Bumbalo) 193
Adamson, Samuel 268, 384
Advice from a Caterpillar (Beane) 201
The Agony & the Agony (Silver) 370
Aguirre-Sacasa, Roberto 328, 371
Albee, Edward 149
Alfaro, Luis Appendix A
All That I Will Ever Be (Ball) 385
The American Plan (Greenberg) 202
Amulets Against the Dragon Forces (Zindel) 194
Ancient Boys (van Itallie) 195
Anderson, Robert 50
Angels in America (Kushner) 209, Appendix B
Another Country (Mitchell) 132
Another Day on Willow St (Polito) 450
Antonio, Salvatore 379
Aretino, Pietro 4
Arigato, Tokyo (MacIvor) 442
Aristophanes 1, 2
Armory 16
Armstrong, Gordon 236
Aron, Geraldine 208
As Bees in Honey Drown (Beane) 277
As Is (Hoffman) 156
As the Beaver (Johnson) 245
As Time Goes By (Greig & Griffiths) 111
At Saint Judas's (Fuller) 11
Auto-da-Fé (Williams) 42
Auto-Erotic Misadventure (Hartland) 148

Baal (Brecht) 20
Babe, Thomas 121
Babies (Harvey) 246
The Backroom (Pagan) 298
Bad Company (Bent) 247
The Baddest of Boys (Holsclaw) 220

Baitz, Jon Robin 356
Ball, Alan 385
The Baltimore Waltz (Vogel) 203
Banana Boys (Placey) 420
Band Fags! (Polito) 433
The Baptism (Jones/Baraka) 63
Baron, Jeff 276
Barr, James 53
Barrett, Andrew 272
Bartlett, Mike 402
Bartlett, Neil 314, Appendix, Appendix B
Bartley, Jim 241
Based on a Totally True Story (Aguirre-Sacasa) 371
Bauer, Wolfgang 81
Beane, Douglas Carter 201, 277, 380, 448
Bearclaw (Mason) 151
Beat the Sunset (MacLennan) 234
Beautiful Child (Silver) 349
Beautiful Thing (Harvey) 235
Beauty of the Father (Cruz) 350
The Bed (Heide) 68
Beer and Rhubarb Pie (Curson) 130
The Beginning of August (Donaghy) 310
Beguelin, Chad 436
Being at Home with Claude (Dubois) 157
Belber, Stephen 355, 401
Bell, Neal 165, 308, 357, 389
The Beloved Disciple (Jacobson) 248
Bennett, Alan 190, 353, 403
Bent (Sherman) 124
Bent, Simon 247, 413
Bentley, Eric 118, 181
Bernitt, Dan Appendix A
Besset, Jean-Marie 210
The Best Brothers (MacIvor) 434
The Best of Schools (Besset) 210
Beyond Therapy (Durang) 133
BFs! (Polito) 433
Big Bill (Gurney) 338
Big Fish, Little Fish (Wheeler) 57
Birimisa, George 70, 109, 119, Appendix A

The Blackmailers (J. Gray & Raffalovich) 10
Blade to the Heat (Mayer) 249
Blessing, Lee 226, 322
Blood and Honour (Harding) 204
Blowing Whistles (Todd) 359
Blow Job (S. Wilson) 87
Blue Dragons (Armstrong) 236
Bobrick, Sam 86
Boom Bang-a-Bang (Harvey) 258
Bootycandy (O'Hara) 421
Bouchard, Michel Marc 177, 261, 290, 430
Bowne, Alan 135
Box 27 (Mann) 237
The Boy in the Basement (Inge) 60
The Boy Who Fell from the Roof (Jenkin) 360
Boys in the Band (Crowley) 78, 147, 334
Bracho, Ricardo A. 398
Bradfield, Jon 452
Bradley, H. Dennis 33
Bradshaw, Thomas 491
Branson, Greg 160
Brassard, Marie 189
Brave Hearts (Rintoul) 211
Bravely Fought the Queen (Dattani) 212
Breaking the Code (Whitemore) 167
Brecht, Bertolt 20, 23
A Bright Room Called Day (Kushner) 174
Brooks, Sam 454
Brown, Arch 127
Bumbalo, Victor 137, 193, 256, 363
Bunbury (Jacobson) 361
Burn This (L. Wilson) 175
Busch, Charles 257, 302, Appendix A
But It Still Goes On (Graves) 32
Butler, Dan Appendix A
Butley (S. Gray) 88

Cabranes-Grant, Leo 282, 299
Camino Real (Williams) 47
Campbell, Alexi Kaye 396

Canary (Harvey) 417
Caprice (Ludlam) 105
Carthaginians 186
Cat on a Hot Tin Roof (Williams) 52
Certain Young Men (Gill) 159
Change (Bauer) 81
Chat Room (Cabranes-Grant) 299
Cherish (Duncum) 339
Chesley, Robert 154, 171
Chinchilla (MacDonald) 112
Chinn, Jimmie 183
Choir Boy (McCraney) 443
Chomi (Nemakonde) 444
Churchill, Caryl 125
Circuitry (Barrett) 372
Citizenship (Ravenhill) 373
Civil Sex (Freeman) 278
Clark, Ron 86
The Clash of Cymbals (Guerrero) 83
Clean (Sánchez) 259
Clocks and Whistles (Adamson) 268
Cloud 9 (Churchill) 125
Cock (Bartlett) 402
Cock-Ups (Moss) 134
The Coffee Lover's Guide to America (J. Hall) 331
Coffeehouse (Jackson) 300
Colman, Robert 347
Comfort and Joy (Heifner) 260
Coming Clean (Elyot) 142
Coming of Age in Soho (Innaurato) 158
Coming Out! (Katz) 90
Compleat Female Stage Beauty (Harcher) 301, Appendix B
Compromised Immunity (Kirby) 176
Concord Floral (Tannahill) 451
Confession (J. Patrick) 106
Confessional (Williams) 84
Congdon, Constance 262
Conpersonas (Lim) 107
The Convergence of Luke (Rintoul) 279
Copi 123
The Coronation Voyage (Bouchard) 261
Corpus Christi (McNally) 288
Courageous (Healey) 418
Coward, Noël 25, 36, 71
Cristofer, Michael 104
Crowley, Mart 78, 334
The Crumple Zone (B. Thomas) 311
Cruz, Nilo 350
Curson, Daniel 130
Curtsy (Drader) 362

Dalliances 386
Dangerous Corner (Priestley) 34
The Dangerous Precaution (Kuzmin) 15
Danny and Chantelle (Still Here) (McMahon) 374
Dattani, Mahesh 212, 297, 306
A Day After the Fair (Purdy) 113
The Death and Resurrection of Mr. Roche (Kilroy) 79
The Death of Peter Pan (Lowe) 196

Deathwatch (Genet) 43
Degrees (Birimisa) 70
Deegan, Loughlin 319
Deemer, Charles 292
de Jongh, Nicholas 395
Delaney, Shelagh 56
de la Roche, Mazo 40
Demchuk, David 173
Deporting the Divas (Reyes) 269
Design for Living (Coward) 36
Diary of a Somebody (Lahr) 168
Die Mommie Die! (Busch) 302
Dietz, Steven 238
Dillon, David 229
DiPietro, Joe 392
Dog Opera (Congdon) 262
Dog Sees God (Royal) 351
Dogeaters (Hagedorn) 289
Dolly West's Kitchen (McGuinness) 303
Domingo, Colman Appendix A
Donaghy, Tom 264, 310
Douglas, Lord Alfred 12, 19, 27, 39, 103, 118, 198, 286
Down Dangerous Passes Road (Bouchard) 290
Drader, Brian 327, 354, 362
The Drag (West) 26
Drake, David Appendix A
The Dressing Gown (Gilbert) 152
The Drowning Room (Mavenawitz) 375
Duberman, Martin 93
Dubois, René-Daniel 157
Duncum, Ken 225, 339
Durang, Christopher 133, 438, Appendix A
Dyer, Charles 72
Dying City (Shinn) 376
The Dying Gaul (Lucas) 291

Eagleton, Terry 198
Eastern Standard (Greenberg) 187
Easy Terms (Vickery) 143
Edith Can Shoot Things and Hit Them (Pamatmat) 422
Edward II (Marlowe) 5, 23, 266, Appendix B
Elagabalus (Duberman) 93
Elizabeth Rex (Findley) 312
Elyot, Kevin 142, 255, 325
The Enclave (Laurents) 94
The End (Palmer) 91
The End of the Tour (Johnson) 340
Enemy! (Maugham) 82
Enright, Nick 215, 251, Appendix B
Entertaining Mr. Sloane (Orton) 64

Fales, Steven Appendix A
Falling in Time (Gatchalian) 423
Family Values (Deemer) 292
The Fastest Clock in the Universe (Ridley) 221
Fierstein, Harvey 141, Appendix B
Fifth of July (L. Wilson) 116
Find Your Way Home (Hopkins) 85
Finding the Sun (Albee) 149

Findley, Timothy 242, 312
Fineberg, Larry 99
Firbank, Ronald 19
The Fire That Consumes (Montherlant) 45
Fisher, John 252, 390
Flamingos (J. Hall) 324
Flaubert's Latest (Parnell) 222
Flesh and Blood (C. Thomas) 213
Flipzoids (Peña) 270
Fobister, Waawaate Appendix A
The Food Chain (Silver) 250
Forever After (D. Wilson) 131
Fortune and Men's Eyes (Herbert) 75
Forty-Deuce (Bowne) 135
Foster, Paul 92
Four (Shinn) 293
Franken, Rose 41
Fraser, Brad 200, 284, 415, Appendix B
Freeman, Brian 278
Friel, Brian 89
From White Plains (Perlman) 435
Fry, Stephen 126
Fucking Men (DiPietro) 392
Fugaté, James Barr 53
Fulford, Robin 182
Fuller, Henry Blake 11
Furious (Gow) 214
Furtive Love (Kenna) 117

Galluccio, Steve 317
Game of Fools (Fugaté) 53
García Lorca, Federico 31, 350
Garnhum, Ken Appendix A
Gatchalian, C.E. 423
Gates of Gold (McGuinness) 332
The Gay Detective (Stembridge) 271
Gellert, Roger 54
Gemini (Innaurato) 108
Genet, Jean 43, 377
The Gentle Island (Friel) 89
The Gentleman of the Chrysanthemums (Armory) 16
The Giant (Sher) 387
Gide, André 2n1, 13, 51
Gilbert, Sky 152, 184, 228, 263, 364, 404, Appendix B
Gill, Peter 159, 178, 330, 335, 456
Go Back to Where You Are (Greenspan) 424
Godfrey, Paul 206
Goedhart-Becker, Johanna Maria 21
Goetz, Ruth & Augustus 51
The Golden Thug (Roy) 377
Good Works (Enright) 251
Goode, Chris Appendix A
Gow, Michael 214
Grace (MacLennan) 280
Granville-Barker, Harley 17
Graves, Robert 32
Gray, John 10
Gray, Simon 77, 88
Green, Julian 49
The Green Bay Tree (Shairp) 37
Greenberg, Richard 187, 202, 336
Greene, Graham 103

Index to entry numbers

Greig, Noël 111
Griffiths, Drew 111
Grimm, David 315, 381, 400, 408
Grimsley, Jim 179
Gross Indecency (Kaufman) 281
Guare, John 207
Guerrero, Wilfrido Maria 83
Gurney, A.R. 6, 216, 338

The Habit of Art (Bennett) 403
Hagedorn, Jessica 289
Hall, Jonathan 324, 331, 341, 344
Hall, Richard 144
Hamilton, Godfrey Appendix A
Hamilton, Patrick 30
Hampton, Christopher 73, 80
Handbag (Ravenhill) 294
Hansberry, Lorraine 67
Happy Birthday, Daddy (R. Hall) 144
Happy Endings Are Extra (Johaardien) 352
Harbor (Beguelin) 436
A Hard Rain (Bradfield & Hooper) 452
Hardcore (J. Hall) 341
Harding, Alex 204, Appendix B
Hare, David 295
Hartland, F.J. 148
Harvey, Jonathan 235, 246, 258, 304, 326, 417, Appendix B
Hatcher, Jeffrey 301
The Haunted Host (R. Patrick) 65
Healey, Michael 418
Heartbreak (Heifner) 223
Heide, Robert 68
The Heidi Chronicles (Wasserstein) 188
Heifner, Jack 223, 260
Herbert, John 75
Hickman, Craig Appendix A
Hicks, James 369
Hijra (Kotak) 313
Hill, Michael 35
Hirschberg, Herbert 14
His Greatness (MacIvor) 388
The History Boys (Bennett) 353
Hoffman, William M. 156
Holding the Man (Murphey) 378
Holsclaw, Doug 220
Home, William Douglas 44
Hooper, Martin 452
Hopkins, John 85
Hosanna (Tremblay) 95
House of the Rising Son (Jacobson) 425
How Does Your Garden Grow (McNeil) 97
Human Remains (Fineberg) 99
Hunter, Samuel D. 440
Hushabye Mountain 304
Hyde in Hollywood (Harvey) 197

I Have Aids (Gilbert) 404
If This Isn't Love! (S. Morris) 145
The Immoralist (Goetzes) 51
In Extremis (Barlett) 314

In Gabriel's Kitchen (Antonio) 379
In Mortality (Cabranes-Grant) 282
In the Blue (Gill) 159
Indiana, Gary Appendix A
Inge, William 60, 74
Innaurato, Albert 108, 158
Innocence (McGuinness) 169
The Intelligent Homosexual's Guide to Capitalism (Kushner) 405
The Invention of Love (Stoppard) 283
Irving (Piñero) 170
It's All Due to Leprechauns (Branson) 160

Jackson, Michael D. 300
Jacobs, Pieter 386
Jacobson, Tom 248, 361, 425, 432
Jeffrey (Rudnick) 224
Jenkin, Juliet 360
Jerker (Chesley) 171
Jim Dandy (Gilbert) 263
Johaardien, Ashraf 352
John, I'm Only Dancing (Duncum) 225
Johnson, Joel Drake 245, 340
Jones, Leroi 62, 63
Joy (Fisher) 252
The Judas Kiss (Hare) 295
Jumpers for Goalposts (Wells) 445

Karam, Stephen 391, 429
Katz, Jonathan 90
Kaufman, Moisés 281, 316
Kearns, Michael Appendix A
Kenna, Peter 100, 117, 215
Kennedy's Children (R. Patrick) 96
Kilroy, Thomas 9, 79, 286
Kilt (J. Wilson) 305
Kirby, Andy 176
Kirkwood, James 102, Appendix B
Kiss of the Spider Woman (Puig) 136
Kit Marlowe (Grimm) 315
The Kitchen Sink (Wells) 426
Knights (Aristophanes) 1
Kondoleon, Harry 192
Kotak, Ash 313
Kramer, Larry 163
Kushner, Tony 174, 209, 405
Kuzmin, Mikhail 15, 18

Lahr, John 168
Lake Street Extension (Blessing) 226
A Language of Their Own (Yew) 253
The Laramie Project (Kaufman) 316
Last Romantics (MacLennan) 342
The Last Sunday in June (Tolins) 343
Late Company (Tannahill) 446
Latin! or Tobacco and Boys (Fry) 126
Laurents, Arthur 30, 94, 346
The Law of Remains (Abdoh) 227
Lepage, Robert 189
Levitation (Mason) 153
Levitt, Harold 48
Liar (Drader) 354
The Life of Edward the Second of England (Brecht) 23

Lilies (Bouchard) 177
Lim, Paul Steven 107
The Lisbon Traviata (McNally) 161
The Little Dog Laughed (Beane) 380
Logan, John 162
Lonely Planet (Dietz) 238
Lonsdale, Frederick 22
Look: We've Come Through (Wheeler) 58
Lord Alfred's Lover (Bentley) 118
Love! Valour! Compassion! (McNally) 254
Lovesong of the Electric Bear (S. Wilson) 333
Lowe, Barry 196
Lucas, Craig 291, Appendix B
Lucie, Doug 155
Ludlam, Charles 105
Lynch, Peter A
The Lyons (Silver) 427

MacArthur, Greg 266
MacDonald, Bryden 219, 416
MacDonald, Robert David 112, 150
MacIvor, Daniel 287, 388, 434, 442, Appendix A, Appendix B
MacLennan, Michael Lewis 234, 280, 329, 342
The Madness of Lady Bright (L. Wilson) 66
The Madras House (Granville-Barker) 17
La Maison Suspendue (Tremblay) 205
Mambo Italiano (Galluccio) 317
Mamet, David 365
Man and Boy (Rattigan) 61
The Man with Straight Hair (Birimisa) 119
Mann, Michael Norman 237
Mantello, Joe Appendix A
Mapa, Alec Appendix A
Marans, Jon 367, 414
Marcus (McCraney) 406
The Marescalco (Aretino) 4
Marlowe, Christopher 5, 231, 248, 315
Martin Yesterday (Fraser) 284
Mary (Bradshaw) 419
Mason, Timothy 151, 153
Match (Belber) 355
Mates (Kenna) 100
Maugham, Robin 82
Mavenawitz, Verity-Alicia 375
Mayer, Oliver 249
Mazumdar, Maxim Appendix A
McCraney, Tarell Alvin 401, 406, 443
McGuinness, Frank 164, 169, 186, 303, 332
McMahon, Phillip 374
McNally, Terrence 98, 161, 254, 288, 383, 447, Appendix B
McNeil, Jim 97, 215
Me, as a Penguin (Wells) 407
Mean Tears (Gill) 178
Measure for Pleasure (Grimm) 381

The Men from the Boys (Crowley) 334
Miller, Terry 138
Miller, Tim Appendix A
Minutes from the Blue Route (Donaghy) 264
The Miracle at Naples (Grimm) 408
"*Mistakes*" (Hirschberg) 14
Mr. Elliott (J. Hall) 344
Mr. Universe (Grimsley) 179
Mitchell, Julian 132
Mongrels (Enright) 215
Monkman, Kent Appendix A
Montherlant, Henry de 45
Moran, Martin Appendix A
Moran, Nick 369
Morris, Mary 233
Morris, Sidney 145
Moss, Simon 134
The Most Fabulous Story Ever Told (Rudnick) 296
Mothers and Sons (McNally) 447
Mouth to Mouth (Elyot) 325
Murphy, Tommy 368, 378
Murray, Steve 307
Muscle (Wainwright) 409
The Muscles in Our Toes (Belber) 410
Mustn't Do It! (Goedhart-Becker) 21
My Big Gay Italian Wedding (Wilkinson) 345
My Night with Reg (Elyot) 255
My Night with Tennessee (Gilbert) 228
Myth of Andrew & Jo (van Eeden) 411

The Nance (Beane) 448
Nasty Little Secrets (Robertson) 180
Nauffts, Geoffrey 412
Nemakonde, Pfarelo 444
Never the Sinner (Logan) 162
News Boy (Brown) 127
Next Fall (Nauffts) 412
Niagara Falls (Bumbalo) 137
Nichols, Peter 114
Night Queen (Dattani) 306
Night Sweat (Chesley) 154
The Normal Heart (Kramer) 163
Norman, Is That You? (Clark & Bobrick) 86
"*Now Barabbas ...*" (Home) 44
Now or Later (Shinn) 393
Now She Dances! (D. Wilson) 59

Observe the Sons of Ulster (McGuinness) 164
Octopus (Yockey) 394
O'Halloran, Mark 431
O'Hara, Robert 421
Okita, Dwight 240
The Old Boy (Gurney) 216
On a Muggy Night in Mambai (Dattani) 297
Once in a While the Odd Thing Happens (Godfrey) 206
One Foot to the Sea (Levitt) 48
O'Neill, Eugene 29
Original Sin (Gill) 335
Orton, Joe 64, 134, 168, 180, 413

Osborne, John 69
Oscar Wilde (Cohen) 27
Oscar Wilde (Stokeses) 39
Osment, Philip 191, 275
Other People (Shinn) 318
Out in the Open (Harvey) 326
Outrageous Fortune (Franken) 41

Pagan, Adrian 298
Palmer, John 91, 320
Pamatmat, A. Rey 422
Panych, Morris 455
The Paris Letter (Baitz) 356
Parnell, Peter 197, 222
Party (Dillon) 229
Passing By (Sherman) 101
Patrick, John 106
Patrick, Robert 65, 96, 122, Appendix A, Appendix B
A Patriot for Me (Osborne) 69
Peña, Ralph B. 270
A Perfect Relationship (D. Wilson) 120
Perlman, Michael 435
Piñero, Miguel 170
Pines '79 (Miller) 138
Pintauro, Joe 146, 217
Placey, Evan 420, 453
Plague Over England (de Jongh) 395
Plato 2n1
The Pleasure Man (West) 28
Pogey Bait (Birimisa) 109
Polito, Frank Anthony 433, 450
Poliziano 3
Polygraph (Lepage & Brassard) 189
Pomo Afro Homos Appendix A
Porcelain (Yew) 230
Postoff, Shawn 366
A Prayer for My Daughter (Babe) 121
Prick Up Your Ears (Bent) 413
The Pride (Campbell) 396
Priestley, J.B. 34
The Princess Zoubaroff (Firbank) 19
The Prisoners of War (Ackerley) 24
Privates on Parade (Nichols) 114
Progress (Lucie) 155
Prok (Drader) 327
Pronoun (Placey) 453
P.S. Your Cat Is Dead (Kirkwood) 102
Pterodactyls (Silver) 239
The Public (García Lorca) 31
Puig, Manuel 136
Purdy, James 113
Py, Olivier 348

Quaint Honour (Gellert) 54
The Queen & Peacock (Deegan) 319
Queer People (Hill) 35
Questa (Bumbalo) 363
A Question of Mercy (Rabe) 285
A Quiet End (Swados) 172

Rabe, David 110, 285
Rademeyer, Philip 439
Raffalovich, Marc-André 10
Raft of the Medusa (Pintauro) 217
The Rainy Season (Okita) 240

Raised in Captivity (Silver) 265
Rao, R. Raj Appendix A
The Rats of Norway (Winter) 38
Rattigan, Terence 61, 428
Rattigan's Nijinsky (Wright) 428
Ravenhill, Mark 272, 294, 373
Raw Youth (Bell) 165
Regrets Only (Rudnick) 382
Reinhart, Robert C. Appendix A
The Relapse (Vanbrugh) 8
Remember Me (Tremblay) 139
Rents (Wilcox) 128
Rescue and Recovery (Murray) 307
The Return of A.J. Raffles (Greene) 103
Reyes, Guillermo 269, Appendix A
Richmond Jim (Yeomans) 129
Riding in Cars with (Mostly Straight) Boys 454
Ridley, Philip 221, 323
Rintoul, Harry 211, 279
The Rise and Fall of Peter Gaveston (MacArthur) 266
The Ritz (McNally) 98
Robertson, Lanie 180
Rocco, Antonio 2n1
Roche, David A
Rochester, Second Earl of 7
Romance (Mamet) 365
Roots and Wings (Vickery) 267
Rope (Hamilton) 30
Rope Enough (Gilbert) 364
Rosenthal, Andrew 46
Round 2 (Bentley) 181
Roy, Ed 377
Royal, Bert V. 351
Rudnick, Paul 224, 296, 358, 382

Sade, Marquis de 2n1
Saint Oscar (Eagleton) 198
The Saints and Apostles (Storey) 218
Sánchez, Edwin 232, 259
Satyricon (Foster) 92
Saul (Gide) 13
Say You Love Satan (Aguirre-Sacasa) 328
Scheffer, Will Appendix A
Schnitzler, Arthur 152, 181, 392
The School of Night (Whelan) 231
The Secret Fall of Constance Wilde (Kilroy) 286
Secrets of the Trade (Tolins) 397
Semi-Monde (Coward) 25
Sextet (Panych) 455
The Shadow Box (Cristofer) 104
Shadow of Himself (Bell) 389
Shaffer, Peter 76
Shairp, Mordaunt 37
Shakespeare, William 6, 231, 248, 312
Sher, Antony 387
Sherman, Martin 101, 124, 166, 273, Appendix B
Shinn, Christopher 293, 318, 337, 376, 393, 449
The Shooting Stage (MacLennan) 329

Index to entry numbers 191

Shopping and Fucking (Ravenhill) 272
Shores, Del 274, 321
The Sign in Sidney Brustein's Window (Hansberry) 67
Silver, Nicky 239, 250, 265, 349, 370, 427
Singapore (Palmer) 320
Single Spies (Bennett) 190
Sir Richard Wadd, Pornographer (Postoff) 366
Sissy (Bracho) 398
Six Degrees of Separation (Guare) 207
Slipping (Talbott) 399
Small Craft Warnings (Williams) 84
Snow Orchid (Pintauro) 146
Sodom (Rochester) 7, Appendix B
The Soldier Dreams (MacIvor) 287
Some Men (McNally) 383
Some Sunny Day (Sherman) 273
Something Cloudy, Something Clear (Williams) 140
Somewhere in the Pacific (Bell) 308
A Song at Twilight (Coward) 71
Sons of the Prophet (Karam) 429
Sordid Lives (Shores) 274
South (Green) 49
Southern Baptist Sissies (Shores) 321
Southwark Fair (Adamson) 384
Spagnoletti, Nicholas 437
Spatter Pattern (Bell) 357
Spears, Steve J. Appendix A
Special Forces (Fisher) 390
Special Thanks to Guests from Afar (Spagnoletti) 437
Speech & Debate (Karam) 391
Spring Cleaning (Lonsdale) 22
Spring's Awakening (Wedekind) 9
Staircase (Dyer) 72
The Stanley Parkers (Aron) 208
Steel Kiss (Fulford) 182
Stembridge, Gerard 271
Stephen & Mr. Wilde (Bartley) 241
Steve & Idi (Grimm) 400
Stevens, David 199
The Stillborn Lover (Findley) 242
Stokes, Leslie & Sewell 39
Stoppard, Tom 283
Storey, Raymond 218
Straight and Narrow (Chinn) 183
A Strange and Separate People (Marans) 367
Strange Interlude (O'Neill) 29
Strangers in Between (Murphey) 368
Streamers (Rabe) 110
Street Theater (D. Wilson) 147
Suddenly Last Summer (Williams) 55
The Sum of Us (Stevens) 199
Swados, Robin 172

T-Shirts (R. Patrick) 122
Take Me Out (Greenberg) 336

Talbott, Daniel 399
The Tale of Orpheus (Poliziano) 3
Tannahill, Jordan 446, 451, Appendix A
A Taste of Honey (Delaney) 56
Tea and Sympathy (Anderson) 50
Teddy Ferrara (Shinn) 449
Telstar (Moran & Hicks) 369
The Temperamentals (Marans) 414
Theatrelife (Gilbert) 184
Thief River (Blessing) 322
Third Person (Rosenthal) 46
This Island's Mine (Osment) 191
Thomas, Buddy 311
Thomas, Collin 213, Appendix A
Todd, Matthew 359
The Toilet (Jones/Baraka) 62
Tolins, Jonathan 243, 343, 397, Appendix A
Tom at the Farm (Bouchard) 430
Torch Song Trilogy (Fierstein) 141
Total Eclipse (Hampton) 80
Touch (Demchuk) 173
A Tower Near Paris (Copi) 122
Trade (O'Halloran) 431
Trafficking in Broken Hearts (Sánchez) 232
Tragedy in Jermyn Street (Hill) 35
Tremblay, Michel 95, 139, 205
Troilus and Cressida (Shakespeare) 6
True Love Lies (Fraser) 415
The Twentieth-Century Way (Jacobson) 432
The Twilight of the Golds (Tolins) 243
2 Lives (Laurents) 346
Two Weeks with the Queen (M. Morris) 233

The Undertaking (Osment) 275
Unidentified Human Remains (Fraser) 200

Valhalla (Rudnick) 358
Vanbrugh, John 8
van Eeden, Gideon 411
Van Itallie, Jean-Claude 195
Vanya and Sonia and Masha and Spike (Durang) 438
The Venetian Madcaps (Kuzmin) 18
Versailles (Gill) 456
Vickery, Frank 143, 267
Vieux Carré (Williams) 115
The View (Rademeyer) 439
Vignale, Antonio 2n1
Vile Bodies (Bradley) 33
Vincent River (Ridley) 323
Visiting Mr. Green (Baron) 276
Vogel, Paula 203

Wainwright, Tom 409
Wasserstein, Wendy 188
Watkins, Neil Appendix A

Webb, Ben Appendix A
Webster (MacDonald) 150
Wedekind, Frank 9, 335
Wells, Tom 407, 426, 445, Appendix A
West, Mae 26, 28
The Whale (Hunter) 440
Whale Riding Weather (MacDonald) 219
What Are Tuesdays Like? (Bumbalo) 256
What's Wrong with Angry? (P. Wilde) 244
Wheeler, Hugh 57, 58
Whelan, Peter 231
When Did You Last See My Mother? (Hampton) 73
When She Danced (Sherman) 166
When the King Comes He Is Welcome (Douglas) 12
Where Do We Live (Shinn) 337
Where's Daddy? (Inge) 74
White Liars (Shaffer) 76
Whitemore, Hugh 167
Whiteoaks (de la Roche) 40
Wig Out! (McCraney) 401
Wilcox, Michael 128
Wilde, Oscar 19, 20, 27, 39, 59, 118, 198, 241, 281, 283, 286, 294, 295, 314, 361, Appendix A
Wilde, Patrick 244
Wilkinson, Anthony J. 345
Williams, Tennessee 42, 47, 52, 55, 84, 115, 140, 228, 388
Wilmot, John (Second Earl of Rochester) 7
Wilson, Doric 59, 120, 131, 147
Wilson, Jonathan 305, Appendix A
Wilson, Lanford 66, 116, 175, Appendix A
Wilson, Snoo 87, 333
Winter, Keith 38
Wise Child (S. Gray) 77
With Bated Breath (MacDonald) 416
Wolves (Yockey) 441
Women at the Thesmophoria Festival (Aristophanes) 2
Wonderland (Yew) 309
Wright, Nicholas 428

Xenophon 2n1

Yeomans, Cal 129
Yew, Chay 230, 253, 309
Yockey, Steve 394, 441
The York Realist (Gill) 330
You Should Be So Lucky (Busch) 257
Your Loving Simon (Colman) 347
Youth (Py) 348

Zero Positive (Kondoleon) 192
Zindel, Paul 194

www.ingramcontent.com/pod-product-compliance
Lightning Source LLC
Chambersburg PA
CBHW081557300426
44116CB00015B/2920